SO-AZV-473

Grimm Fairy Tales

Return to Wonderland

Grimm Fairy Tales: Return to Wonderland. Published by Zenescope Entertainment Inc., 501 Office Center Drive, Ste. 8, Ft. Washington,
PA 19034. Zenescope and its logos are ® and © 2009 Zenescope Entertainment Inc. all rights reserved. Grimm Fairy Tales, its logo and
all related characters, names and their likeness are trademarks of Zenescope Entertainment. Any similarities to persons (living or dead),
events, institutions, or locales are purely coincidental. No portion of this publication my be reproduced or transmitted, in any form or by
any means, without the express written permission of Zenescope Entertainment Inc except for artwork used for review purposes.
Printed in Canada.

'But I don't want to go among mad people,' Alice remarked.

'Oh, you can't help that,' said the Cat: 'we're all mad here. I'm mad. You're mad.'

'How do you know I'm mad?' said Alice.

'You must be,' said the Cat, 'or you wouldn't have come here.'

- Alice's Adventures in Wonderland - Lewis Carroll

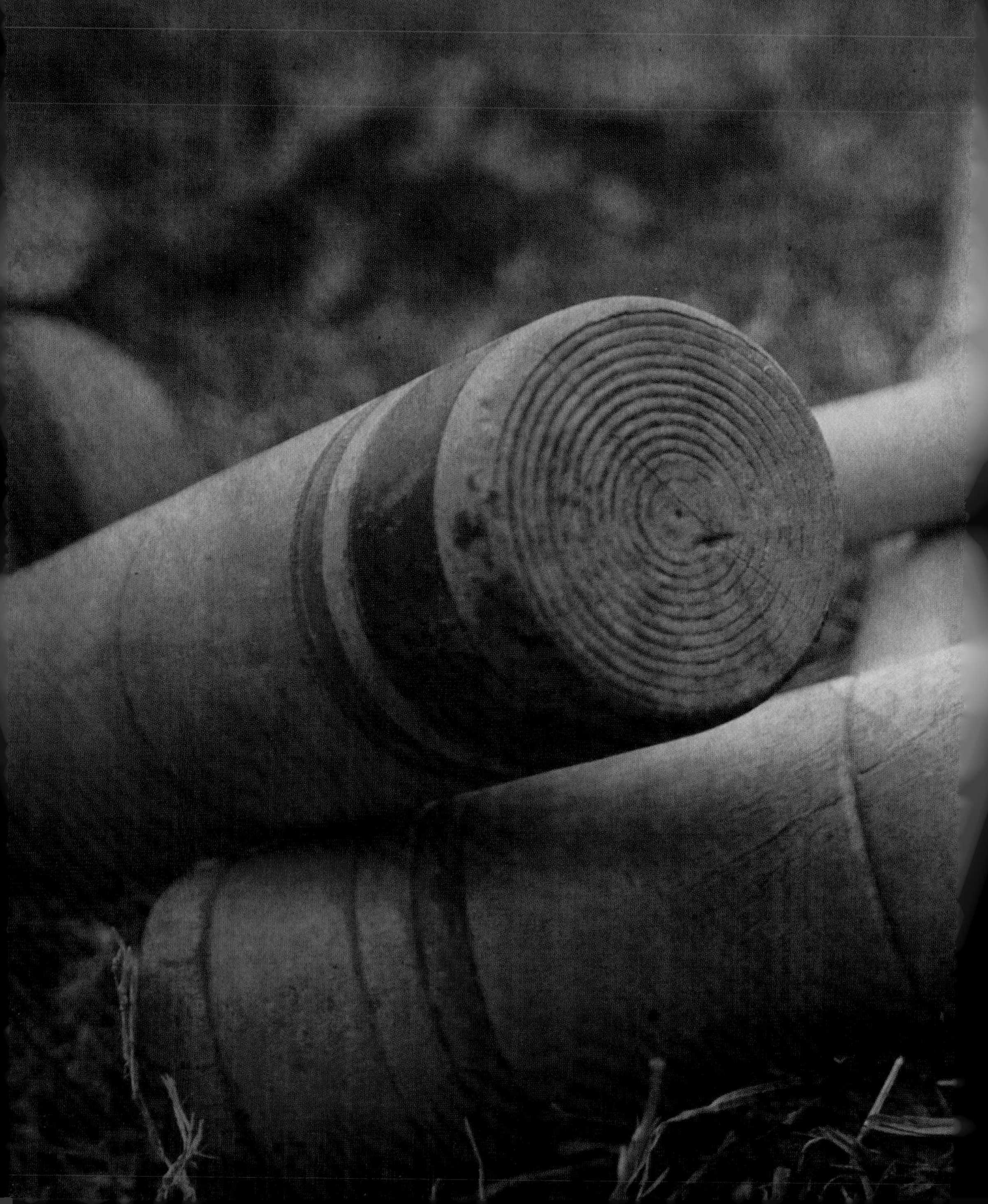

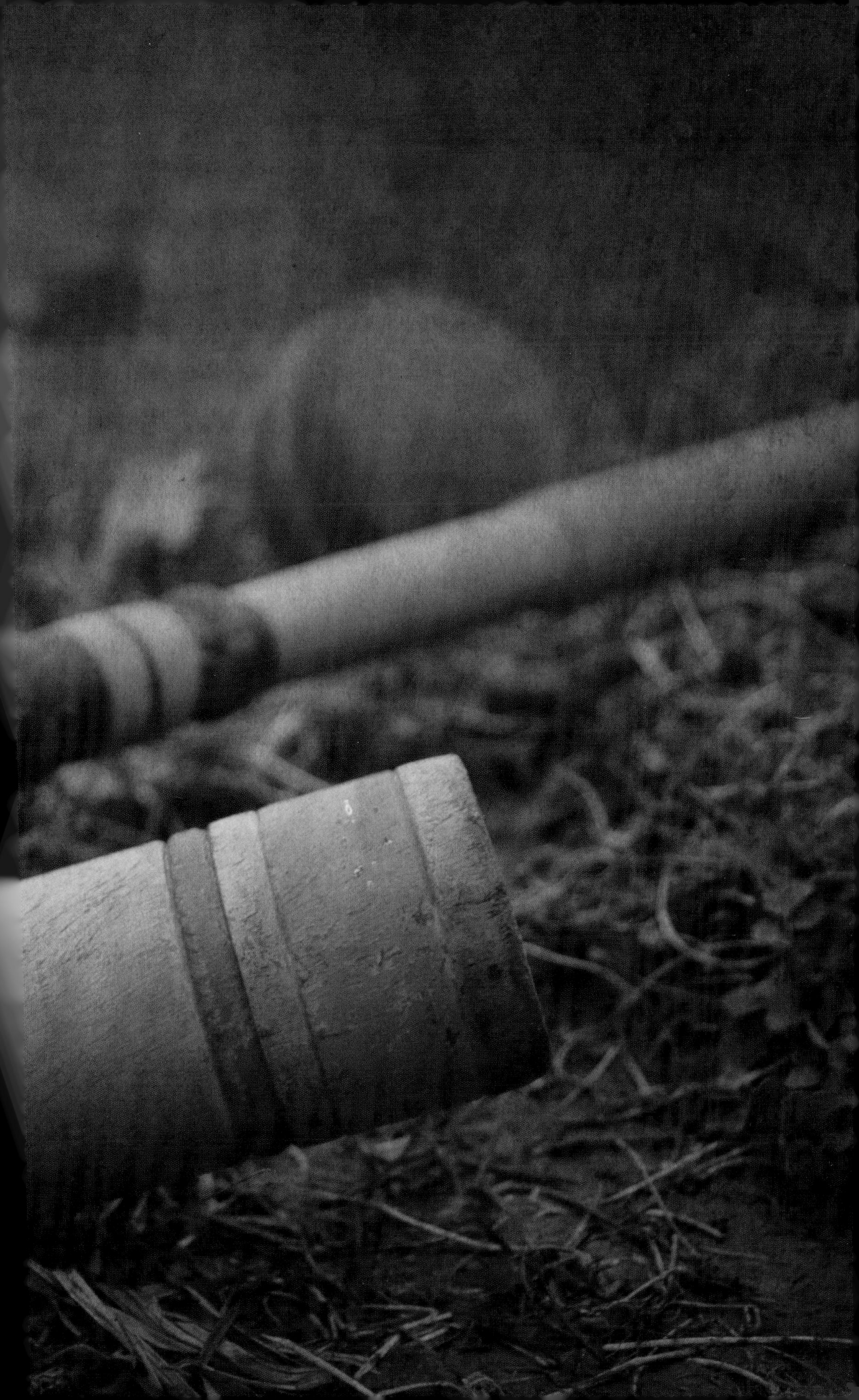

Published by Zenescope Entertainment • Paperback Third Edition, NOV. 2010 • ISBN 978-0-9817550-5-2

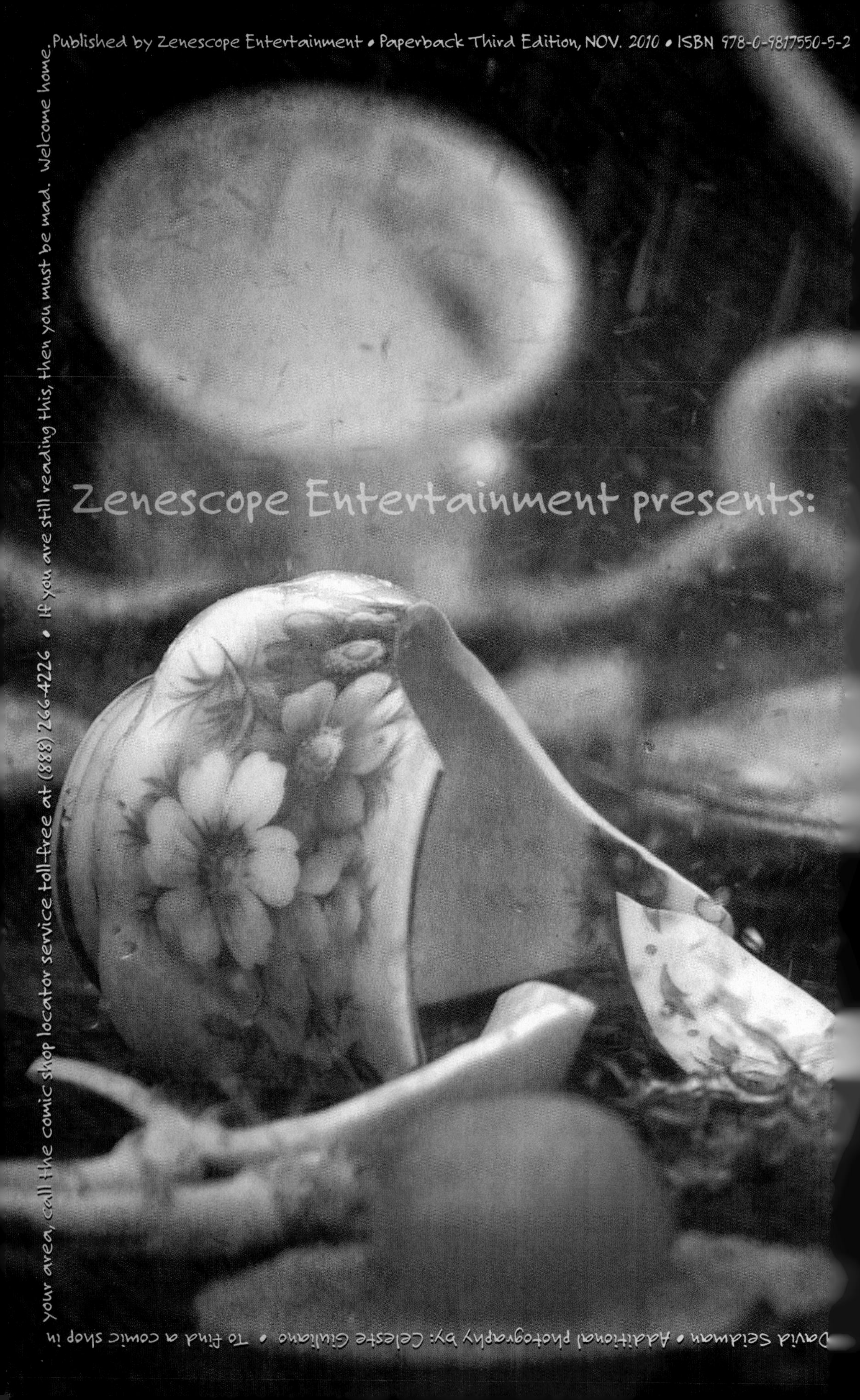

Zenescope Entertainment presents:

your area, call the comic shop locator service toll-free at (888) 266-4226 • If you are still reading this, then you must be mad. Welcome home.

David Seidman • Additional photography by: Celeste Giuliano • To find a comic shop in

This volume collects the complete comic book series Return to Wonderland from Zenescope Entertainment • President: Joe Brusha, V.P./ Editor-in-Chief: Ralph Tedesco, Art Director: David Seidman, Executive Editor: Raven Gregory, Production Assistant: Jenna Sibel • Collection designer & supplemental art:

RETURN TO WONDERLAND

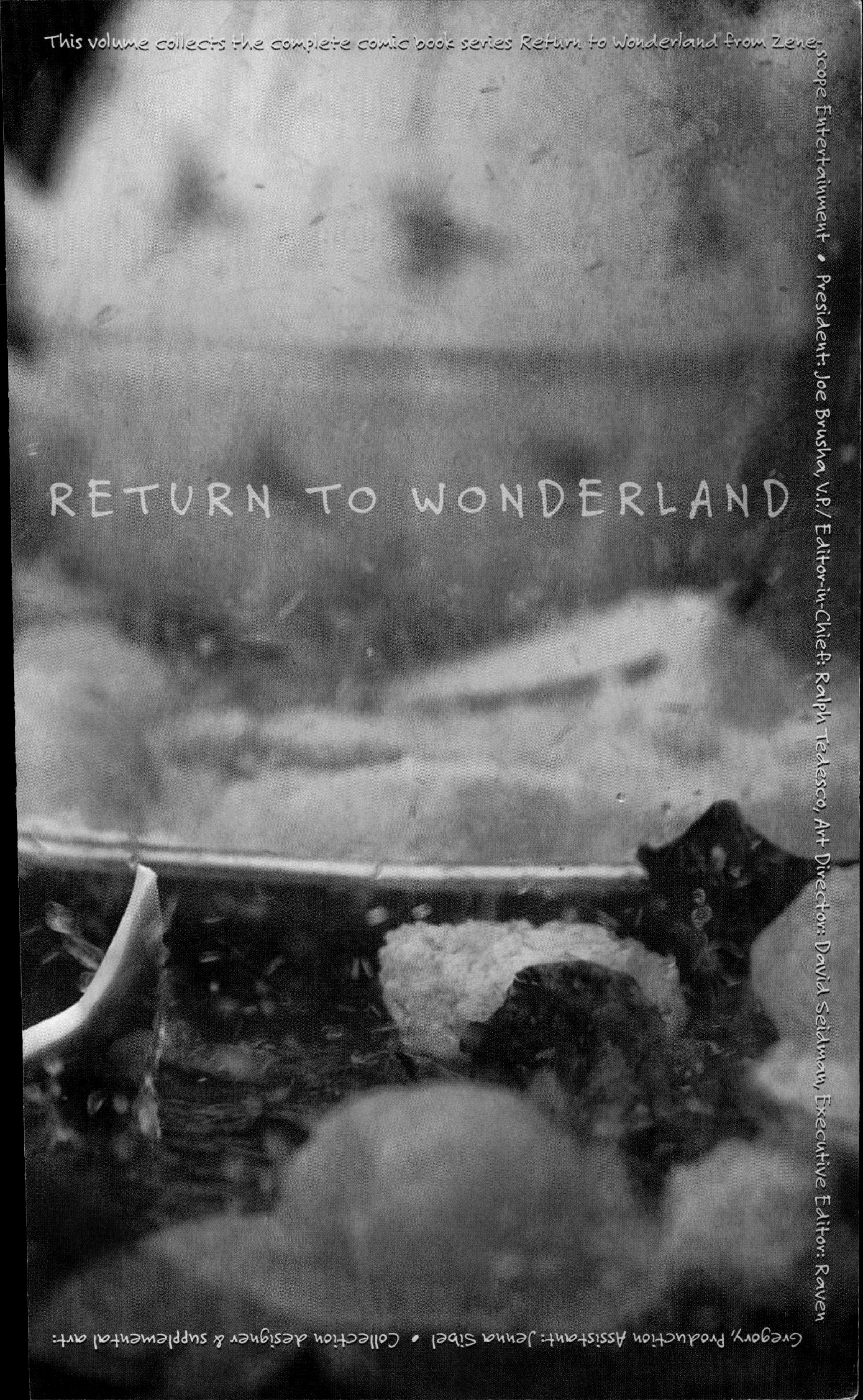

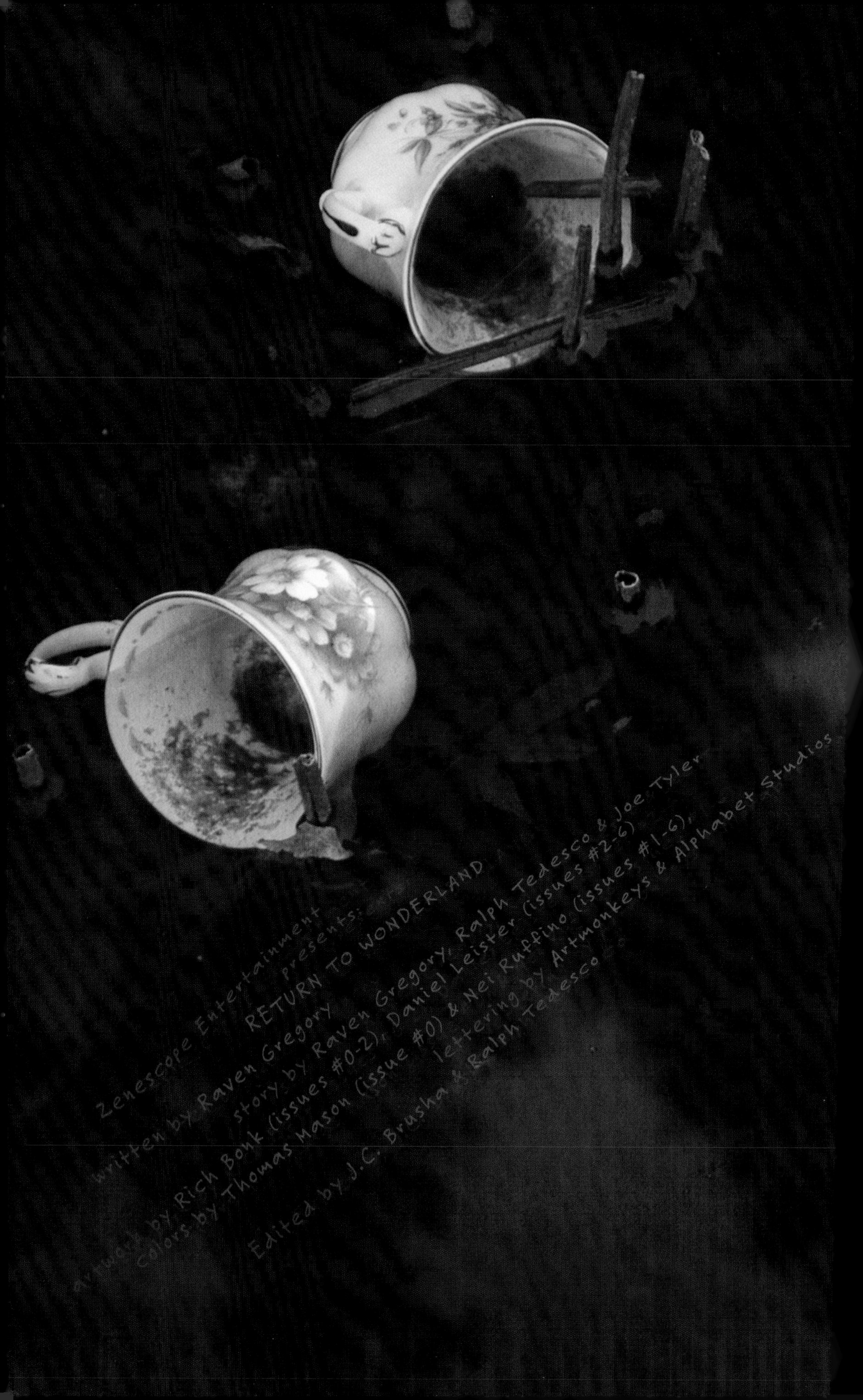

Zenescope Entertainment
presents:
RETURN TO WONDERLAND
written by Raven Gregory, Ralph Tedesco & Joe Tyler
story by Raven Gregory
artwork by Rich Bonk (issues #0-2), Daniel Leister (issues #2-6)
Colors by Thomas Mason (issue #0) & Nei Ruffino (issues #1-6),
lettering by Artmonkeys & Alphabet Studios
Edited by J.C. Brusha & Ralph Tedesco

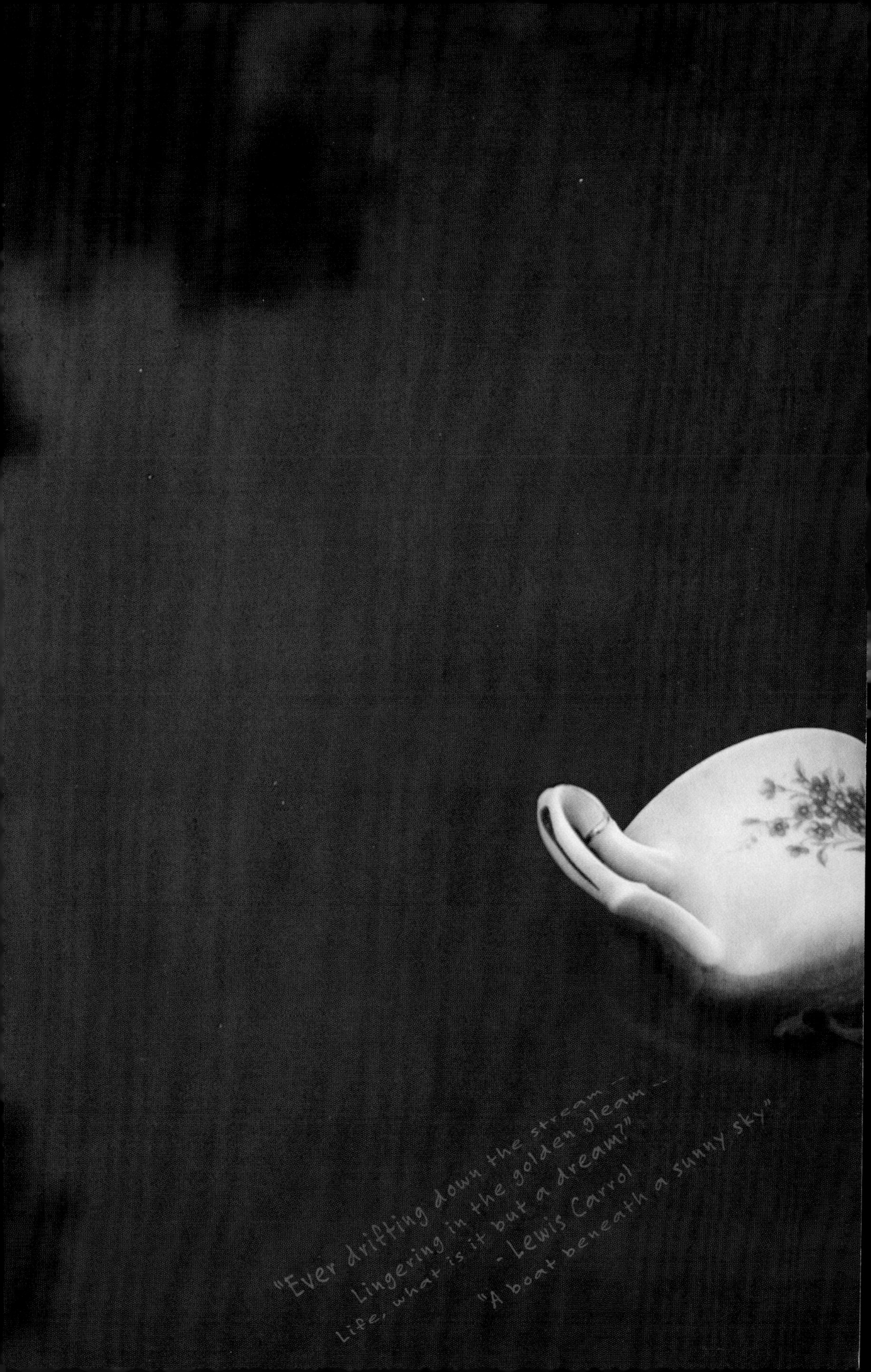
"Ever drifting down the stream --
Lingering in the golden gleam --
Life, what is it but a dream?"
- Lewis Carrol
"A boat beneath a sunny sky"

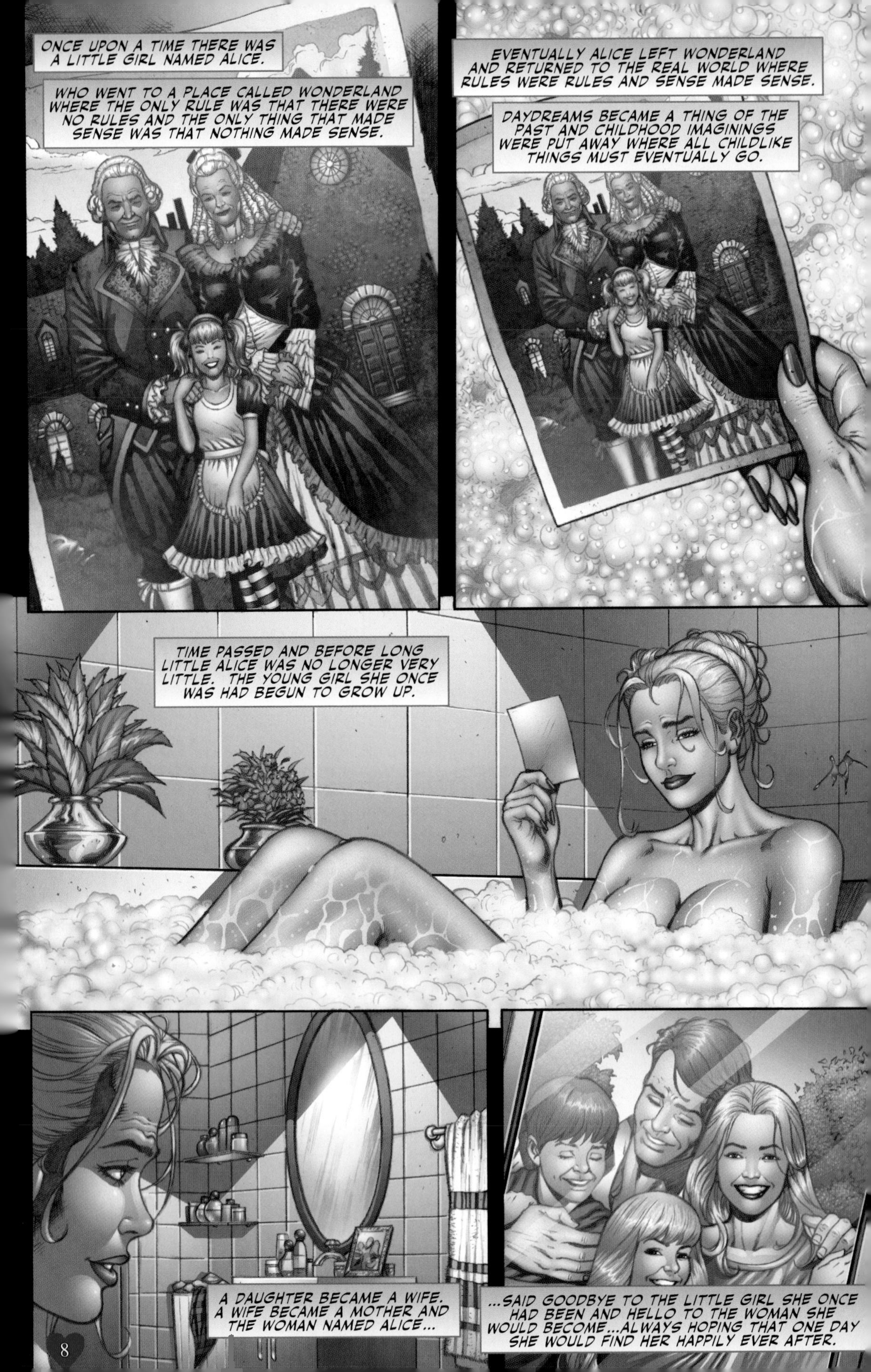
ONCE UPON A TIME THERE WAS A LITTLE GIRL NAMED ALICE.
WHO WENT TO A PLACE CALLED WONDERLAND WHERE THE ONLY RULE WAS THAT THERE WERE NO RULES AND THE ONLY THING THAT MADE SENSE WAS THAT NOTHING MADE SENSE.
EVENTUALLY ALICE LEFT WONDERLAND AND RETURNED TO THE REAL WORLD WHERE RULES WERE RULES AND SENSE MADE SENSE.
DAYDREAMS BECAME A THING OF THE PAST AND CHILDHOOD IMAGININGS WERE PUT AWAY WHERE ALL CHILDLIKE THINGS MUST EVENTUALLY GO.
TIME PASSED AND BEFORE LONG LITTLE ALICE WAS NO LONGER VERY LITTLE. THE YOUNG GIRL SHE ONCE WAS HAD BEGUN TO GROW UP.
A DAUGHTER BECAME A WIFE. A WIFE BECAME A MOTHER AND THE WOMAN NAMED ALICE...
...SAID GOODBYE TO THE LITTLE GIRL SHE ONCE HAD BEEN AND HELLO TO THE WOMAN SHE WOULD BECOME...ALWAYS HOPING THAT ONE DAY SHE WOULD FIND HER HAPPILY EVER AFTER.

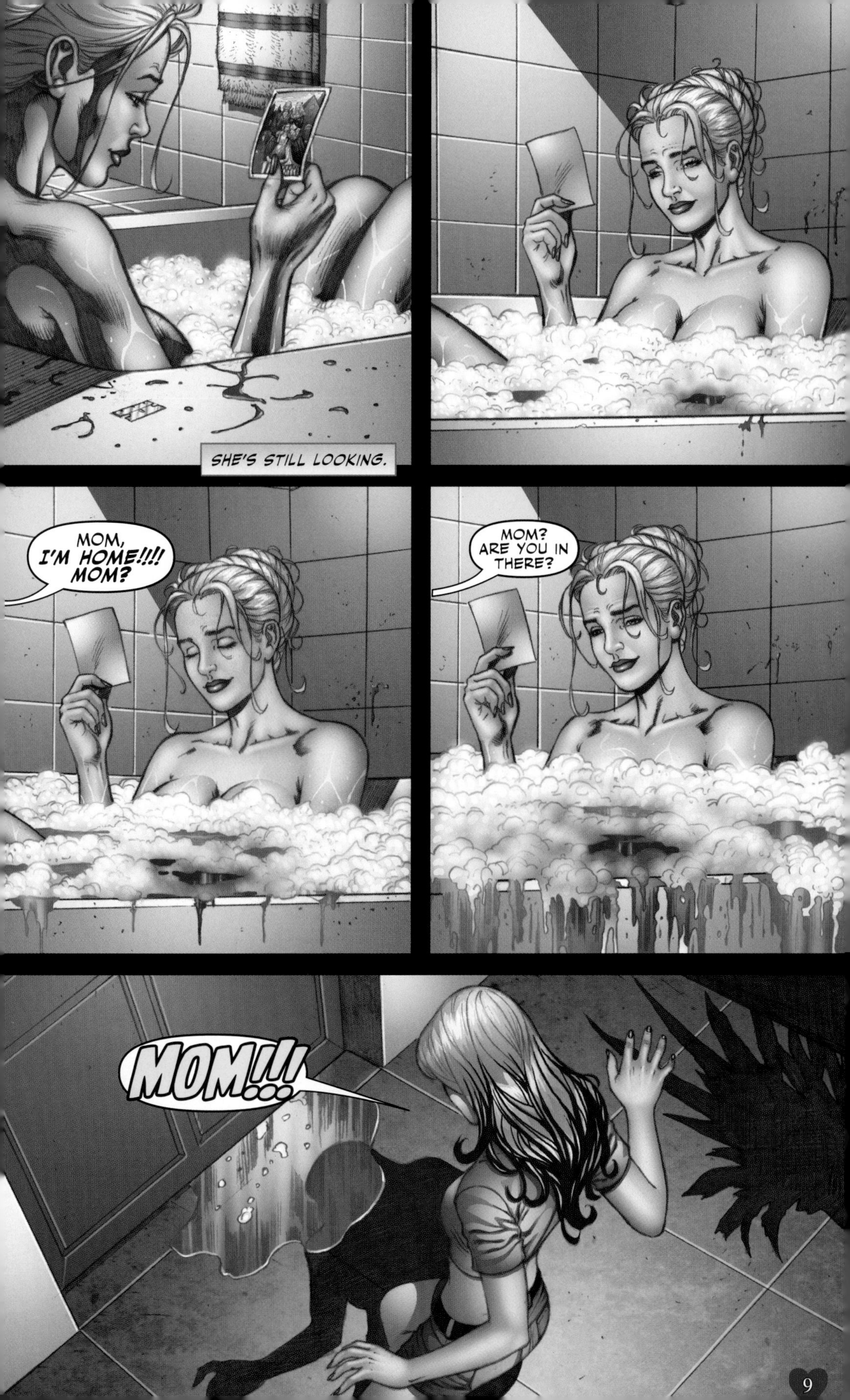
SHE'S STILL LOOKING.
MOM, I'M HOME!!!! MOM?
MOM? ARE YOU IN THERE?
MOM!!!...

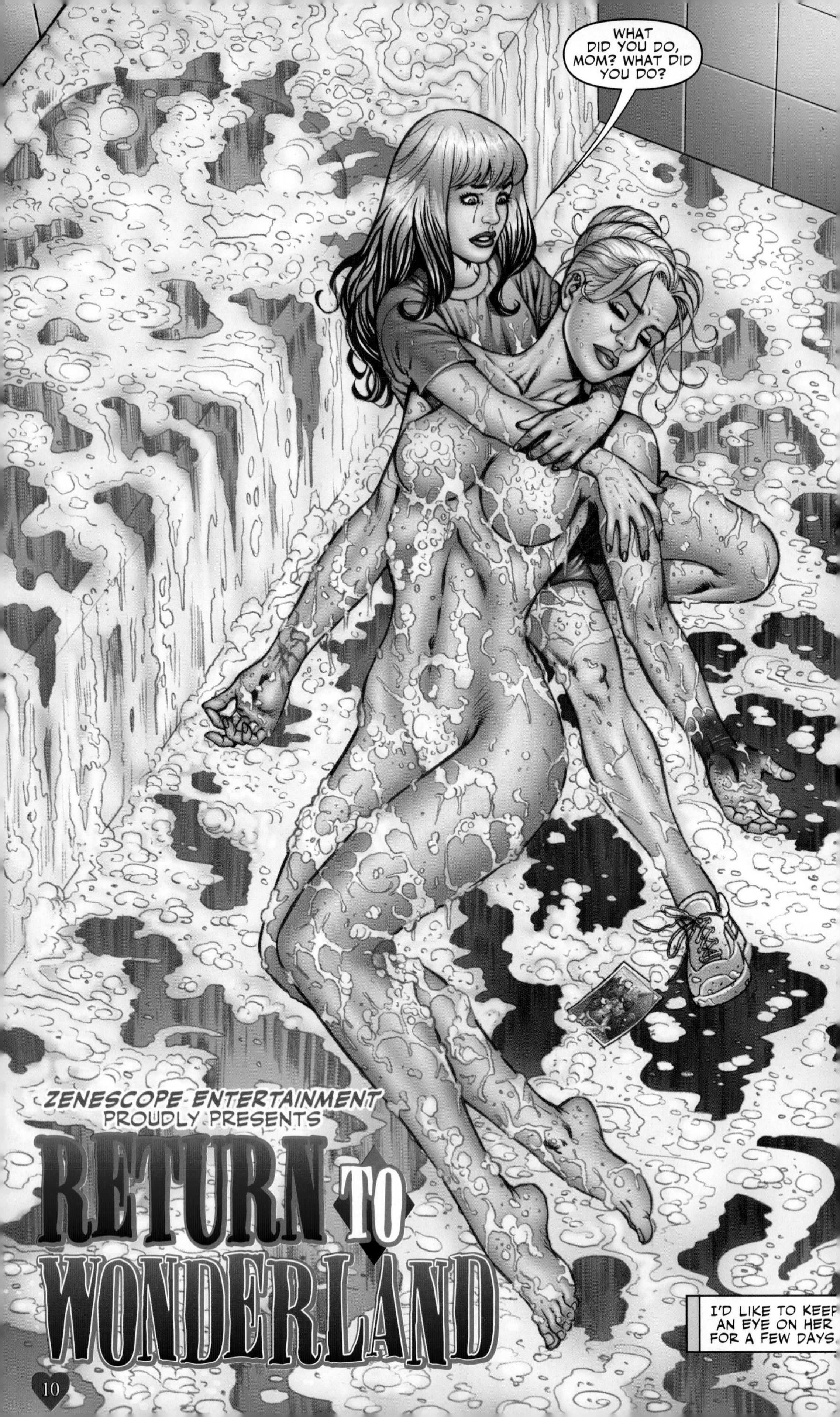
WHAT DID YOU DO, MOM? WHAT DID YOU DO?
ZENESCOPE ENTERTAINMENT PROUDLY PRESENTS
RETURN TO WONDERLAND
I'D LIKE TO KEEP AN EYE ON HER FOR A FEW DAYS.

I THINK THE BEST THING TO DO WOULD BE TO PUT HER IN OBSERVATION OVER THE NEXT WEEK AND SEE HOW SHE RESPONDS TO THE NEW MEDICATION.

WHATEVER YOU THINK IS BEST, DOCTOR YING.

≠SOB≠ WHY DID SHE DO IT, DAD? WHY?

I DON'T KNOW, HONEY. I JUST...I JUST DON'T KNOW.

IF EVERYTHING GOES WELL, WE'LL HAVE HER BACK HOME IN NO...

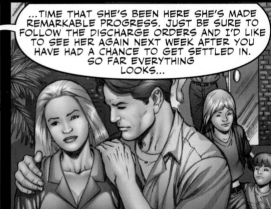

...TIME THAT SHE'S BEEN HERE SHE'S MADE REMARKABLE PROGRESS. JUST BE SURE TO FOLLOW THE DISCHARGE ORDERS AND I'D LIKE TO SEE HER AGAIN NEXT WEEK AFTER YOU HAVE HAD A CHANCE TO GET SETTLED IN. SO FAR EVERYTHING LOOKS...

...GOOD IDEA MIGHT BE TO GET HER SOME KIND OF PET. I THINK IT WILL BE VERY THERAPEUTIC FOR HER. DURING OUR SESSIONS SHE'S MENTIONED A...

SO, DO YOU LIKE HIM?

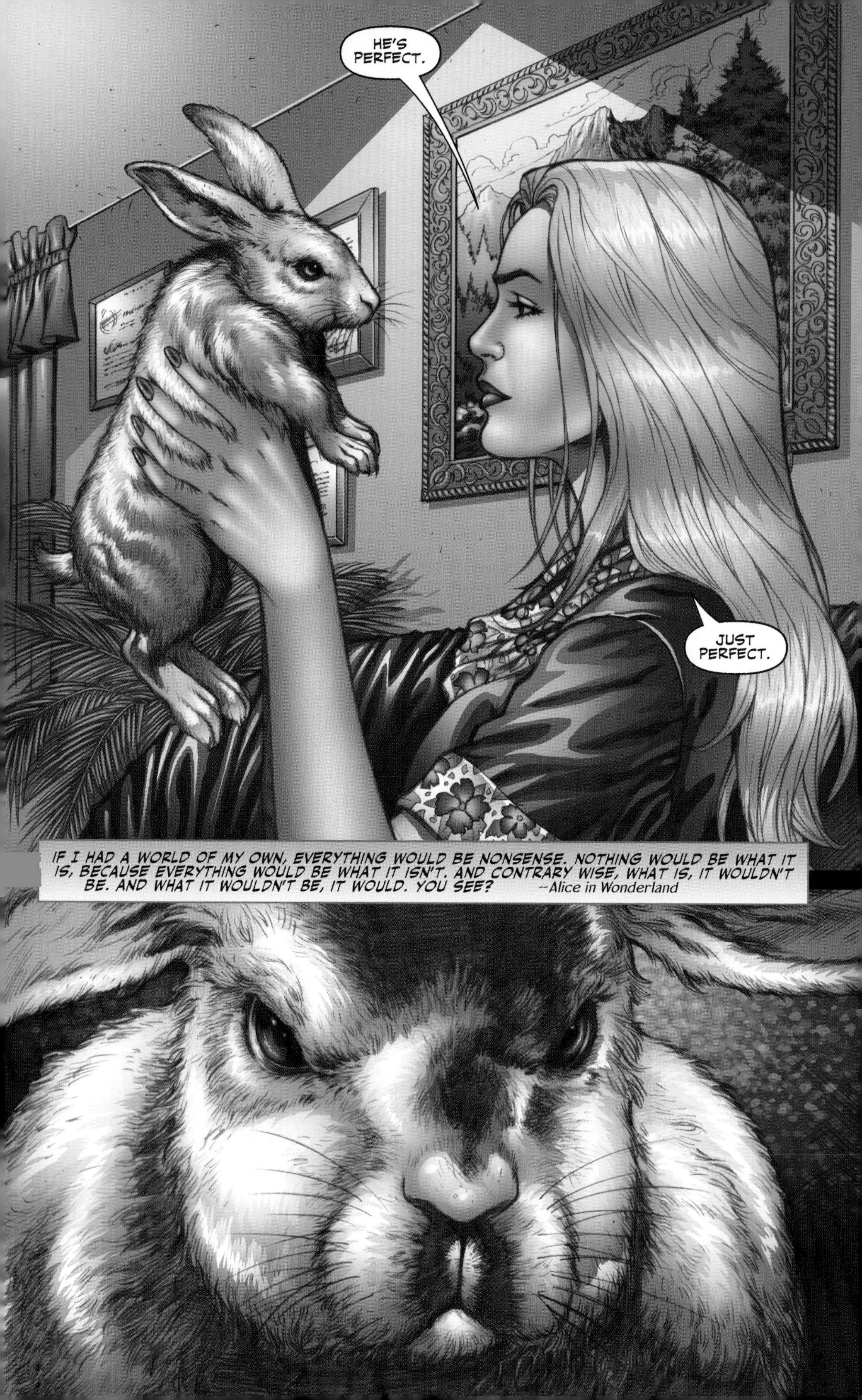
HE'S PERFECT.
JUST PERFECT.
IF I HAD A WORLD OF MY OWN, EVERYTHING WOULD BE NONSENSE. NOTHING WOULD BE WHAT IT IS, BECAUSE EVERYTHING WOULD BE WHAT IT ISN'T. AND CONTRARY WISE, WHAT IS, IT WOULDN'T BE. AND WHAT IT WOULDN'T BE, IT WOULD. YOU SEE? --Alice in Wonderland

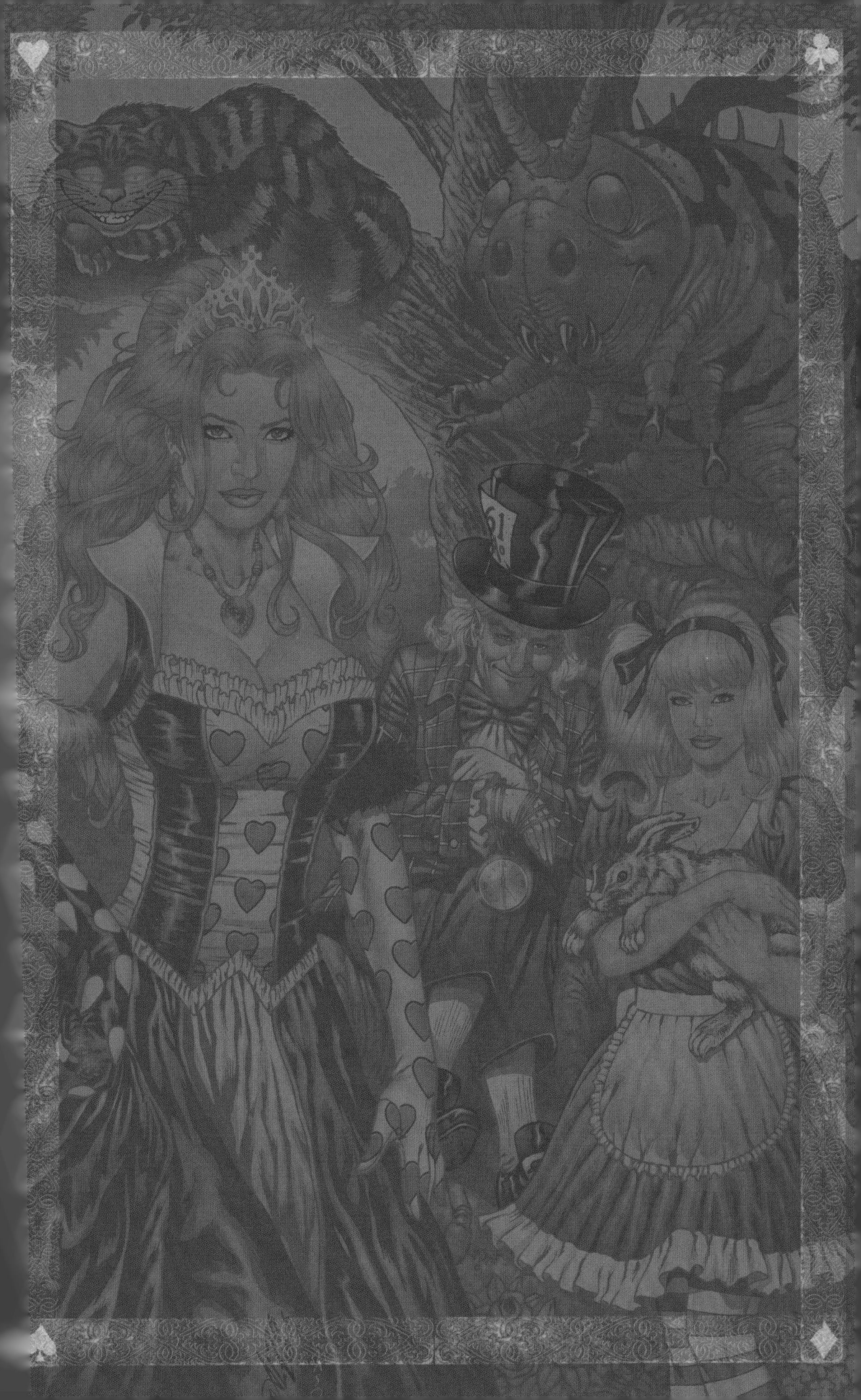

March 17

Grandpappy just arrived today. He gave me this really nice pencil case with some really nice color pencils inside. He said it was an early birthday gift. Grandpappy always gives me gifts even when I don't have a birthday coming up. I love my Grandpappy and I love my mom and dad. They all like to give me a lot of things to play with and use. I think I'm going to use the color pencils to draw Grandpappy a picture of me and him and another one for Mom and Dad. I hope they like it.

April 1

Mom and Dad had some friends over the house today. Grandpappy told Mom and Dad to tell me to say HI to all the people in the house. They were all very nice. I wanted to stay with the guest but Grandpappy told me to go to my room because I didn't need to deal with the adult stuff. But I wanted to know what they were talking about so I hid in the hallway. I wanted to hear something about my birthday party but I couldn't make out what they were saying, it was like they were talking in a different language. It kind of scared me because their voices changed. Maybe that's the adult way of talking, I'm not too sure. I didn't want to stay so I went to my room. I guess I didn't need to deal with all the adult stuff after all.

April 21

o Dad went to a store with Grandpappy today and brought home this BIG MIRROR. I asked them why they had brought this in the house. Grandpappy just said it would look nice in the house. I really don't like that mirror because when I looked at myself in that mirror I didn't look pretty. I told mom that that mirror makes people look ugly but she said I was just having a wild imagenation. I really don't like that mirror and I hope Dad will move it further away from my room.

May 3

Today is the day before my birthday and I can't wait to see what mom and dad got for me. I know it's going to be great. They always know what to get me. I really really hope they got me what I wanted. Mom told me tommorrow will be a great day. She said that I will be going to a fair tomorrow and that should be a lot of fun. I really can't wait.

May 4

Today is my BIRTHDAY! I'm ten years old! I'm so HAPPY!
I'm going to the fair now...

May 4

The FAIR was a lot of fun. I got to dress up like the little girls use
to dress up back in the old days. I even got to keep one of the
dress! We walked around and did a lot of fun things. We also went
on a walk I guess it was a tour or some kind I'm not sure
what it was because I wasn't feeling too good. I'm still not
feeling too good right now to. But we saw some really nice things
on the walk. A lot of pretty flowers and a funny little squirrel
and I also saw a rabbit hole. I really didn't like the rabbit
hole that much because it looked scary to me. I don't remember
too well all the other things I saw. I think I should have
mom make some lemonade. Mom makes the best lemonade that
will make anyone feel better.

May 4

I just had another glass of Mom's lemonade. It was really good.
Grandpappy came to my room earlier to see how I was doing.
He is really great. Grandpappy told me that I would feel a lot
better soon. He said after I got some rest that I would wake
up feeling good. I told Grandpappy about how after seeing that
hole during the walk that I started to not feel well. I told
him the hole scared me because it was so dark and big. He
told me not to be scared of the hole. He said that I
shouldn't let something that I didn't know much about scare
me. He said sometimes the darkest places have the most
wonderful things and that all we need to do in order to
see them is to simply turn on a light. So that hole I saw
might not be so bad at all. Maybe Grandpappy is right.
Maybe just maybe somewhere deep down in that hole there is
something wonderful in that dark place.

CALIE'S BLOG

10 march 2007
A possible cure for my boredom?

So today was almost like any other day…boring, unexciting, redundant, and everything else that seems to define boring. I wanted to hang out with my boyfriend Brandon but he was busy with lord knows what. Brandon if you're reading this, I hope you got something good for the both of us…please none of that weak ass shit you got us last time. So anyhow when I got home from prison today, oops I mean school, I decided that today was going to be the day that I was going to explore my attic. Why you say? I guess I just felt that that would somehow cure my boredom. So upon rummaging through some old stuff in the attic I came across this really old looking type of journal. Anyhow it's a journal for sure, so when I opened it up I realized that it was an old journal that my mom kept when she was a kid. I guess you can say I was both surprised and amused that my mom kept a journal. It's cool to see that my mom had somewhat of a normal childhood unlike now I guess. A couple of years ago my mom attempted suicide and she's been in and out of the hospital ever since. Don't feel sorry for me, because I'm really okay. But anyhow back to the cure to my boredom. So with this journal that I've found, I think I'm going to start writing my own stuff. I'm just going to continue from where my mom left off. I think that can possibly help me with my boredom crisis.

13 march 2007
What's the deal with mirrors?

No I'm not going to go on some rant about how mirrors are evil and how they "SUPPOSINGLY" make skinny girls look fat (I overheard a girl in my school the other day say something to that degree, gez). So anyway my Dad, and my brother Johnny and I just found out today from my Mom's Doctor that she doesn't like mirrors. And of course I'm thinking WTF? So Dad and Johnny had to move this big mirror in our house downstairs to the basement. I thought it was kind of messed up to move a gift from my Grandpa downstairs to the basement where no one will see it, but if mom doesn't like it, I guess its worth putting away. So yeah since my mom is coming home tomorrow the Doc said we should get rid of the mirrors and possibly get her a pet. Now my DAD is spending his Saturday looking for the RIGHT pet for mom. Well whatever it is I hope it's worth getting.

About me
Email

Archives
April 2007
March 2007
February 2007
January 2007
December 2006
November 2006
October 2006
August 2006
July 2006
June 2006

CALIE'S BLOG

14 march 2007

A freaking WHITE RABBIT?

What the hell? So Dad came back with this hideous looking white rabbit. Gez maybe I should have went with him to pick out a nicer looking rabbit, but than again what the hell do I know about rabbits. I've never touched or even thought about having a rabbit, bunny or whatever you want to call those little things as a pet. But for some reason the Doc told Dad that mom really wants a rabbit. This rabbit better be worth all the trouble.

16 march 2007

What color should I dye my hair today?

I think I'm really leaning towards more black streaks. I don't seem to have enough of those in my hair.

20 march 2007

Since when did I become a babysitter?

I'm so frustrated that my Dad expects me to keep an eye on mom like every freaking day. I mean I have a life too. Since when did I become a babysitter? I mean don't get me wrong, I love my mom, I care about her and I don't want her to do something stupid. But I'm really tired of having to worry about her or just having to constantly wonder if she is okay. I'm just really tired I guess...

26 march 2007

CREEPY??

I think my mom is stuck to that Rabbit like crazy clue. Ever since we gave her that thing she doesn't seem to want to part with it...creepy to me on so many levels.

About me

Email

Archives

April 2007

March 2007

February 2007

January 2007

December 2006

November 2006

October 2006

August 2006

July 2006

June 2006

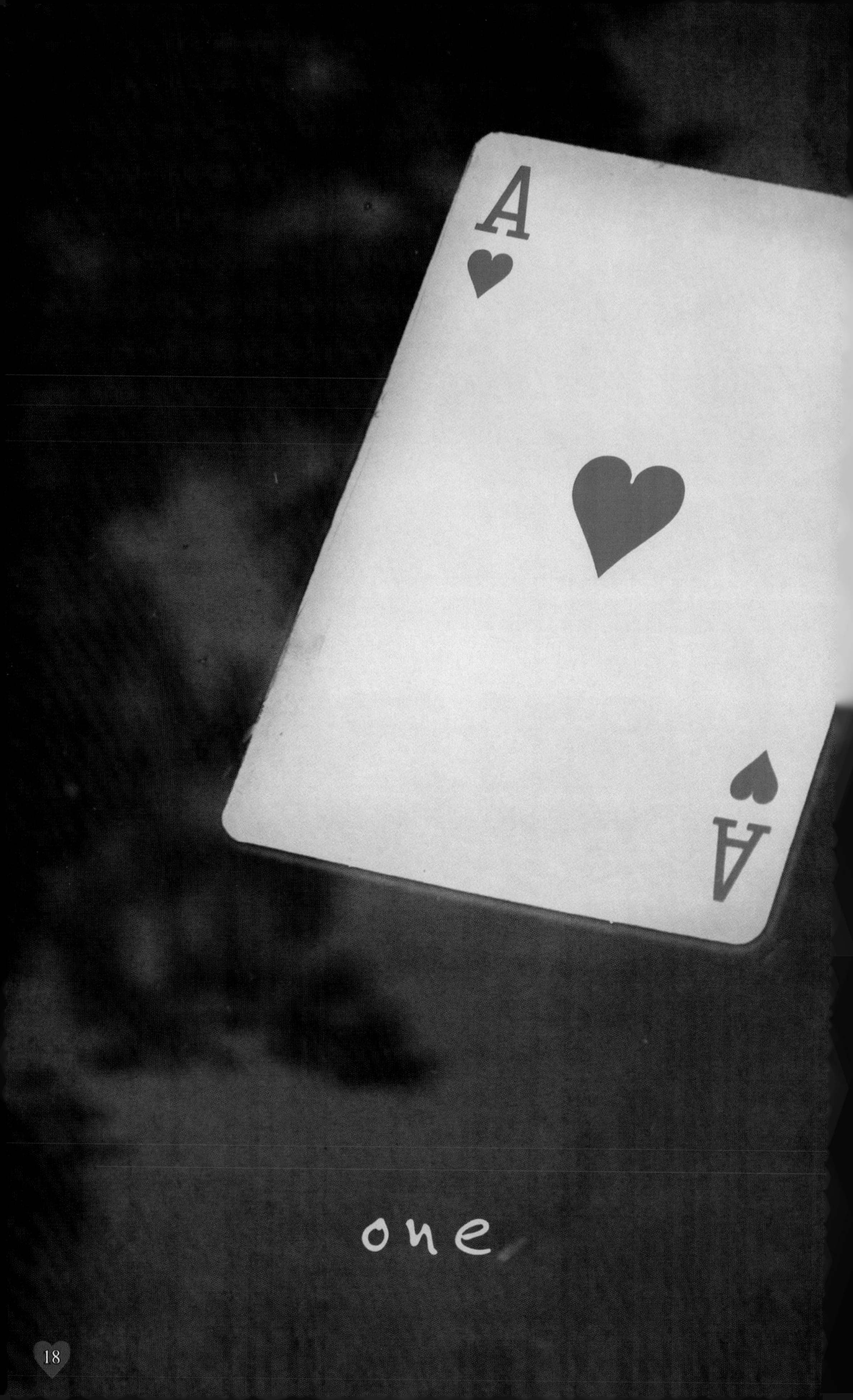

one

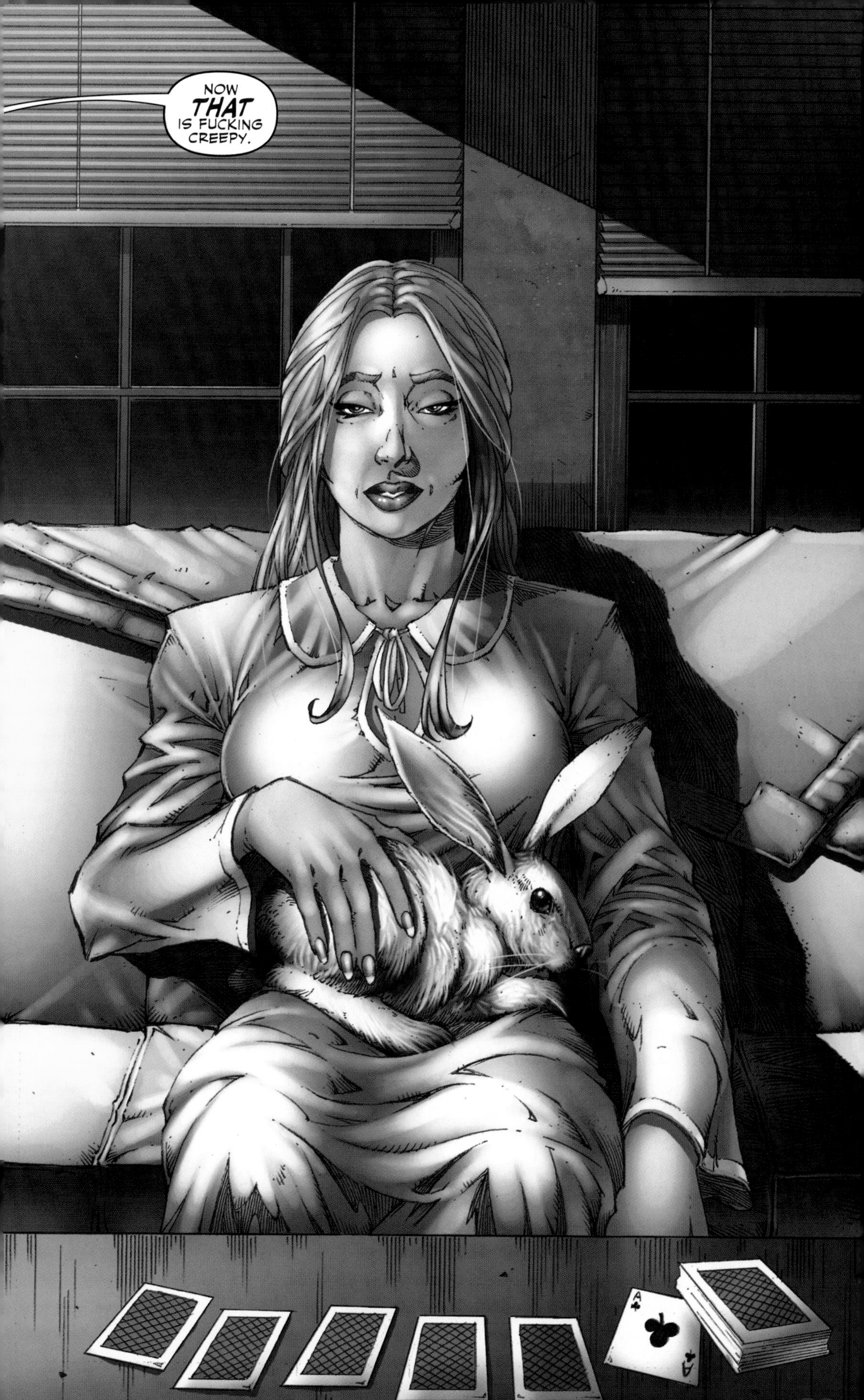
NOW THAT IS FUCKING CREEPY.

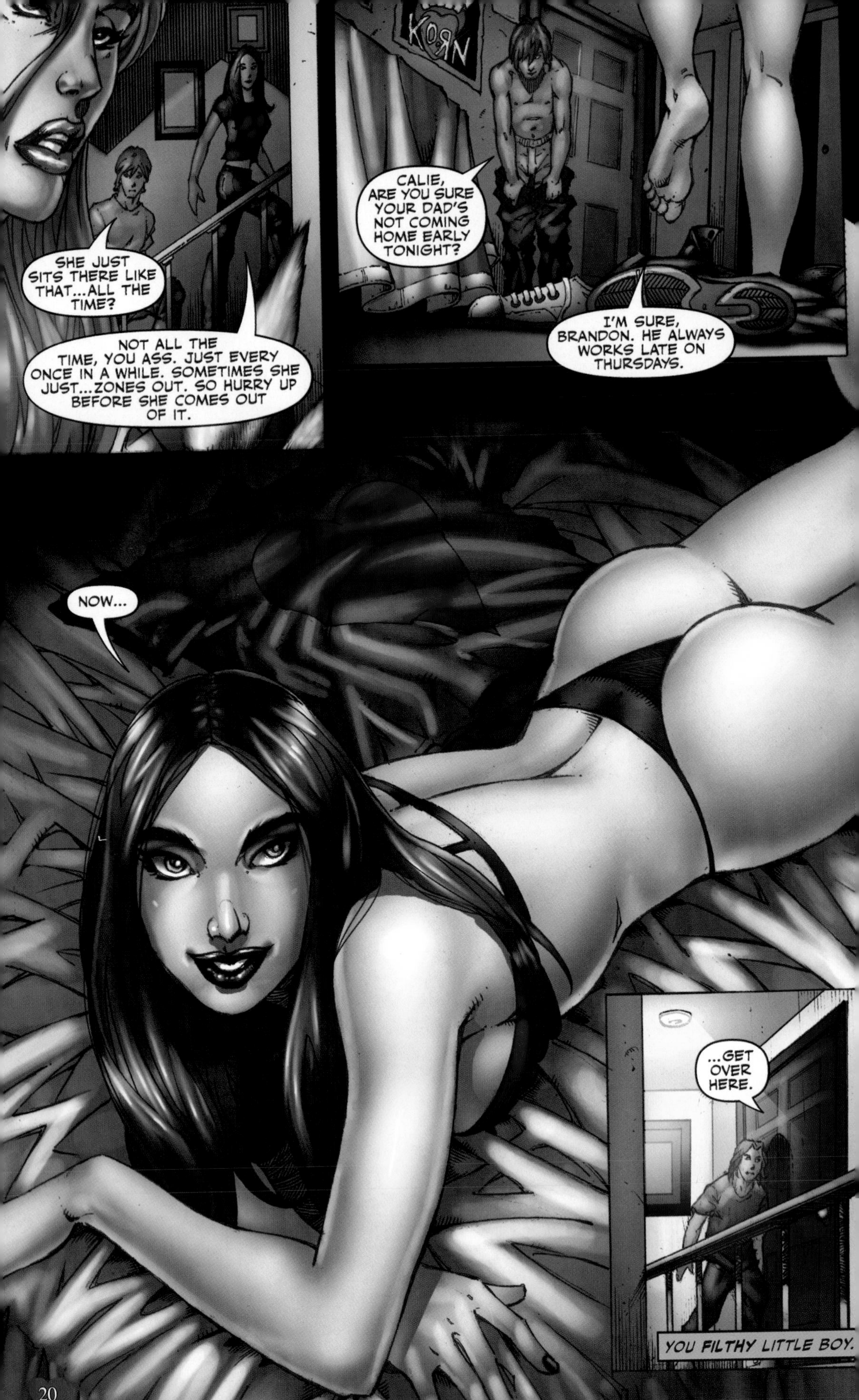
SHE JUST SITS THERE LIKE THAT...ALL THE TIME?
NOT ALL THE TIME, YOU ASS. JUST EVERY ONCE IN A WHILE. SOMETIMES SHE JUST...ZONES OUT. SO HURRY UP BEFORE SHE COMES OUT OF IT.
KORN
CALIE, ARE YOU SURE YOUR DAD'S NOT COMING HOME EARLY TONIGHT?
I'M SURE, BRANDON. HE ALWAYS WORKS LATE ON THURSDAYS.
NOW...
...GET OVER HERE.
YOU *FILTHY* LITTLE BOY.

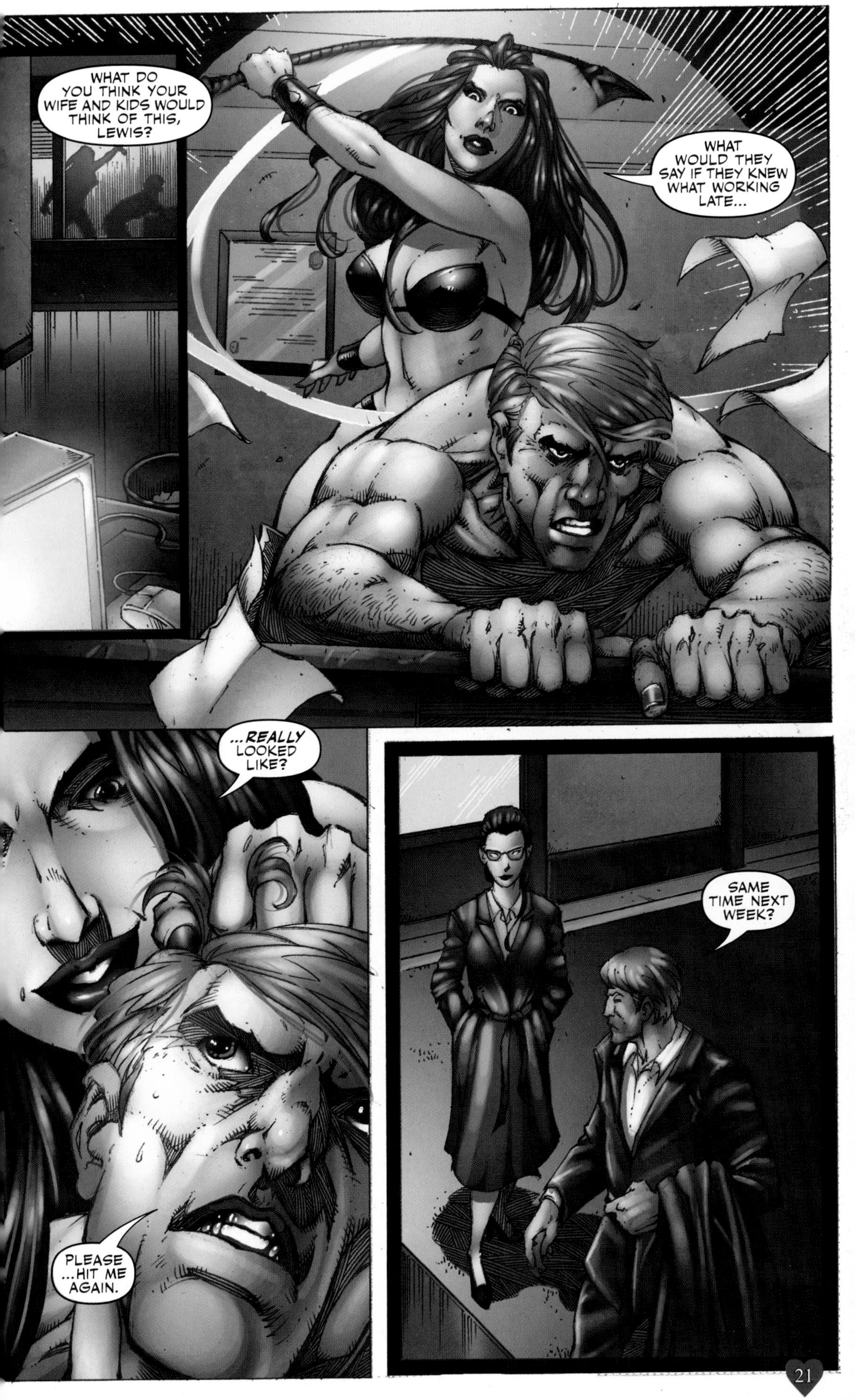
WHAT DO YOU THINK YOUR WIFE AND KIDS WOULD THINK OF THIS, LEWIS?
WHAT WOULD THEY SAY IF THEY KNEW WHAT WORKING LATE...
...*REALLY* LOOKED LIKE?
PLEASE ...HIT ME AGAIN.
SAME TIME NEXT WEEK?

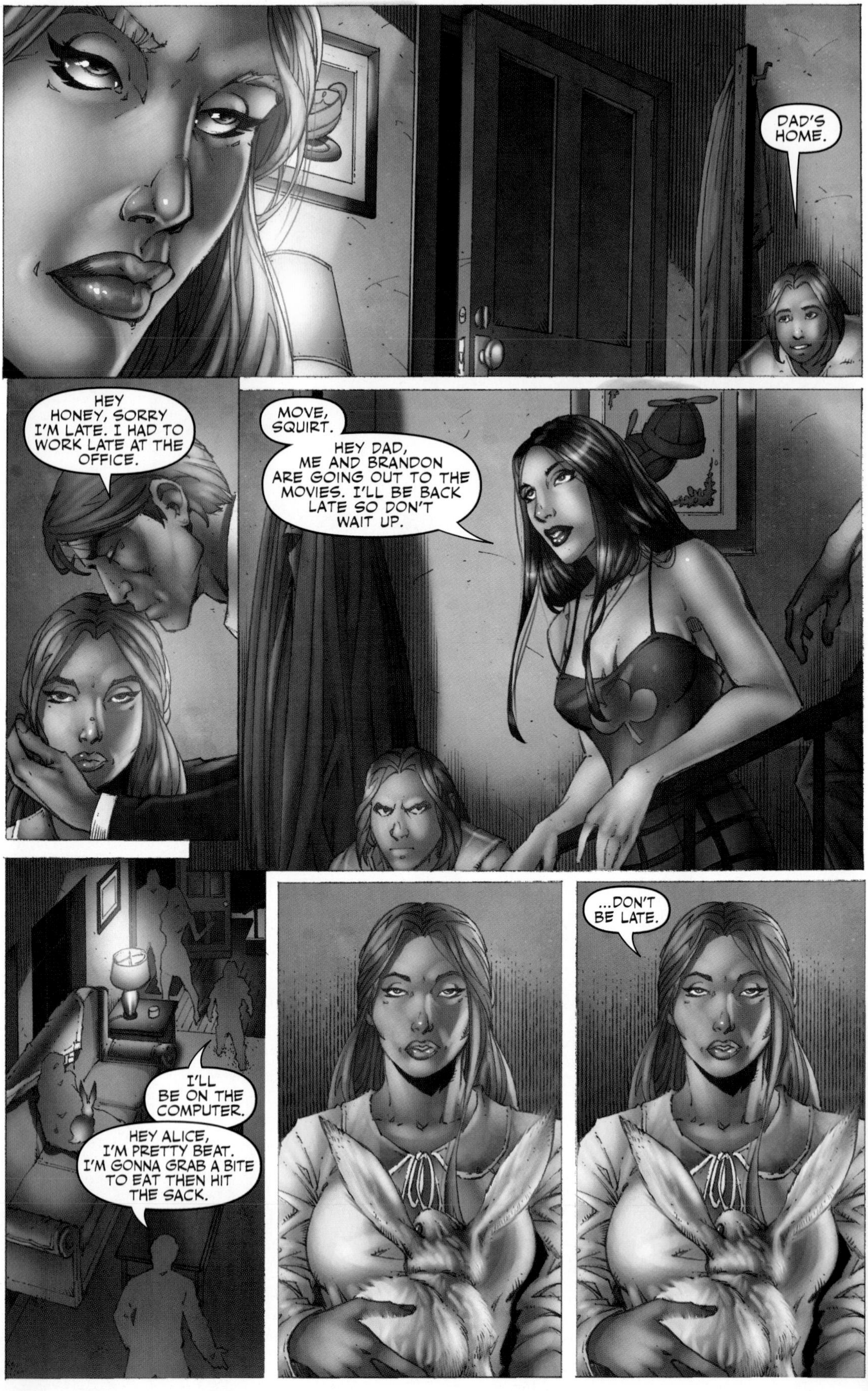
DAD'S HOME.
HEY HONEY, SORRY I'M LATE. I HAD TO WORK LATE AT THE OFFICE.
MOVE, SQUIRT.
HEY DAD, ME AND BRANDON ARE GOING OUT TO THE MOVIES. I'LL BE BACK LATE SO DON'T WAIT UP.
I'LL BE ON THE COMPUTER.
HEY ALICE, I'M PRETTY BEAT. I'M GONNA GRAB A BITE TO EAT THEN HIT THE SACK.
...DON'T BE LATE.

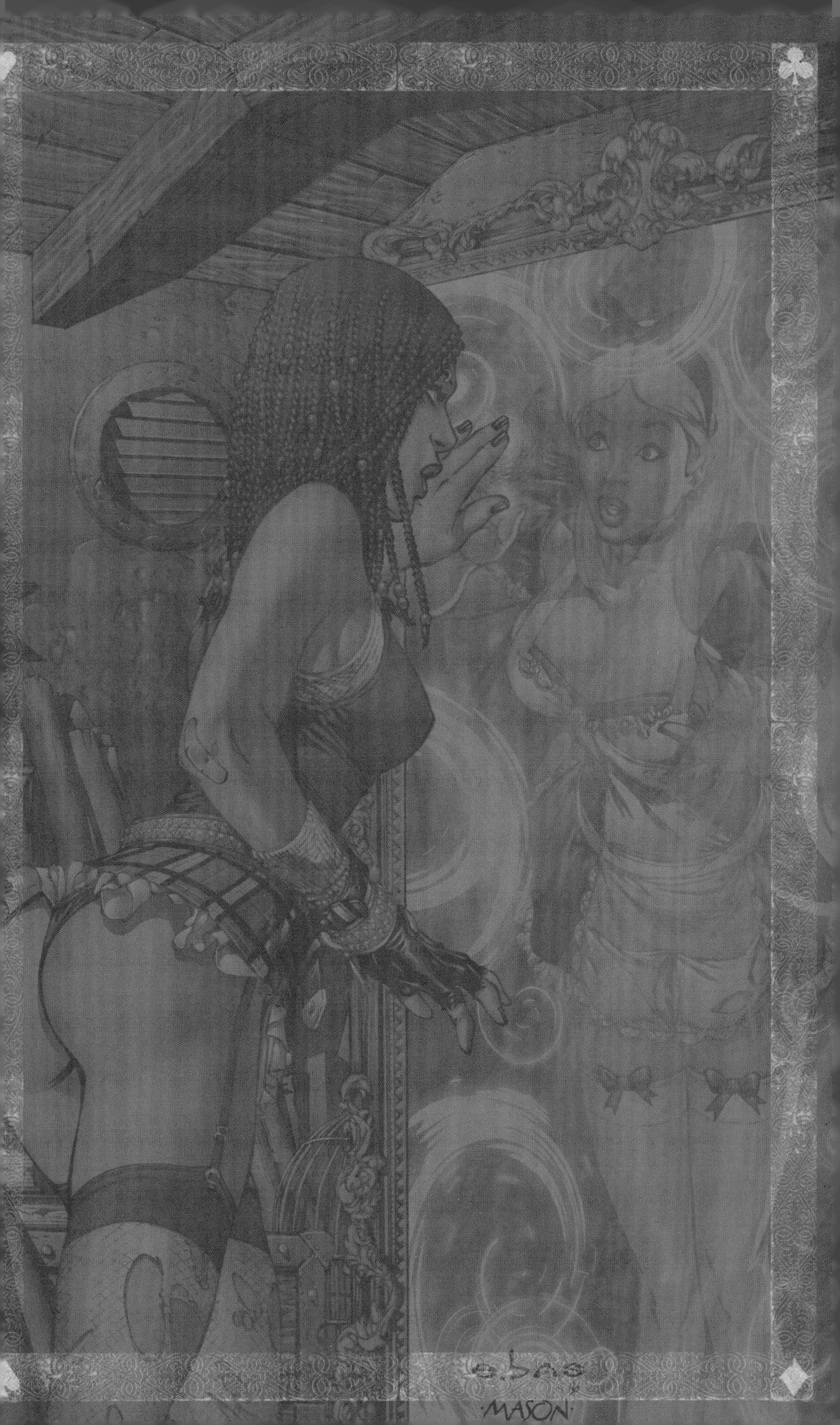
MASON

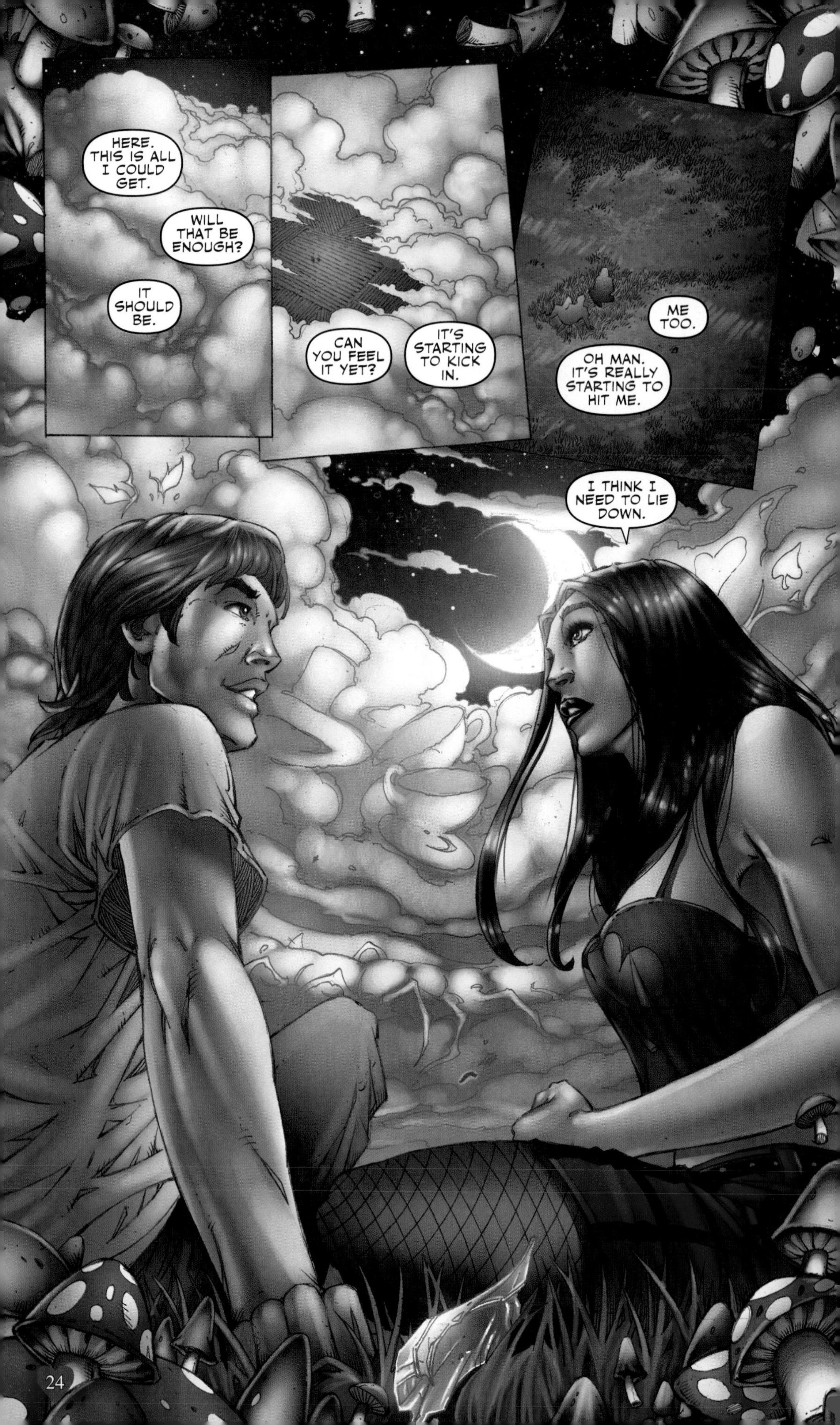
HERE. THIS IS ALL I COULD GET.
WILL THAT BE ENOUGH?
IT SHOULD BE.
CAN YOU FEEL IT YET?
IT'S STARTING TO KICK IN.
ME TOO.
OH MAN. IT'S REALLY STARTING TO HIT ME.
I THINK I NEED TO LIE DOWN.

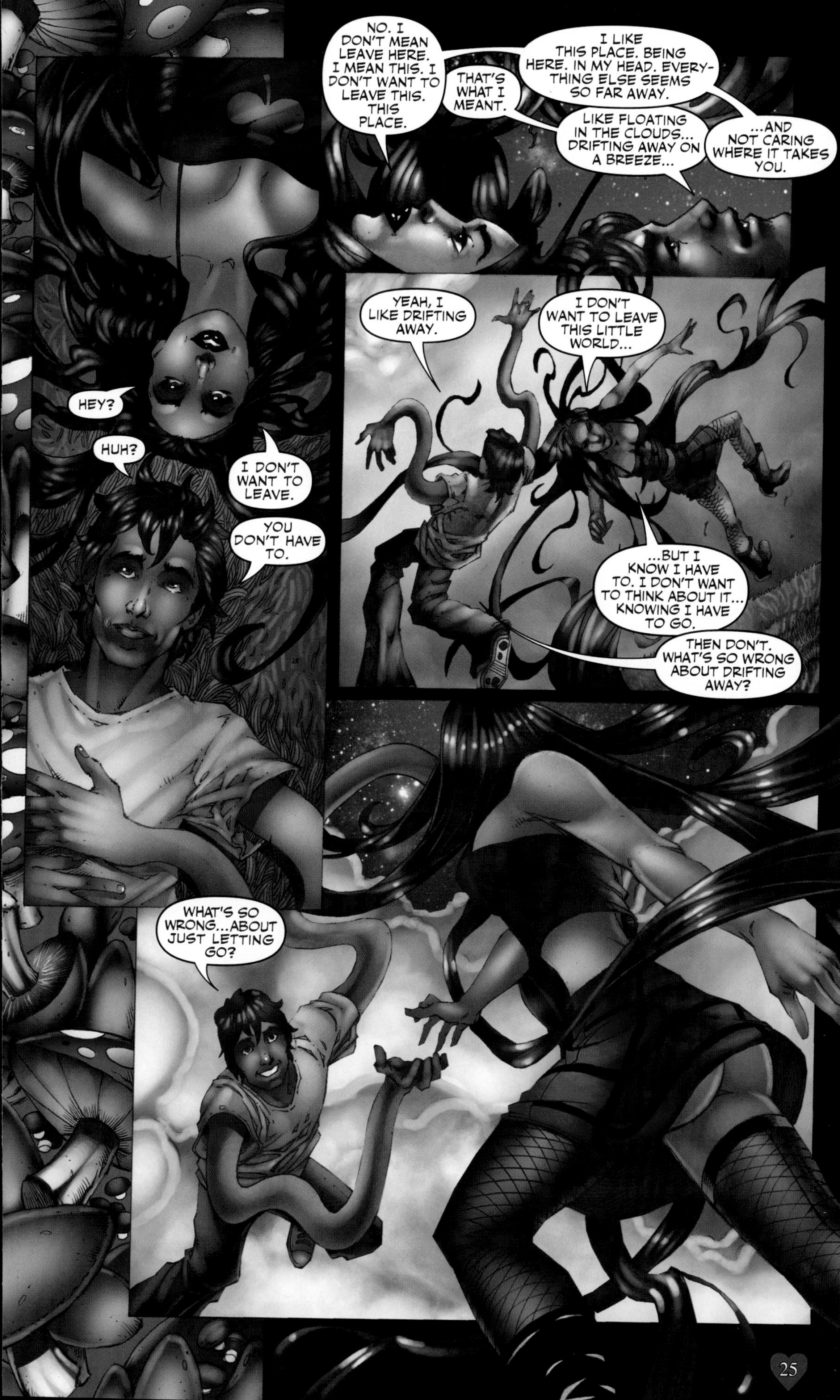
NO. I DON'T MEAN LEAVE HERE. I MEAN THIS. I DON'T WANT TO LEAVE THIS. THIS PLACE.
THAT'S WHAT I MEANT.
I LIKE THIS PLACE. BEING HERE. IN MY HEAD. EVERYTHING ELSE SEEMS SO FAR AWAY.
LIKE FLOATING IN THE CLOUDS... DRIFTING AWAY ON A BREEZE...
...AND NOT CARING WHERE IT TAKES YOU.
HEY?
HUH?
I DON'T WANT TO LEAVE.
YOU DON'T HAVE TO.
YEAH, I LIKE DRIFTING AWAY.
I DON'T WANT TO LEAVE THIS LITTLE WORLD...
...BUT I KNOW I HAVE TO. I DON'T WANT TO THINK ABOUT IT... KNOWING I HAVE TO GO.
THEN DON'T. WHAT'S SO WRONG ABOUT DRIFTING AWAY?
WHAT'S SO WRONG...ABOUT JUST LETTING GO?

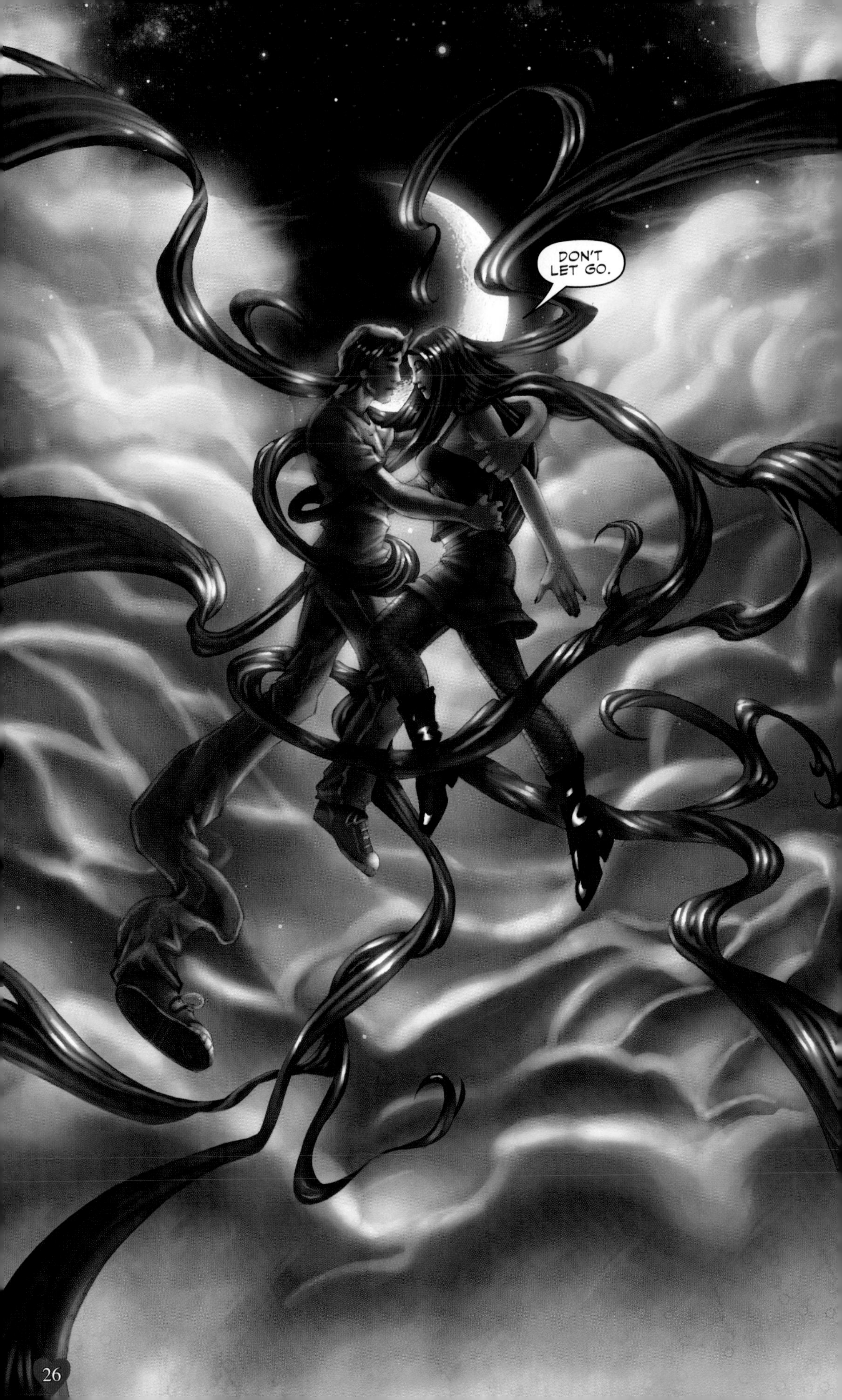
DON'T LET GO.

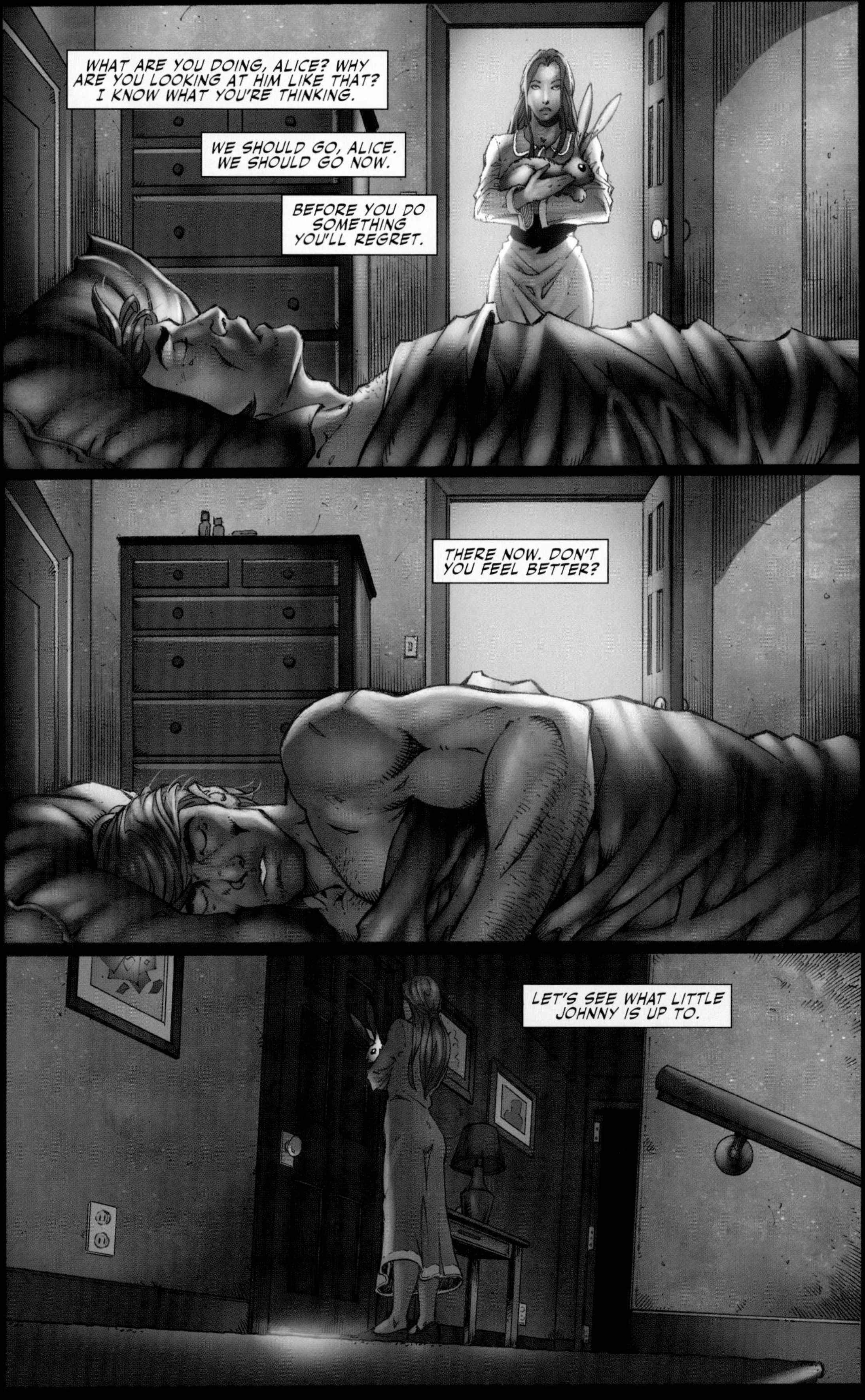
WHAT ARE YOU DOING, ALICE? WHY ARE YOU LOOKING AT HIM LIKE THAT? I KNOW WHAT YOU'RE THINKING.
WE SHOULD GO, ALICE. WE SHOULD GO NOW.
BEFORE YOU DO SOMETHING YOU'LL REGRET.
THERE NOW. DON'T YOU FEEL BETTER?
LET'S SEE WHAT LITTLE JOHNNY IS UP TO.

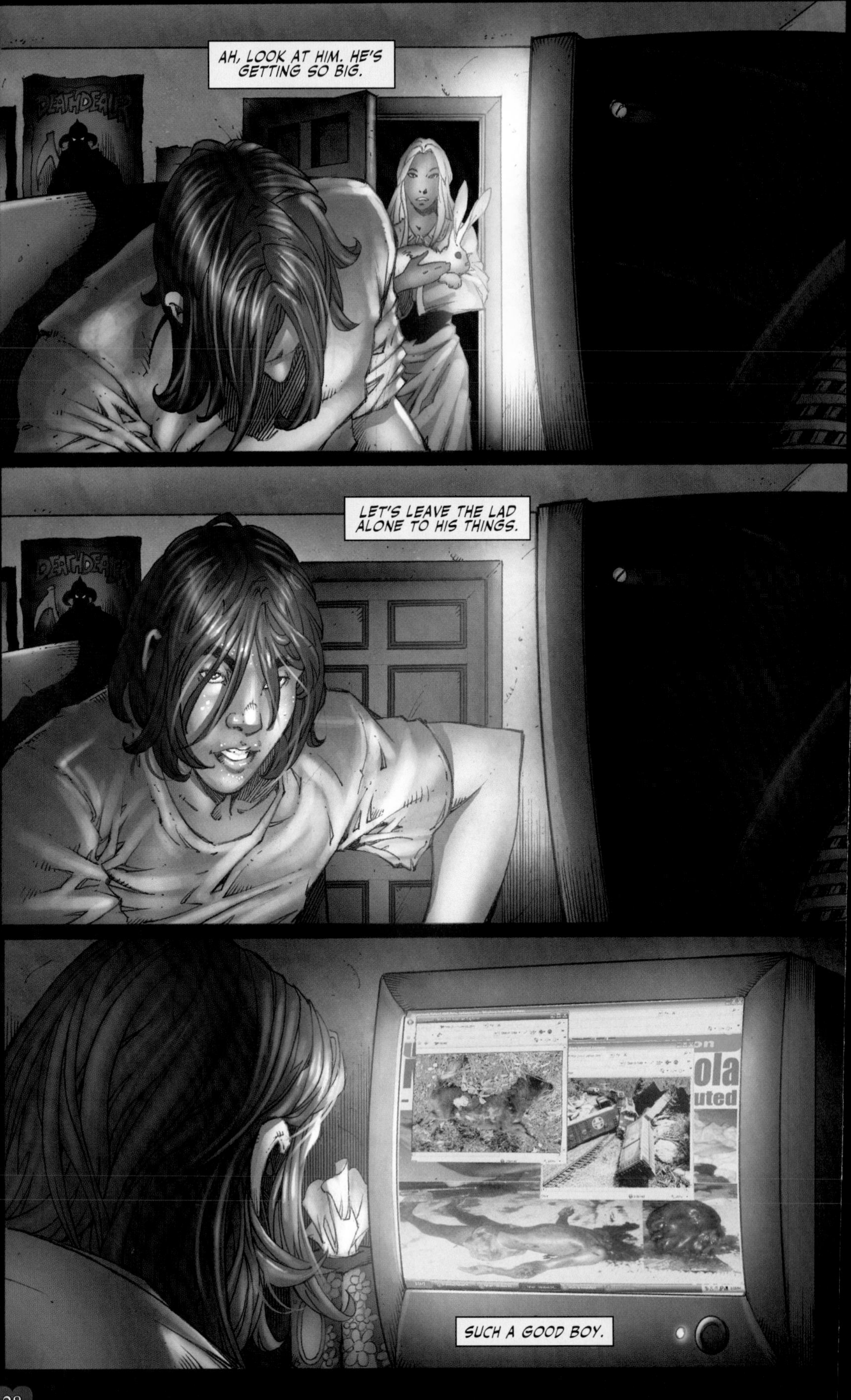
AH, LOOK AT HIM. HE'S GETTING SO BIG.
LET'S LEAVE THE LAD ALONE TO HIS THINGS.
SUCH A GOOD BOY.

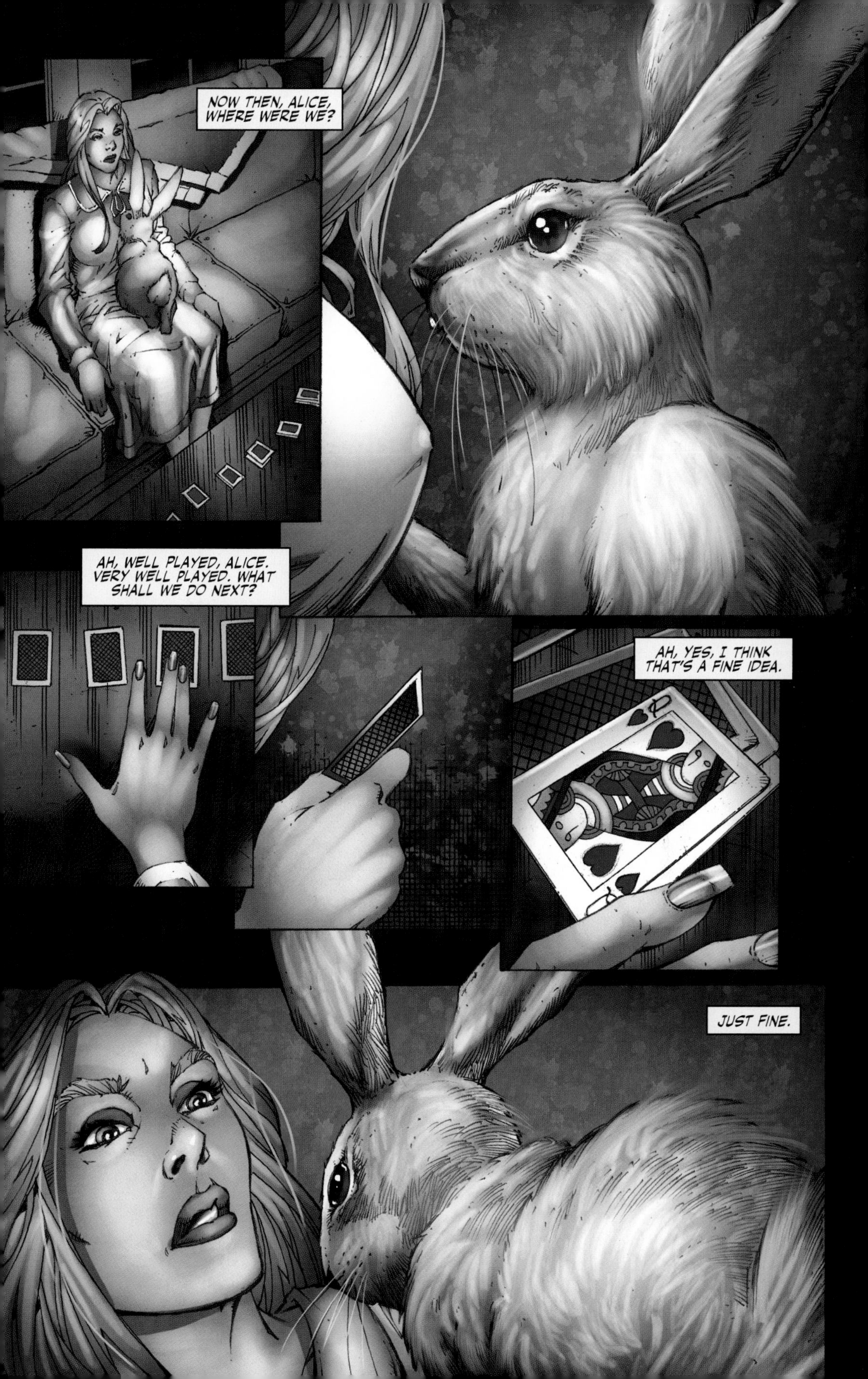
NOW THEN, ALICE, WHERE WERE WE?
AH, WELL PLAYED, ALICE. VERY WELL PLAYED. WHAT SHALL WE DO NEXT?
AH, YES, I THINK THAT'S A FINE IDEA.
JUST FINE.

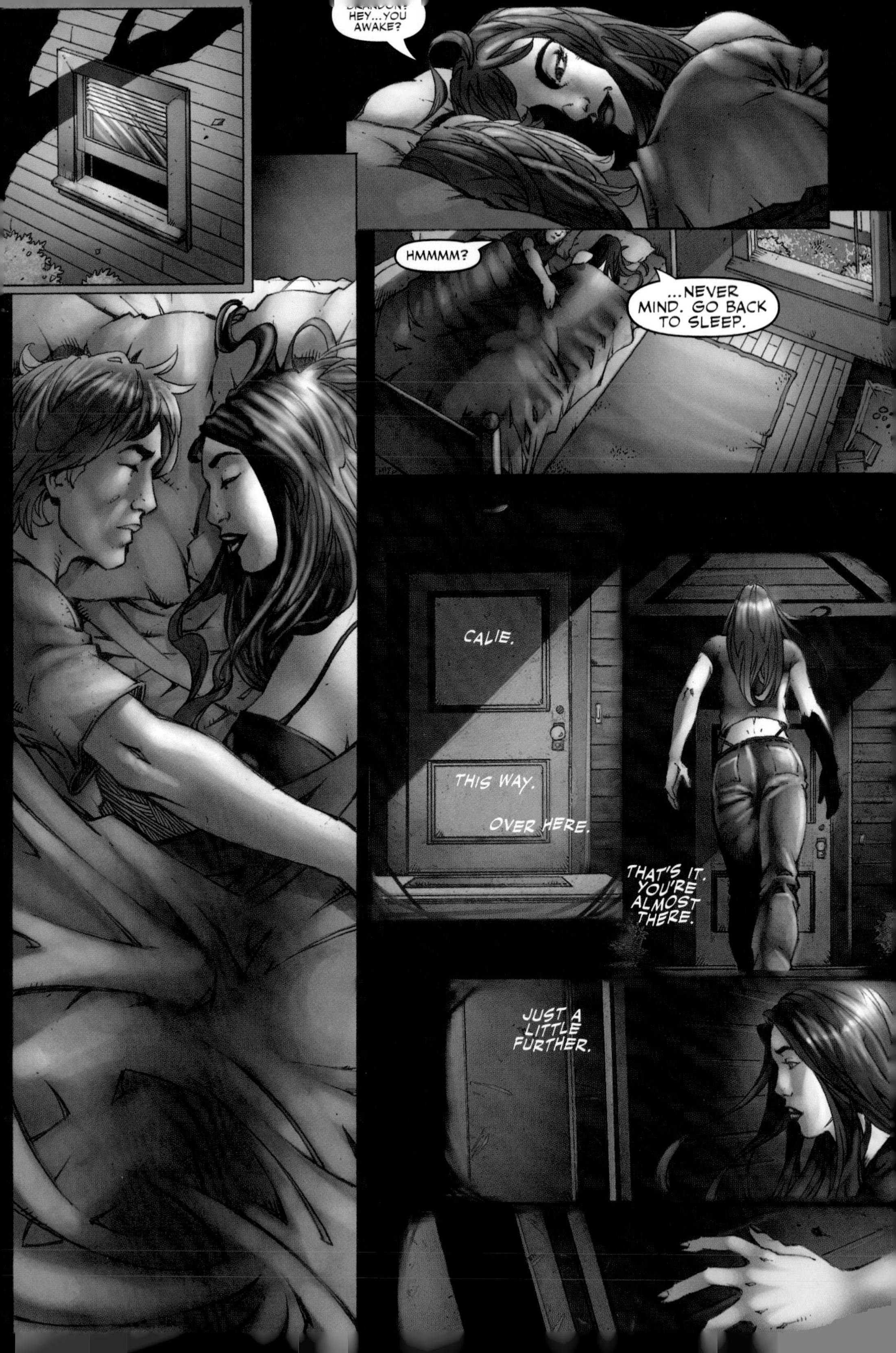
HEY...YOU AWAKE?
HMMMM?
...NEVER MIND. GO BACK TO SLEEP.
CALIE.
THIS WAY.
OVER HERE.
THAT'S IT. YOU'RE ALMOST THERE.
JUST A LITTLE FURTHER.

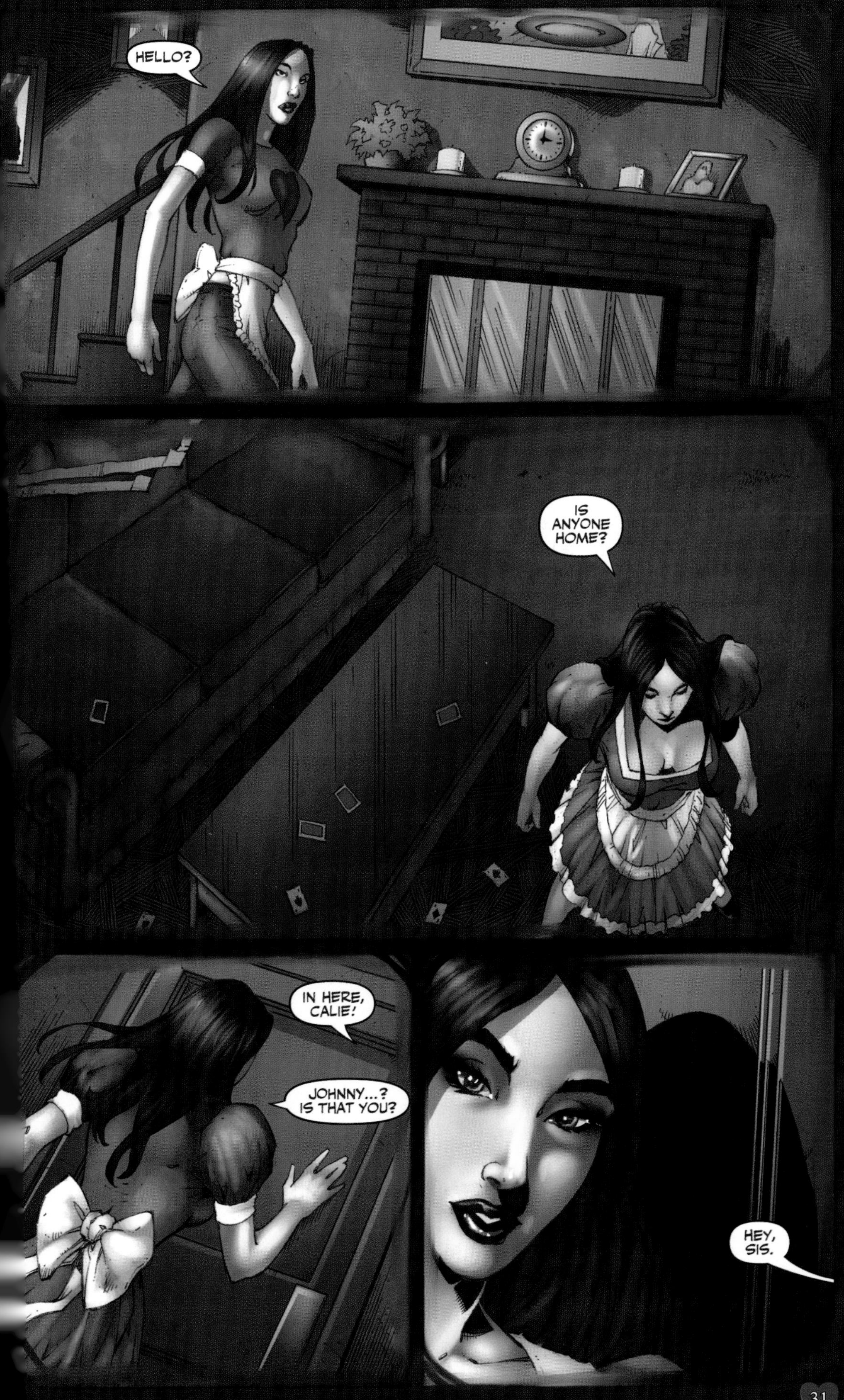
HELLO?
IS ANYONE HOME?
IN HERE, CALIE!
JOHNNY...? IS THAT YOU?
HEY, SIS.

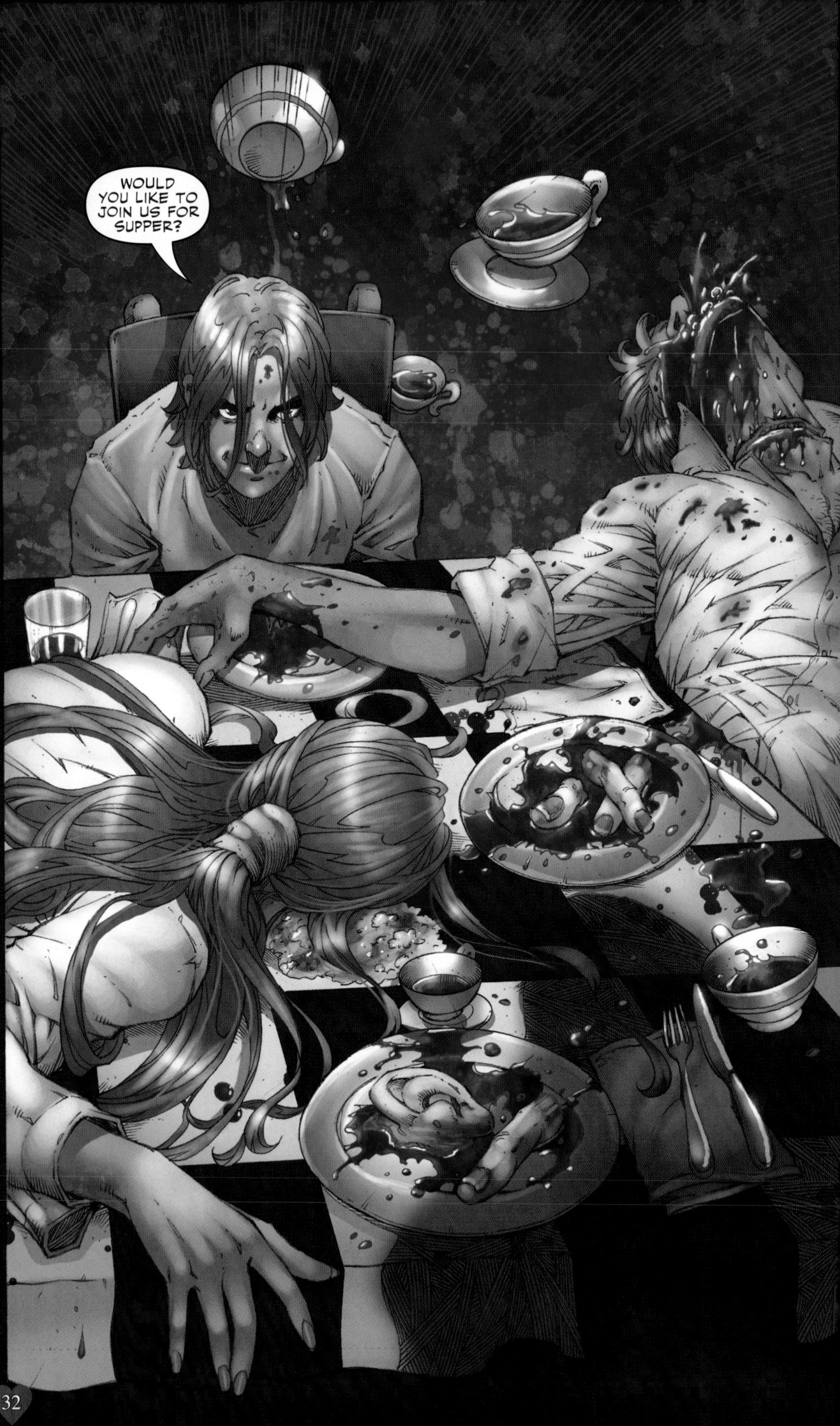
WOULD YOU LIKE TO JOIN US FOR SUPPER?

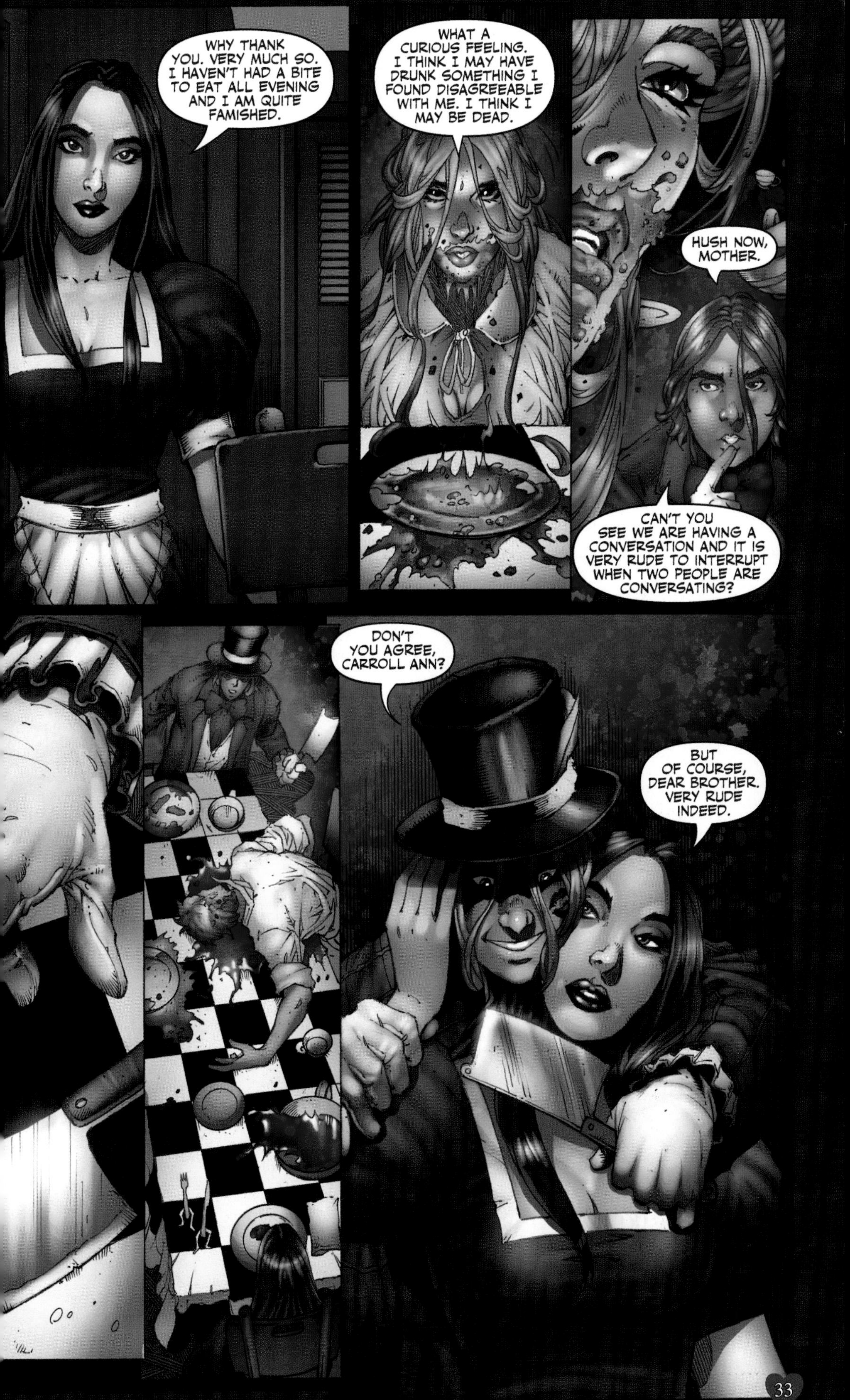

WHY THANK YOU. VERY MUCH SO. I HAVEN'T HAD A BITE TO EAT ALL EVENING AND I AM QUITE FAMISHED.
WHAT A CURIOUS FEELING. I THINK I MAY HAVE DRUNK SOMETHING I FOUND DISAGREEABLE WITH ME. I THINK I MAY BE DEAD.
HUSH NOW, MOTHER.
CAN'T YOU SEE WE ARE HAVING A CONVERSATION AND IT IS VERY RUDE TO INTERRUPT WHEN TWO PEOPLE ARE CONVERSATING?
DON'T YOU AGREE, CARROLL ANN?
BUT OF COURSE, DEAR BROTHER. VERY RUDE INDEED.

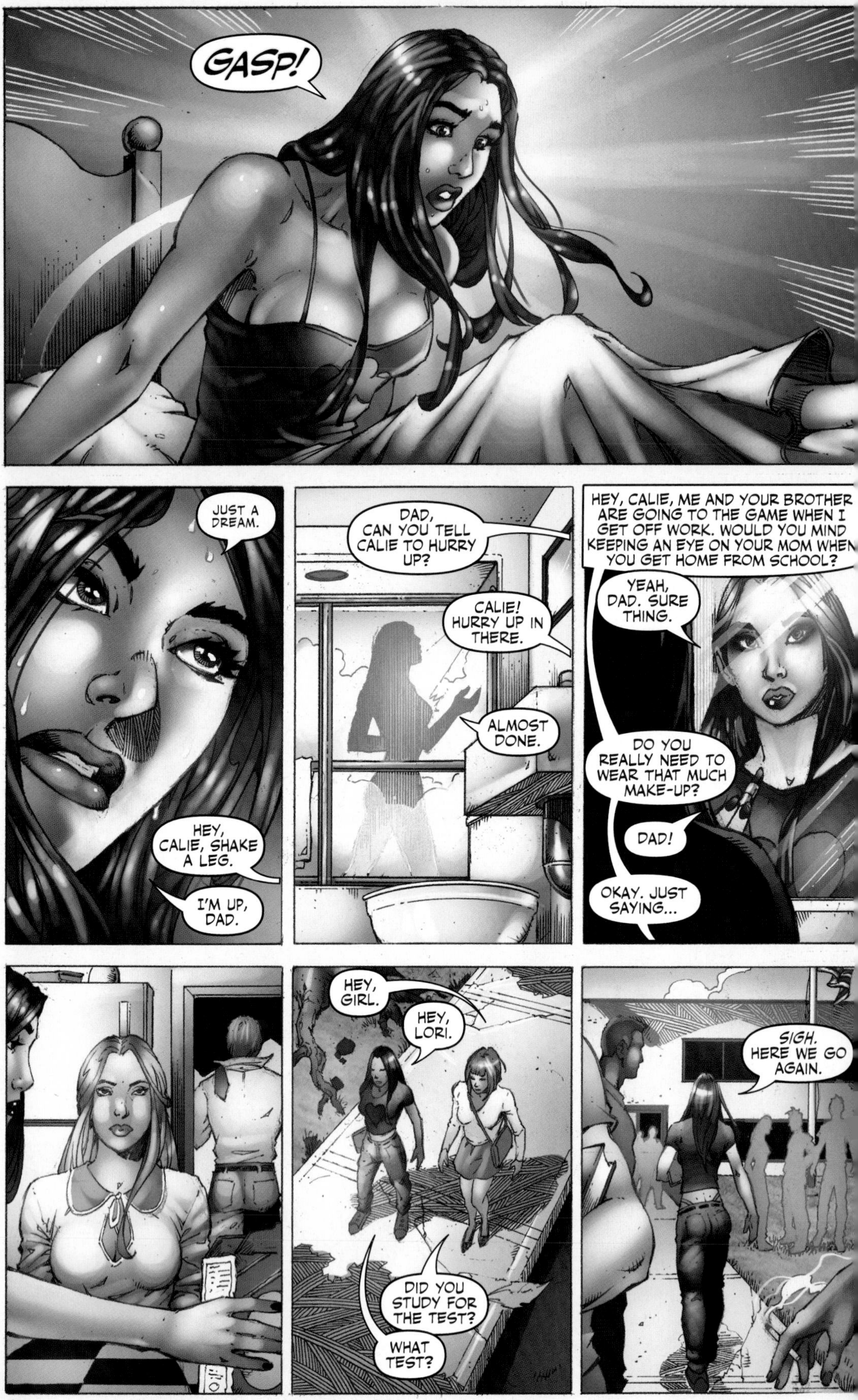
GASP!
JUST A DREAM.
HEY, CALIE, SHAKE A LEG.
I'M UP, DAD.
DAD, CAN YOU TELL CALIE TO HURRY UP?
CALIE! HURRY UP IN THERE.
ALMOST DONE.
HEY, CALIE, ME AND YOUR BROTHER ARE GOING TO THE GAME WHEN I GET OFF WORK. WOULD YOU MIND KEEPING AN EYE ON YOUR MOM WHEN YOU GET HOME FROM SCHOOL?
YEAH, DAD. SURE THING.
DO YOU REALLY NEED TO WEAR THAT MUCH MAKE-UP?
DAD!
OKAY. JUST SAYING...
HEY, GIRL.
HEY, LORI.
DID YOU STUDY FOR THE TEST?
WHAT TEST?
SIGH. HERE WE GO AGAIN.

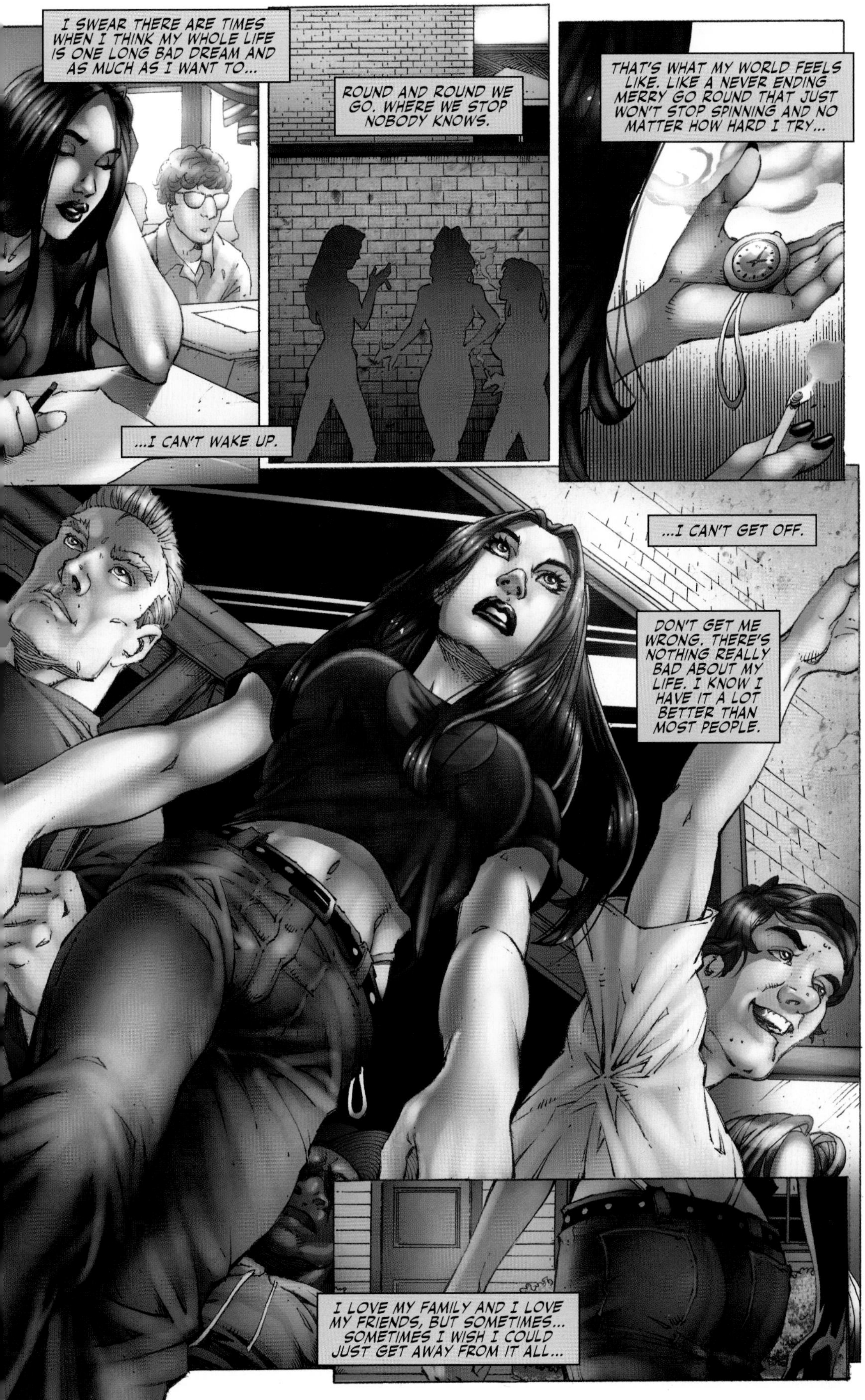
I SWEAR THERE ARE TIMES WHEN I THINK MY WHOLE LIFE IS ONE LONG BAD DREAM AND AS MUCH AS I WANT TO...
...I CAN'T WAKE UP.
ROUND AND ROUND WE GO. WHERE WE STOP NOBODY KNOWS.
THAT'S WHAT MY WORLD FEELS LIKE. LIKE A NEVER ENDING MERRY GO ROUND THAT JUST WON'T STOP SPINNING AND NO MATTER HOW HARD I TRY...
...I CAN'T GET OFF.
DON'T GET ME WRONG. THERE'S NOTHING REALLY BAD ABOUT MY LIFE. I KNOW I HAVE IT A LOT BETTER THAN MOST PEOPLE.
I LOVE MY FAMILY AND I LOVE MY FRIENDS, BUT SOMETIMES... SOMETIMES I WISH I COULD JUST GET AWAY FROM IT ALL...

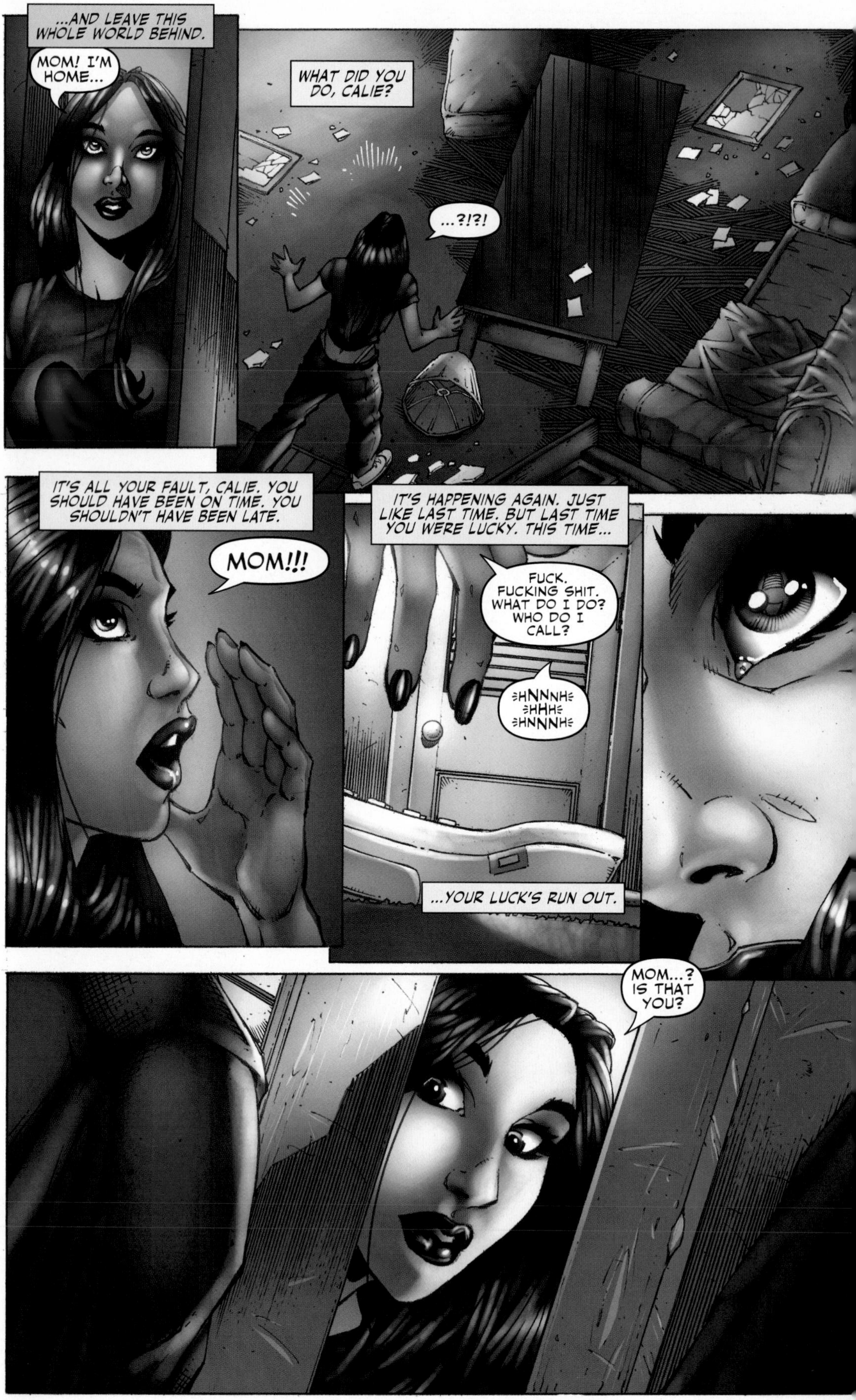
...AND LEAVE THIS WHOLE WORLD BEHIND.
MOM! I'M HOME...
WHAT DID YOU DO, CALIE?
...?!?!
IT'S ALL YOUR FAULT, CALIE. YOU SHOULD HAVE BEEN ON TIME. YOU SHOULDN'T HAVE BEEN LATE.
MOM!!!
IT'S HAPPENING AGAIN. JUST LIKE LAST TIME. BUT LAST TIME YOU WERE LUCKY. THIS TIME...
FUCK. FUCKING SHIT. WHAT DO I DO? WHO DO I CALL?
HNNNH HHH HNNNH
...YOUR LUCK'S RUN OUT.
MOM...? IS THAT YOU?

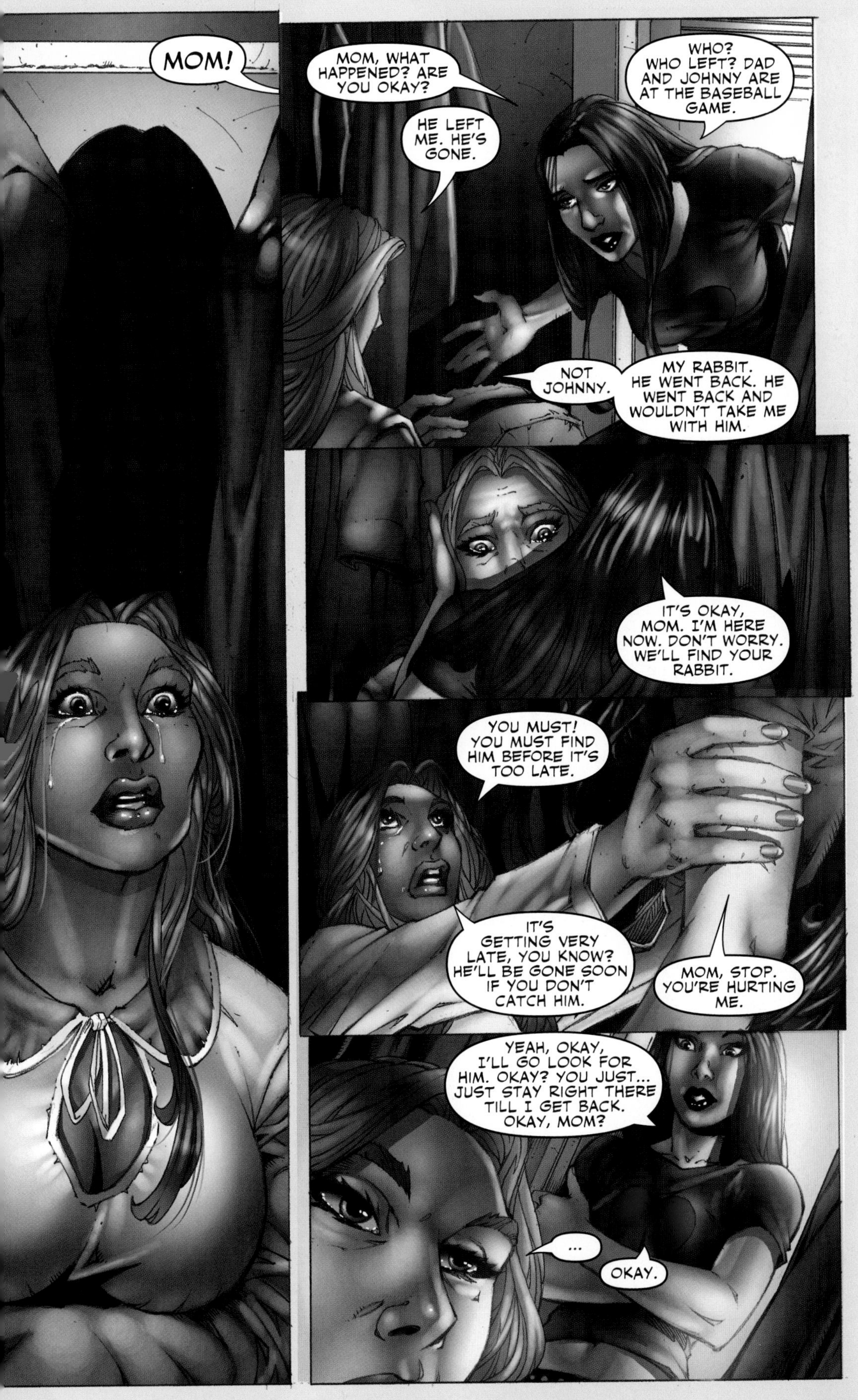
MOM!
MOM, WHAT HAPPENED? ARE YOU OKAY?
HE LEFT ME. HE'S GONE.
WHO? WHO LEFT? DAD AND JOHNNY ARE AT THE BASEBALL GAME.
NOT JOHNNY.
MY RABBIT. HE WENT BACK. HE WENT BACK AND WOULDN'T TAKE ME WITH HIM.
IT'S OKAY, MOM. I'M HERE NOW. DON'T WORRY. WE'LL FIND YOUR RABBIT.
YOU MUST! YOU MUST FIND HIM BEFORE IT'S TOO LATE.
IT'S GETTING VERY LATE, YOU KNOW? HE'LL BE GONE SOON IF YOU DON'T CATCH HIM.
MOM, STOP. YOU'RE HURTING ME.
YEAH, OKAY, I'LL GO LOOK FOR HIM. OKAY? YOU JUST... JUST STAY RIGHT THERE TILL I GET BACK. OKAY, MOM?
...
OKAY.

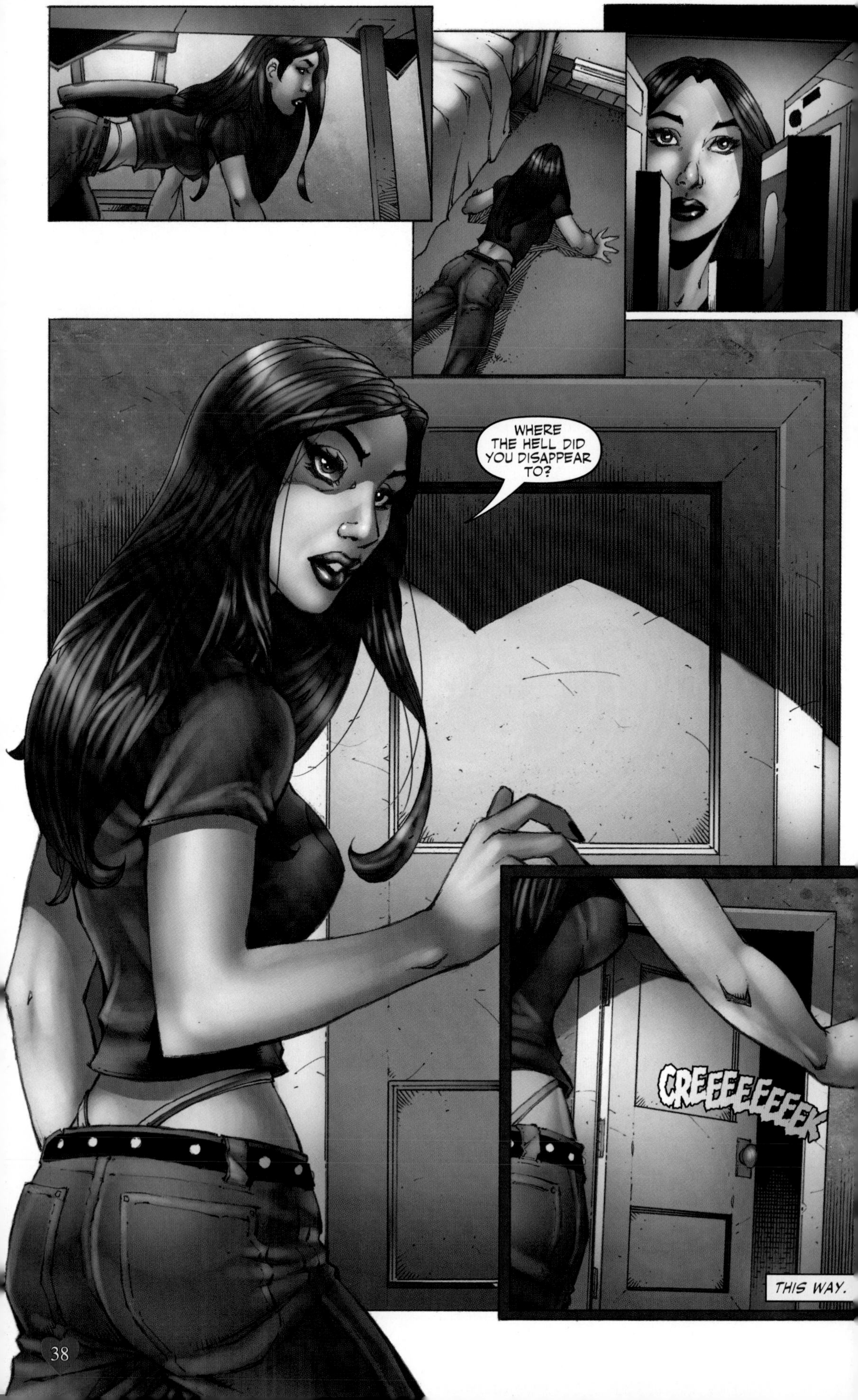
WHERE THE HELL DID YOU DISAPPEAR TO?
CREEEEEEEEK
THIS WAY.

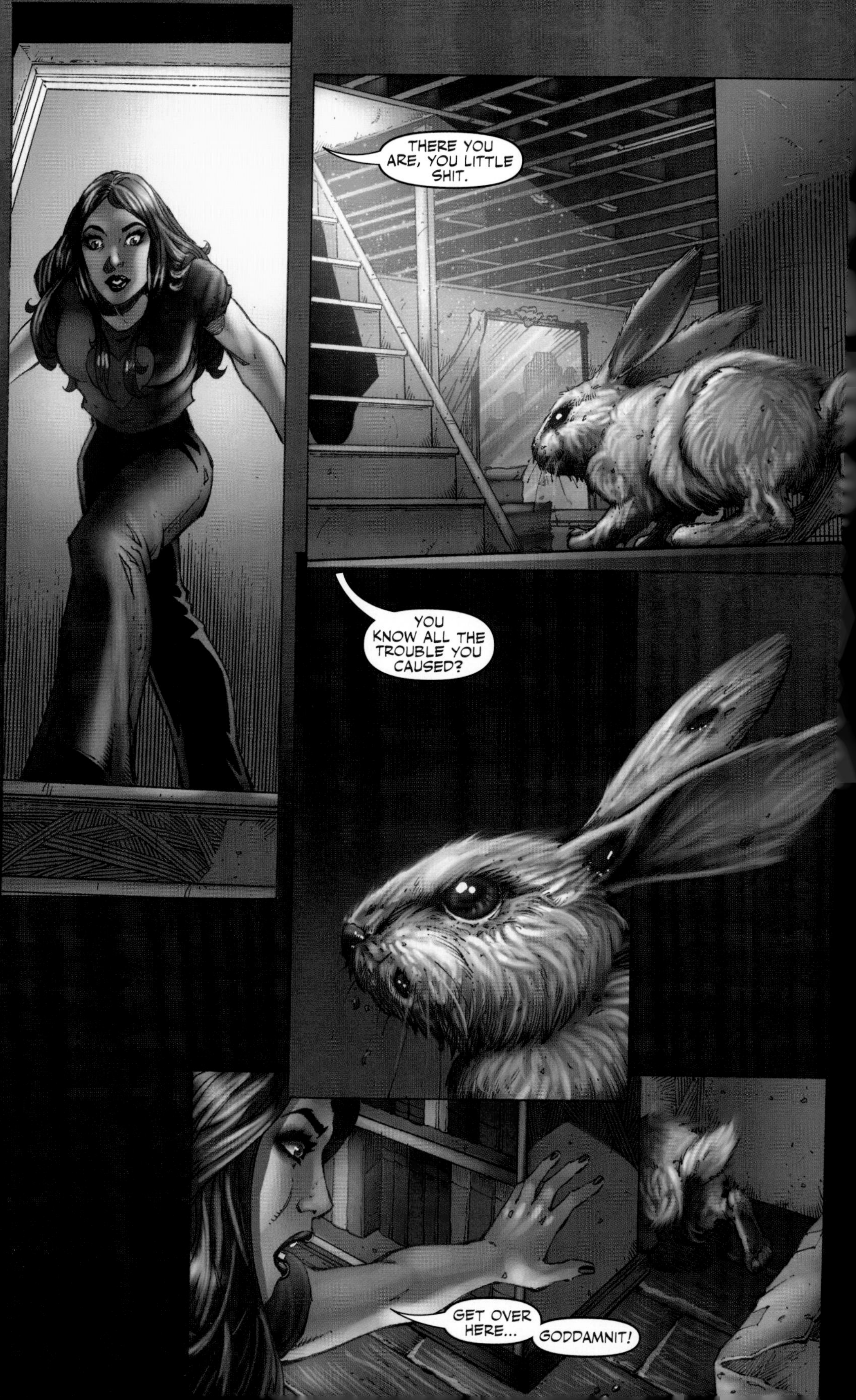
THERE YOU ARE, YOU LITTLE SHIT.
YOU KNOW ALL THE TROUBLE YOU CAUSED?
GET OVER HERE...
GODDAMNIT!

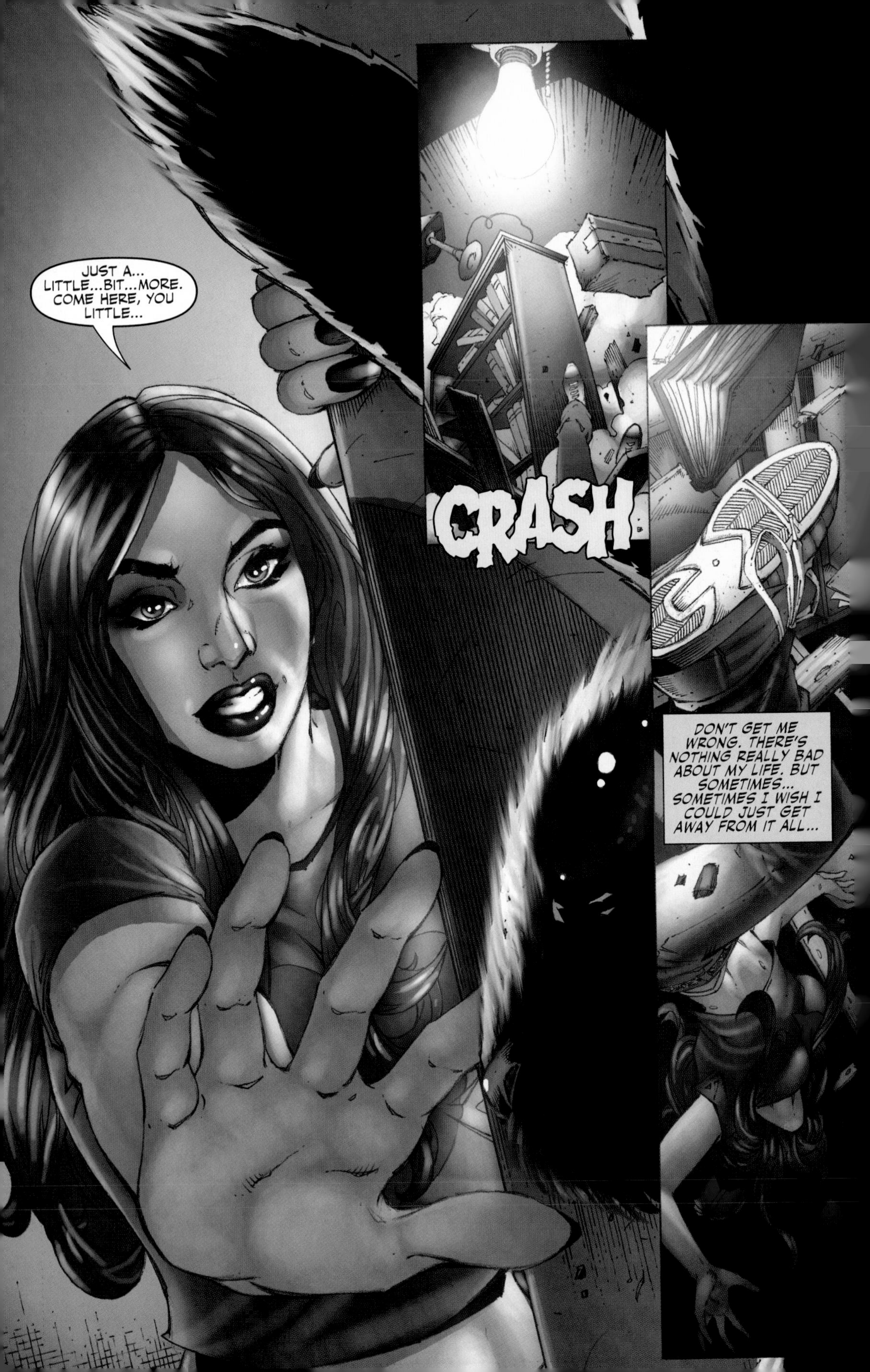
JUST A... LITTLE...BIT...MORE. COME HERE, YOU LITTLE...
CRASH
DON'T GET ME WRONG. THERE'S NOTHING REALLY BAD ABOUT MY LIFE. BUT SOMETIMES... SOMETIMES I WISH I COULD JUST GET AWAY FROM IT ALL...

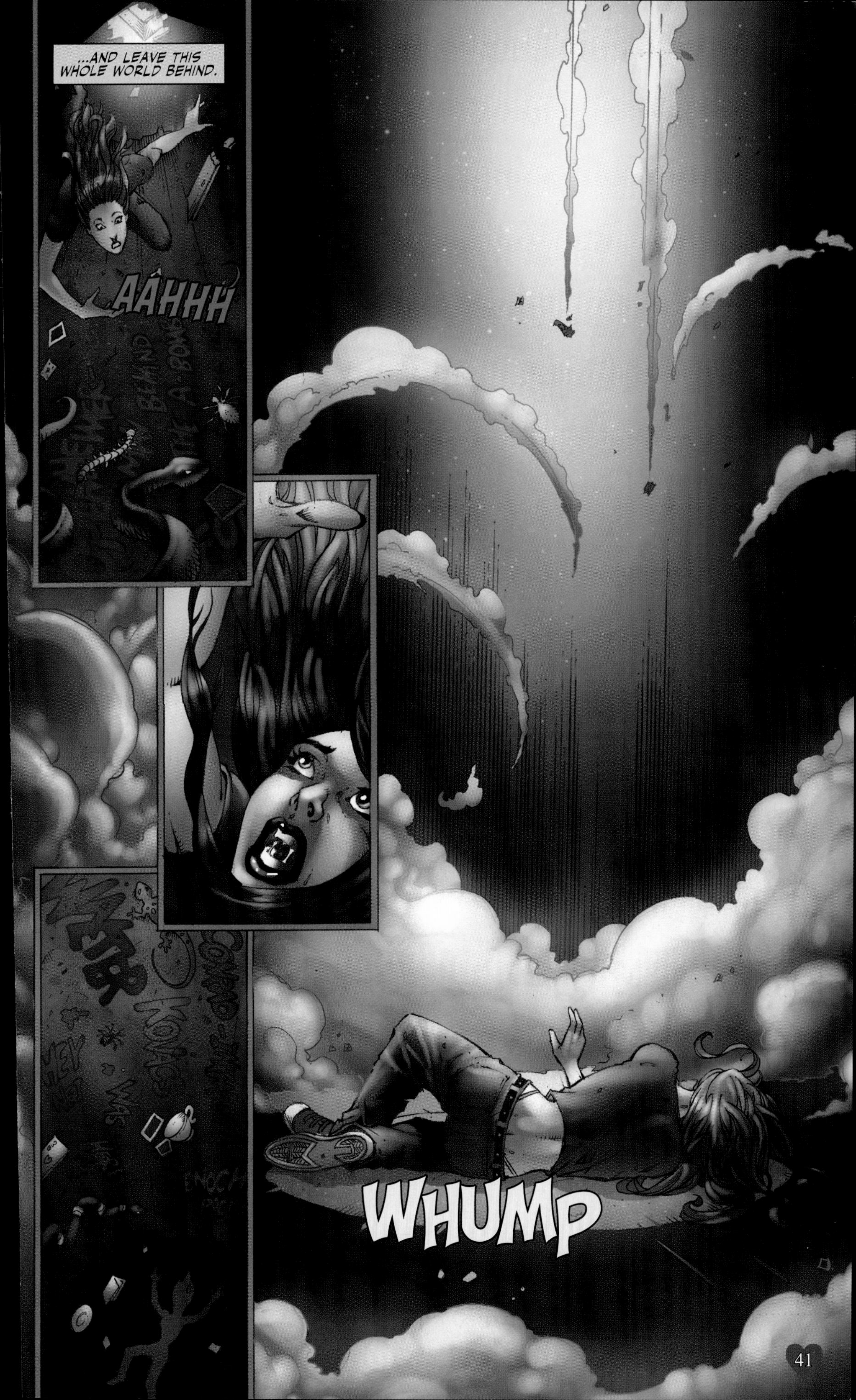
...AND LEAVE THIS WHOLE WORLD BEHIND.
AAHHH
WHUMP

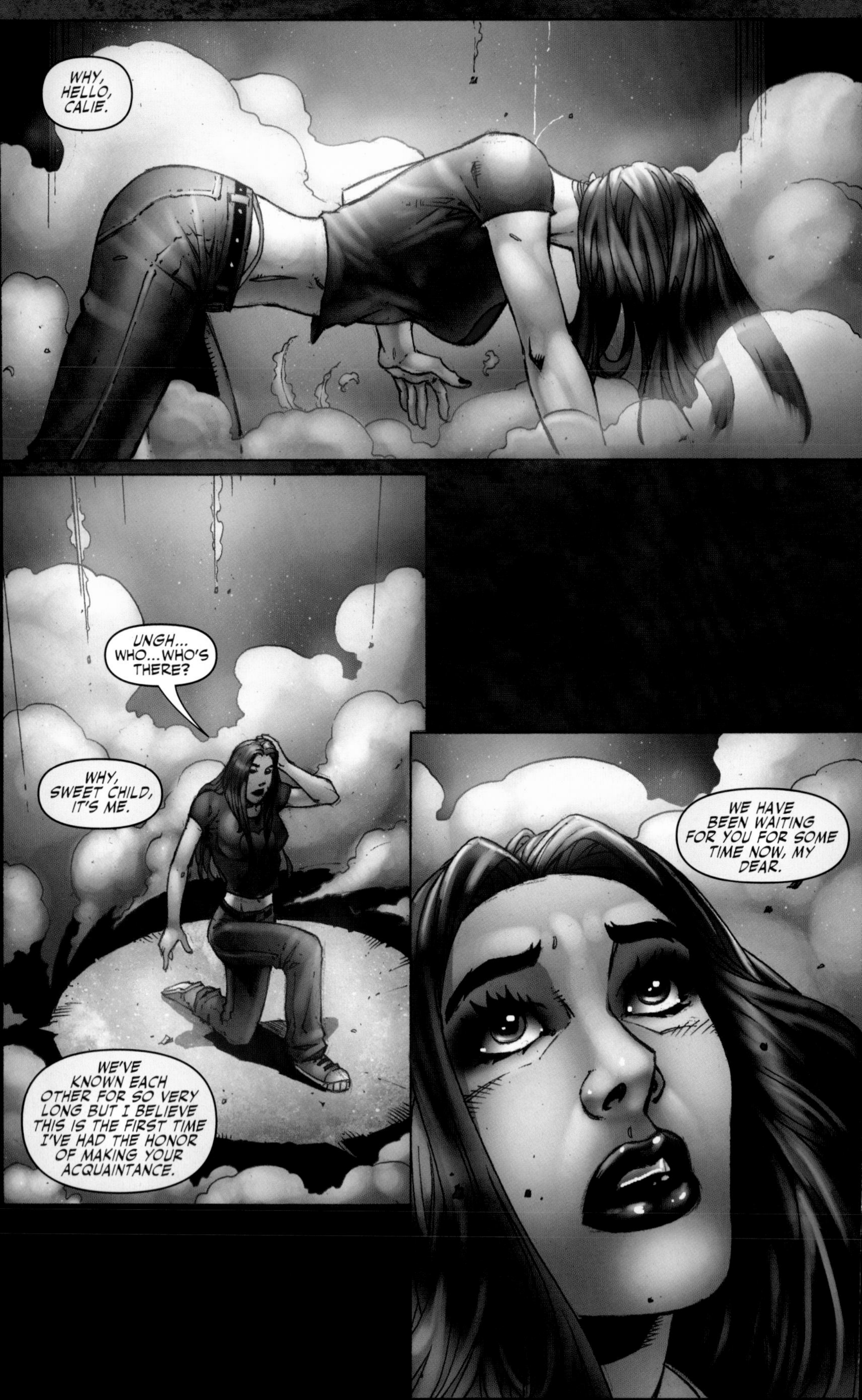
WHY, HELLO, CALIE.
UNGH... WHO...WHO'S THERE?
WHY, SWEET CHILD, IT'S ME.
WE'VE KNOWN EACH OTHER FOR SO VERY LONG BUT I BELIEVE THIS IS THE FIRST TIME I'VE HAD THE HONOR OF MAKING YOUR ACQUAINTANCE.
WE HAVE BEEN WAITING FOR YOU FOR SOME TIME NOW, MY DEAR.

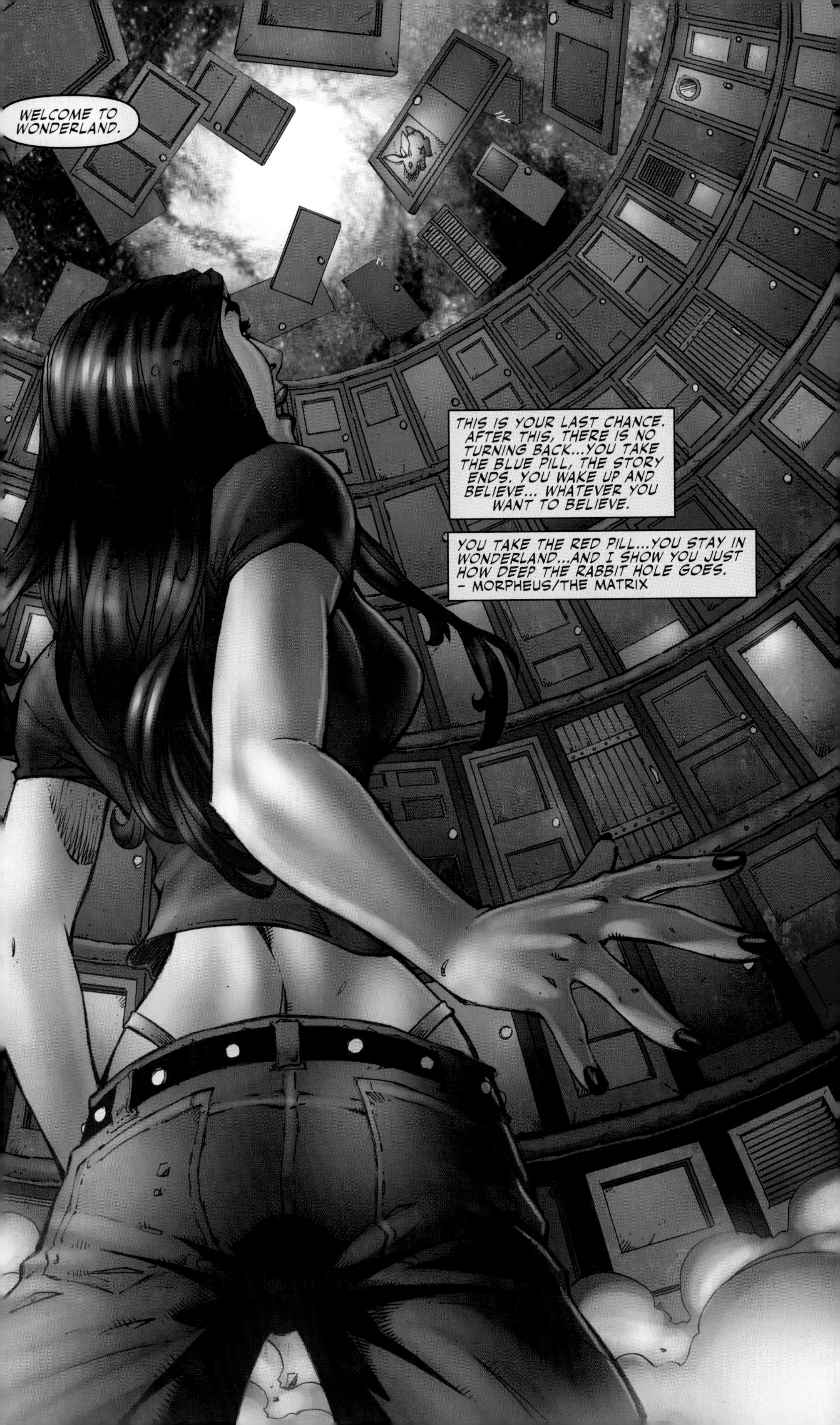
WELCOME TO WONDERLAND.
THIS IS YOUR LAST CHANCE. AFTER THIS, THERE IS NO TURNING BACK...YOU TAKE THE BLUE PILL, THE STORY ENDS. YOU WAKE UP AND BELIEVE... WHATEVER YOU WANT TO BELIEVE.
YOU TAKE THE RED PILL...YOU STAY IN WONDERLAND...AND I SHOW YOU JUST HOW DEEP THE RABBIT HOLE GOES.
- MORPHEUS/THE MATRIX

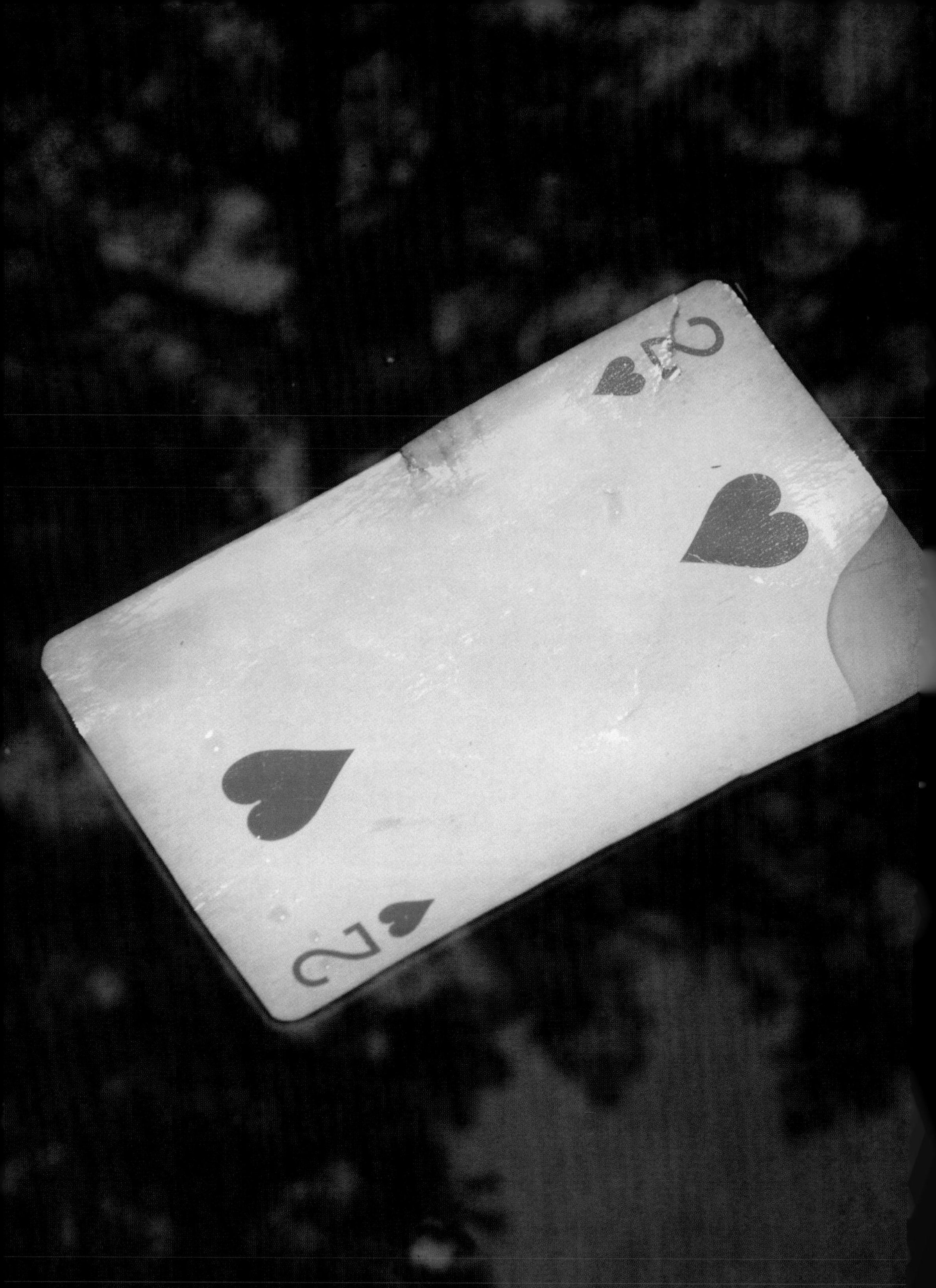

two

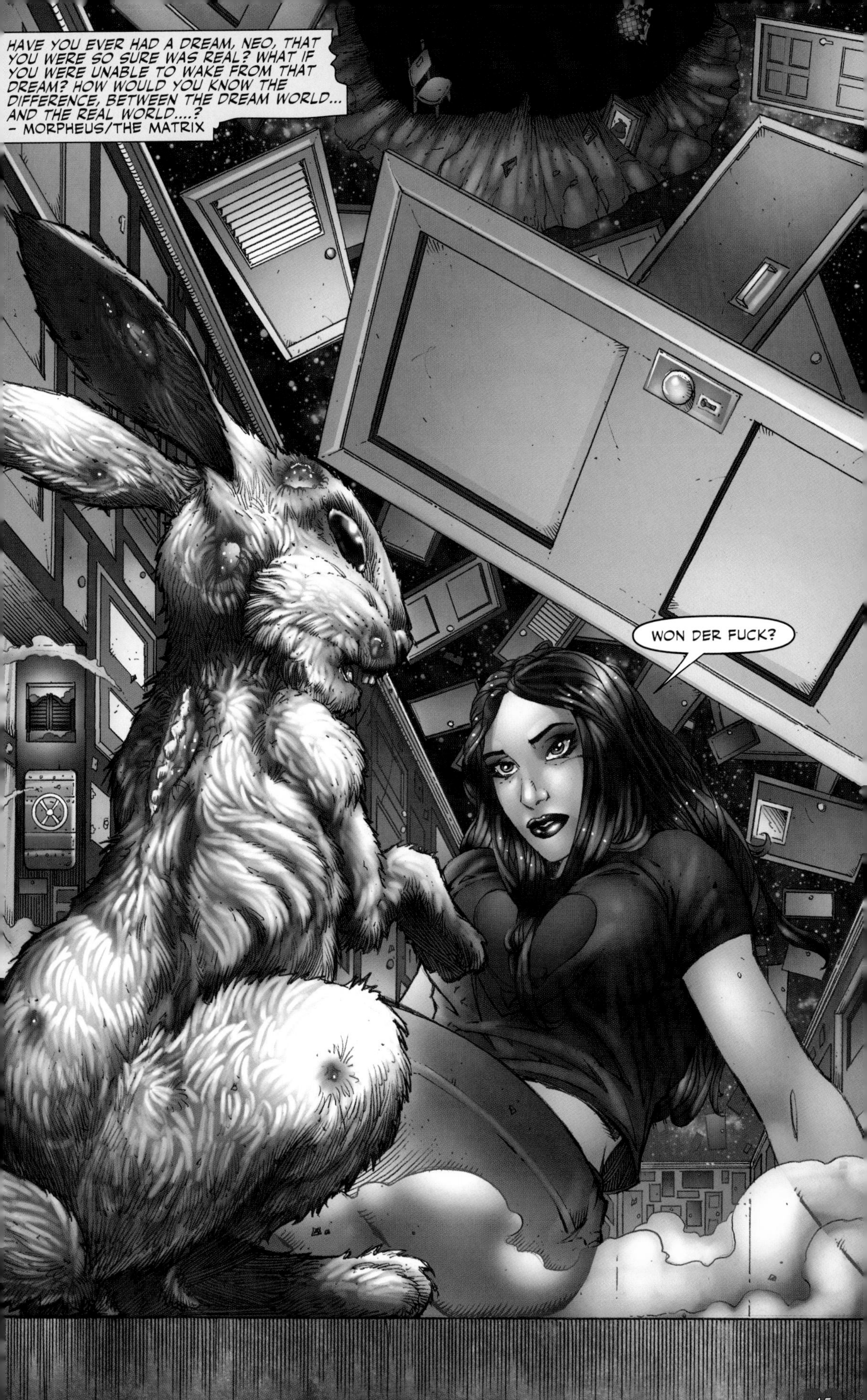
HAVE YOU EVER HAD A DREAM, NEO, THAT YOU WERE SO SURE WAS REAL? WHAT IF YOU WERE UNABLE TO WAKE FROM THAT DREAM? HOW WOULD YOU KNOW THE DIFFERENCE, BETWEEN THE DREAM WORLD... AND THE REAL WORLD....?
- MORPHEUS/THE MATRIX
WON DER FUCK?

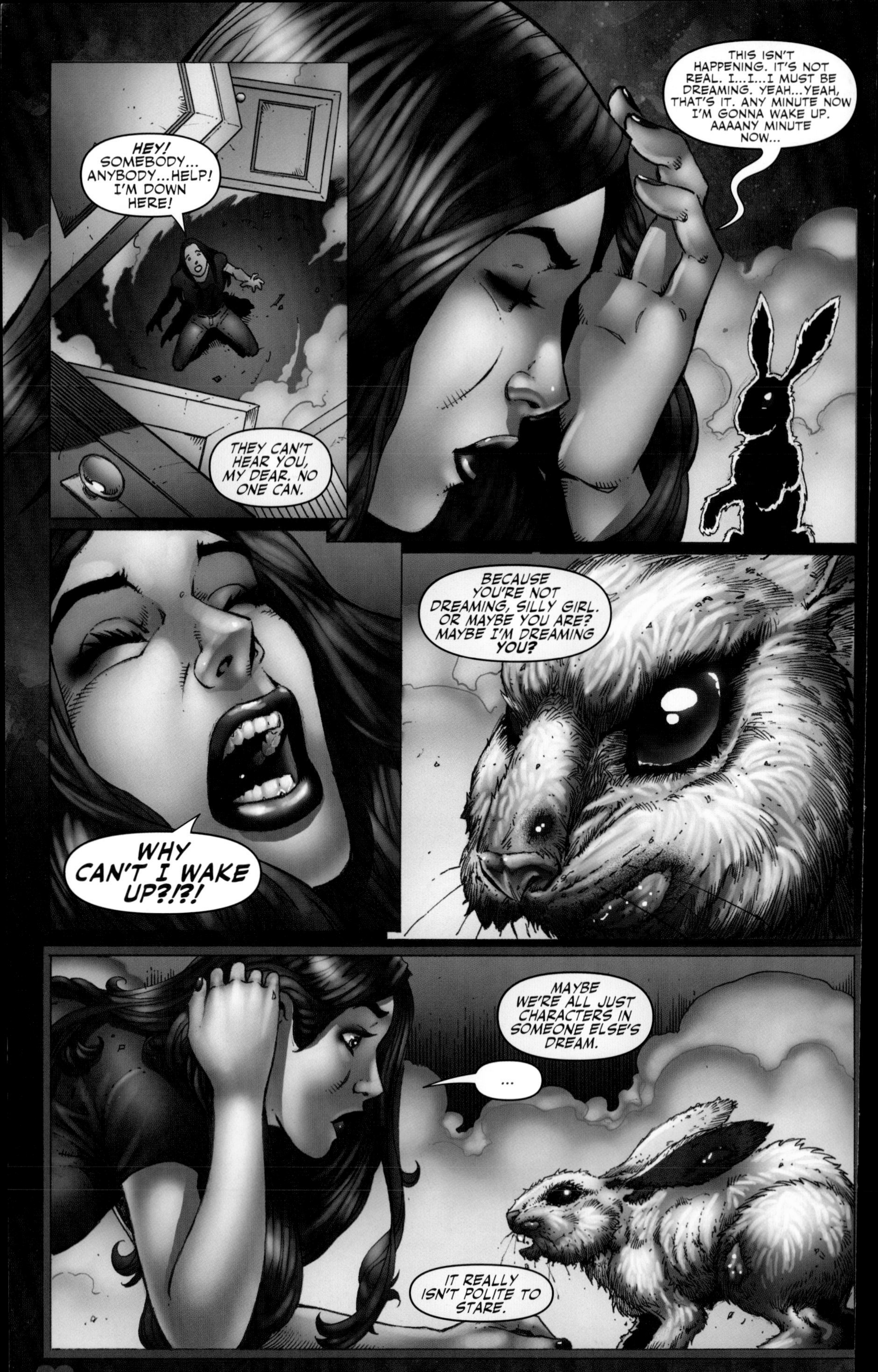
HEY! SOMEBODY... ANYBODY...HELP! I'M DOWN HERE!
THIS ISN'T HAPPENING. IT'S NOT REAL. I...I...I MUST BE DREAMING. YEAH...YEAH, THAT'S IT. ANY MINUTE NOW I'M GONNA WAKE UP. AAAANY MINUTE NOW...
THEY CAN'T HEAR YOU, MY DEAR. NO ONE CAN.
WHY CAN'T I WAKE UP?!?!
BECAUSE YOU'RE NOT DREAMING, SILLY GIRL. OR MAYBE YOU ARE? MAYBE I'M DREAMING YOU?
MAYBE WE'RE ALL JUST CHARACTERS IN SOMEONE ELSE'S DREAM.
...
IT REALLY ISN'T POLITE TO STARE.

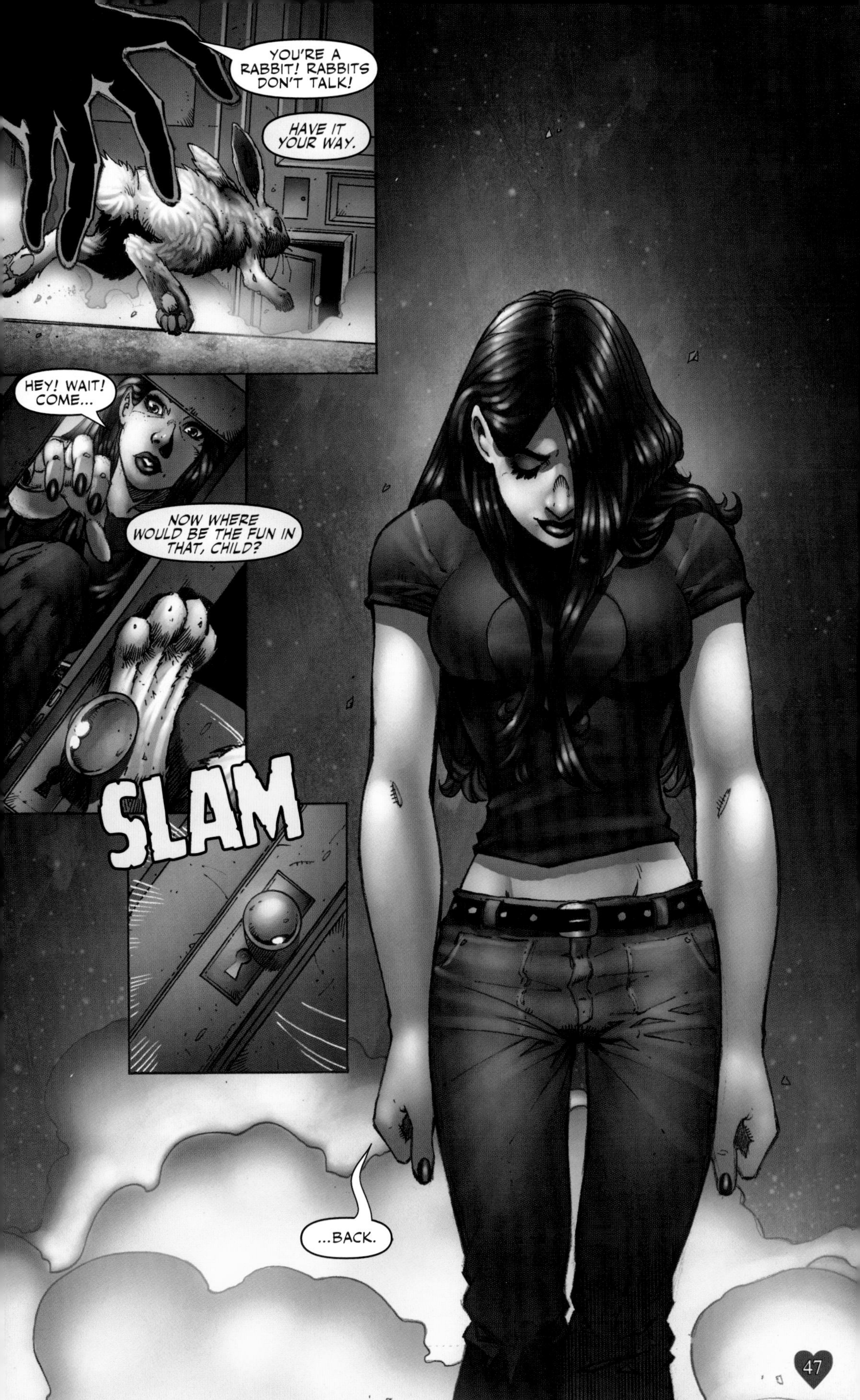
YOU'RE A RABBIT! RABBITS DON'T TALK!
HAVE IT YOUR WAY.
HEY! WAIT! COME...
NOW WHERE WOULD BE THE FUN IN THAT, CHILD?
SLAM
...BACK.

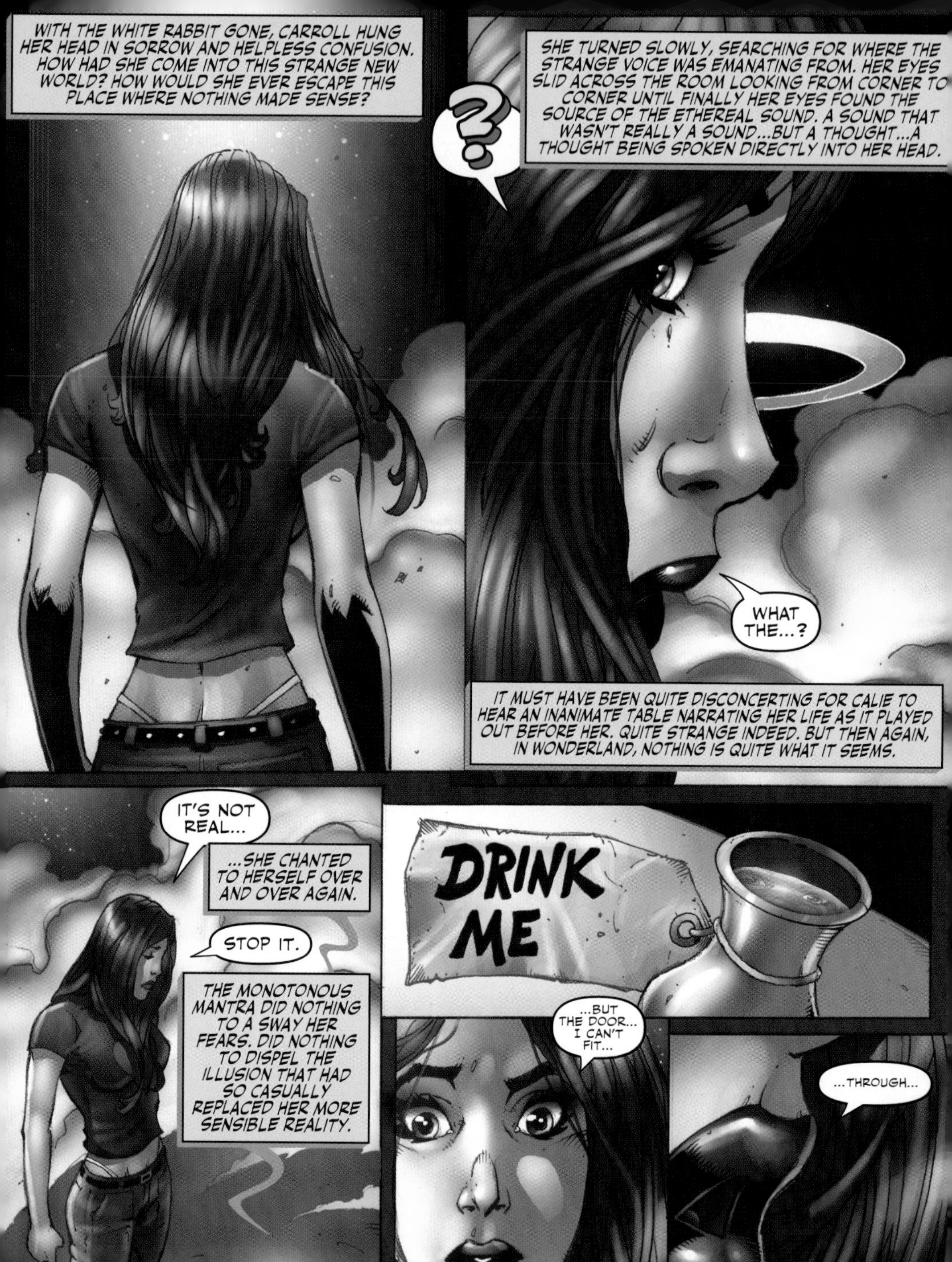
WITH THE WHITE RABBIT GONE, CARROLL HUNG HER HEAD IN SORROW AND HELPLESS CONFUSION. HOW HAD SHE COME INTO THIS STRANGE NEW WORLD? HOW WOULD SHE EVER ESCAPE THIS PLACE WHERE NOTHING MADE SENSE?
?
SHE TURNED SLOWLY, SEARCHING FOR WHERE THE STRANGE VOICE WAS EMANATING FROM. HER EYES SLID ACROSS THE ROOM LOOKING FROM CORNER TO CORNER UNTIL FINALLY HER EYES FOUND THE SOURCE OF THE ETHEREAL SOUND. A SOUND THAT WASN'T REALLY A SOUND...BUT A THOUGHT...A THOUGHT BEING SPOKEN DIRECTLY INTO HER HEAD.
WHAT THE...?
IT MUST HAVE BEEN QUITE DISCONCERTING FOR CALIE TO HEAR AN INANIMATE TABLE NARRATING HER LIFE AS IT PLAYED OUT BEFORE HER. QUITE STRANGE INDEED. BUT THEN AGAIN, IN WONDERLAND, NOTHING IS QUITE WHAT IT SEEMS.
IT'S NOT REAL...
...SHE CHANTED TO HERSELF OVER AND OVER AGAIN.
STOP IT.
THE MONOTONOUS MANTRA DID NOTHING TO A SWAY HER FEARS. DID NOTHING TO DISPEL THE ILLUSION THAT HAD SO CASUALLY REPLACED HER MORE SENSIBLE REALITY.
WHY IS THIS HAPPENING TO ME?
ONLY THE BOTTLE WOULD DO THAT. ONLY BY FOLLOWING THE WHITE RABBIT WOULD SHE FIND THE ANSWERS SHE SO DESPERATELY NEEDED.
DRINK ME
...BUT THE DOOR... I CAN'T FIT...
...THROUGH...

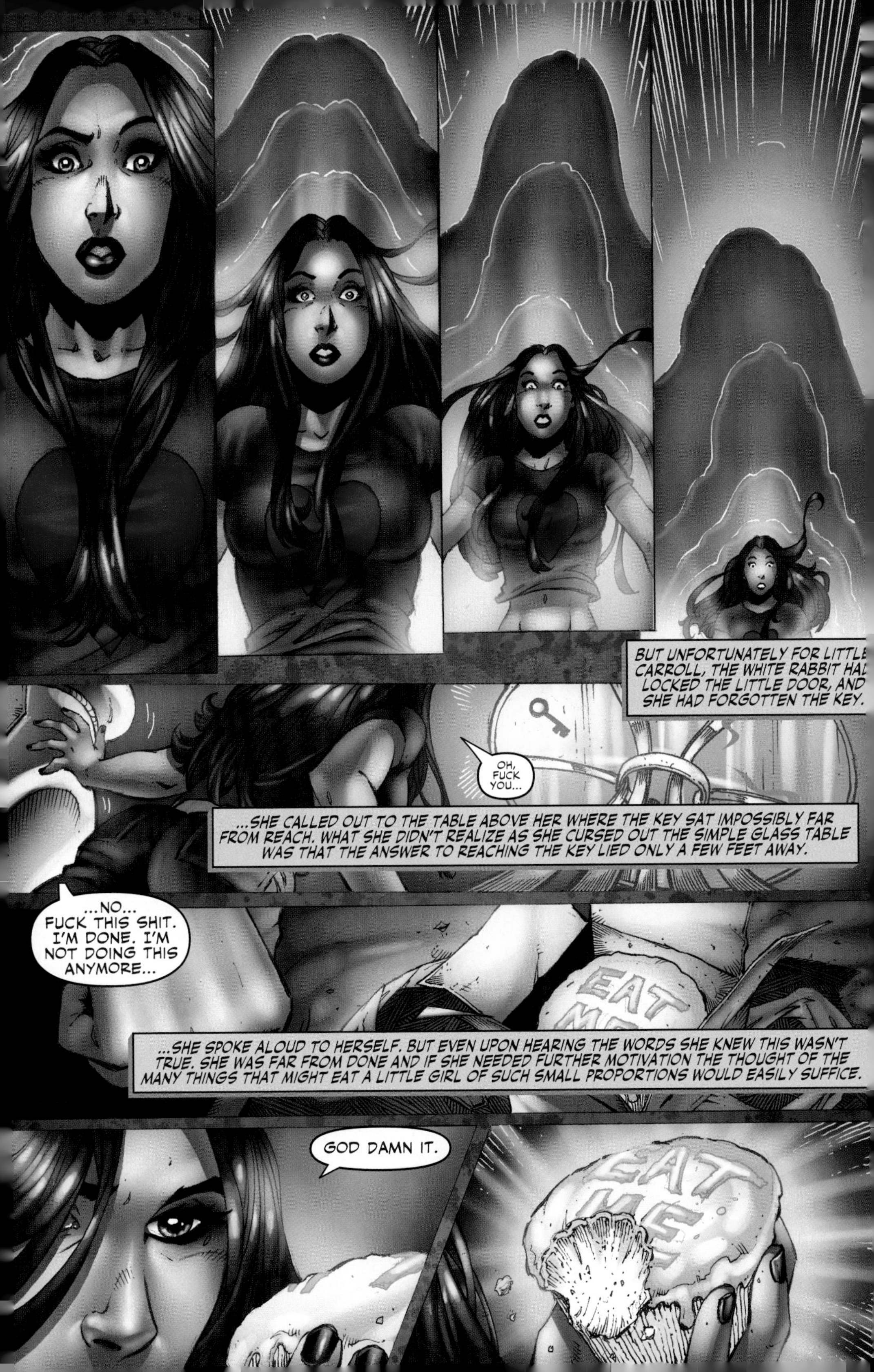
BUT UNFORTUNATELY FOR LITTLE CARROLL, THE WHITE RABBIT HAD LOCKED THE LITTLE DOOR, AND SHE HAD FORGOTTEN THE KEY.
OH, FUCK YOU...
...SHE CALLED OUT TO THE TABLE ABOVE HER WHERE THE KEY SAT IMPOSSIBLY FAR FROM REACH. WHAT SHE DIDN'T REALIZE AS SHE CURSED OUT THE SIMPLE GLASS TABLE WAS THAT THE ANSWER TO REACHING THE KEY LIED ONLY A FEW FEET AWAY.
...NO... FUCK THIS SHIT. I'M DONE. I'M NOT DOING THIS ANYMORE...
...SHE SPOKE ALOUD TO HERSELF. BUT EVEN UPON HEARING THE WORDS SHE KNEW THIS WASN'T TRUE. SHE WAS FAR FROM DONE AND IF SHE NEEDED FURTHER MOTIVATION THE THOUGHT OF THE MANY THINGS THAT MIGHT EAT A LITTLE GIRL OF SUCH SMALL PROPORTIONS WOULD EASILY SUFFICE.
GOD DAMN IT.
EAT ME

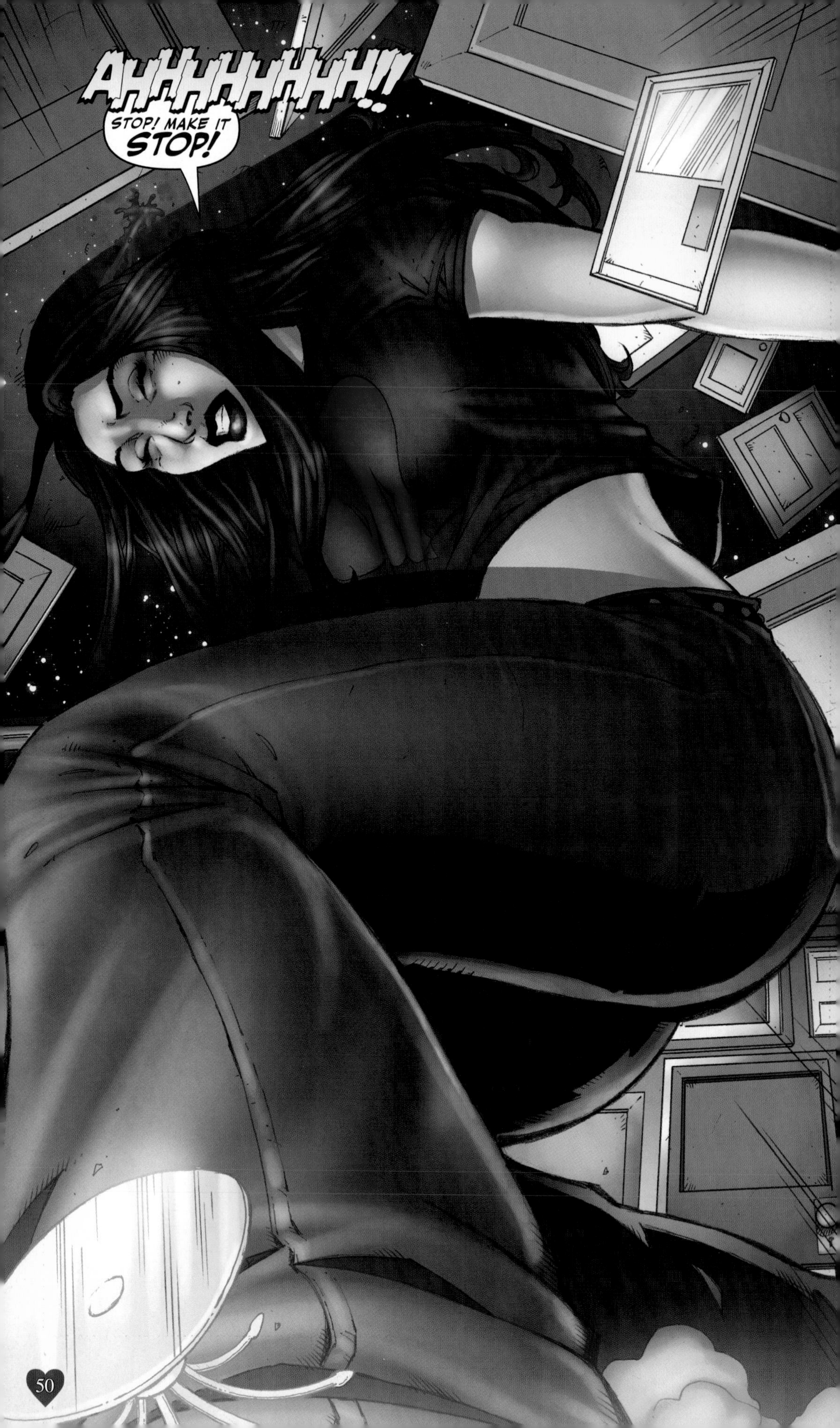
AHHHHHHHH!!
STOP! MAKE IT STOP!

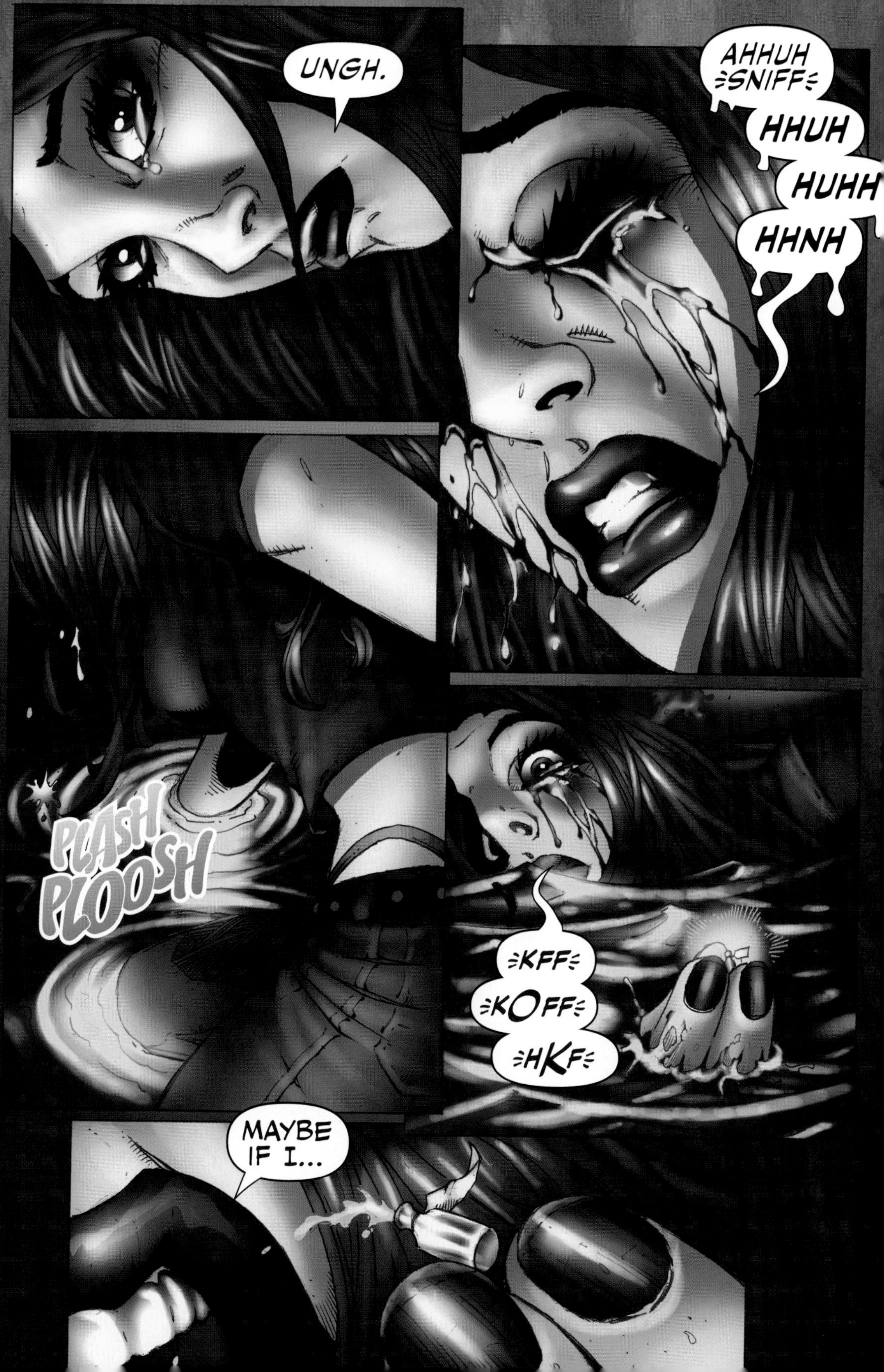
UNGH.
AHHUH SNIFF
HHUH
HUHH
HHNH
PLASH
PLOOSH
KFF
KOFF
HKF
MAYBE IF I...

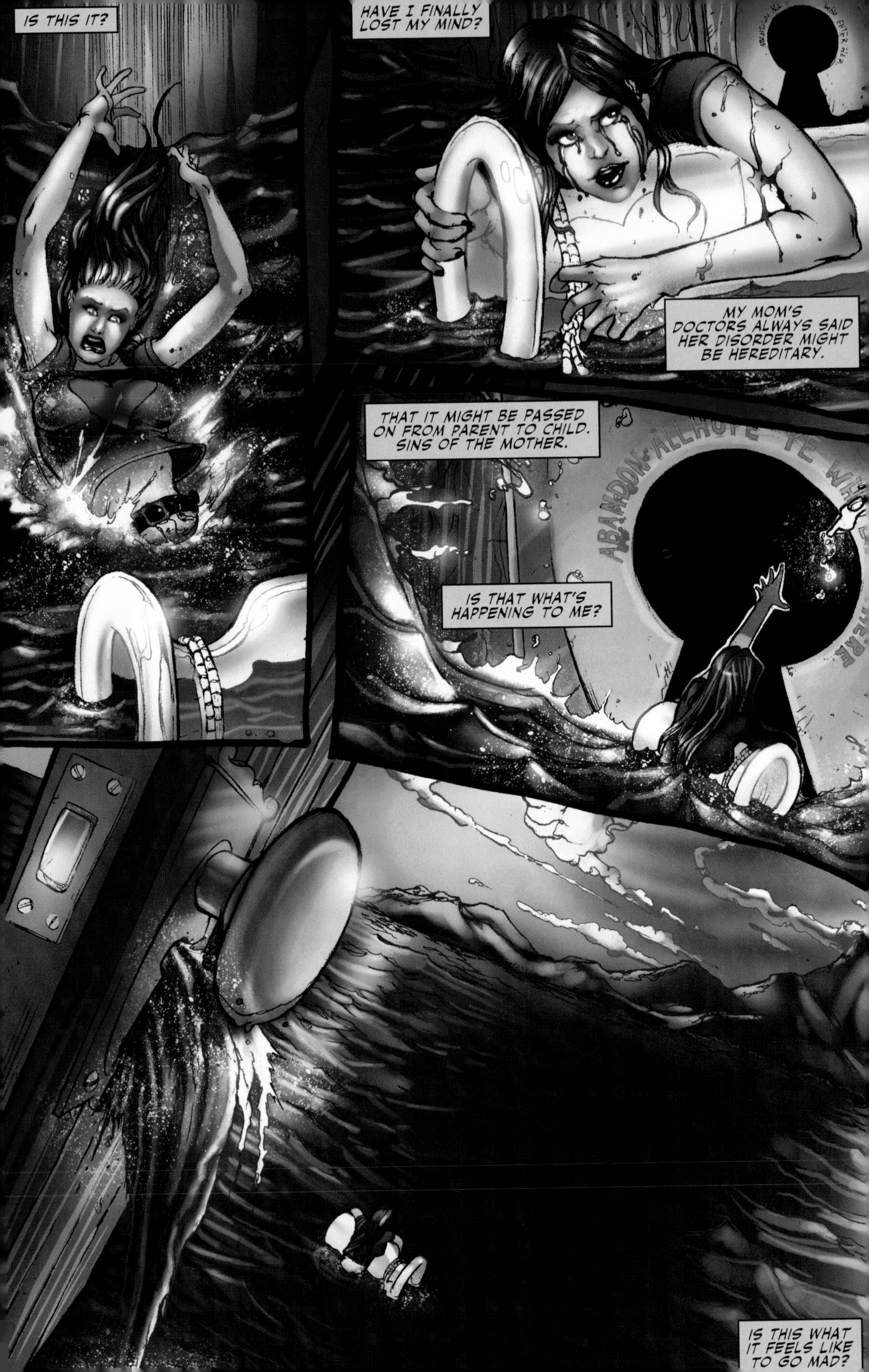
IS THIS IT?
HAVE I FINALLY LOST MY MIND?
MY MOM'S DOCTORS ALWAYS SAID HER DISORDER MIGHT BE HEREDITARY.
THAT IT MIGHT BE PASSED ON FROM PARENT TO CHILD. SINS OF THE MOTHER.
ABANDON ALL HOPE YE
IS THAT WHAT'S HAPPENING TO ME?
IS THIS WHAT IT FEELS LIKE TO GO MAD?

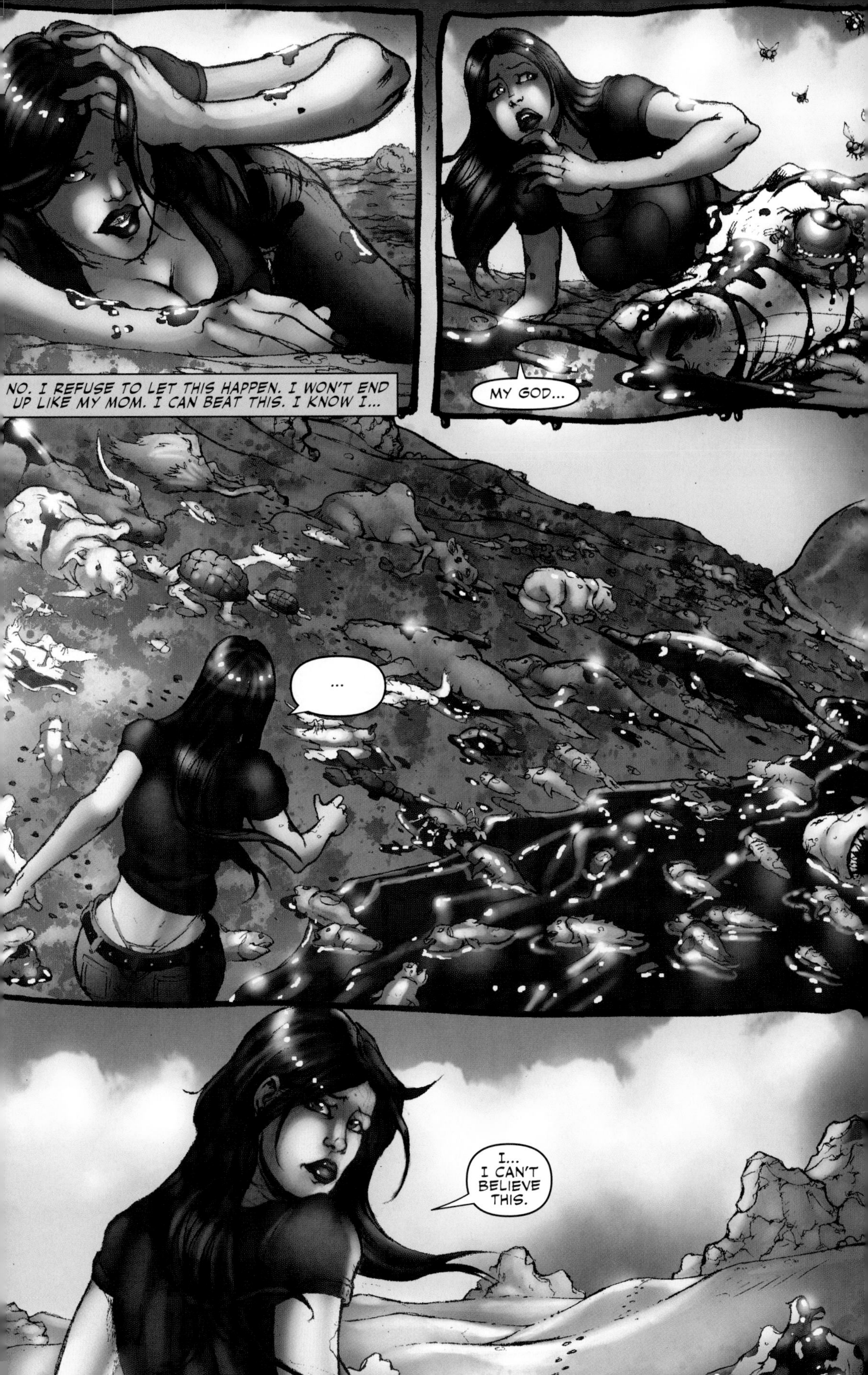
NO. I REFUSE TO LET THIS HAPPEN. I WON'T END UP LIKE MY MOM. I CAN BEAT THIS. I KNOW I...
MY GOD...
...
I... I CAN'T BELIEVE THIS.

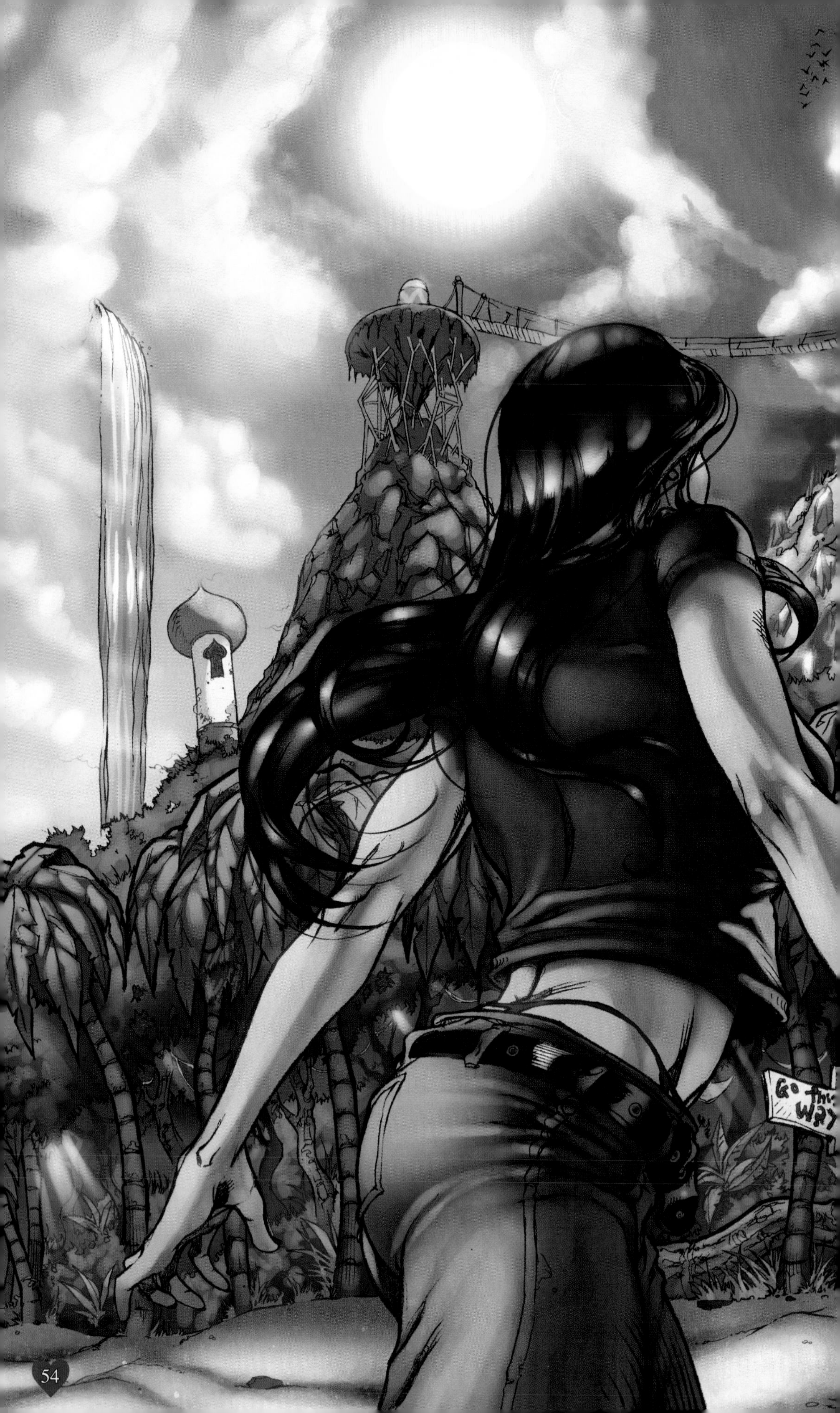

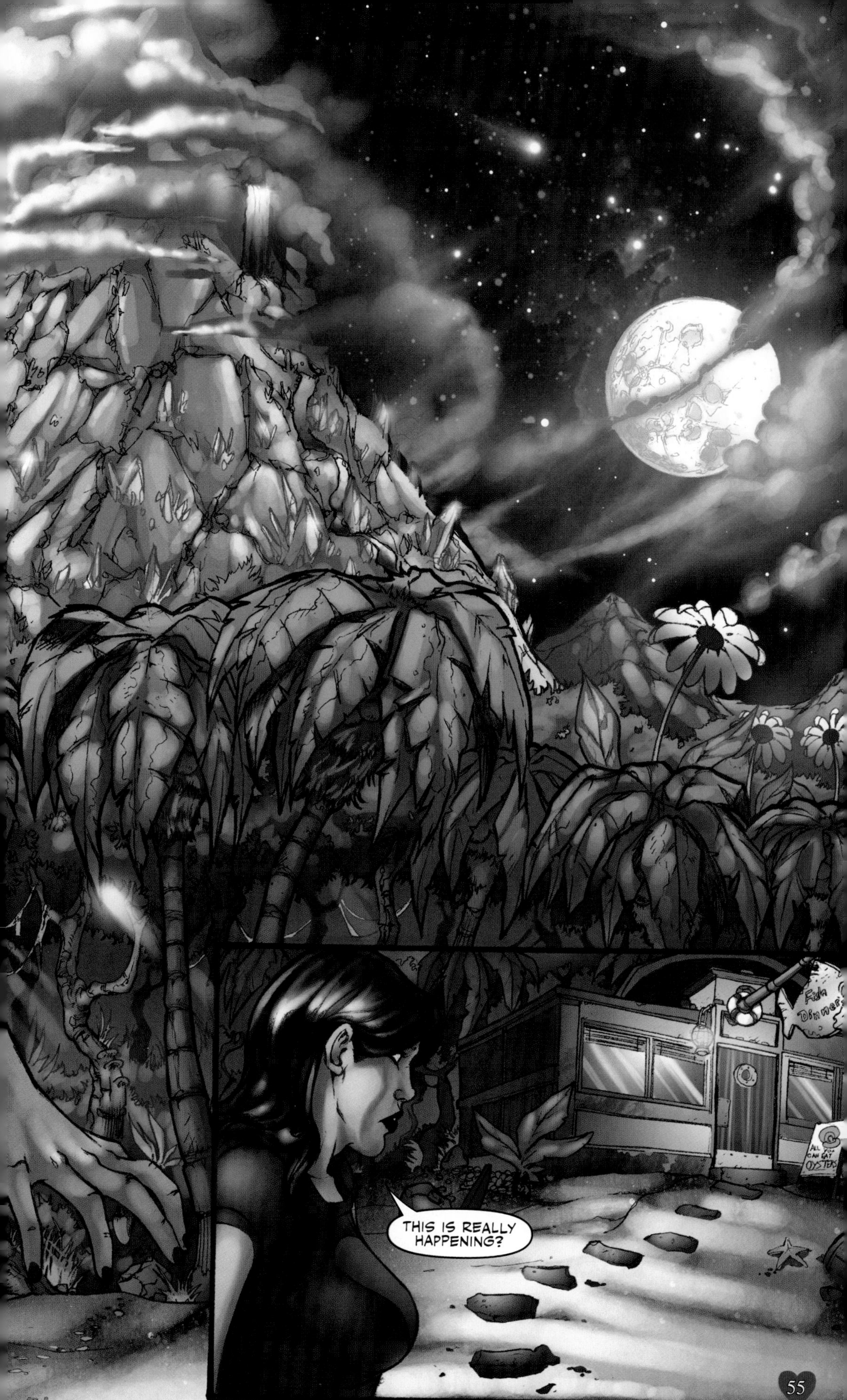
Fish Dinner
THIS IS REALLY HAPPENING?

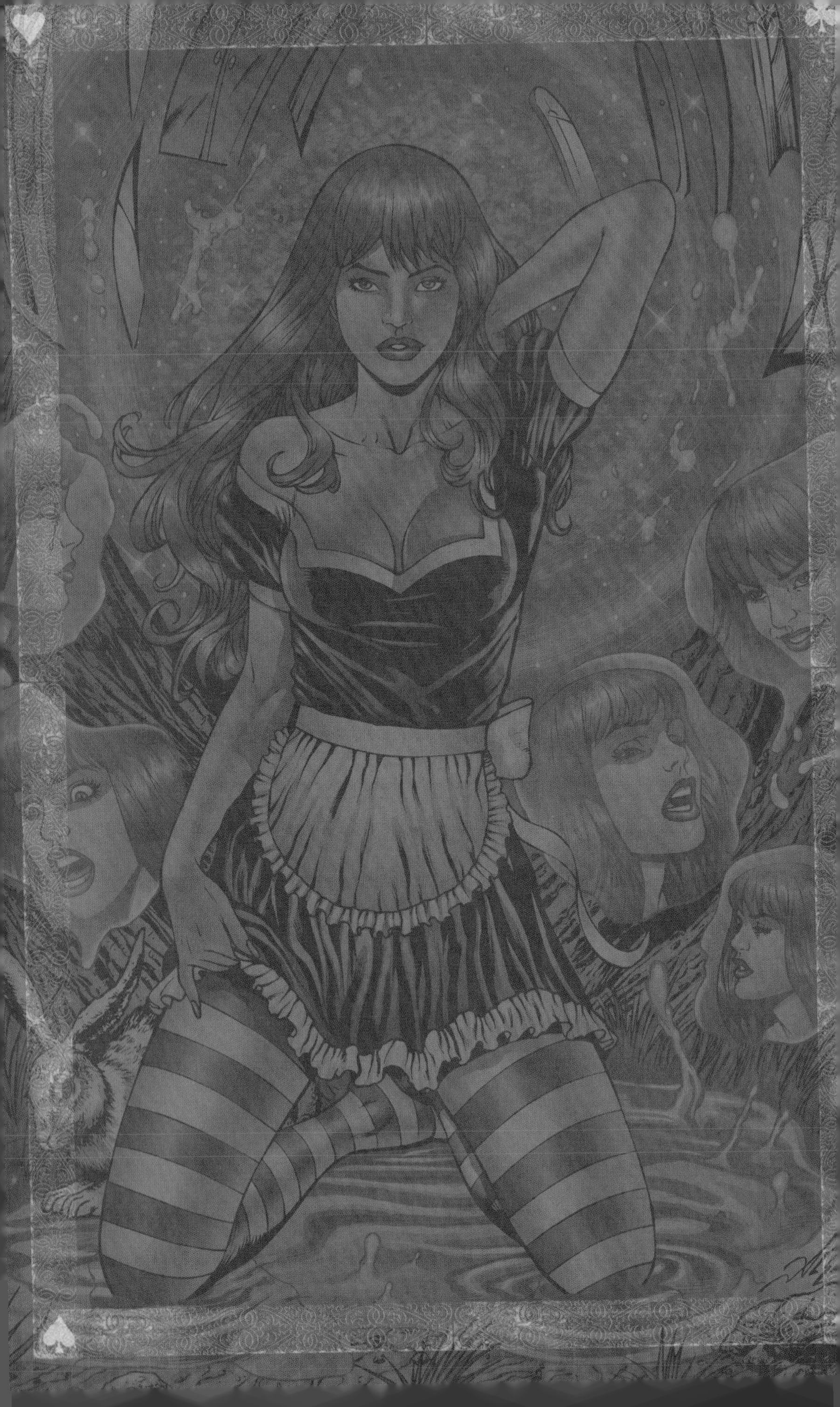

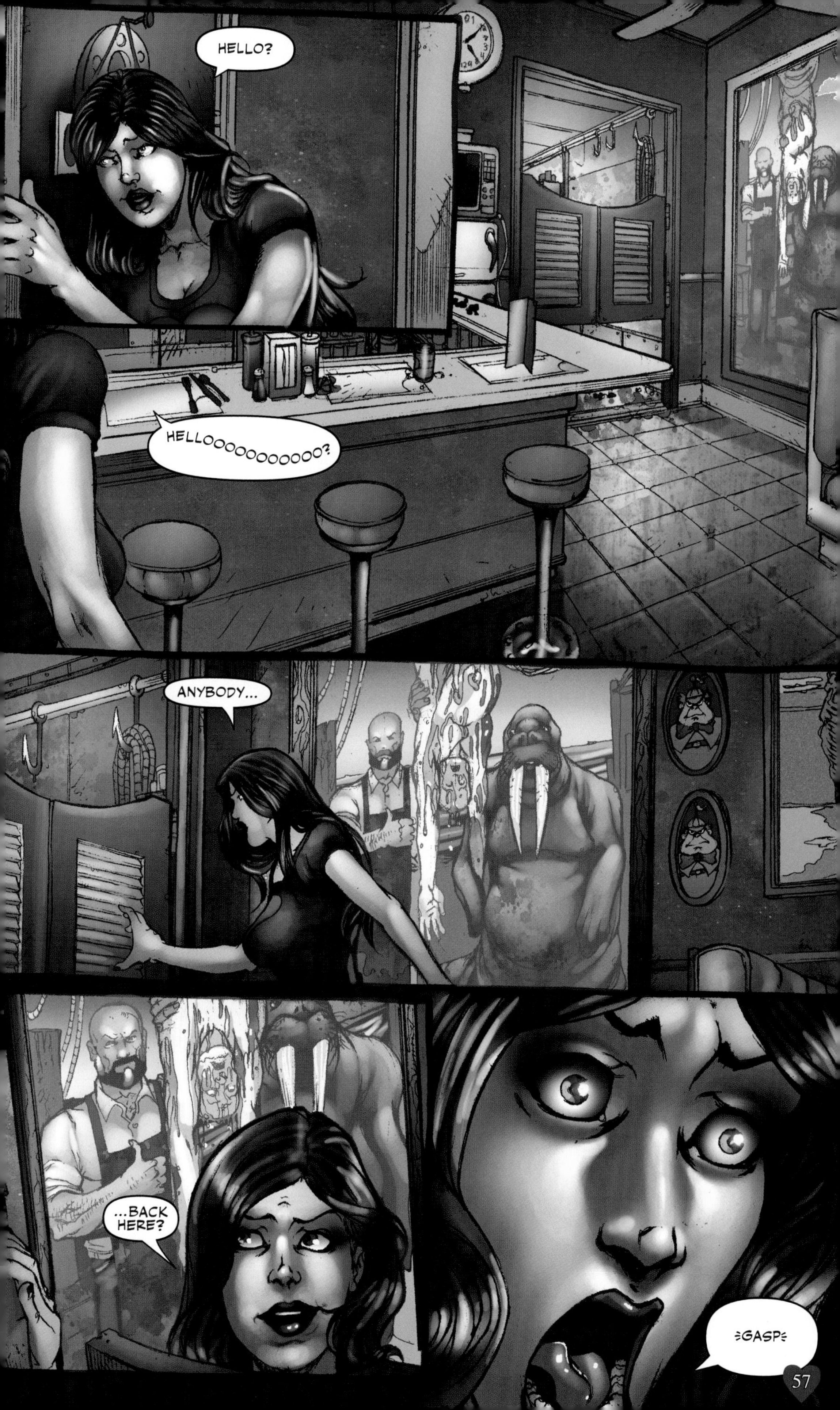
HELLO?
HELLOOOOOOOOOOOO?
ANYBODY...
...BACK HERE?
=GASP=

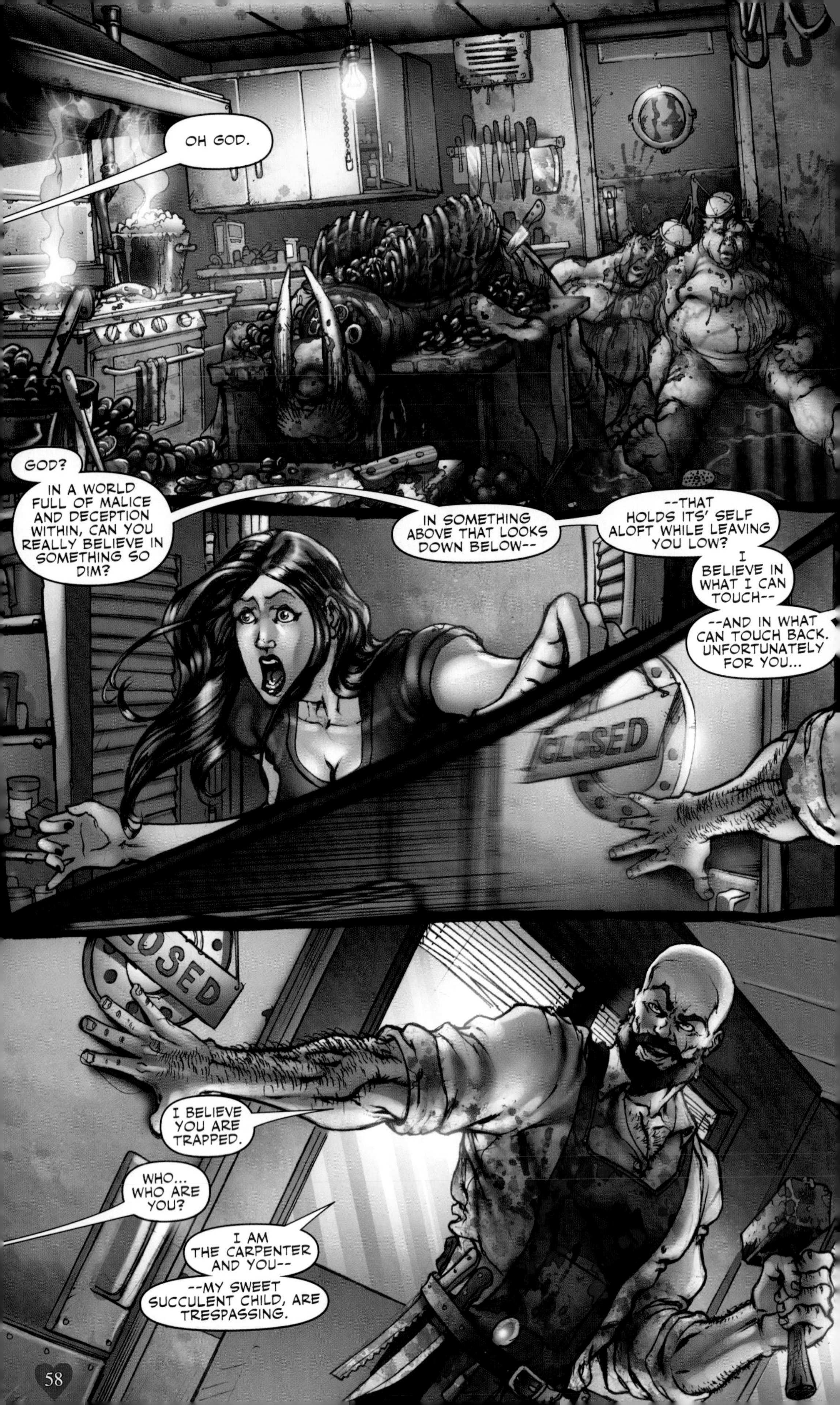
OH GOD.
GOD?
IN A WORLD FULL OF MALICE AND DECEPTION WITHIN, CAN YOU REALLY BELIEVE IN SOMETHING SO DIM?
IN SOMETHING ABOVE THAT LOOKS DOWN BELOW--
--THAT HOLDS ITS' SELF ALOFT WHILE LEAVING YOU LOW?
I BELIEVE IN WHAT I CAN TOUCH--
--AND IN WHAT CAN TOUCH BACK. UNFORTUNATELY FOR YOU...
CLOSED
I BELIEVE YOU ARE TRAPPED.
WHO... WHO ARE YOU?
I AM THE CARPENTER AND YOU--
--MY SWEET SUCCULENT CHILD, ARE TRESPASSING.

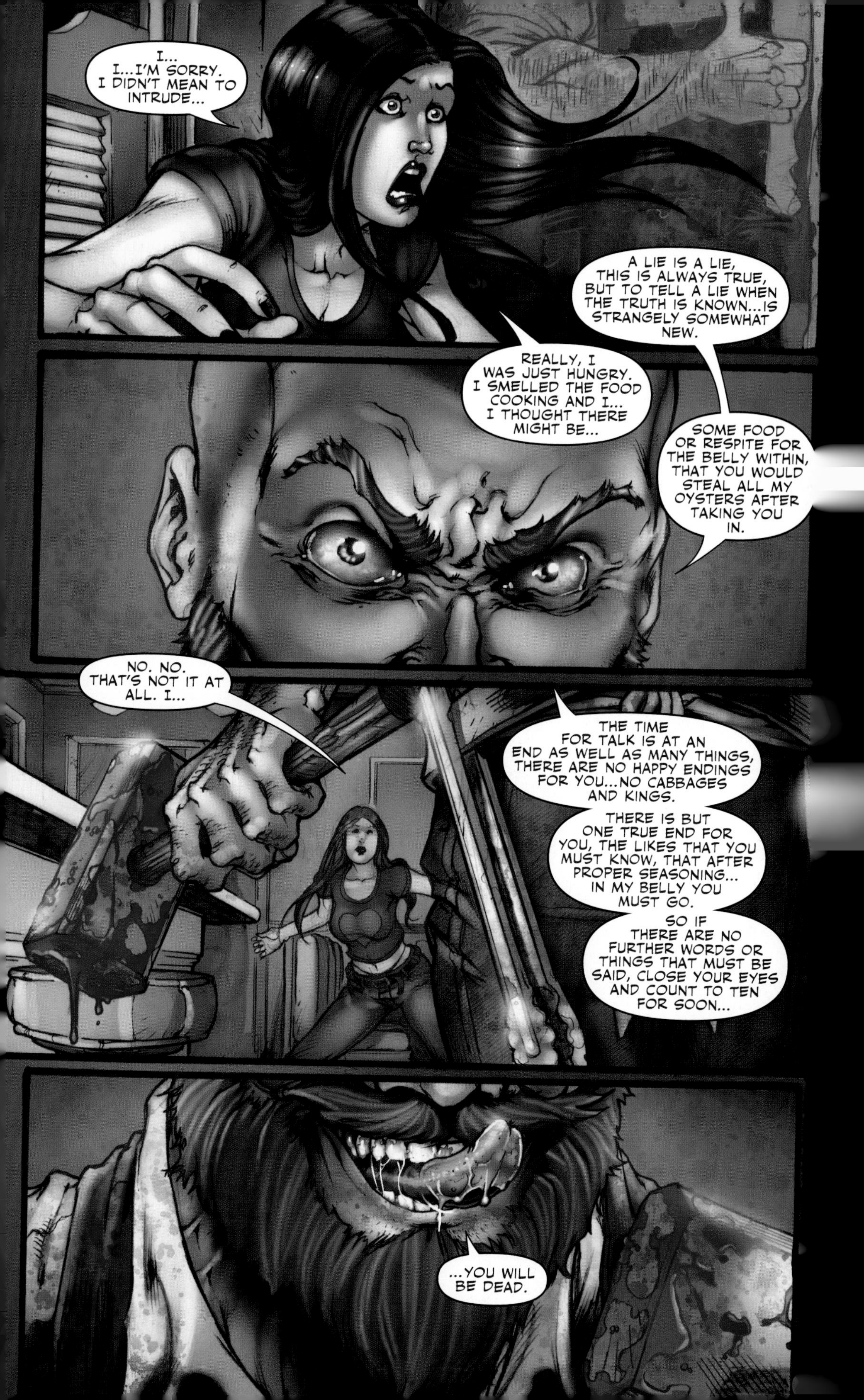
I... I...I'M SORRY. I DIDN'T MEAN TO INTRUDE...
A LIE IS A LIE, THIS IS ALWAYS TRUE, BUT TO TELL A LIE WHEN THE TRUTH IS KNOWN...IS STRANGELY SOMEWHAT NEW.
REALLY, I WAS JUST HUNGRY. I SMELLED THE FOOD COOKING AND I... I THOUGHT THERE MIGHT BE...
SOME FOOD OR RESPITE FOR THE BELLY WITHIN, THAT YOU WOULD STEAL ALL MY OYSTERS AFTER TAKING YOU IN.
NO. NO. THAT'S NOT IT AT ALL. I...
THE TIME FOR TALK IS AT AN END AS WELL AS MANY THINGS, THERE ARE NO HAPPY ENDINGS FOR YOU...NO CABBAGES AND KINGS.
THERE IS BUT ONE TRUE END FOR YOU, THE LIKES THAT YOU MUST KNOW, THAT AFTER PROPER SEASONING... IN MY BELLY YOU MUST GO.
SO IF THERE ARE NO FURTHER WORDS OR THINGS THAT MUST BE SAID, CLOSE YOUR EYES AND COUNT TO TEN FOR SOON...
...YOU WILL BE DEAD.

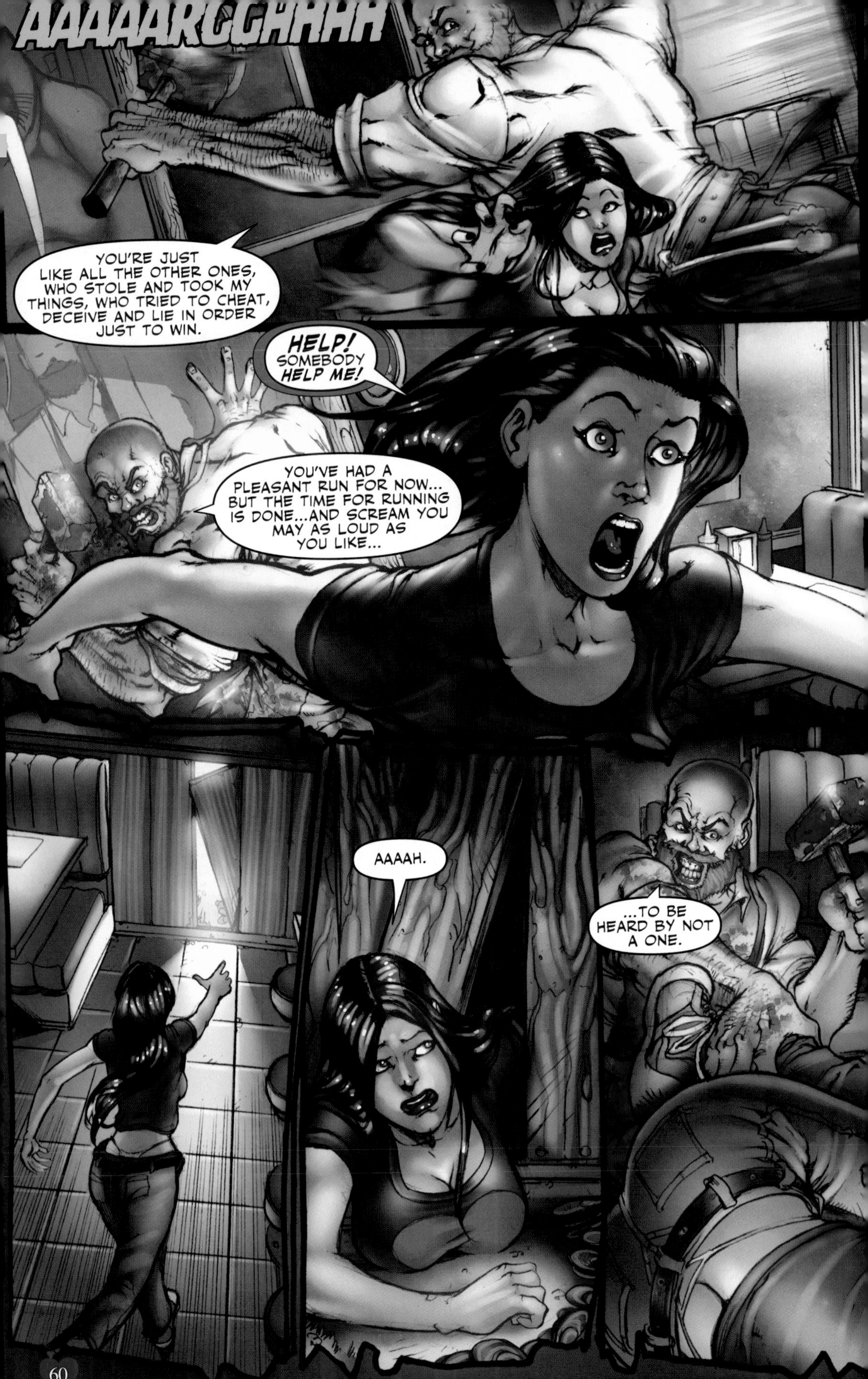
AAAAARGGHHHH
YOU'RE JUST LIKE ALL THE OTHER ONES, WHO STOLE AND TOOK MY THINGS, WHO TRIED TO CHEAT, DECEIVE AND LIE IN ORDER JUST TO WIN.
HELP! SOMEBODY HELP ME!
YOU'VE HAD A PLEASANT RUN FOR NOW... BUT THE TIME FOR RUNNING IS DONE...AND SCREAM YOU MAY AS LOUD AS YOU LIKE...
AAAAH.
...TO BE HEARD BY NOT A ONE.

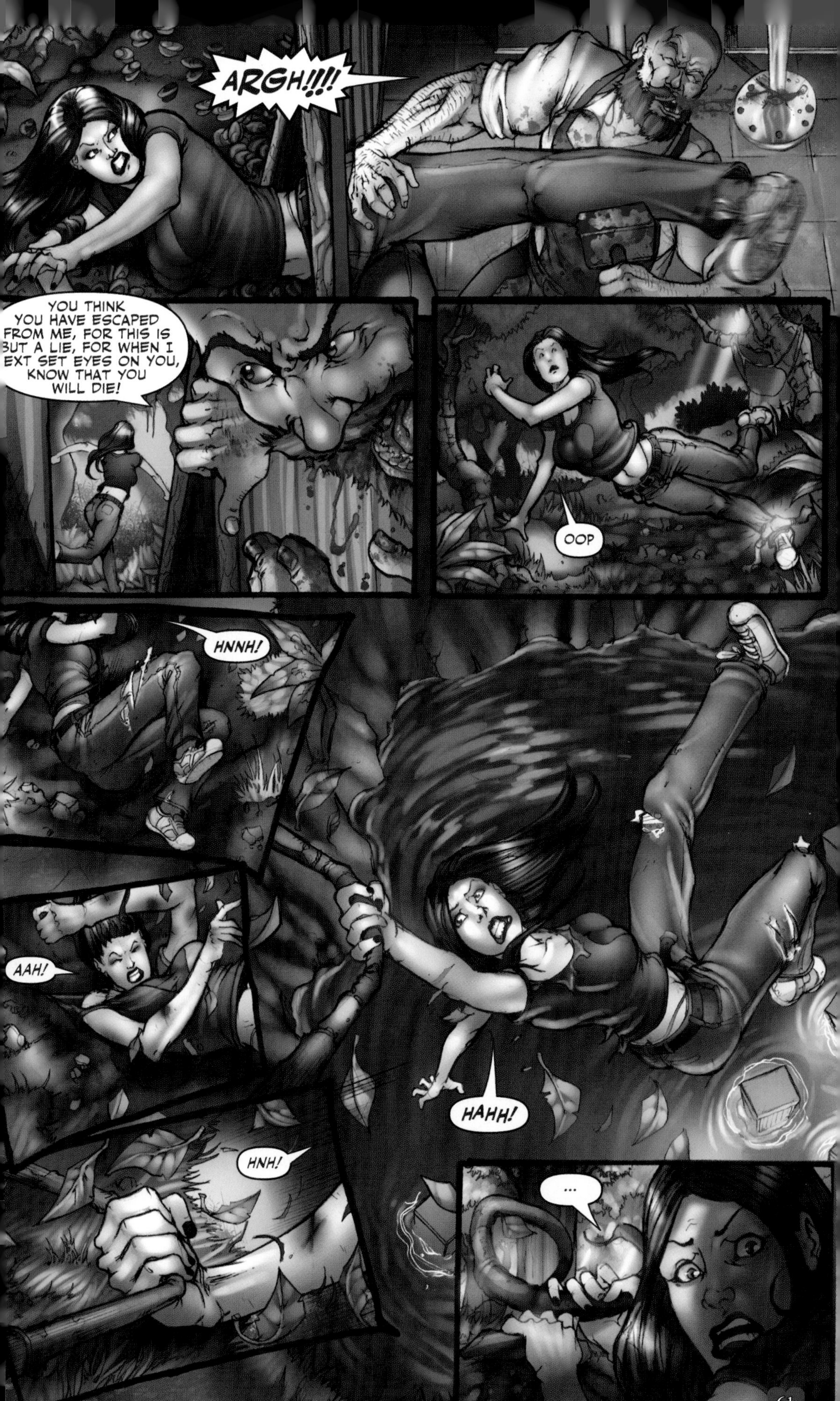
ARGH!!!!
YOU THINK YOU HAVE ESCAPED FROM ME, FOR THIS IS BUT A LIE, FOR WHEN I EXT SET EYES ON YOU, KNOW THAT YOU WILL DIE!
OOP
HNNH!
AAH!
HAHH!
HNH!
...

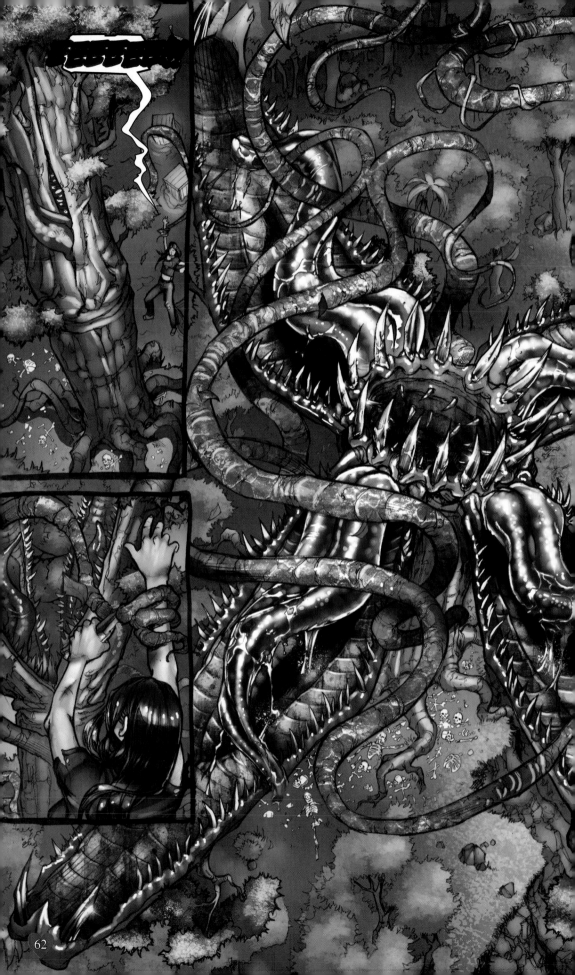

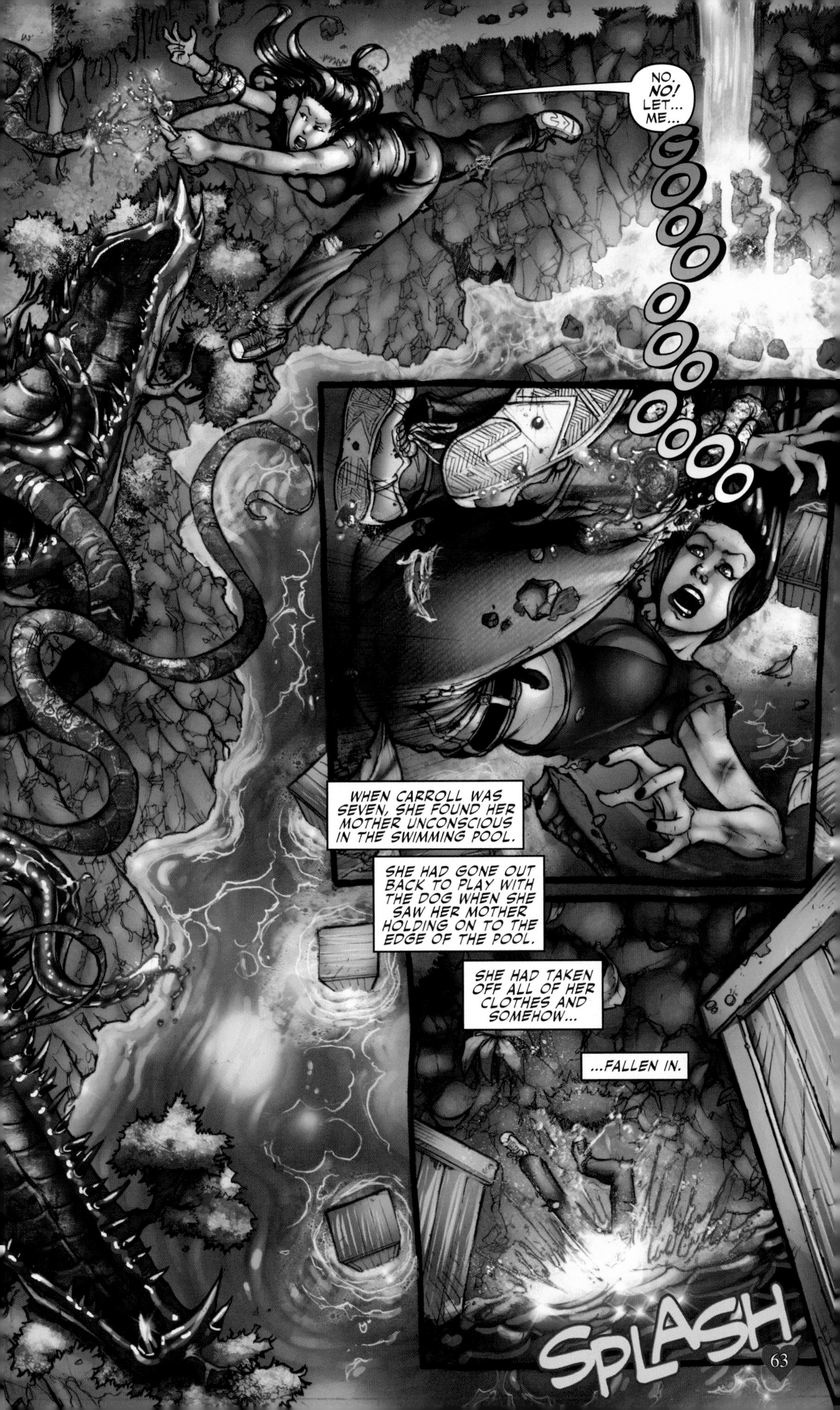
NO. NO! LET... ME...
GOOOOOOOOOOOO
WHEN CARROLL WAS SEVEN, SHE FOUND HER MOTHER UNCONSCIOUS IN THE SWIMMING POOL.
SHE HAD GONE OUT BACK TO PLAY WITH THE DOG WHEN SHE SAW HER MOTHER HOLDING ON TO THE EDGE OF THE POOL.
SHE HAD TAKEN OFF ALL OF HER CLOTHES AND SOMEHOW...
...FALLEN IN.
SPLASH

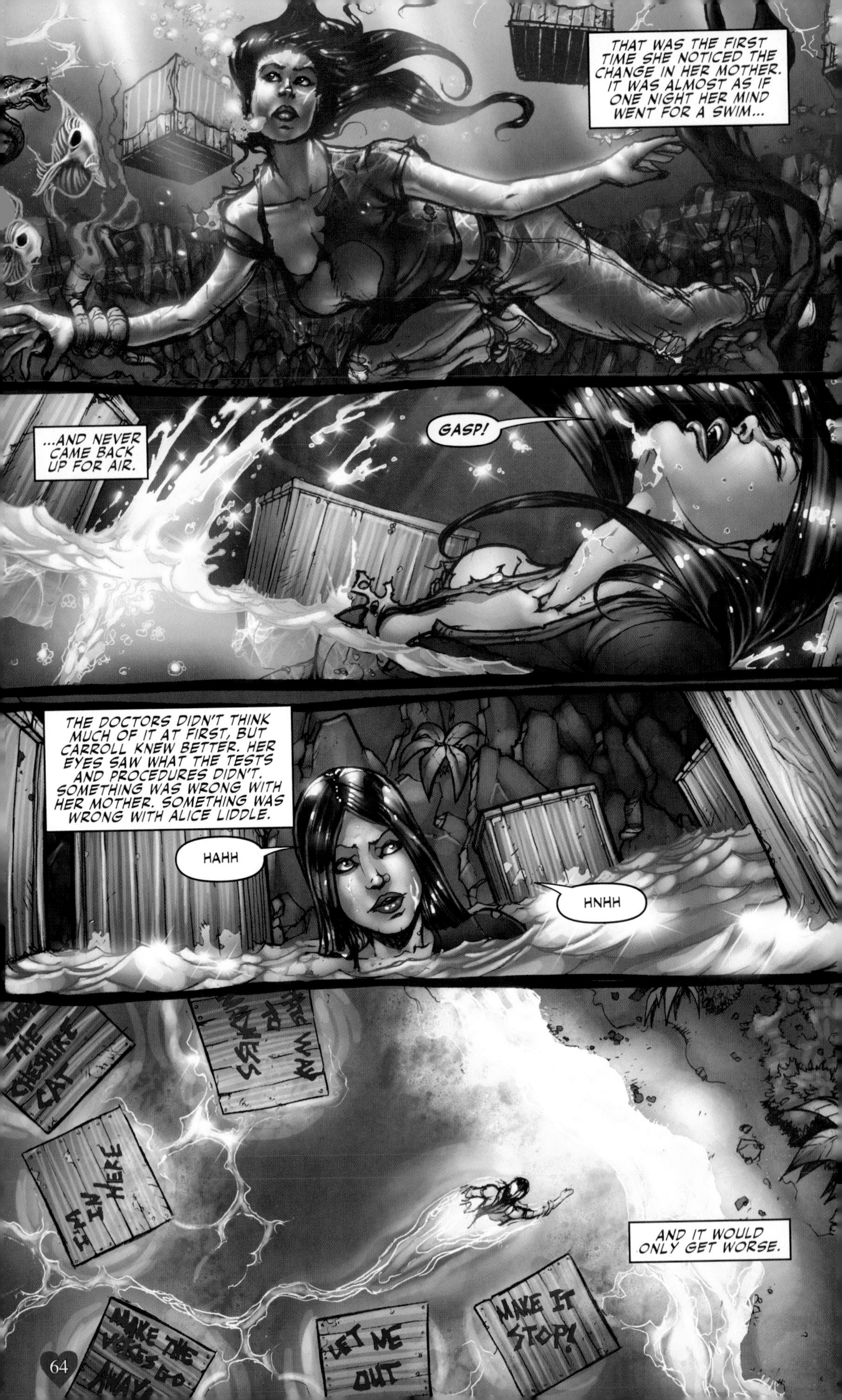
THAT WAS THE FIRST TIME SHE NOTICED THE CHANGE IN HER MOTHER. IT WAS ALMOST AS IF ONE NIGHT HER MIND WENT FOR A SWIM...
...AND NEVER CAME BACK UP FOR AIR.
GASP!
THE DOCTORS DIDN'T THINK MUCH OF IT AT FIRST, BUT CARROLL KNEW BETTER. HER EYES SAW WHAT THE TESTS AND PROCEDURES DIDN'T. SOMETHING WAS WRONG WITH HER MOTHER. SOMETHING WAS WRONG WITH ALICE LIDDLE.
HAHH
HNHH
THE CHESHIRE CAT
I'M IN HERE
AND IT WOULD ONLY GET WORSE.
MAKE THE VOICES GO AWAY!
LET ME OUT
MAKE IT STOP!

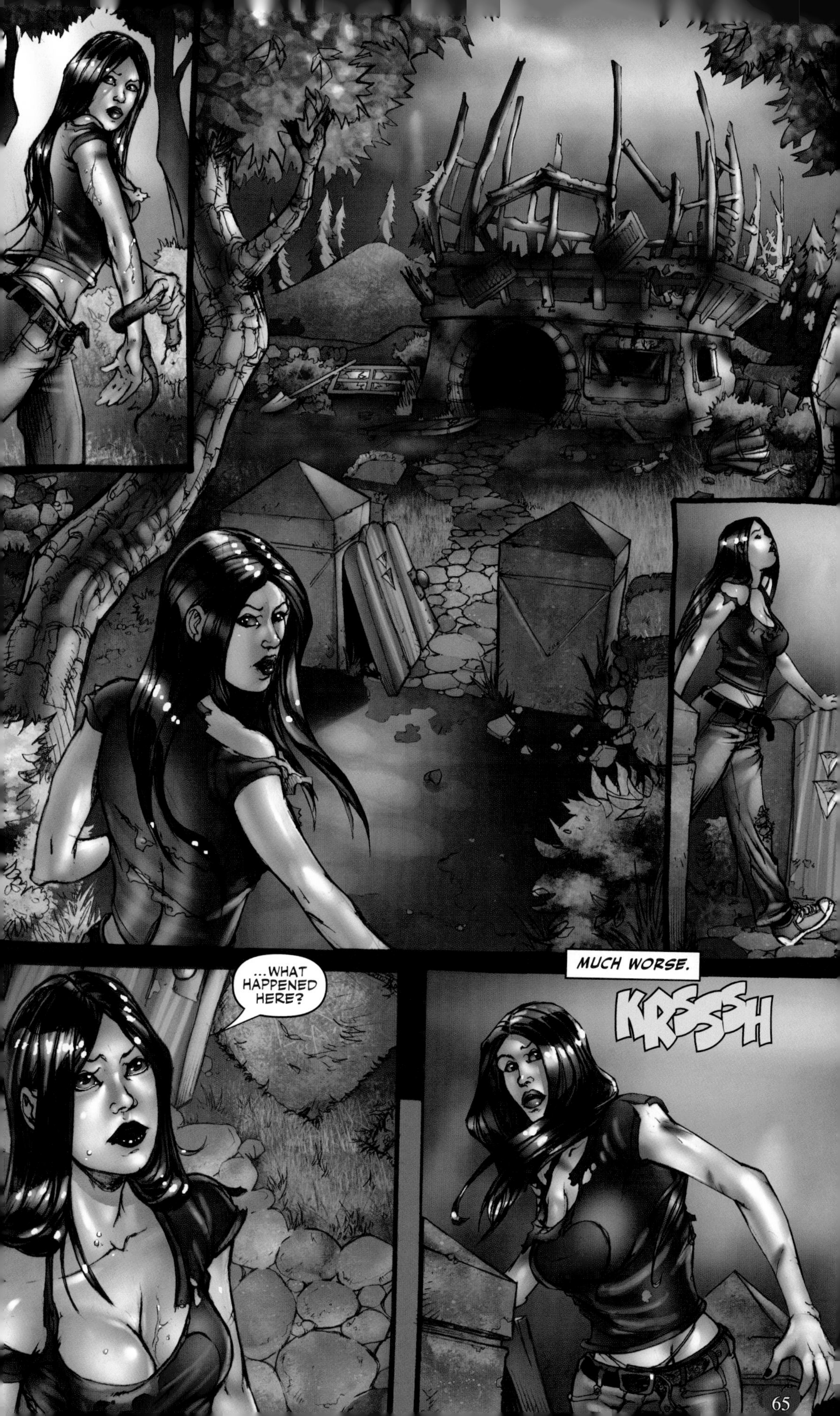
...WHAT HAPPENED HERE?
MUCH WORSE.
KRSSH

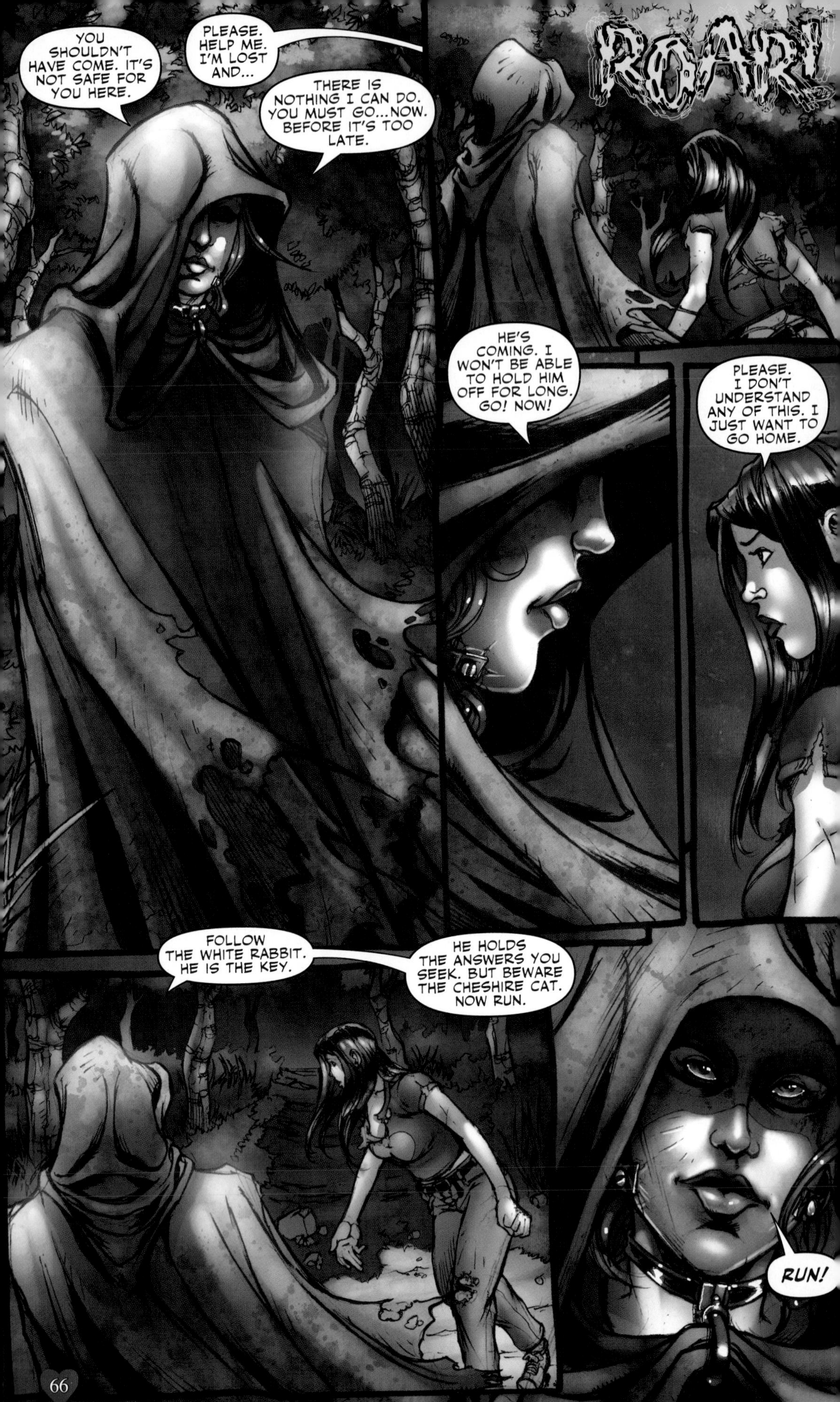
YOU SHOULDN'T HAVE COME. IT'S NOT SAFE FOR YOU HERE.
PLEASE. HELP ME. I'M LOST AND...
THERE IS NOTHING I CAN DO. YOU MUST GO...NOW. BEFORE IT'S TOO LATE.
ROAR!
HE'S COMING. I WON'T BE ABLE TO HOLD HIM OFF FOR LONG. GO! NOW!
PLEASE. I DON'T UNDERSTAND ANY OF THIS. I JUST WANT TO GO HOME.
FOLLOW THE WHITE RABBIT. HE IS THE KEY.
HE HOLDS THE ANSWERS YOU SEEK. BUT BEWARE THE CHESHIRE CAT. NOW RUN.
RUN!

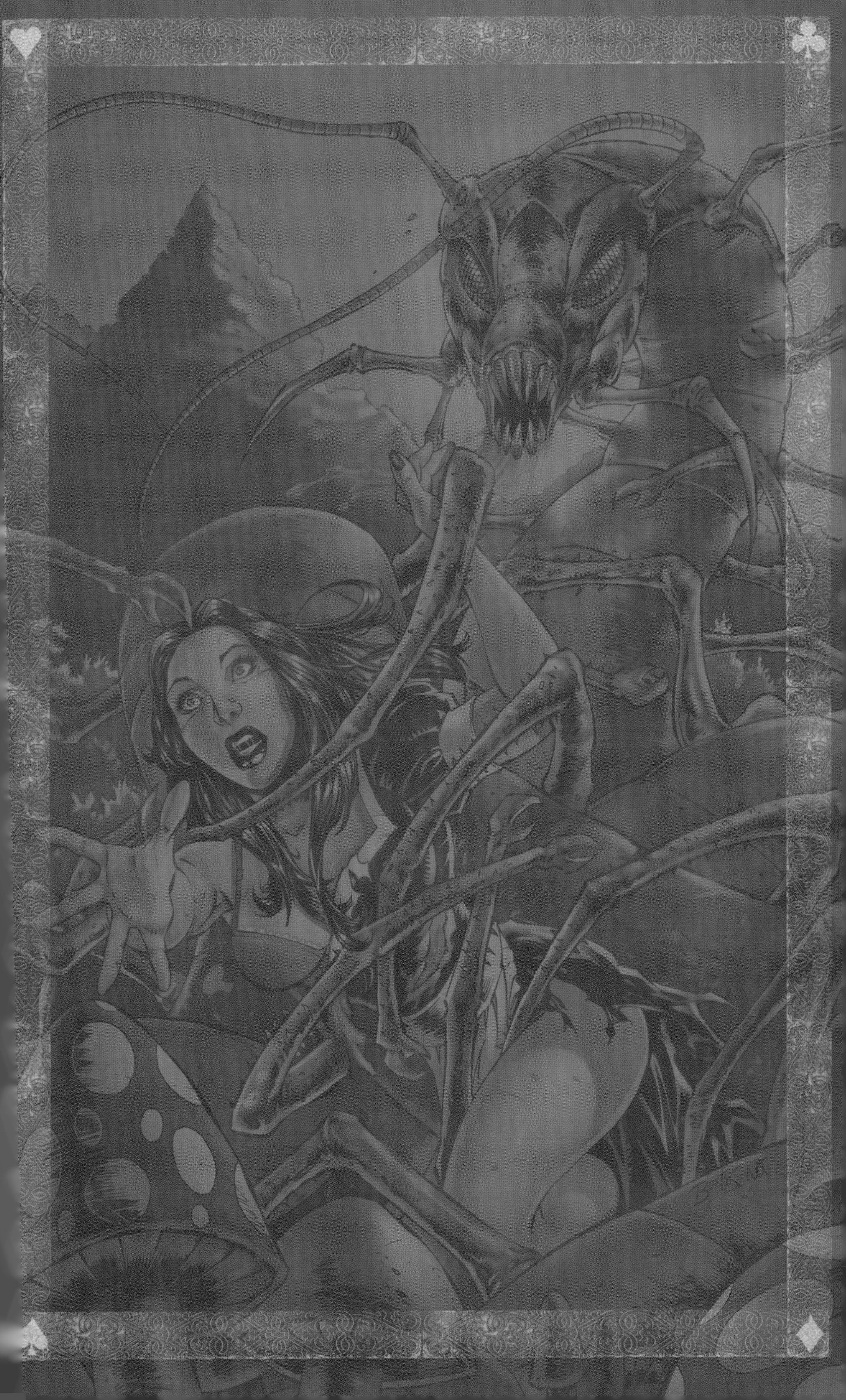

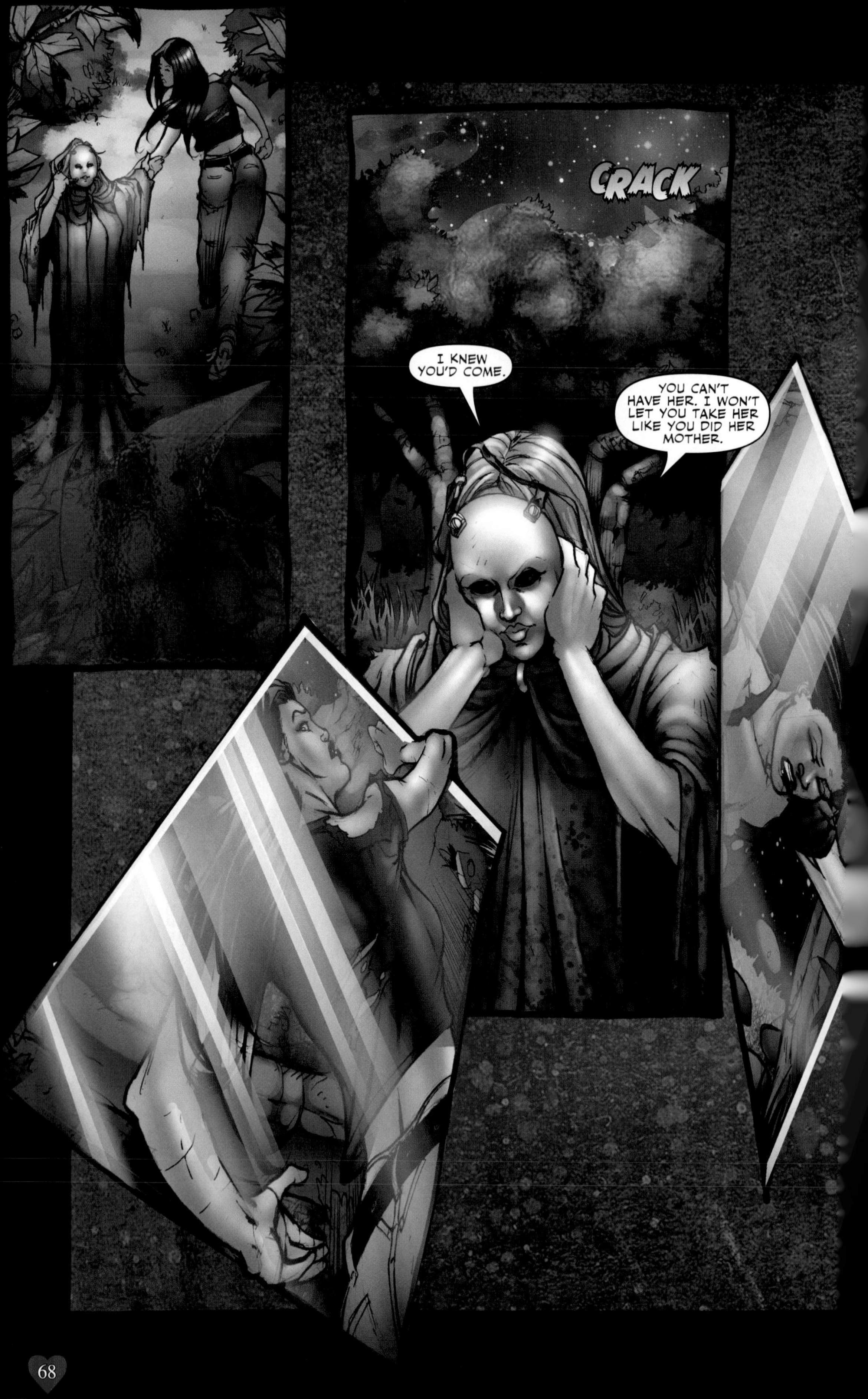
CRACK
I KNEW YOU'D COME.
YOU CAN'T HAVE HER. I WON'T LET YOU TAKE HER LIKE YOU DID HER MOTHER.

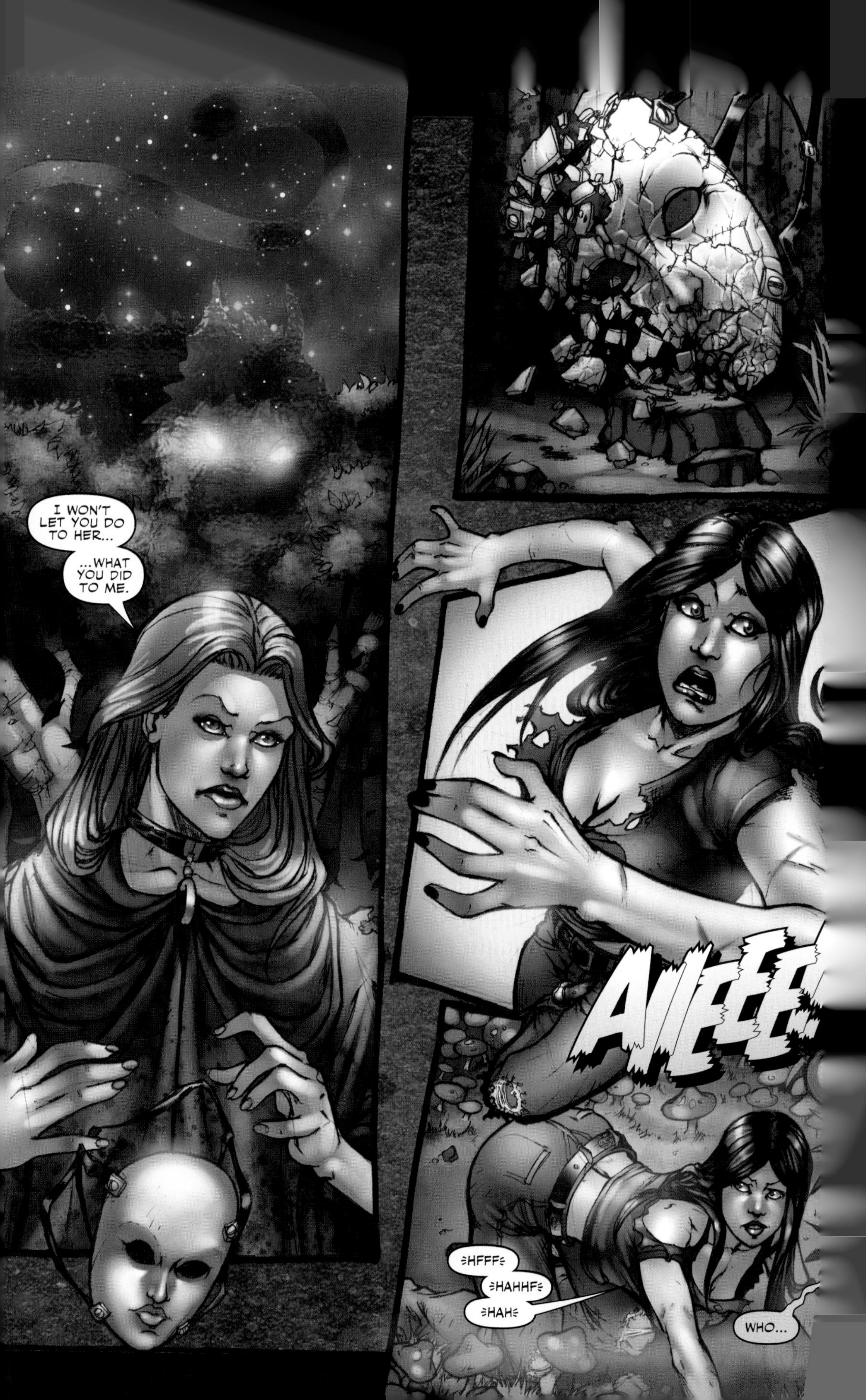
I WON'T LET YOU DO TO HER...
...WHAT YOU DID TO ME.
AIEEE
HFFF
HAHHF
HAH
WHO...

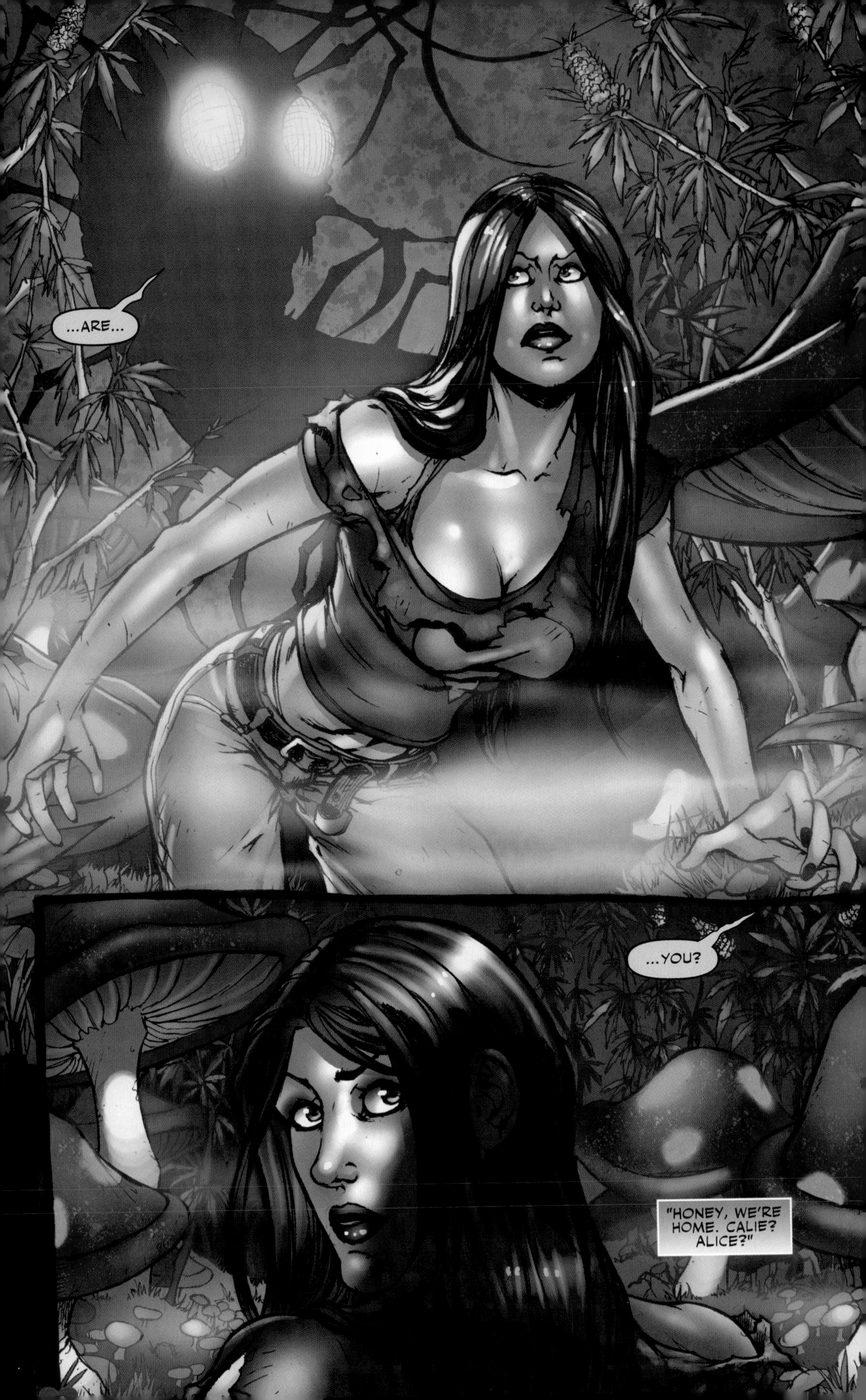
...ARE...
...YOU?
"HONEY, WE'RE HOME. CALIE? ALICE?"

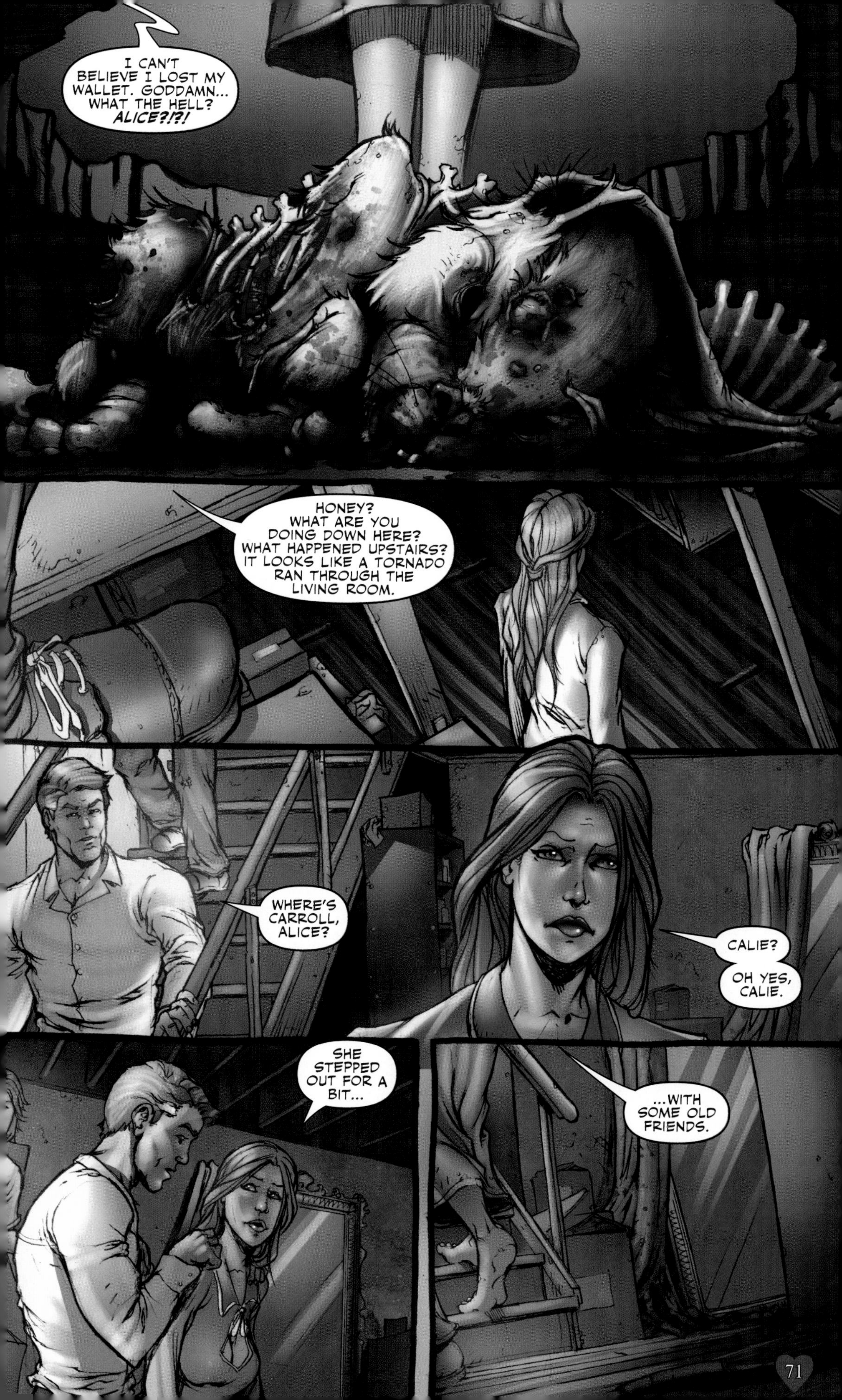
I CAN'T BELIEVE I LOST MY WALLET. GODDAMN... WHAT THE HELL? ALICE?!?!
HONEY? WHAT ARE YOU DOING DOWN HERE? WHAT HAPPENED UPSTAIRS? IT LOOKS LIKE A TORNADO RAN THROUGH THE LIVING ROOM.
WHERE'S CARROLL, ALICE?
CALIE?
OH YES, CALIE.
SHE STEPPED OUT FOR A BIT...
...WITH SOME OLD FRIENDS.

three

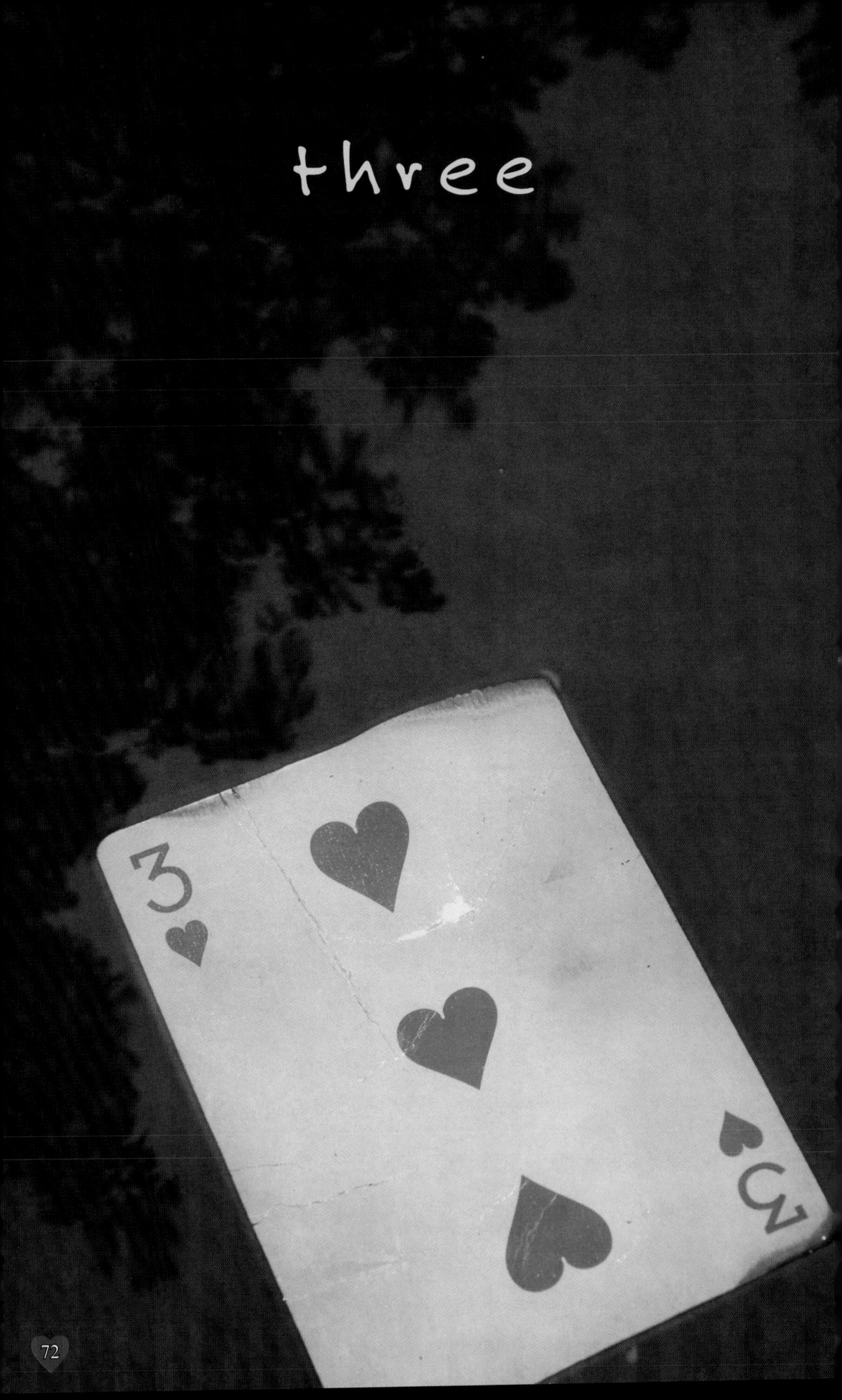

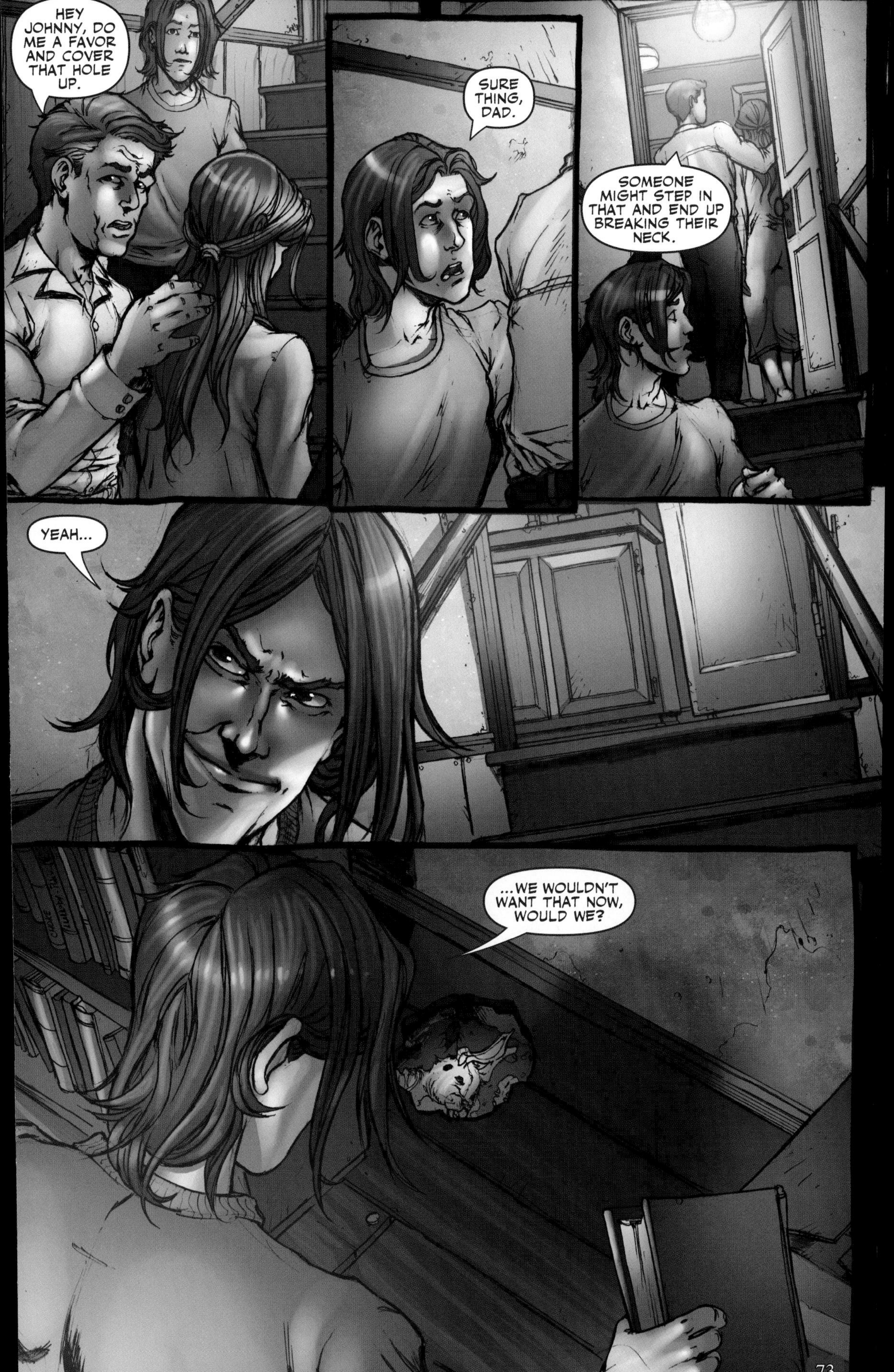
HEY JOHNNY, DO ME A FAVOR AND COVER THAT HOLE UP.
SURE THING, DAD.
SOMEONE MIGHT STEP IN THAT AND END UP BREAKING THEIR NECK.
YEAH...
...WE WOULDN'T WANT THAT NOW, WOULD WE?

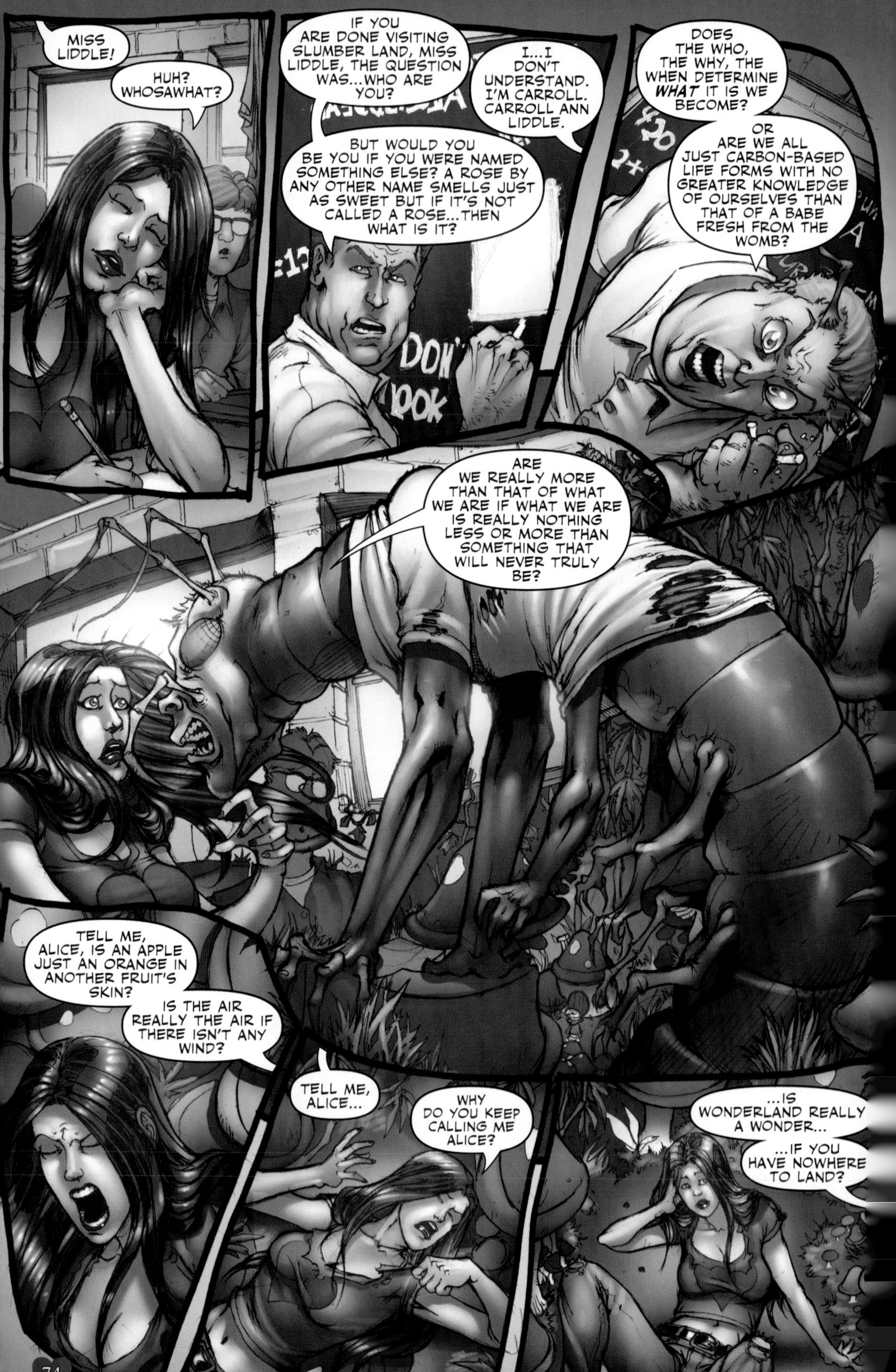
MISS LIDDLE!
HUH? WHOSAWHAT?
IF YOU ARE DONE VISITING SLUMBER LAND, MISS LIDDLE, THE QUESTION WAS...WHO ARE YOU?
I...I DON'T UNDERSTAND. I'M CARROLL. CARROLL ANN LIDDLE.
BUT WOULD YOU BE YOU IF YOU WERE NAMED SOMETHING ELSE? A ROSE BY ANY OTHER NAME SMELLS JUST AS SWEET BUT IF IT'S NOT CALLED A ROSE...THEN WHAT IS IT?
DON'T LOOK
DOES THE WHO, THE WHY, THE WHEN DETERMINE *WHAT* IT IS WE BECOME?
OR ARE WE ALL JUST CARBON-BASED LIFE FORMS WITH NO GREATER KNOWLEDGE OF OURSELVES THAN THAT OF A BABE FRESH FROM THE WOMB?
ARE WE REALLY MORE THAN THAT OF WHAT WE ARE IF WHAT WE ARE IS REALLY NOTHING LESS OR MORE THAN SOMETHING THAT WILL NEVER TRULY BE?
TELL ME, ALICE, IS AN APPLE JUST AN ORANGE IN ANOTHER FRUIT'S SKIN?
IS THE AIR REALLY THE AIR IF THERE ISN'T ANY WIND?
TELL ME, ALICE...
WHY DO YOU KEEP CALLING ME ALICE?
...IS WONDERLAND REALLY A WONDER...
...IF YOU HAVE NOWHERE TO LAND?

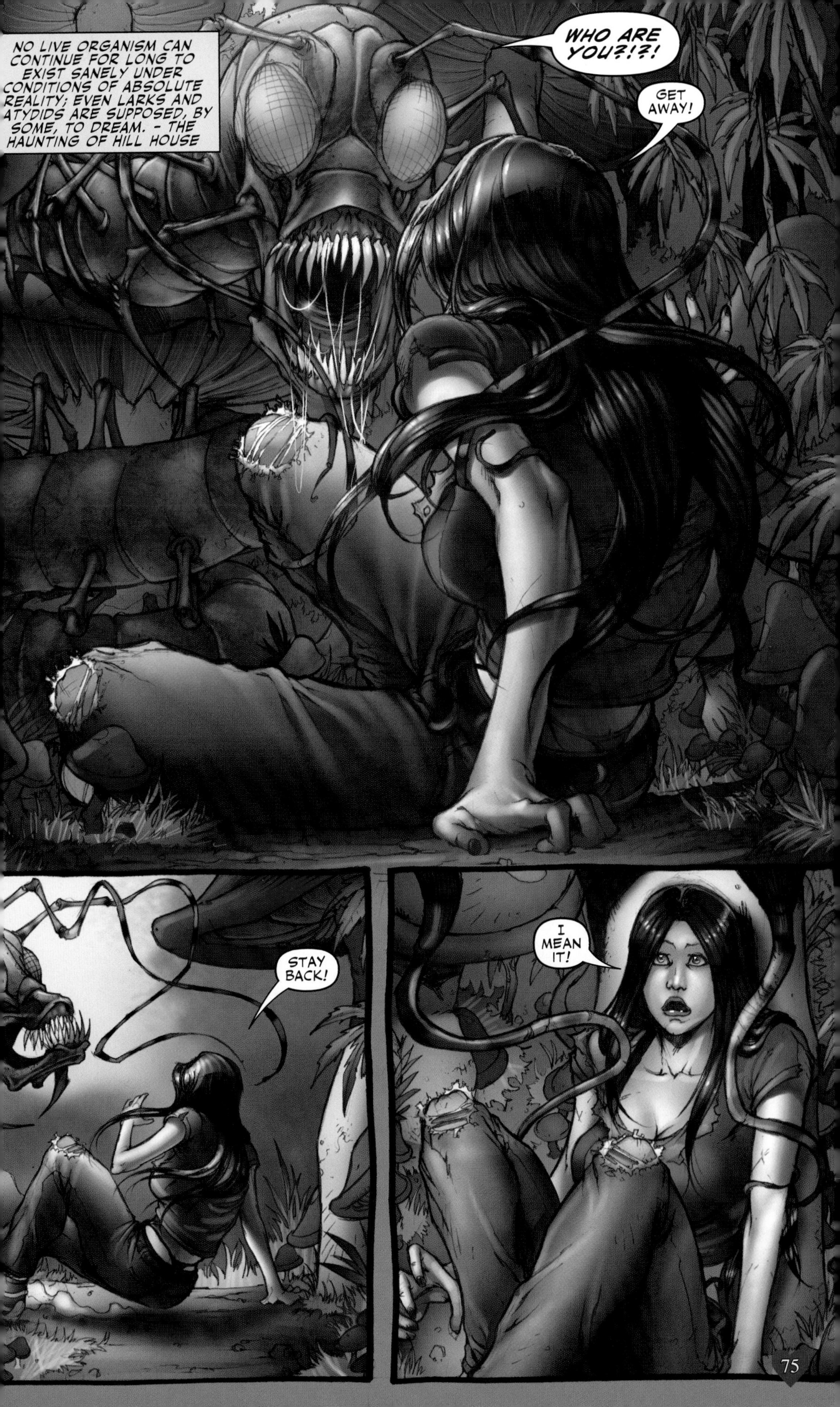
NO LIVE ORGANISM CAN CONTINUE FOR LONG TO EXIST SANELY UNDER CONDITIONS OF ABSOLUTE REALITY; EVEN LARKS AND ATYDIDS ARE SUPPOSED, BY SOME, TO DREAM. - THE HAUNTING OF HILL HOUSE
WHO ARE YOU?!?!
GET AWAY!
STAY BACK!
I MEAN IT!

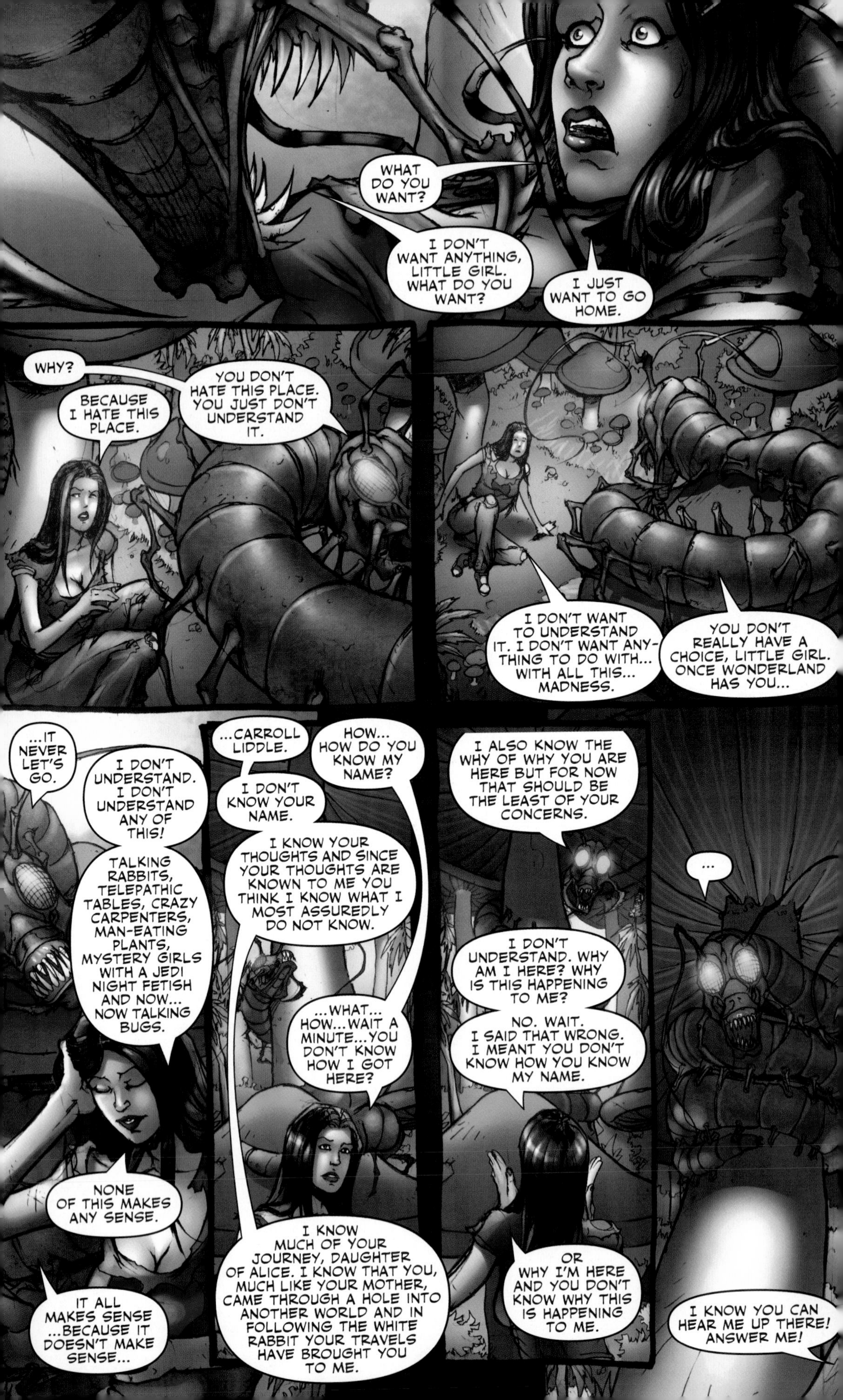
WHAT DO YOU WANT?
I DON'T WANT ANYTHING, LITTLE GIRL. WHAT DO YOU WANT?
I JUST WANT TO GO HOME.
WHY?
BECAUSE I HATE THIS PLACE.
YOU DON'T HATE THIS PLACE. YOU JUST DON'T UNDERSTAND IT.
I DON'T WANT TO UNDERSTAND IT. I DON'T WANT ANY-THING TO DO WITH... WITH ALL THIS... MADNESS.
YOU DON'T REALLY HAVE A CHOICE, LITTLE GIRL. ONCE WONDERLAND HAS YOU...
...IT NEVER LET'S GO.
I DON'T UNDERSTAND. I DON'T UNDERSTAND ANY OF THIS!
TALKING RABBITS, TELEPATHIC TABLES, CRAZY CARPENTERS, MAN-EATING PLANTS, MYSTERY GIRLS WITH A JEDI NIGHT FETISH AND NOW... NOW TALKING BUGS.
NONE OF THIS MAKES ANY SENSE.
IT ALL MAKES SENSE ...BECAUSE IT DOESN'T MAKE SENSE...
...CARROLL LIDDLE.
HOW... HOW DO YOU KNOW MY NAME?
I DON'T KNOW YOUR NAME.
I KNOW YOUR THOUGHTS AND SINCE YOUR THOUGHTS ARE KNOWN TO ME YOU THINK I KNOW WHAT I MOST ASSUREDLY DO NOT KNOW.
...WHAT... HOW...WAIT A MINUTE...YOU DON'T KNOW HOW I GOT HERE?
I KNOW MUCH OF YOUR JOURNEY, DAUGHTER OF ALICE. I KNOW THAT YOU, MUCH LIKE YOUR MOTHER, CAME THROUGH A HOLE INTO ANOTHER WORLD AND IN FOLLOWING THE WHITE RABBIT YOUR TRAVELS HAVE BROUGHT YOU TO ME.
I ALSO KNOW THE WHY OF WHY YOU ARE HERE BUT FOR NOW THAT SHOULD BE THE LEAST OF YOUR CONCERNS.
I DON'T UNDERSTAND. WHY AM I HERE? WHY IS THIS HAPPENING TO ME?
NO. WAIT. I SAID THAT WRONG. I MEANT YOU DON'T KNOW HOW YOU KNOW MY NAME.
OR WHY I'M HERE AND YOU DON'T KNOW WHY THIS IS HAPPENING TO ME.
...
I KNOW YOU CAN HEAR ME UP THERE! ANSWER ME!

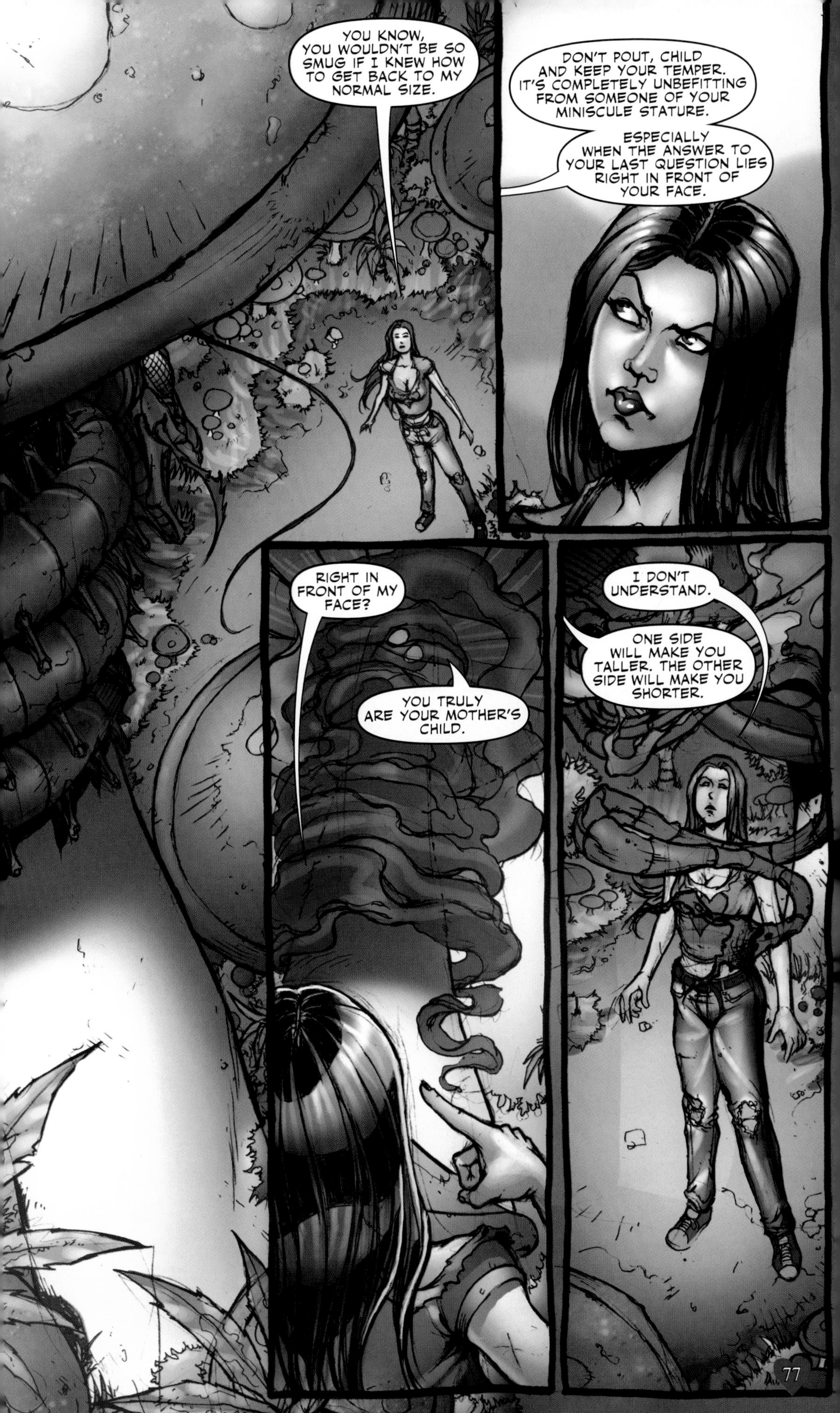
YOU KNOW, YOU WOULDN'T BE SO SMUG IF I KNEW HOW TO GET BACK TO MY NORMAL SIZE.
DON'T POUT, CHILD AND KEEP YOUR TEMPER. IT'S COMPLETELY UNBEFITTING FROM SOMEONE OF YOUR MINISCULE STATURE.
ESPECIALLY WHEN THE ANSWER TO YOUR LAST QUESTION LIES RIGHT IN FRONT OF YOUR FACE.
RIGHT IN FRONT OF MY FACE?
YOU TRULY ARE YOUR MOTHER'S CHILD.
I DON'T UNDERSTAND.
ONE SIDE WILL MAKE YOU TALLER. THE OTHER SIDE WILL MAKE YOU SHORTER.

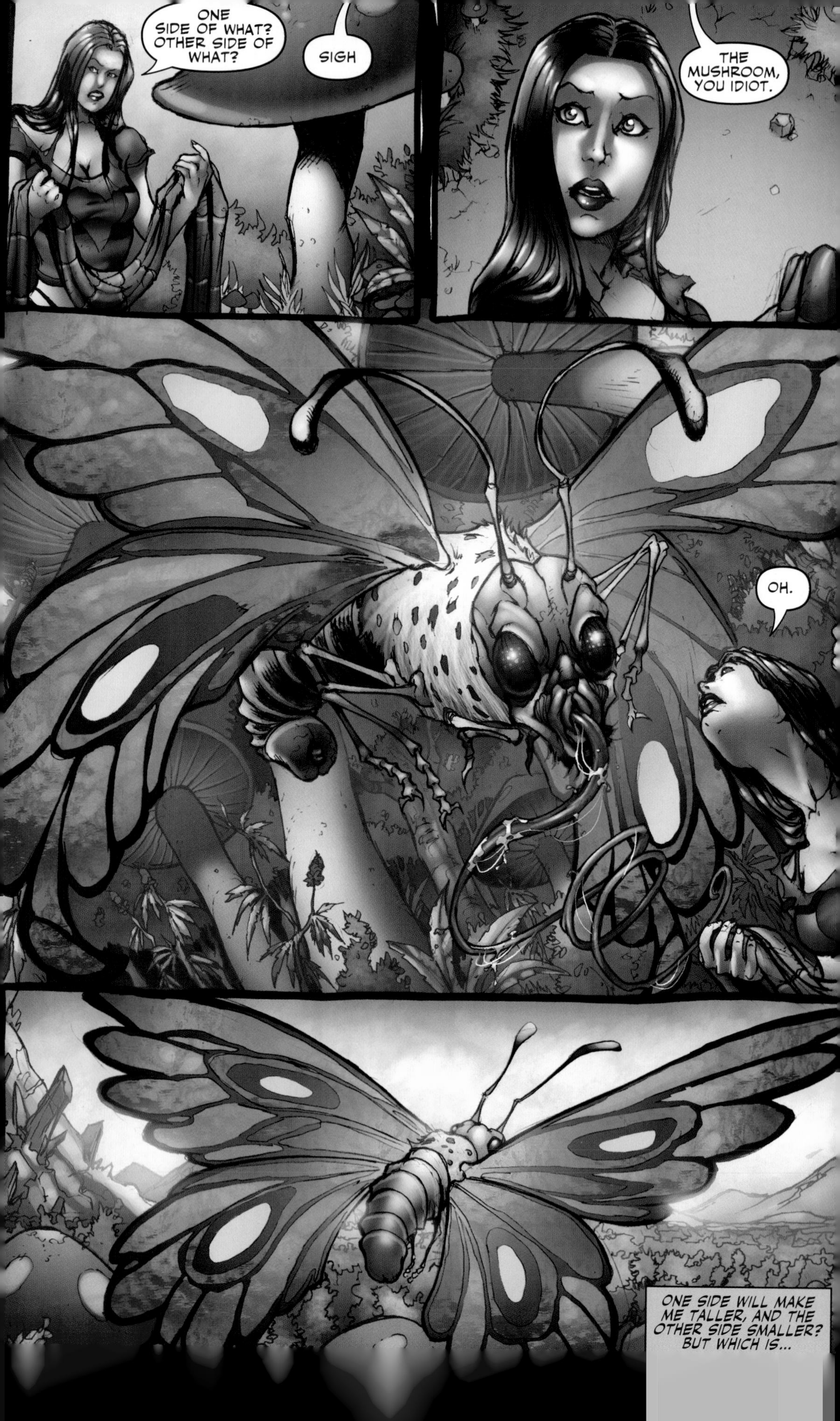

ONE SIDE OF WHAT? OTHER SIDE OF WHAT?
SIGH
THE MUSHROOM, YOU IDIOT.
OH.
ONE SIDE WILL MAKE ME TALLER, AND THE OTHER SIDE SMALLER? BUT WHICH IS...

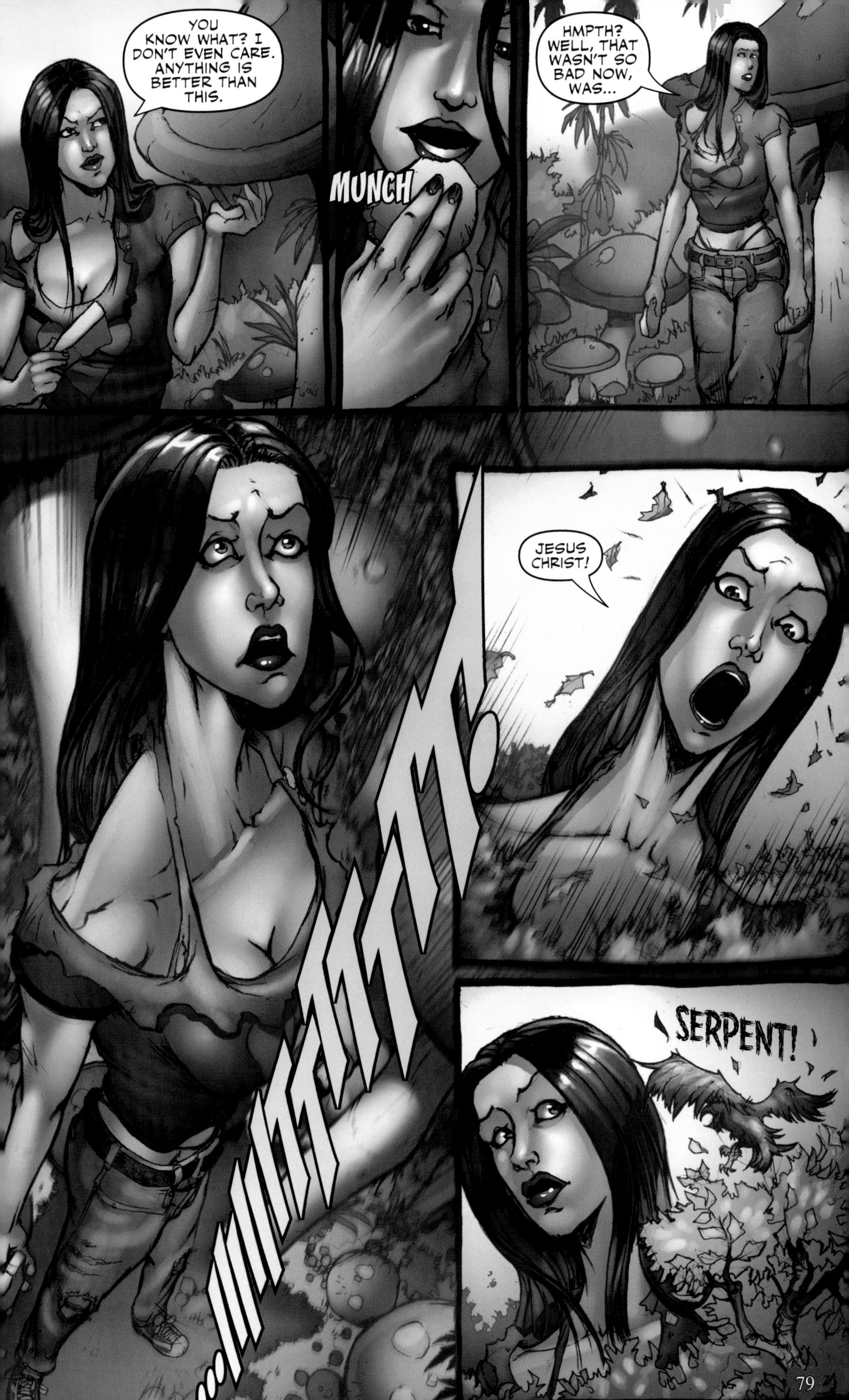
YOU KNOW WHAT? I DON'T EVEN CARE. ANYTHING IS BETTER THAN THIS.
MUNCH
HMPTH? WELL, THAT WASN'T SO BAD NOW, WAS...
...HHHSSSSTTT!
JESUS CHRIST!
SERPENT!

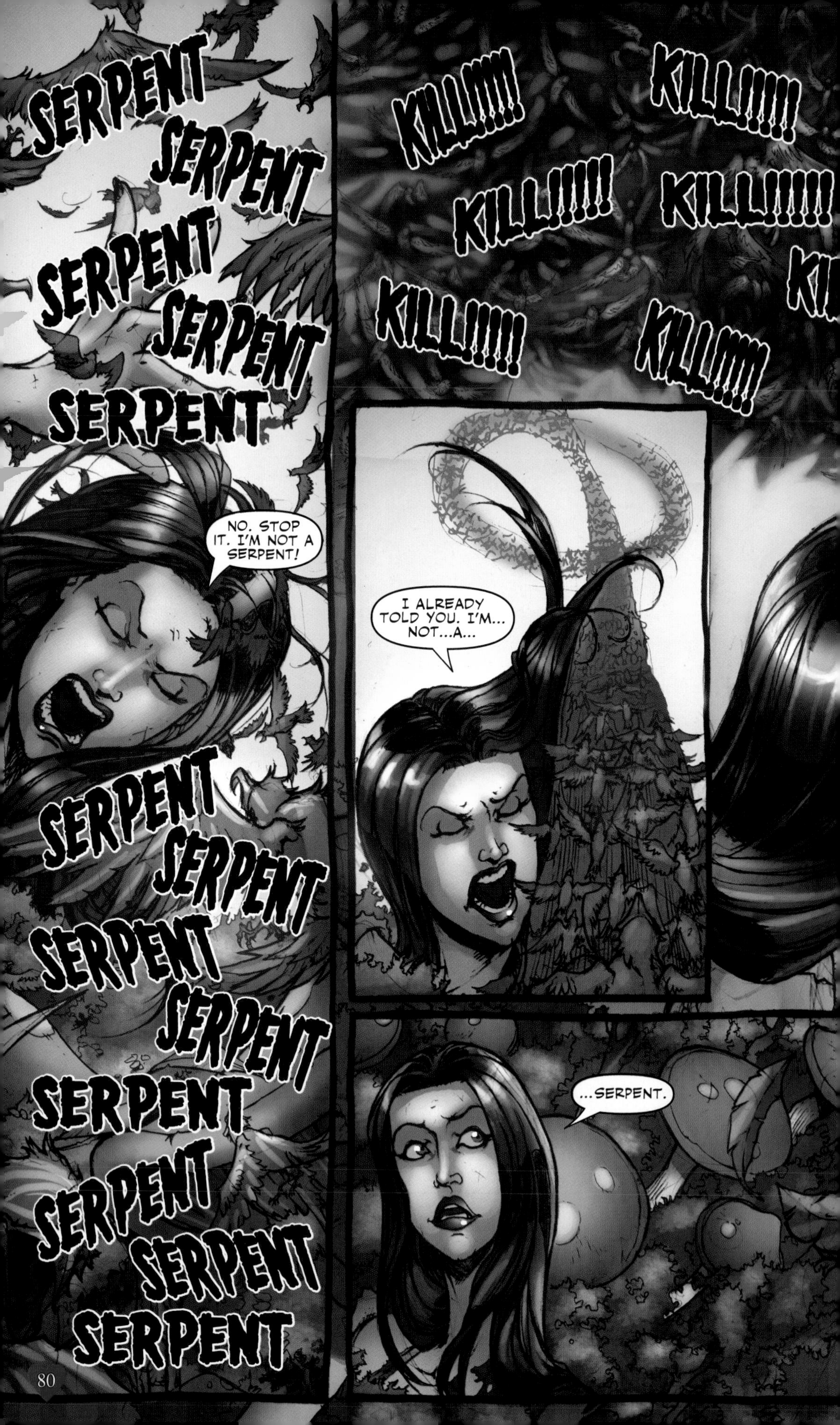

SERPENT
SERPENT
SERPENT
SERPENT
SERPENT
NO. STOP IT. I'M NOT A SERPENT!
SERPENT
SERPENT
SERPENT
SERPENT
SERPENT
SERPENT
SERPENT
SERPENT
KILL!!!!!
KILL!!!!!
KILL!!!!!
KILL!!!!!
KILL!!!!!
KILL!!!!!
I ALREADY TOLD YOU. I'M... NOT...A...
...SERPENT.

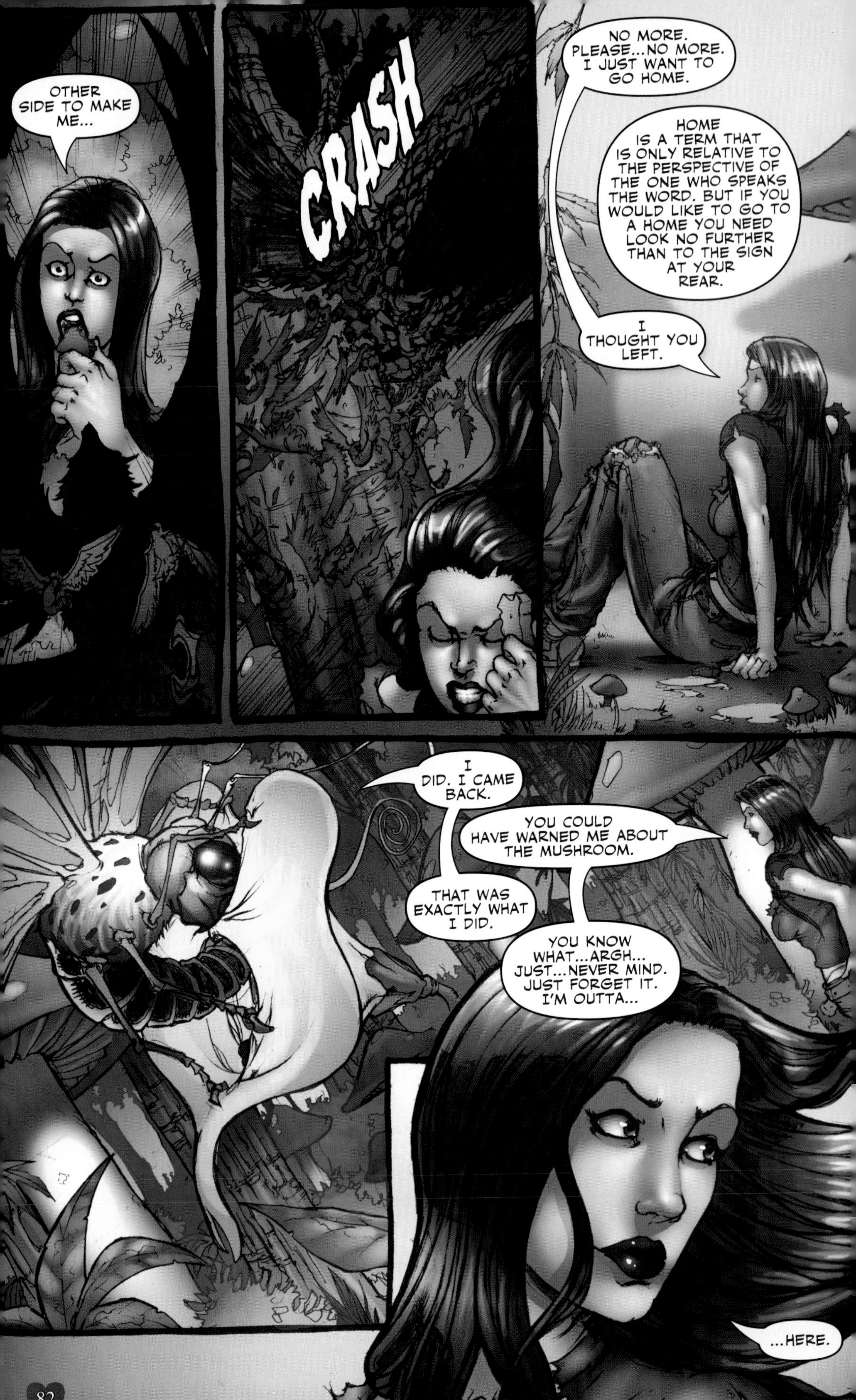
OTHER SIDE TO MAKE ME...
CRASH
NO MORE. PLEASE...NO MORE. I JUST WANT TO GO HOME.
HOME IS A TERM THAT IS ONLY RELATIVE TO THE PERSPECTIVE OF THE ONE WHO SPEAKS THE WORD. BUT IF YOU WOULD LIKE TO GO TO A HOME YOU NEED LOOK NO FURTHER THAN TO THE SIGN AT YOUR REAR.
I THOUGHT YOU LEFT.
I DID. I CAME BACK.
YOU COULD HAVE WARNED ME ABOUT THE MUSHROOM.
THAT WAS EXACTLY WHAT I DID.
YOU KNOW WHAT...ARGH... JUST...NEVER MIND. JUST FORGET IT. I'M OUTTA...
...HERE.

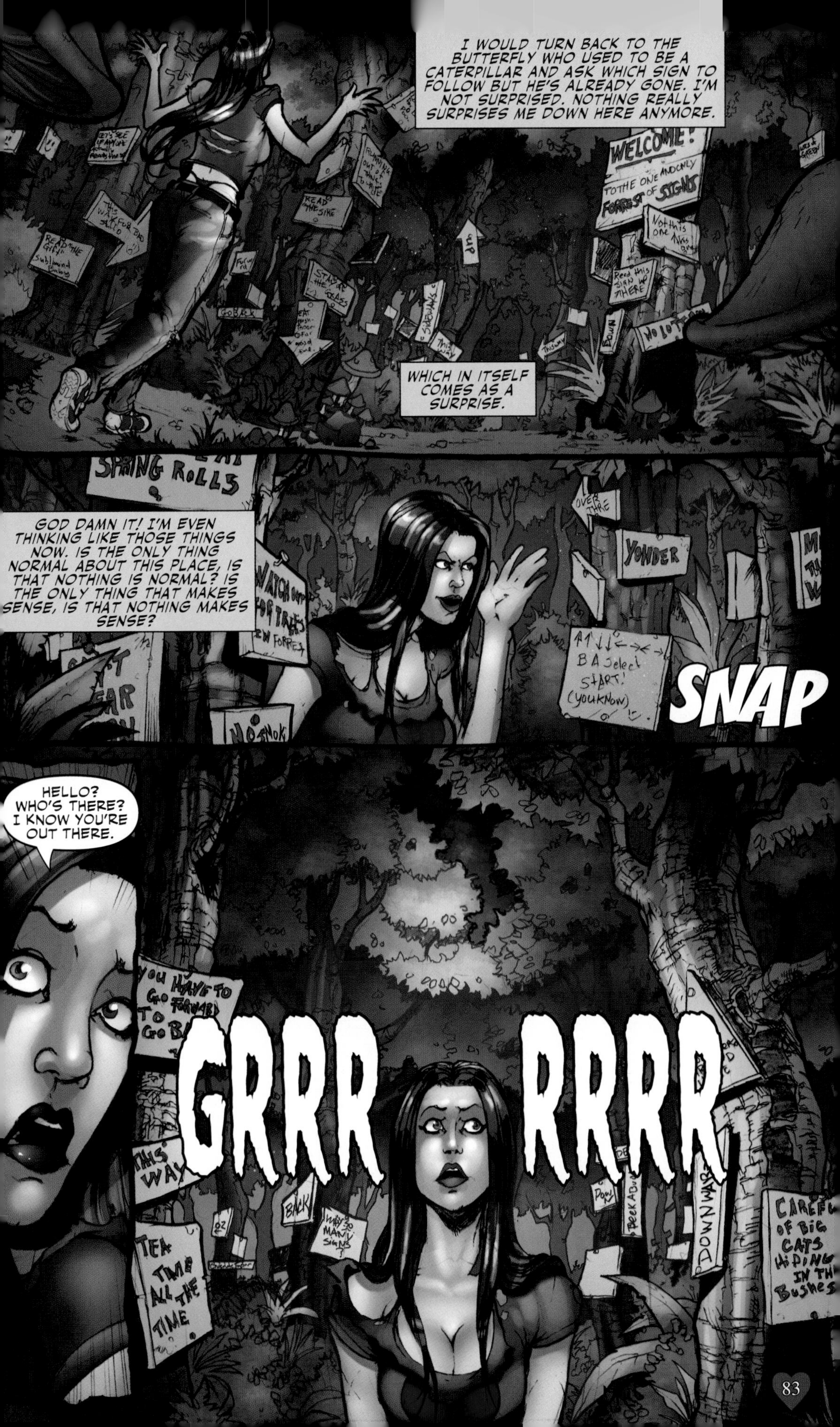
I WOULD TURN BACK TO THE BUTTERFLY WHO USED TO BE A CATERPILLAR AND ASK WHICH SIGN TO FOLLOW BUT HE'S ALREADY GONE. I'M NOT SURPRISED. NOTHING REALLY SURPRISES ME DOWN HERE ANYMORE.
WELCOME! TO THE ONE AND ONLY FORREST OF SIGNS
WHICH IN ITSELF COMES AS A SURPRISE.
SPRING ROLLS
GOD DAMN IT! I'M EVEN THINKING LIKE THOSE THINGS NOW. IS THE ONLY THING NORMAL ABOUT THIS PLACE, IS THAT NOTHING IS NORMAL? IS THE ONLY THING THAT MAKES SENSE, IS THAT NOTHING MAKES SENSE?
YONDER
SNAP
HELLO? WHO'S THERE? I KNOW YOU'RE OUT THERE.
GRRR RRRR
TEA TIME ALL THE TIME
DOWNWARD

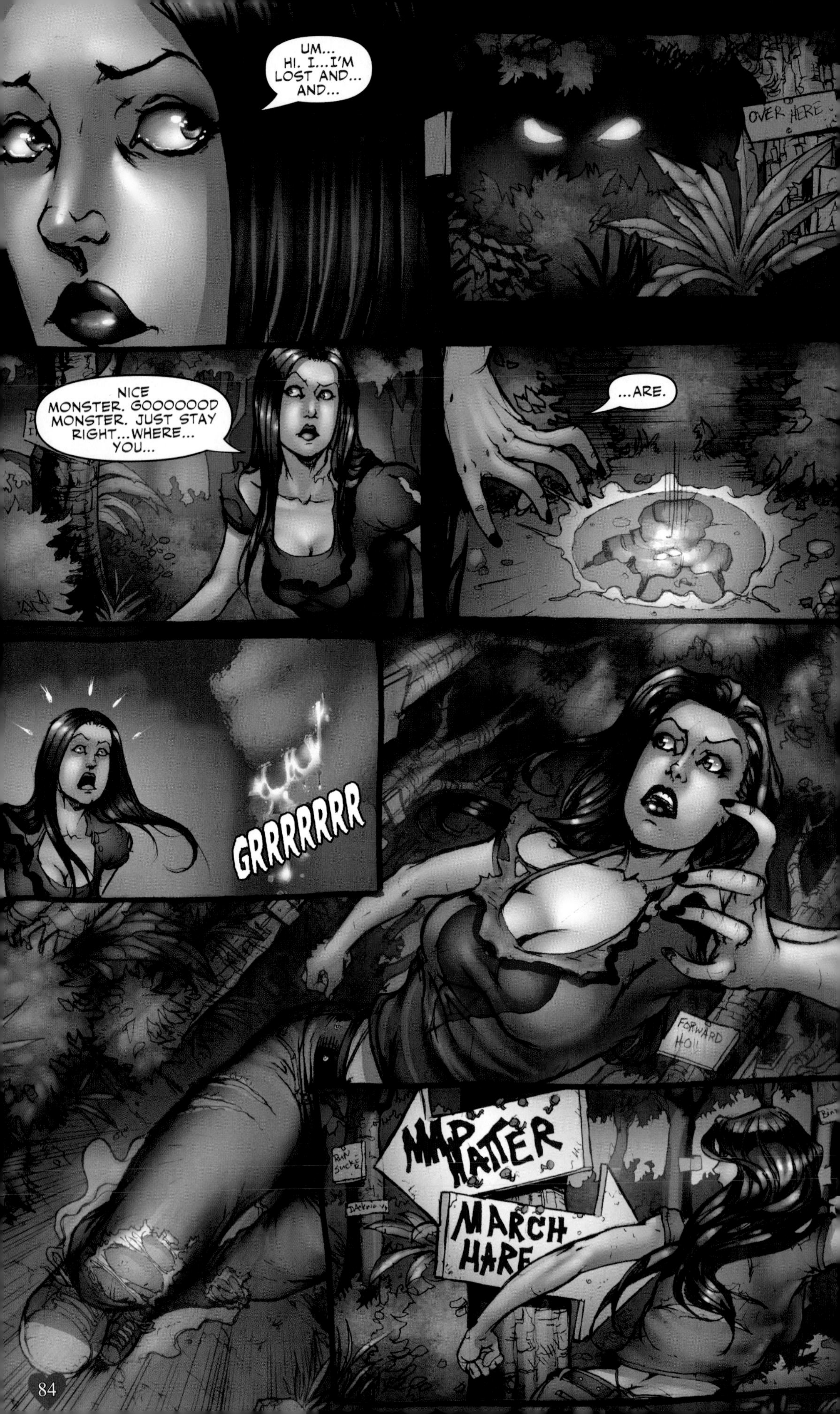
UM... HI. I...I'M LOST AND... AND...
OVER HERE
NICE MONSTER. GOOOOOOD MONSTER. JUST STAY RIGHT...WHERE... YOU...
...ARE.
GRRRRRRR
FORWARD HO!!
MADHATTER
MARCH HARE

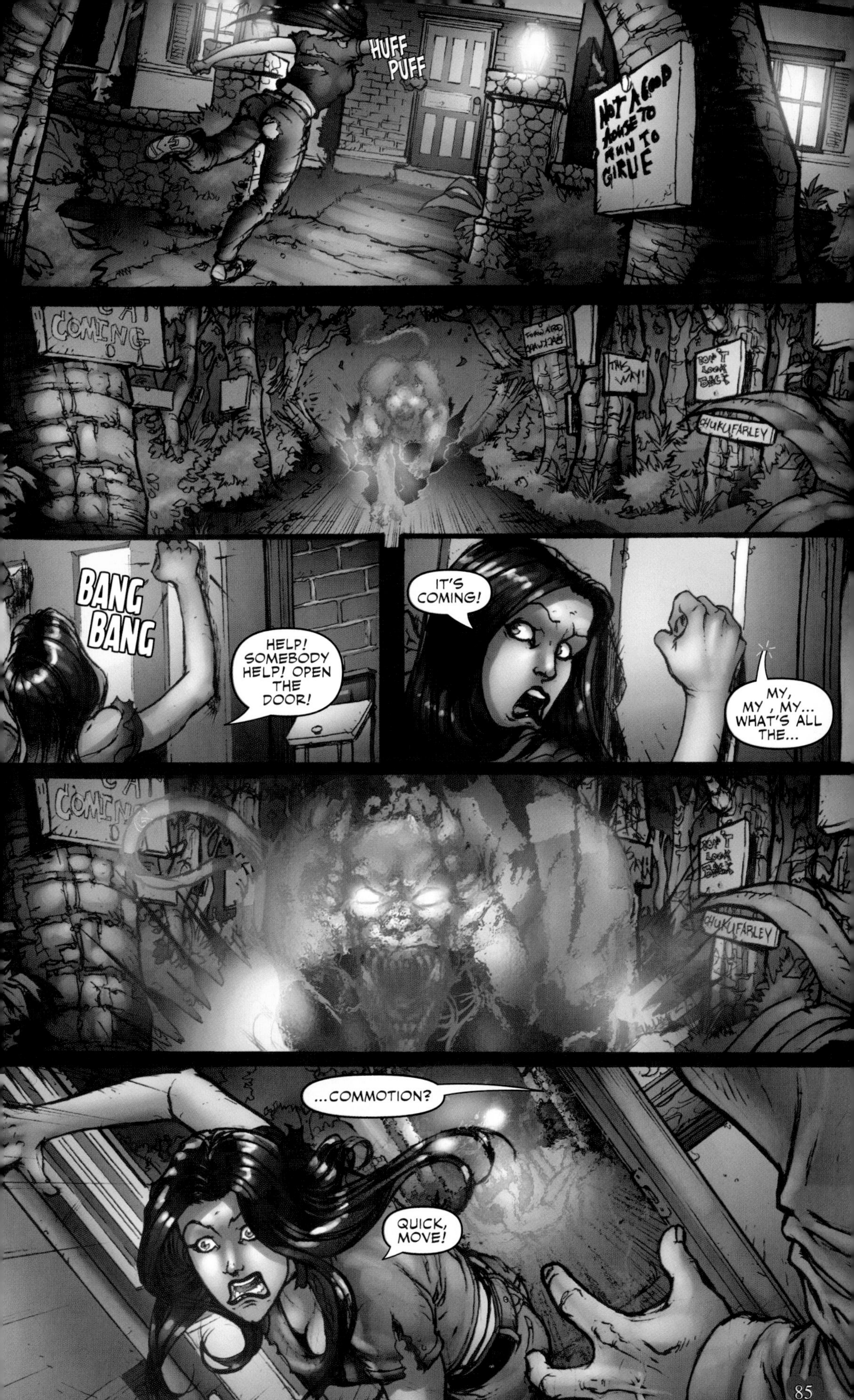

HUFF PUFF
NOT A GOOD HOUSE TO RUN TO GIRLIE
COMING
THIS WAY!
DON'T LOOK BACK
CHUKU FARLEY
BANG BANG
HELP! SOMEBODY HELP! OPEN THE DOOR!
IT'S COMING!
MY, MY, MY... WHAT'S ALL THE...
...COMMOTION?
QUICK, MOVE!

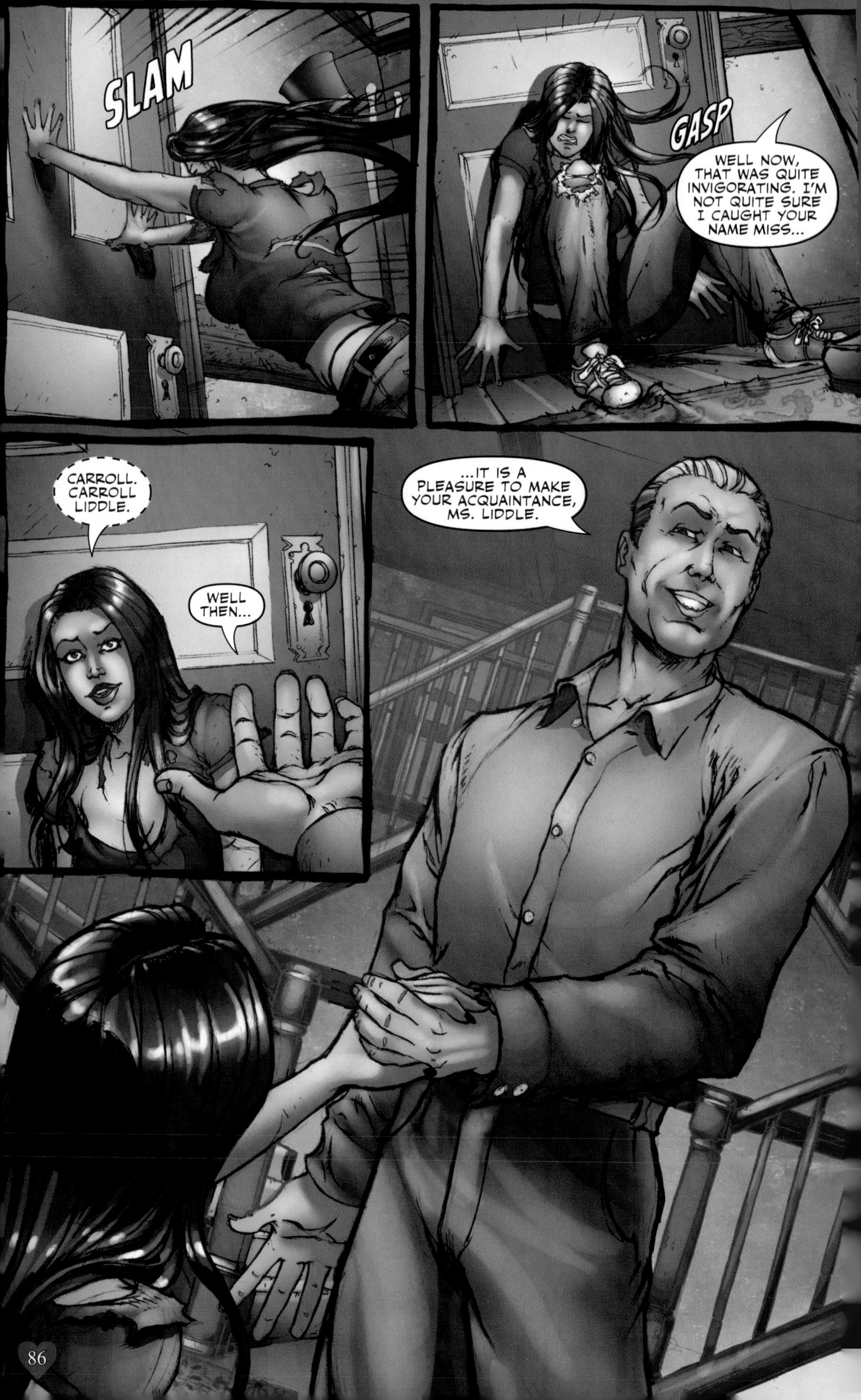
SLAM
GASP
WELL NOW, THAT WAS QUITE INVIGORATING. I'M NOT QUITE SURE I CAUGHT YOUR NAME MISS...
CARROLL. CARROLL LIDDLE.
WELL THEN...
...IT IS A PLEASURE TO MAKE YOUR ACQUAINTANCE, MS. LIDDLE.

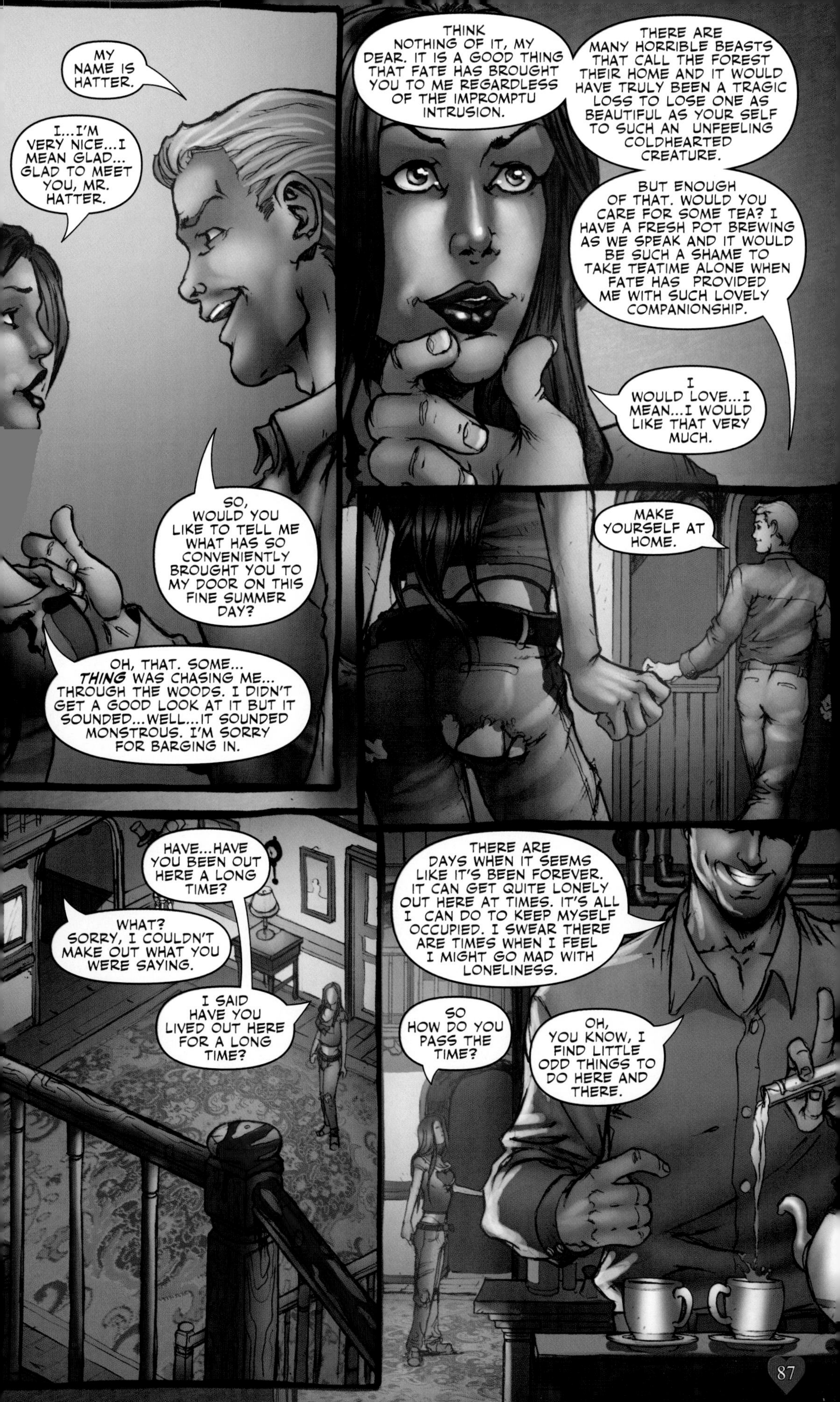
MY NAME IS HATTER.
I...I'M VERY NICE...I MEAN GLAD... GLAD TO MEET YOU, MR. HATTER.
THINK NOTHING OF IT, MY DEAR. IT IS A GOOD THING THAT FATE HAS BROUGHT YOU TO ME REGARDLESS OF THE IMPROMPTU INTRUSION.
THERE ARE MANY HORRIBLE BEASTS THAT CALL THE FOREST THEIR HOME AND IT WOULD HAVE TRULY BEEN A TRAGIC LOSS TO LOSE ONE AS BEAUTIFUL AS YOUR SELF TO SUCH AN UNFEELING COLDHEARTED CREATURE.
BUT ENOUGH OF THAT. WOULD YOU CARE FOR SOME TEA? I HAVE A FRESH POT BREWING AS WE SPEAK AND IT WOULD BE SUCH A SHAME TO TAKE TEATIME ALONE WHEN FATE HAS PROVIDED ME WITH SUCH LOVELY COMPANIONSHIP.
I WOULD LOVE...I MEAN...I WOULD LIKE THAT VERY MUCH.
SO, WOULD YOU LIKE TO TELL ME WHAT HAS SO CONVENIENTLY BROUGHT YOU TO MY DOOR ON THIS FINE SUMMER DAY?
OH, THAT. SOME... *THING* WAS CHASING ME... THROUGH THE WOODS. I DIDN'T GET A GOOD LOOK AT IT BUT IT SOUNDED...WELL...IT SOUNDED MONSTROUS. I'M SORRY FOR BARGING IN.
MAKE YOURSELF AT HOME.
HAVE...HAVE YOU BEEN OUT HERE A LONG TIME?
WHAT? SORRY, I COULDN'T MAKE OUT WHAT YOU WERE SAYING.
I SAID HAVE YOU LIVED OUT HERE FOR A LONG TIME?
THERE ARE DAYS WHEN IT SEEMS LIKE IT'S BEEN FOREVER. IT CAN GET QUITE LONELY OUT HERE AT TIMES. IT'S ALL I CAN DO TO KEEP MYSELF OCCUPIED. I SWEAR THERE ARE TIMES WHEN I FEEL I MIGHT GO MAD WITH LONELINESS.
SO HOW DO YOU PASS THE TIME?
OH, YOU KNOW, I FIND LITTLE ODD THINGS TO DO HERE AND THERE.

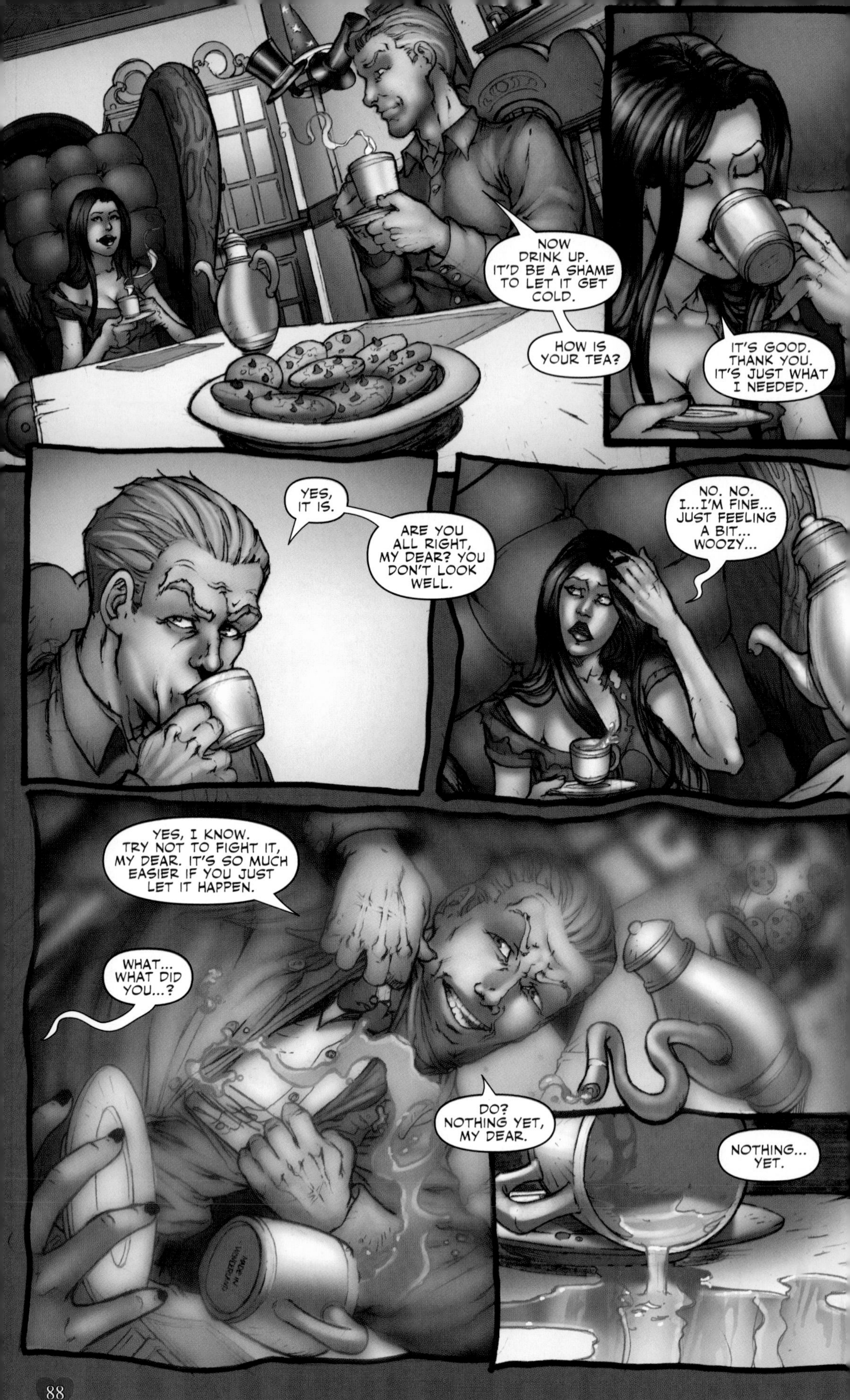
NOW DRINK UP. IT'D BE A SHAME TO LET IT GET COLD.
HOW IS YOUR TEA?
IT'S GOOD. THANK YOU. IT'S JUST WHAT I NEEDED.
YES, IT IS.
ARE YOU ALL RIGHT, MY DEAR? YOU DON'T LOOK WELL.
NO. NO. I...I'M FINE... JUST FEELING A BIT... WOOZY...
YES, I KNOW. TRY NOT TO FIGHT IT, MY DEAR. IT'S SO MUCH EASIER IF YOU JUST LET IT HAPPEN.
WHAT... WHAT DID YOU...?
DO? NOTHING YET, MY DEAR.
NOTHING... YET.

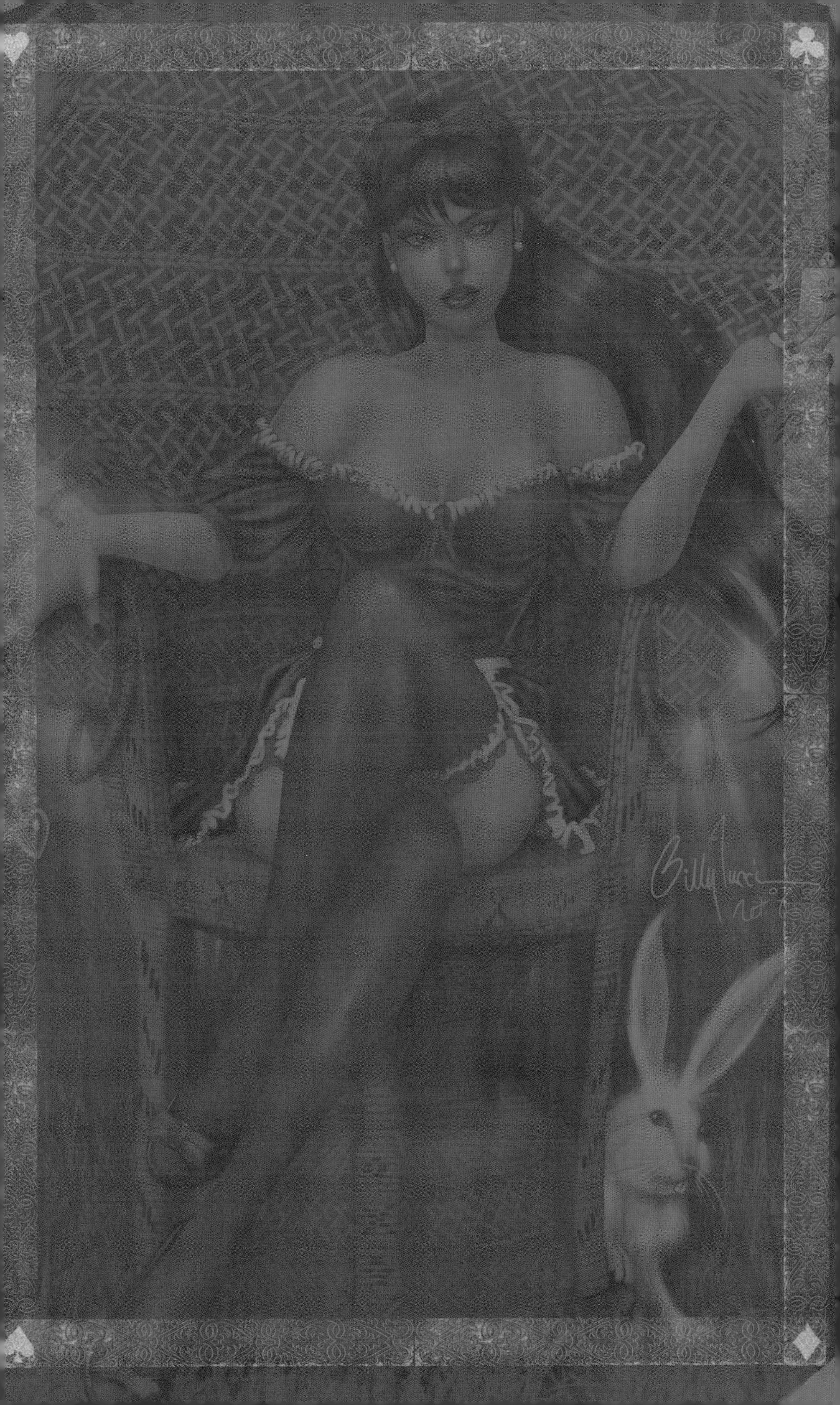

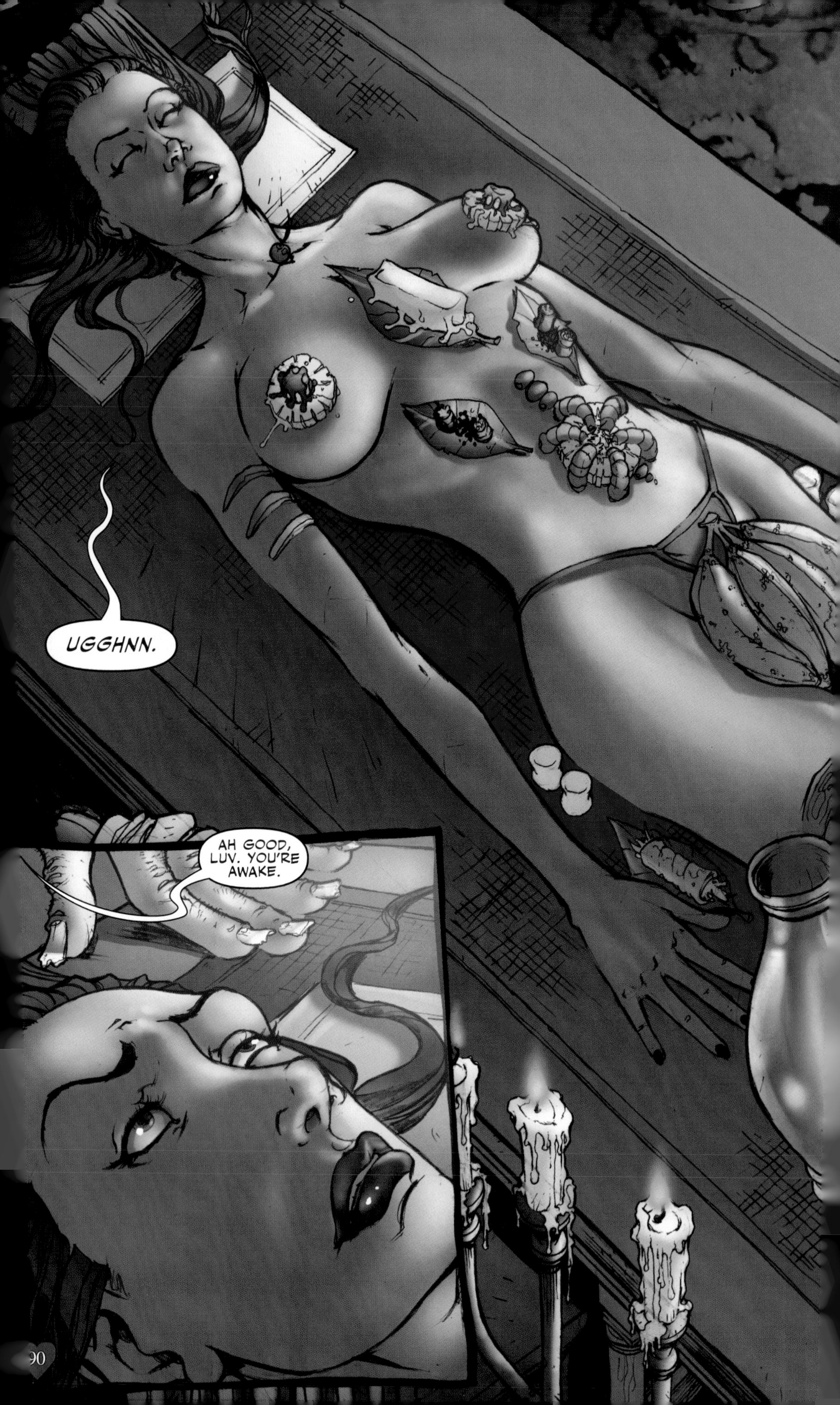
UGGHNN.
AH GOOD, LUV. YOU'RE AWAKE.

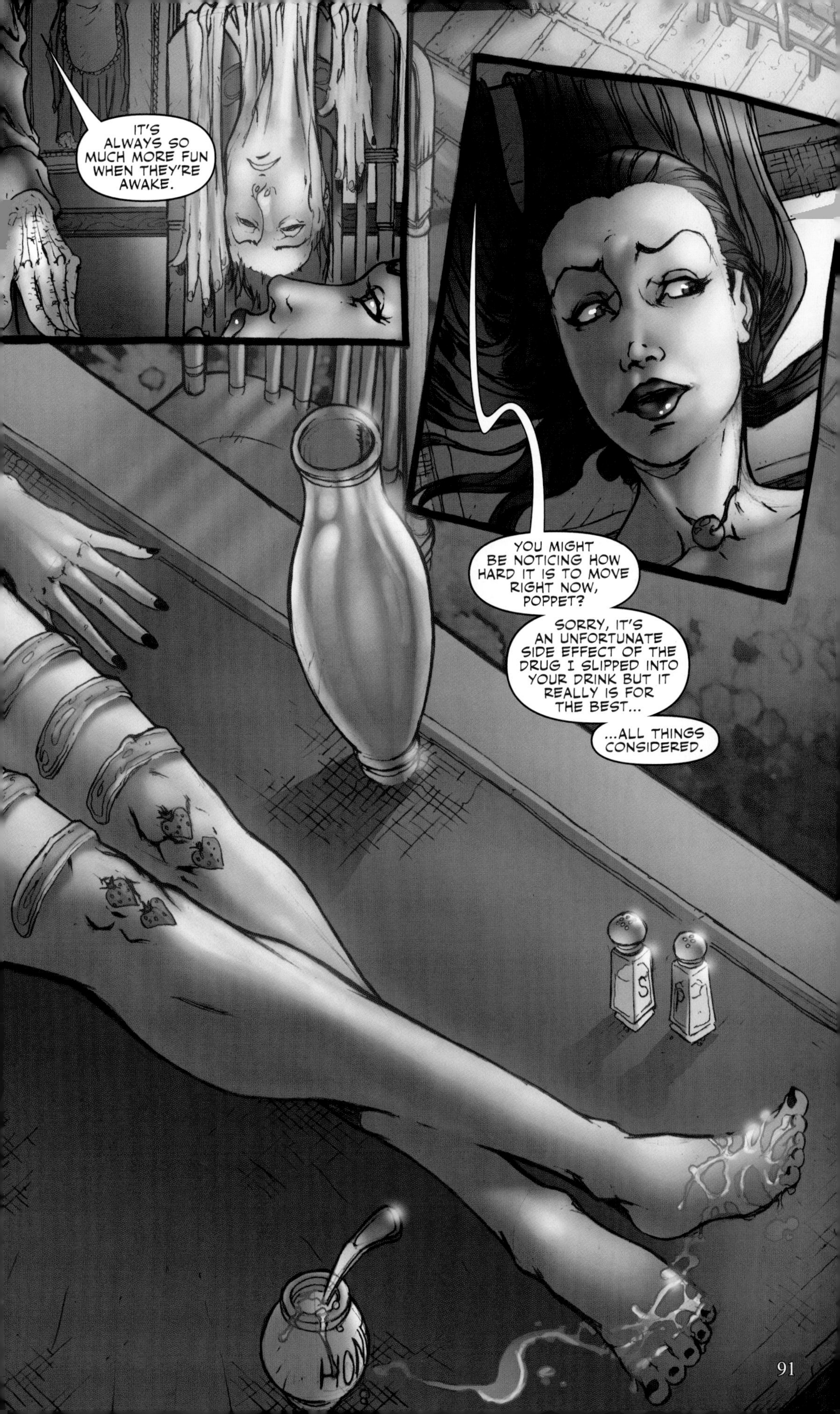
IT'S ALWAYS SO MUCH MORE FUN WHEN THEY'RE AWAKE.
YOU MIGHT BE NOTICING HOW HARD IT IS TO MOVE RIGHT NOW, POPPET?
SORRY, IT'S AN UNFORTUNATE SIDE EFFECT OF THE DRUG I SLIPPED INTO YOUR DRINK BUT IT REALLY IS FOR THE BEST...
...ALL THINGS CONSIDERED.

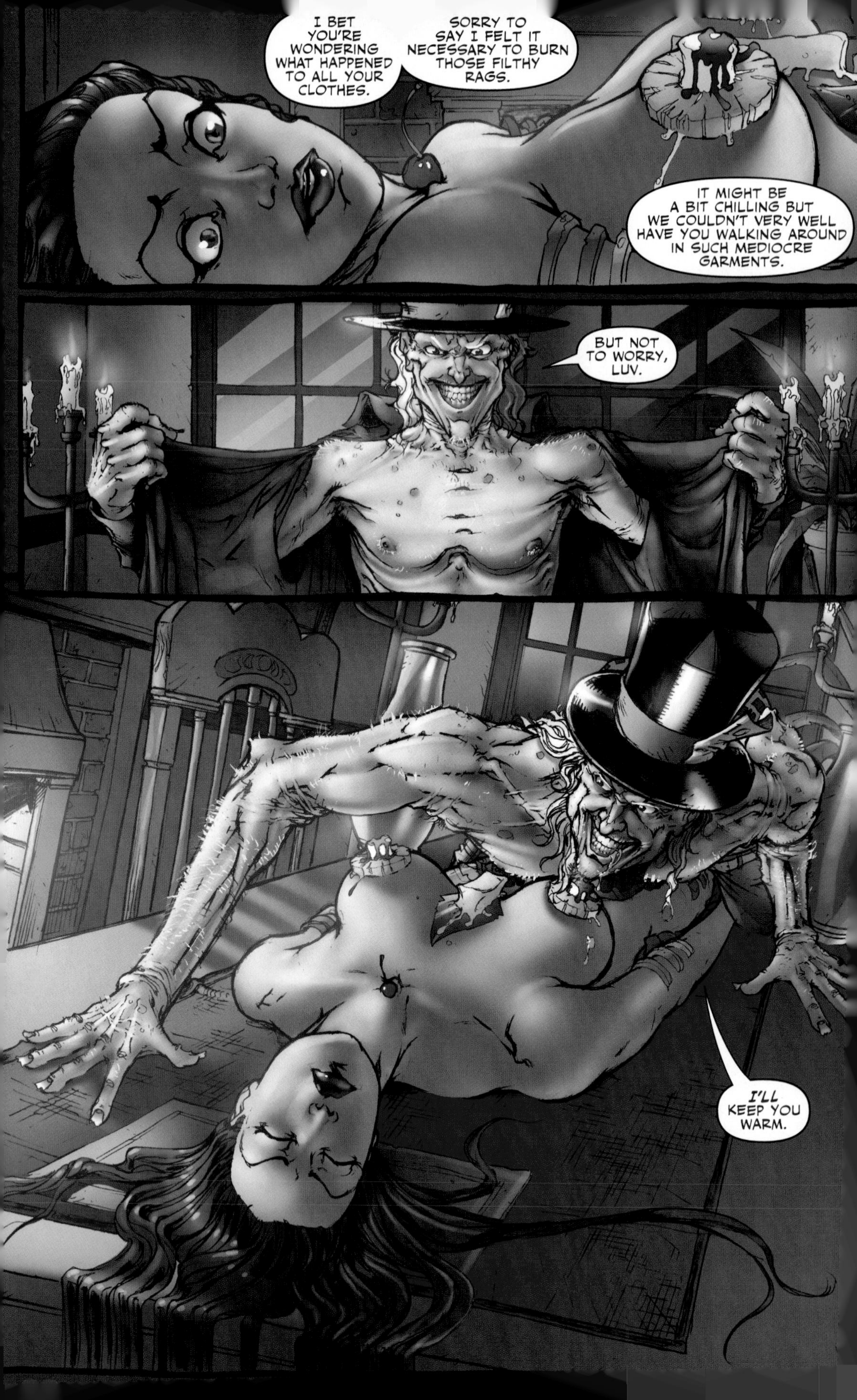
I BET YOU'RE WONDERING WHAT HAPPENED TO ALL YOUR CLOTHES.
SORRY TO SAY I FELT IT NECESSARY TO BURN THOSE FILTHY RAGS.
IT MIGHT BE A BIT CHILLING BUT WE COULDN'T VERY WELL HAVE YOU WALKING AROUND IN SUCH MEDIOCRE GARMENTS.
BUT NOT TO WORRY, LUV.
I'LL KEEP YOU WARM.

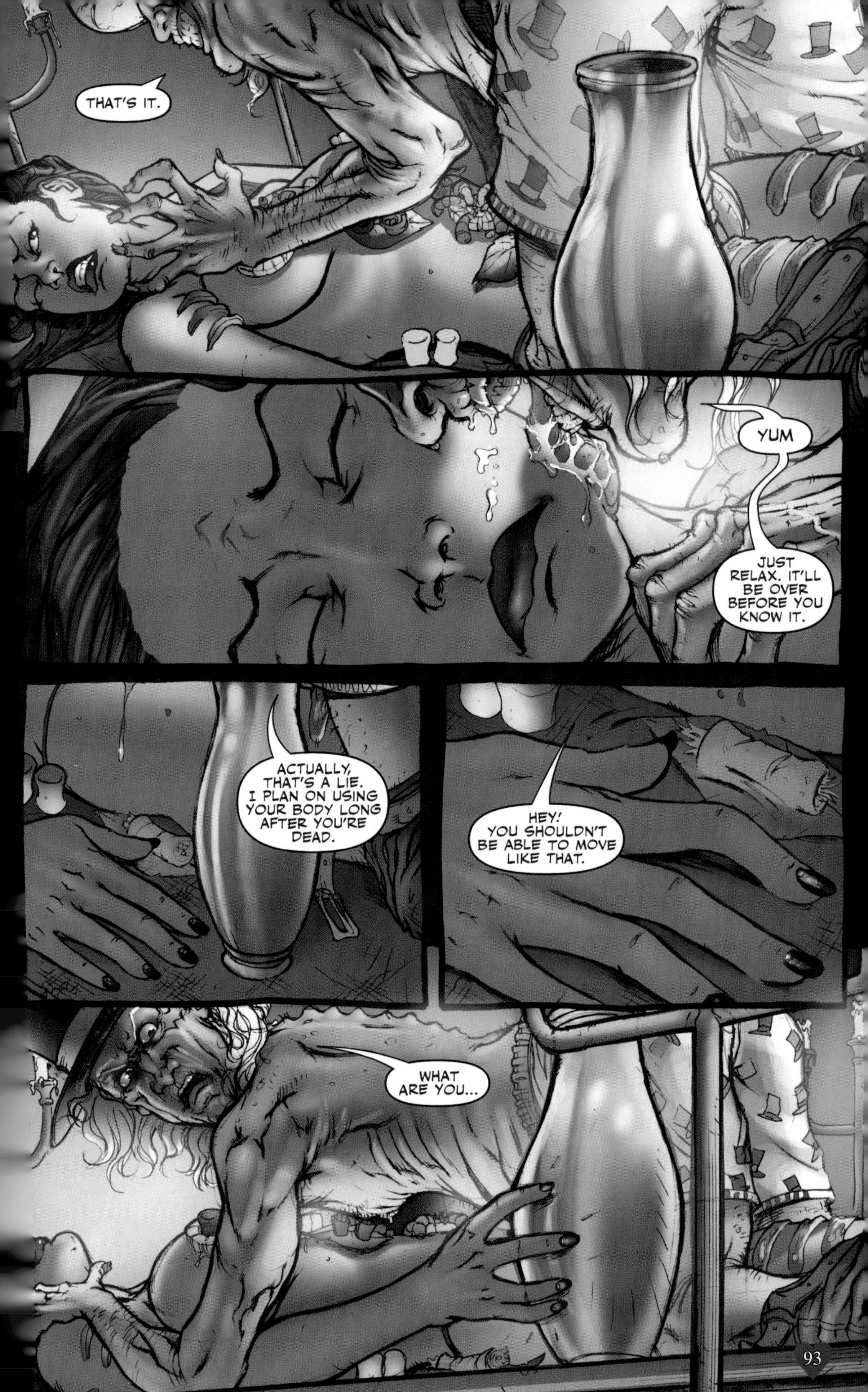
THAT'S IT.
YUM
JUST RELAX. IT'LL BE OVER BEFORE YOU KNOW IT.
ACTUALLY, THAT'S A LIE. I PLAN ON USING YOUR BODY LONG AFTER YOU'RE DEAD.
HEY! YOU SHOULDN'T BE ABLE TO MOVE LIKE THAT.
WHAT ARE YOU...

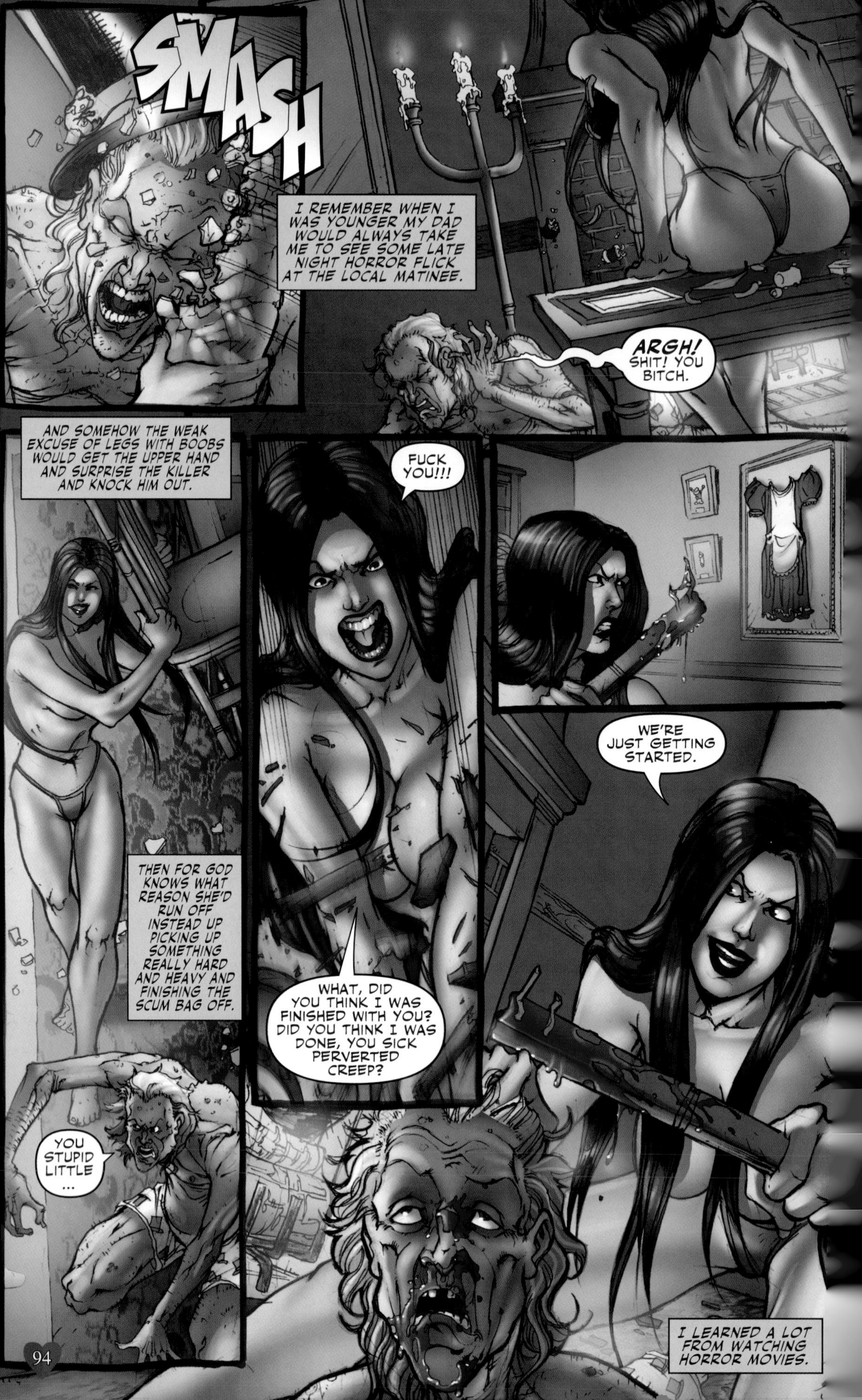
SMASH
I REMEMBER WHEN I WAS YOUNGER MY DAD WOULD ALWAYS TAKE ME TO SEE SOME LATE NIGHT HORROR FLICK AT THE LOCAL MATINEE.
ARGH! SHIT! YOU BITCH.
AND SOMEHOW THE WEAK EXCUSE OF LEGS WITH BOOBS WOULD GET THE UPPER HAND AND SURPRISE THE KILLER AND KNOCK HIM OUT.
THEN FOR GOD KNOWS WHAT REASON SHE'D RUN OFF INSTEAD UP PICKING UP SOMETHING REALLY HARD AND HEAVY AND FINISHING THE SCUM BAG OFF.
YOU STUPID LITTLE ...
FUCK YOU!!!
WHAT, DID YOU THINK I WAS FINISHED WITH YOU? DID YOU THINK I WAS DONE, YOU SICK PERVERTED CREEP?
WE'RE JUST GETTING STARTED.
I LEARNED A LOT FROM WATCHING HORROR MOVIES.

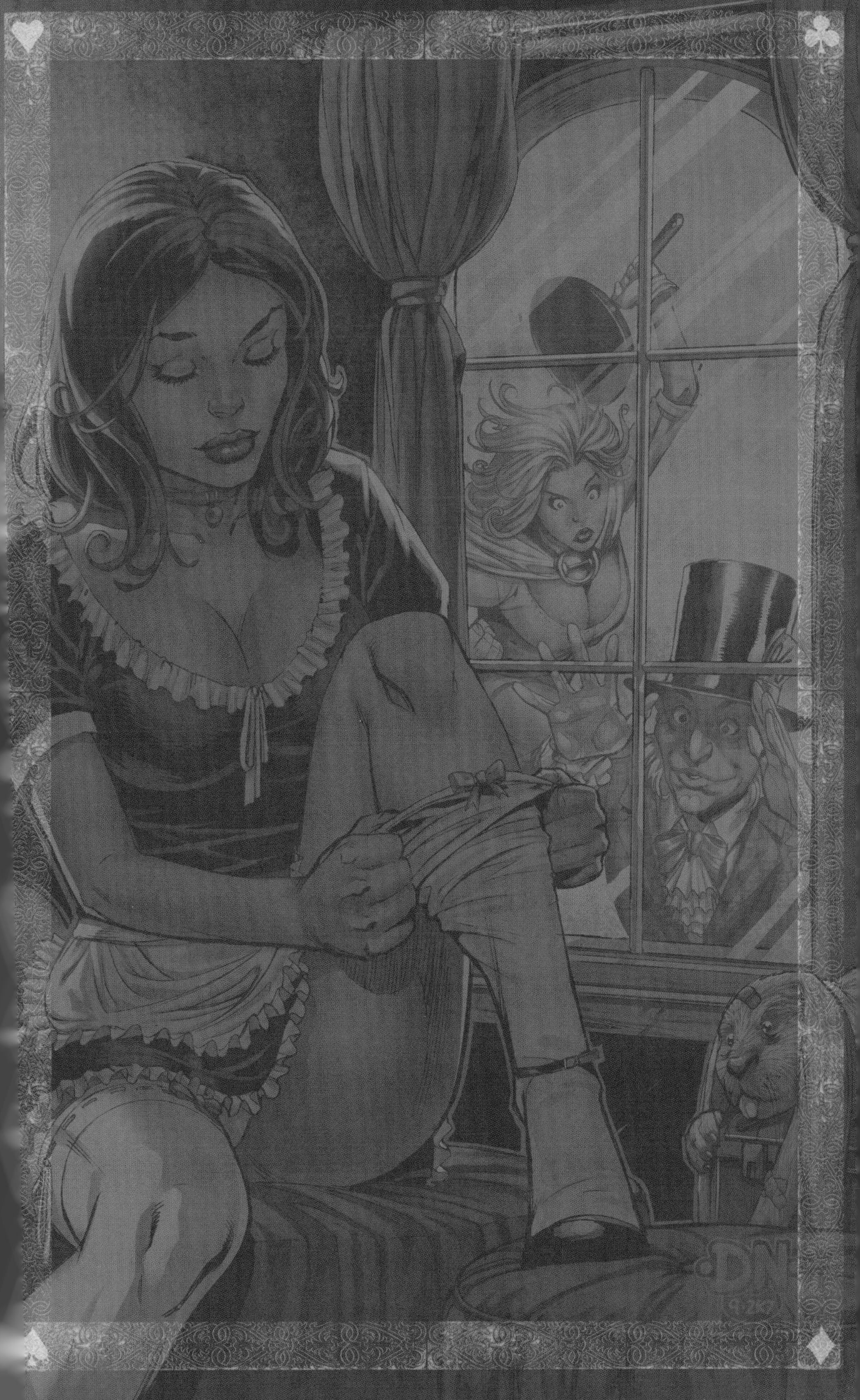

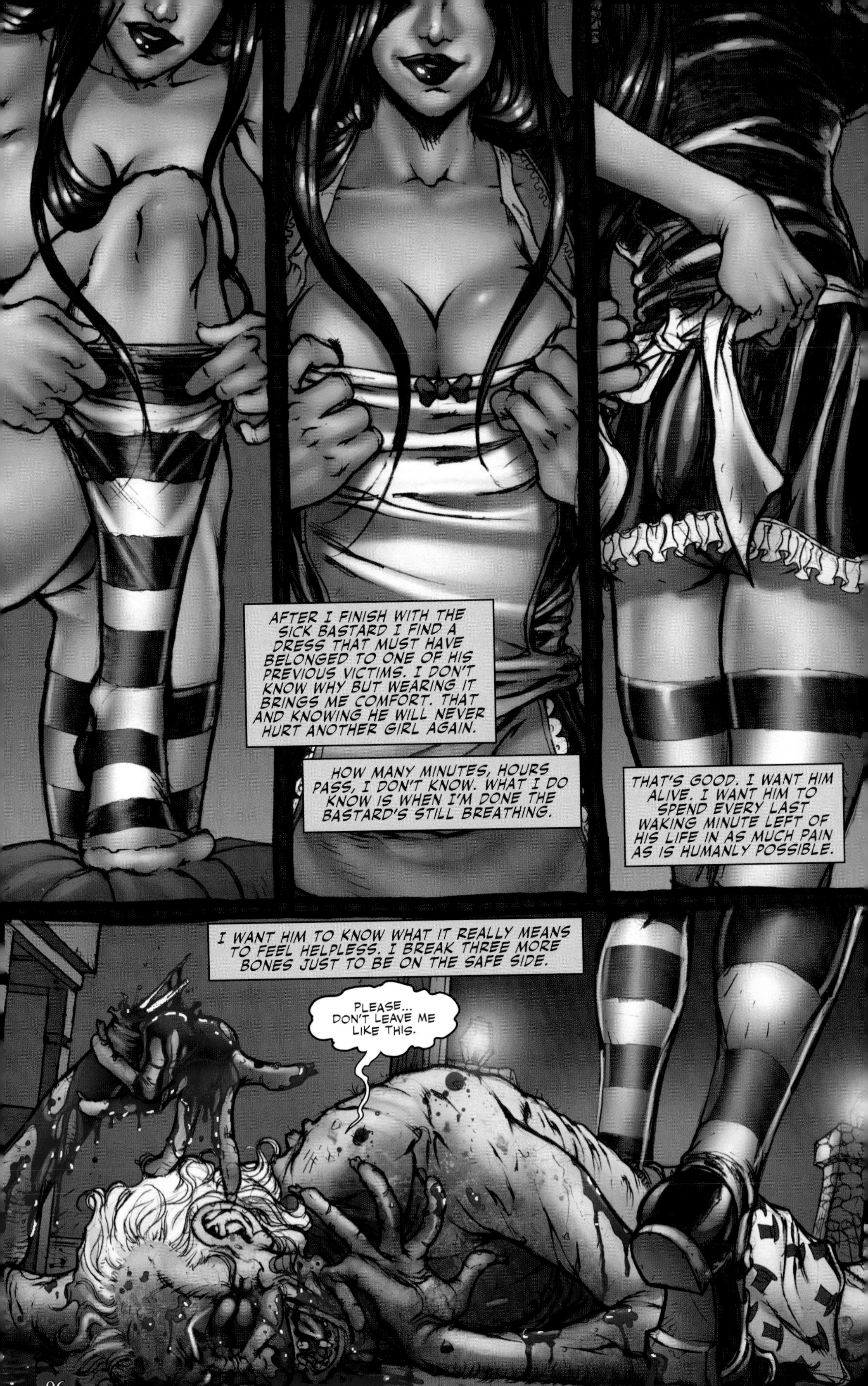

AFTER I FINISH WITH THE SICK BASTARD I FIND A DRESS THAT MUST HAVE BELONGED TO ONE OF HIS PREVIOUS VICTIMS. I DON'T KNOW WHY BUT WEARING IT BRINGS ME COMFORT. THAT AND KNOWING HE WILL NEVER HURT ANOTHER GIRL AGAIN.
HOW MANY MINUTES, HOURS PASS, I DON'T KNOW. WHAT I DO KNOW IS WHEN I'M DONE THE BASTARD'S STILL BREATHING.
THAT'S GOOD. I WANT HIM ALIVE. I WANT HIM TO SPEND EVERY LAST WAKING MINUTE LEFT OF HIS LIFE IN AS MUCH PAIN AS IS HUMANLY POSSIBLE.
I WANT HIM TO KNOW WHAT IT REALLY MEANS TO FEEL HELPLESS. I BREAK THREE MORE BONES JUST TO BE ON THE SAFE SIDE.
PLEASE... DON'T LEAVE ME LIKE THIS.

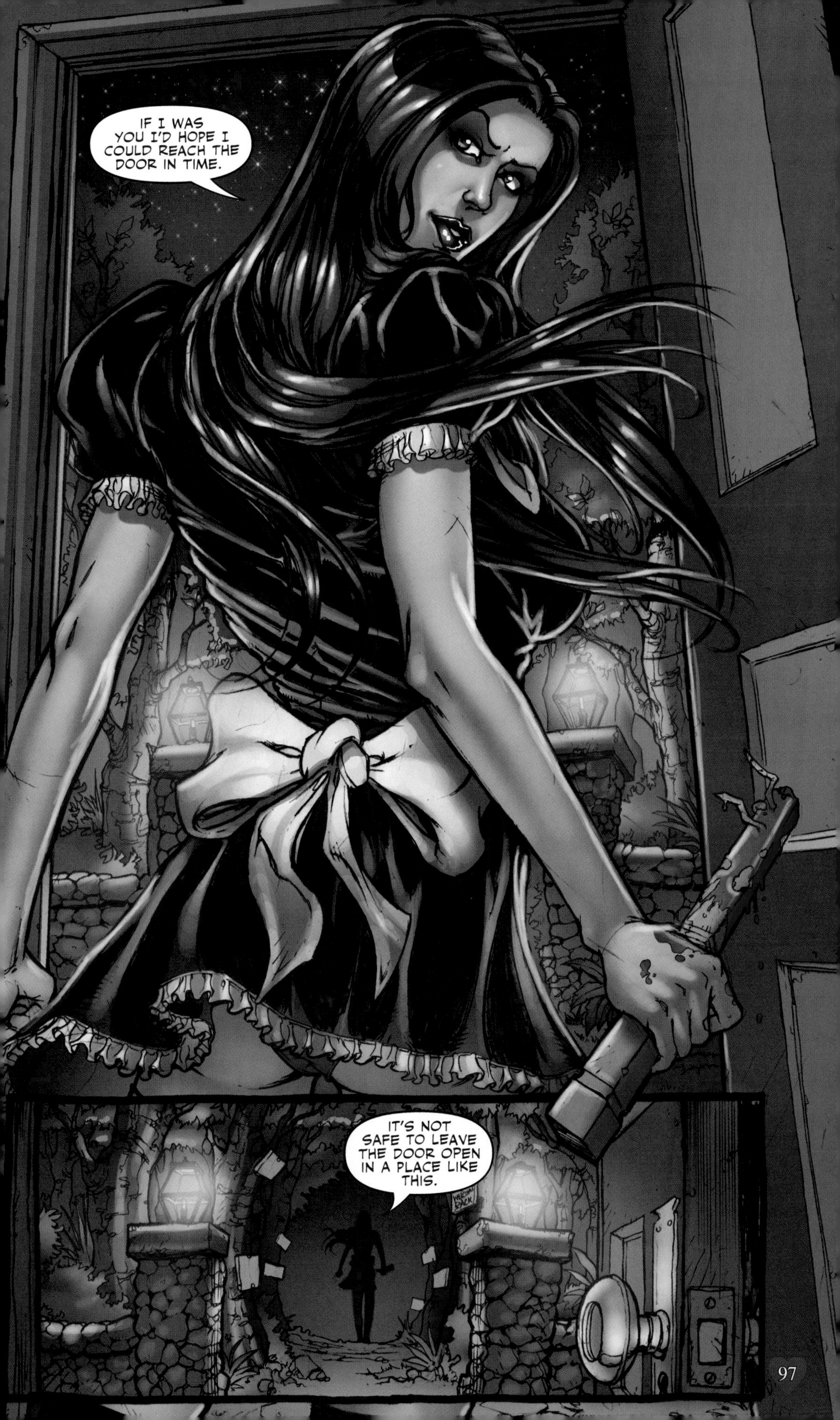
IF I WAS YOU I'D HOPE I COULD REACH THE DOOR IN TIME.
IT'S NOT SAFE TO LEAVE THE DOOR OPEN IN A PLACE LIKE THIS.

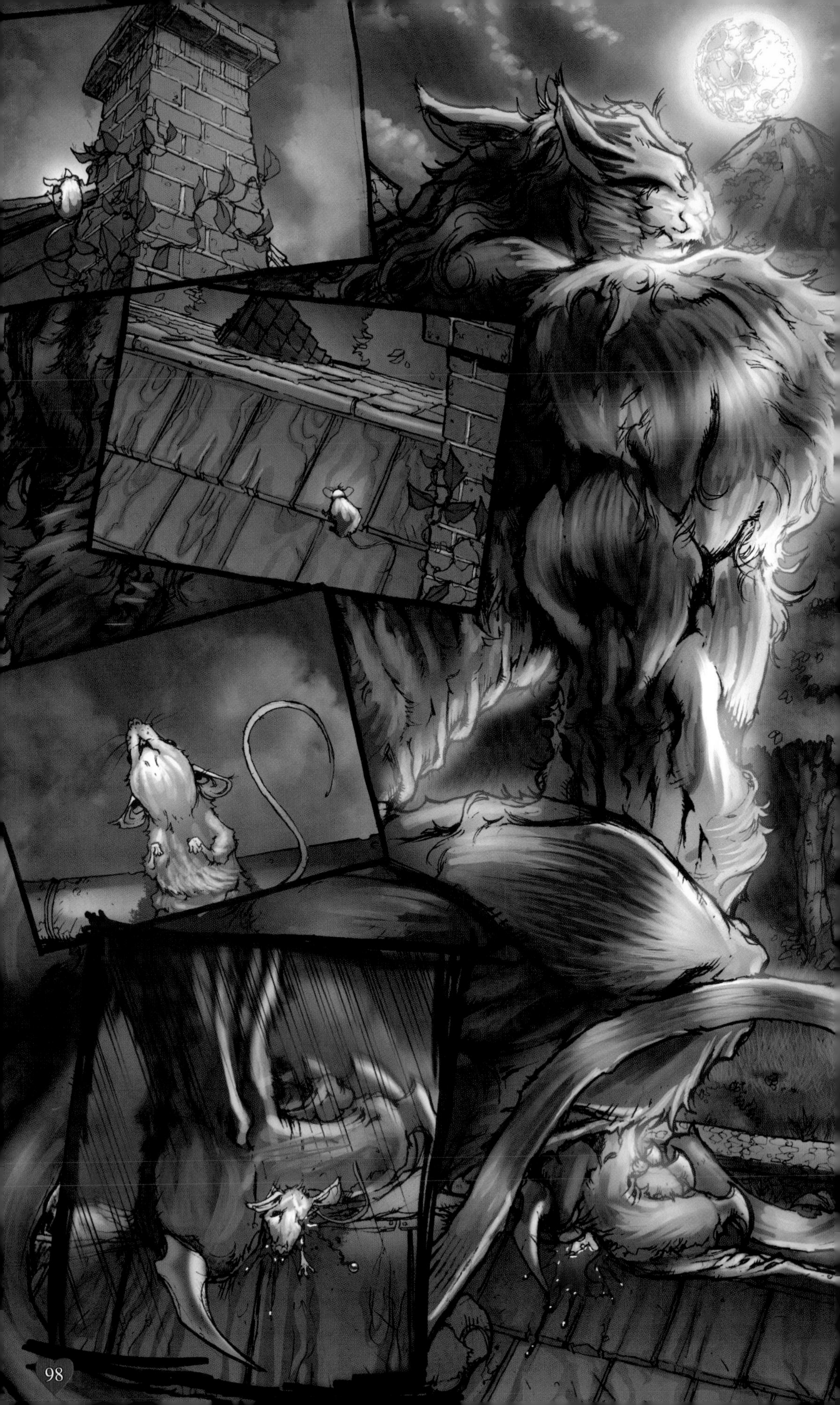

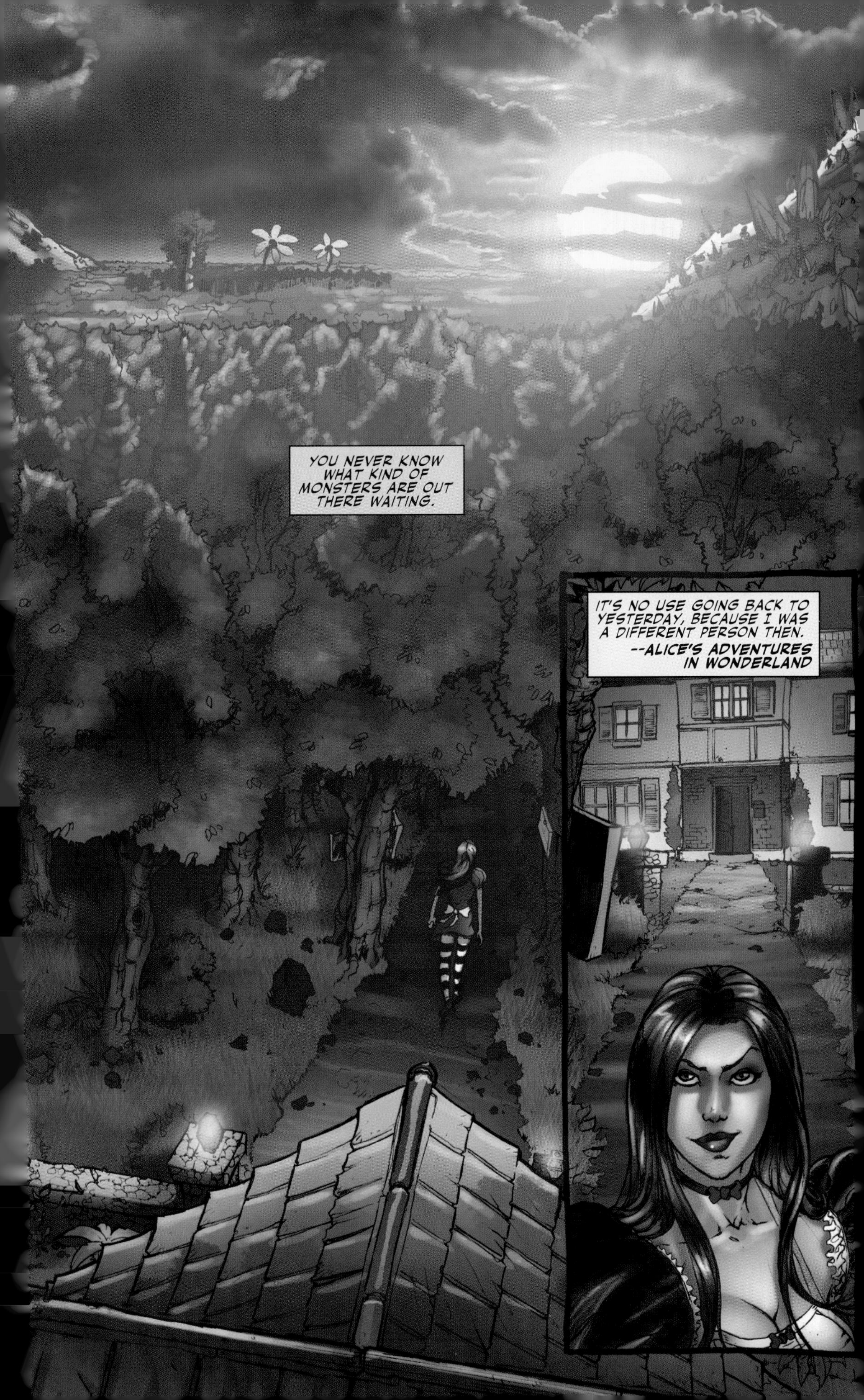
YOU NEVER KNOW WHAT KIND OF MONSTERS ARE OUT THERE WAITING.
IT'S NO USE GOING BACK TO YESTERDAY, BECAUSE I WAS A DIFFERENT PERSON THEN.
--ALICE'S ADVENTURES IN WONDERLAND

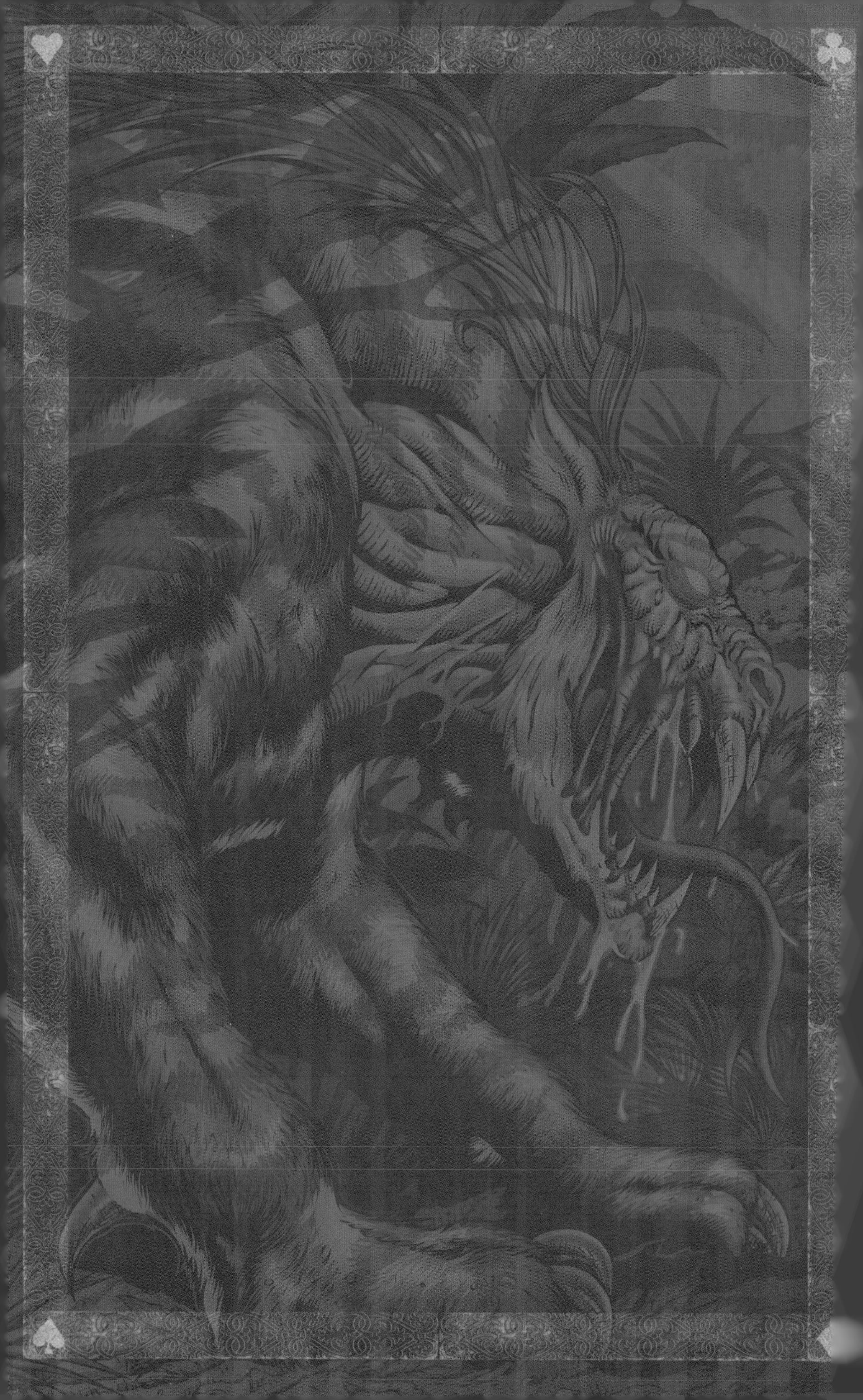

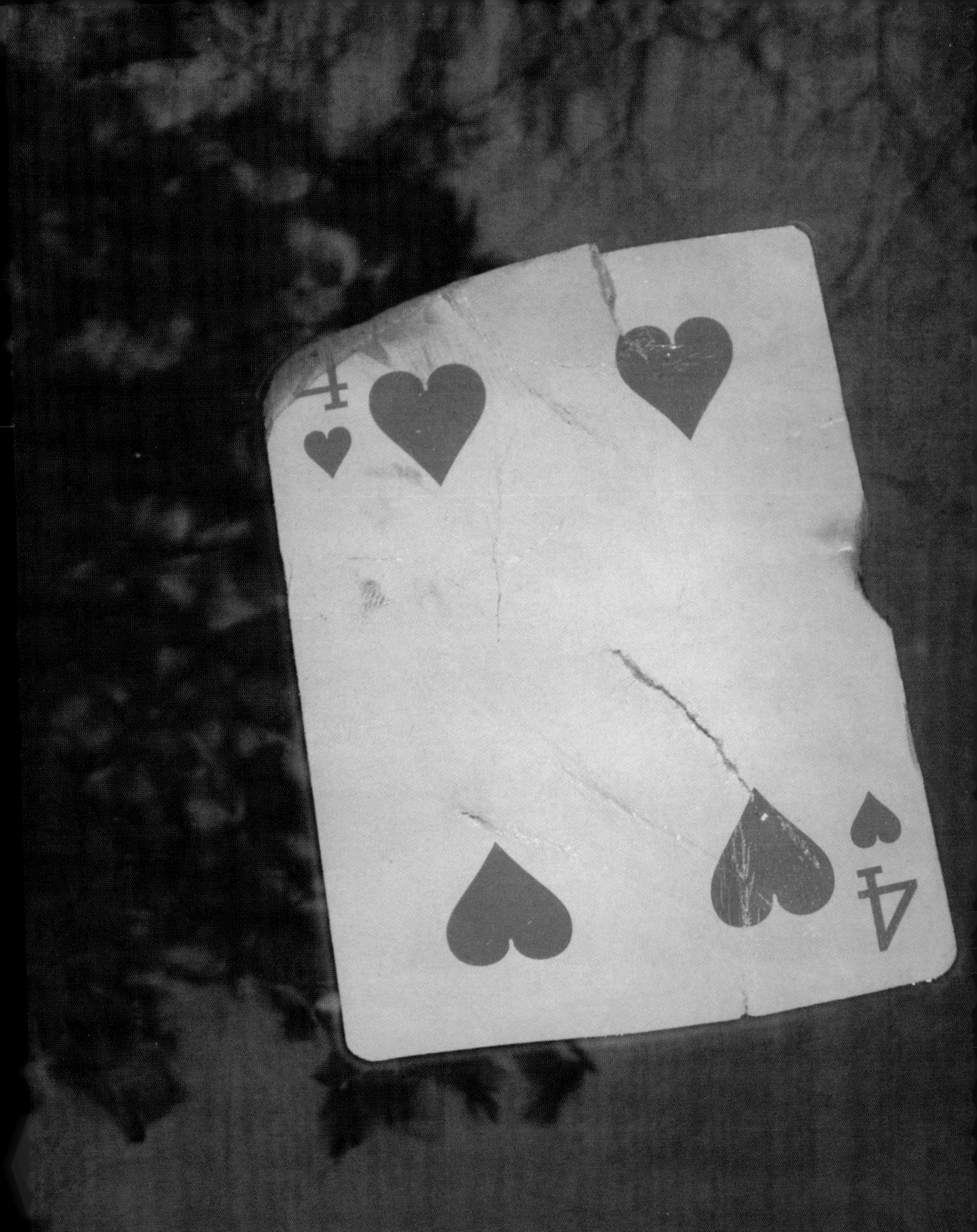

four

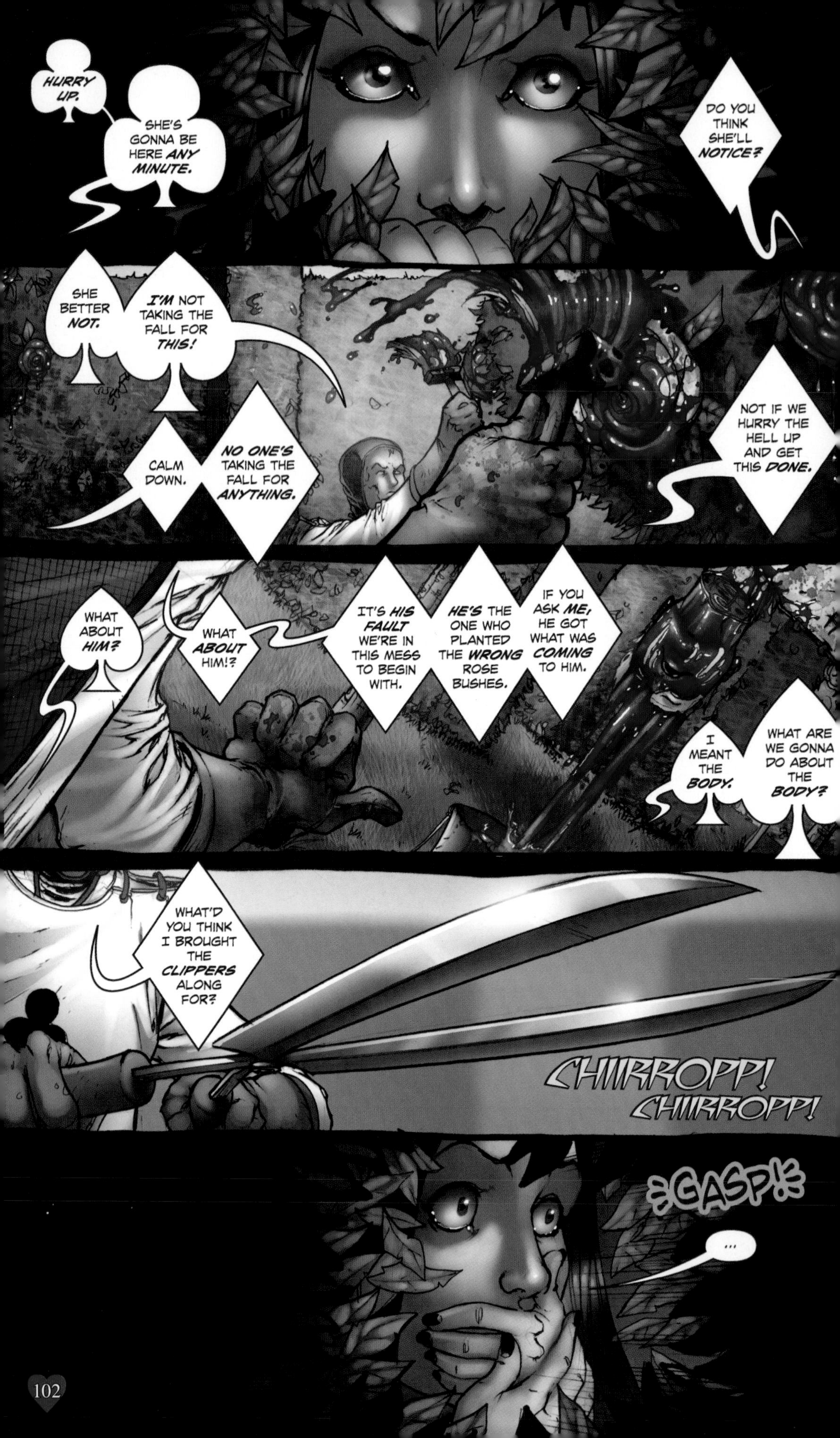
HURRY UP.
SHE'S GONNA BE HERE ANY MINUTE.
DO YOU THINK SHE'LL NOTICE?
SHE BETTER NOT.
I'M NOT TAKING THE FALL FOR THIS!
CALM DOWN.
NO ONE'S TAKING THE FALL FOR ANYTHING.
NOT IF WE HURRY THE HELL UP AND GET THIS DONE.
WHAT ABOUT HIM?
WHAT ABOUT HIM!?
IT'S HIS FAULT WE'RE IN THIS MESS TO BEGIN WITH.
HE'S THE ONE WHO PLANTED THE WRONG ROSE BUSHES.
IF YOU ASK ME, HE GOT WHAT WAS COMING TO HIM.
WHAT ARE WE GONNA DO ABOUT THE BODY?
I MEANT THE BODY.
WHAT'D YOU THINK I BROUGHT THE CLIPPERS ALONG FOR?
CHIIRROPP!
CHIIRROPP!
GASP!
...

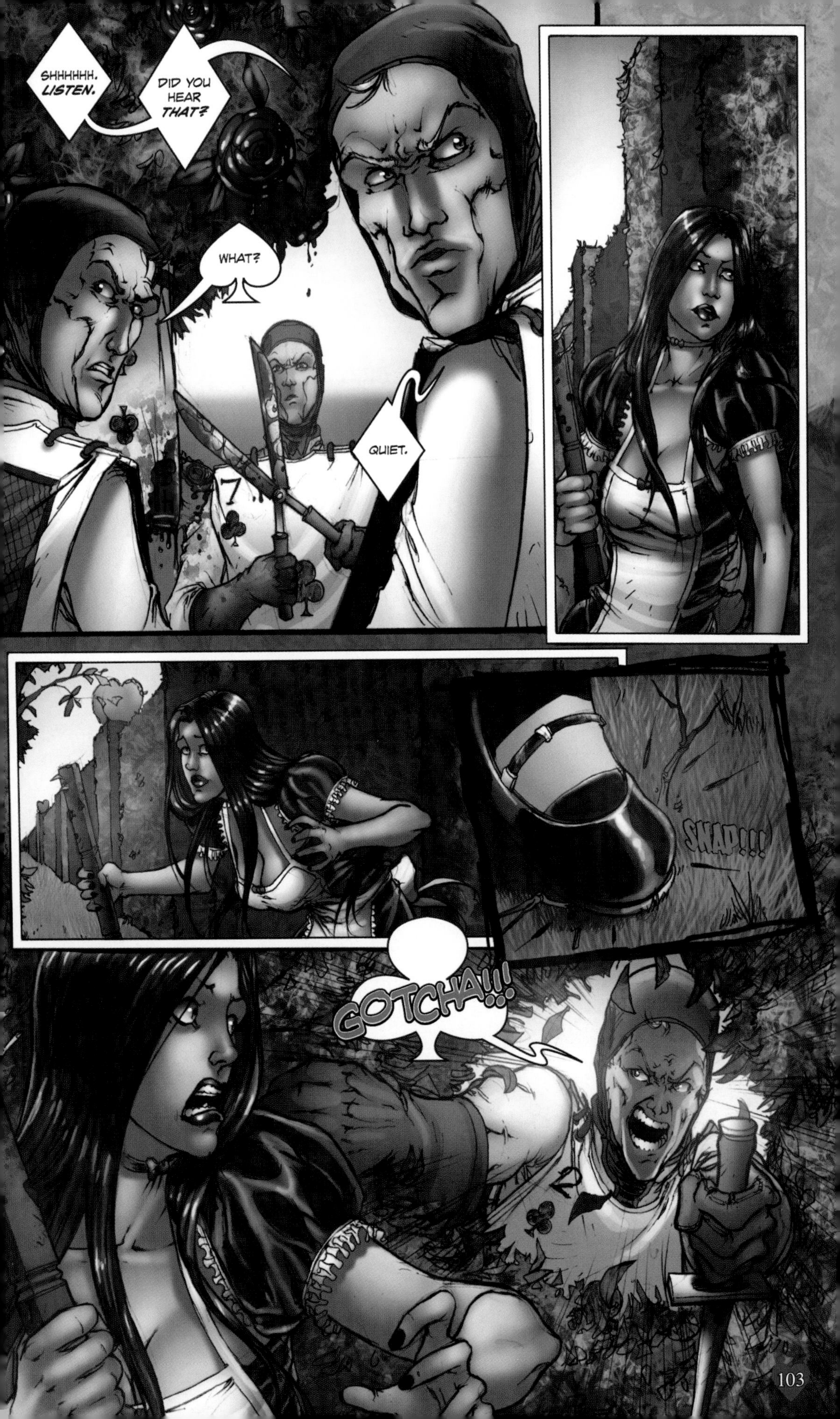
SHHHHHH. *LISTEN.*
DID YOU HEAR *THAT?*
WHAT?
QUIET.
SNAP!!!
GOTCHA!!!

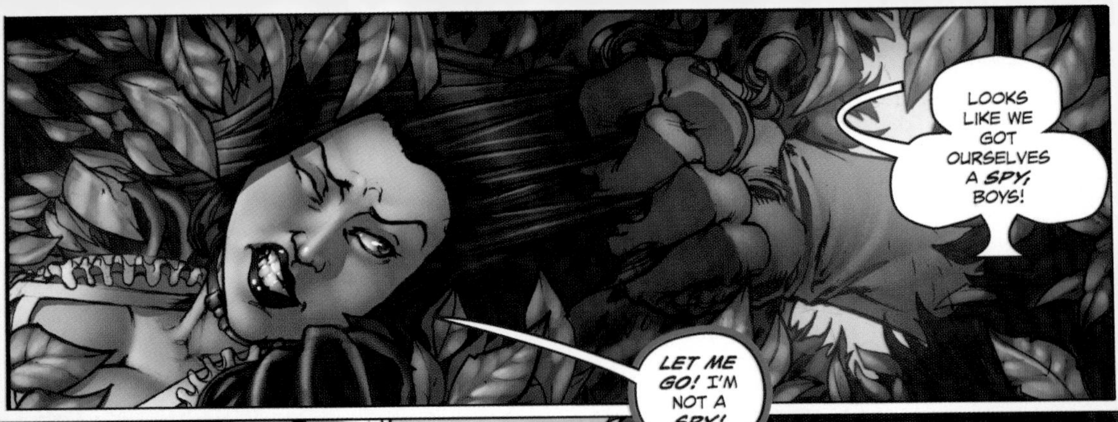
LOOKS LIKE WE GOT OURSELVES A SPY, BOYS!
LET ME GO! I'M NOT A SPY!

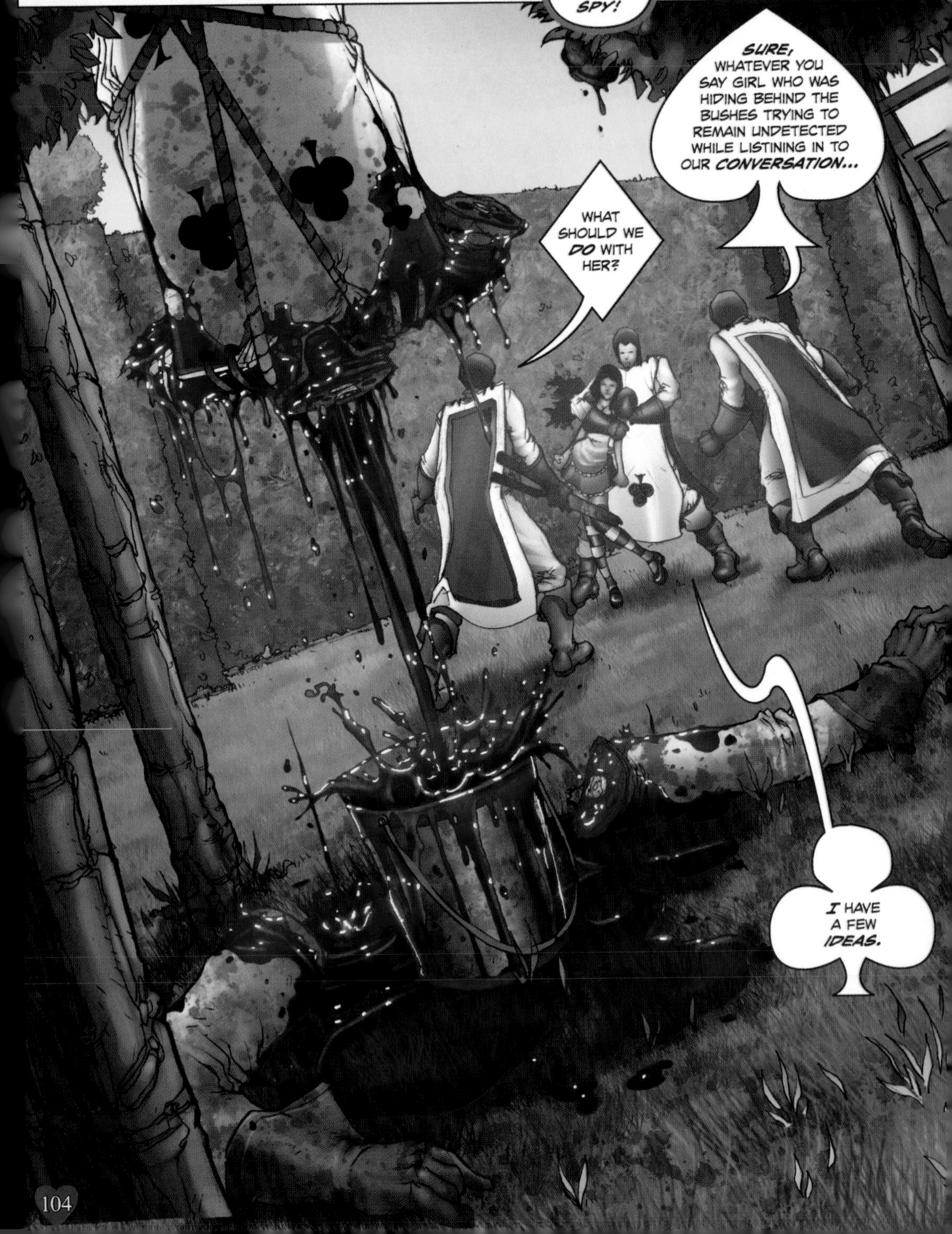
SURE, WHATEVER YOU SAY GIRL WHO WAS HIDING BEHIND THE BUSHES TRYING TO REMAIN UNDETECTED WHILE LISTINING IN TO OUR CONVERSATION...
WHAT SHOULD WE DO WITH HER?
I HAVE A FEW IDEAS.

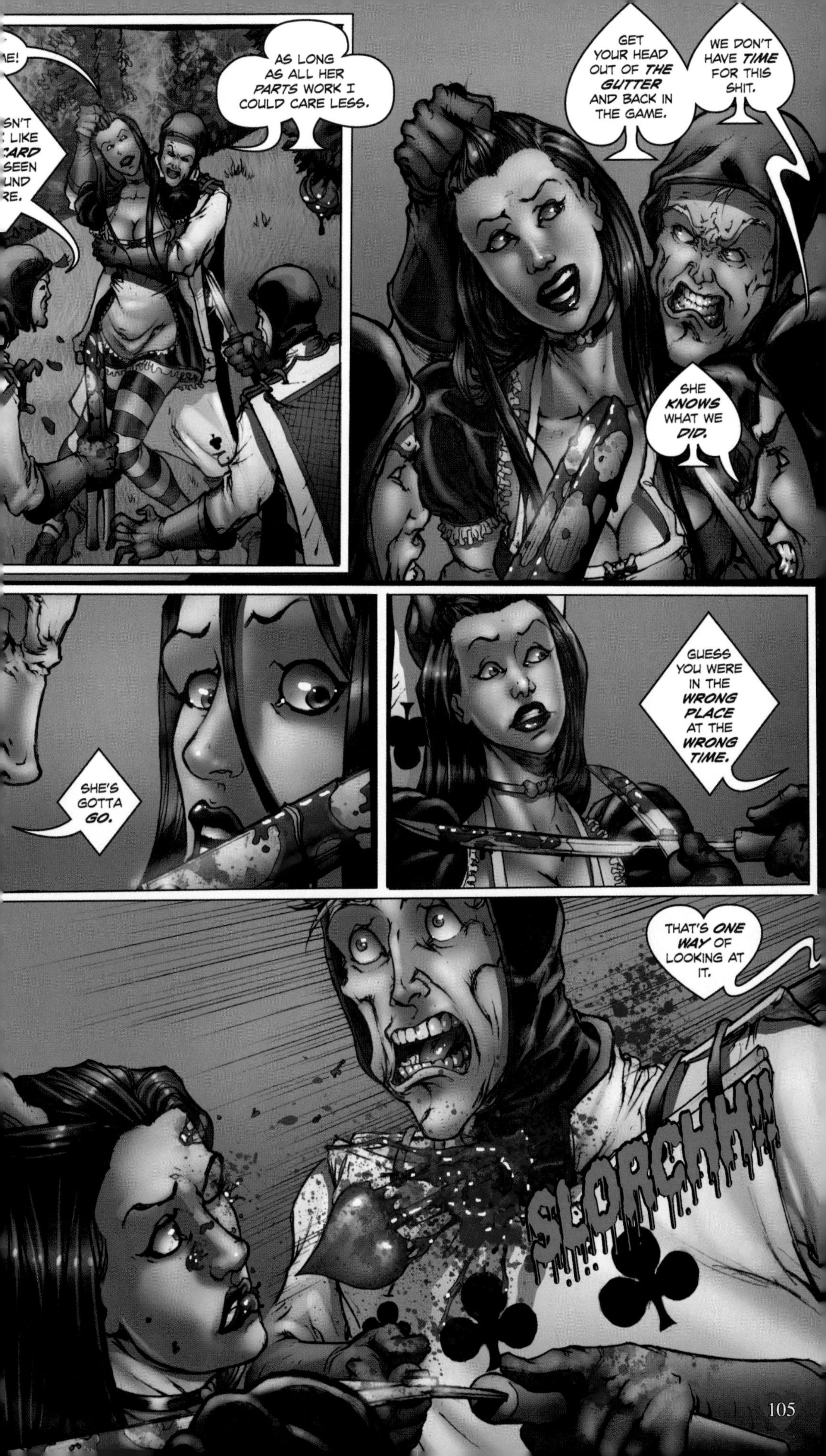
AS LONG AS ALL HER *PARTS* WORK I COULD CARE LESS.
GET YOUR HEAD OUT OF *THE GUTTER* AND BACK IN THE GAME.
WE DON'T HAVE *TIME* FOR THIS SHIT.
SHE *KNOWS* WHAT WE *DID.*
SHE'S GOTTA *GO.*
GUESS YOU WERE IN THE *WRONG PLACE* AT THE *WRONG TIME.*
THAT'S *ONE WAY* OF LOOKING AT IT.
SLORCH!!

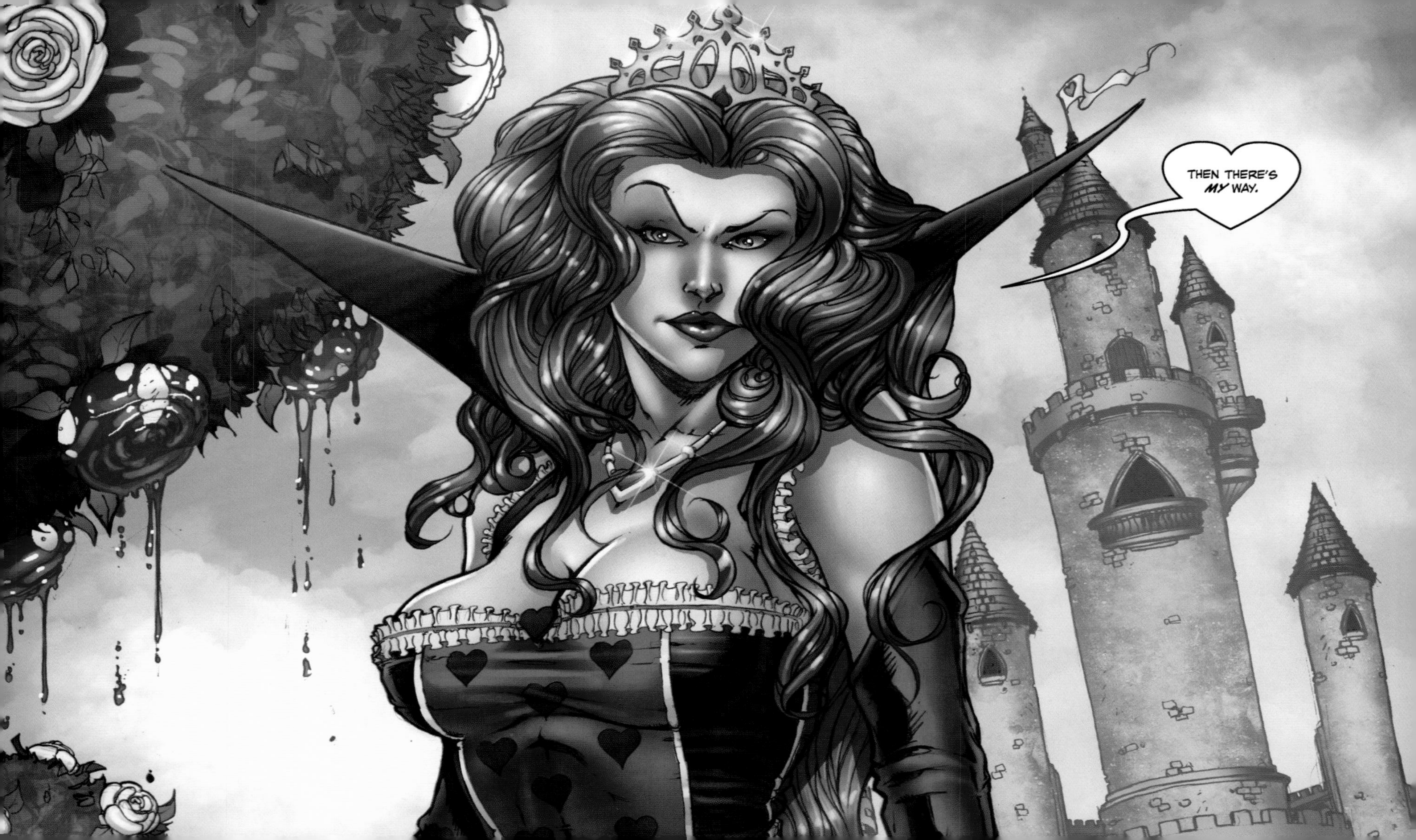
THEN THERE'S *MY* WAY.

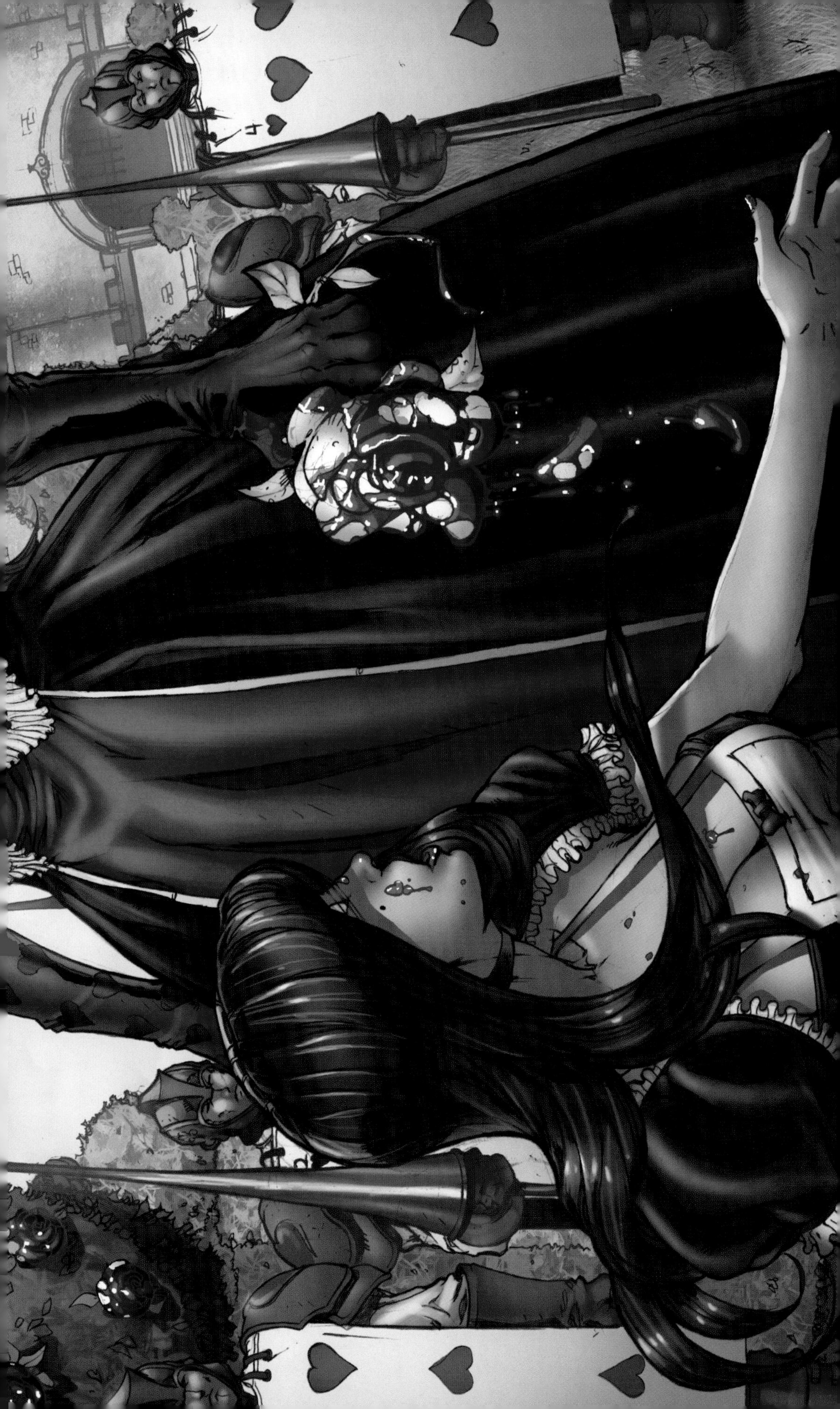

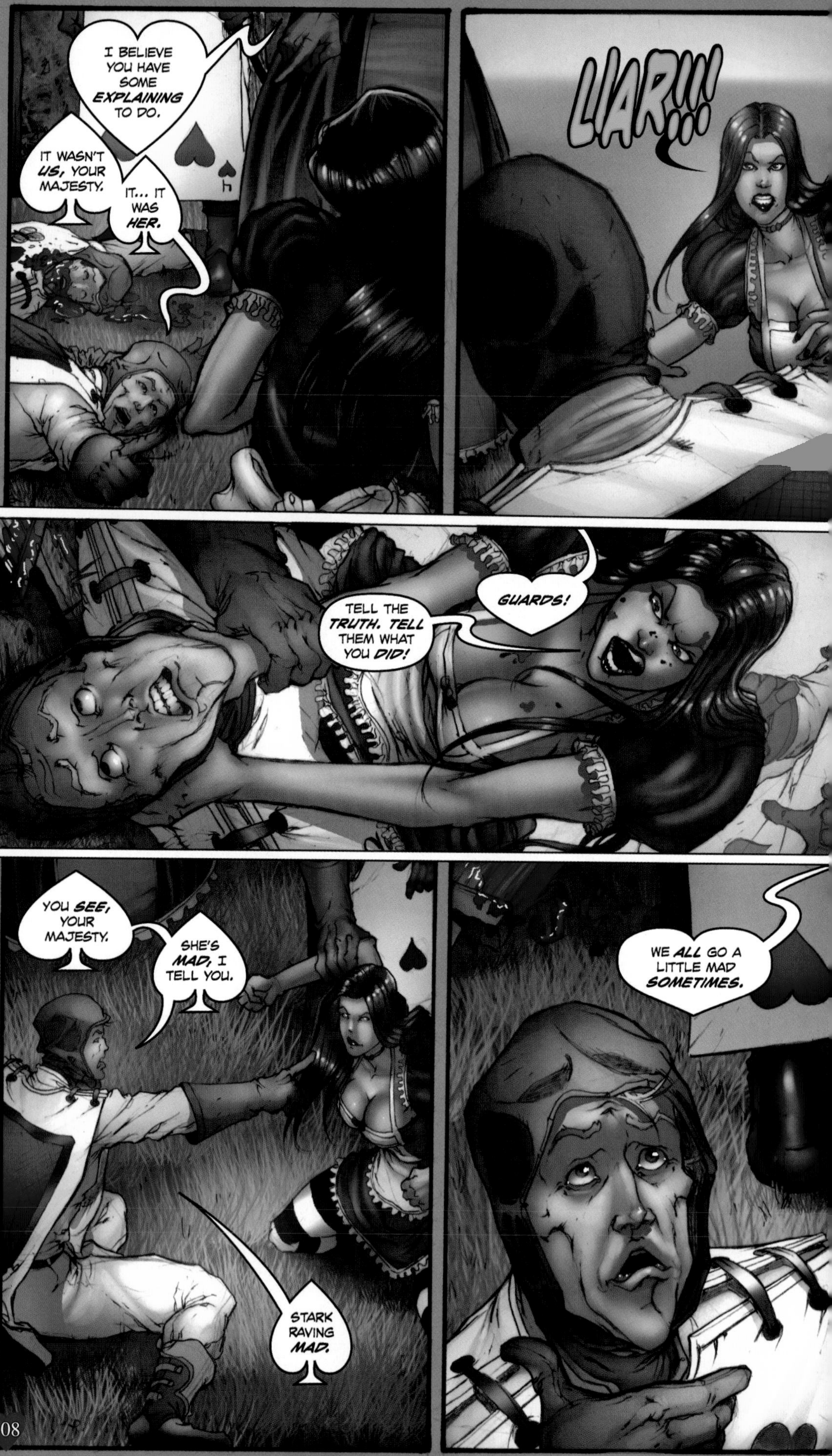
I BELIEVE YOU HAVE SOME EXPLAINING TO DO.
IT WASN'T US, YOUR MAJESTY.
IT... IT WAS HER.
LIAR!!!
TELL THE TRUTH. TELL THEM WHAT YOU DID!
GUARDS!
YOU SEE, YOUR MAJESTY.
SHE'S MAD, I TELL YOU.
STARK RAVING MAD.
WE ALL GO A LITTLE MAD SOMETIMES.

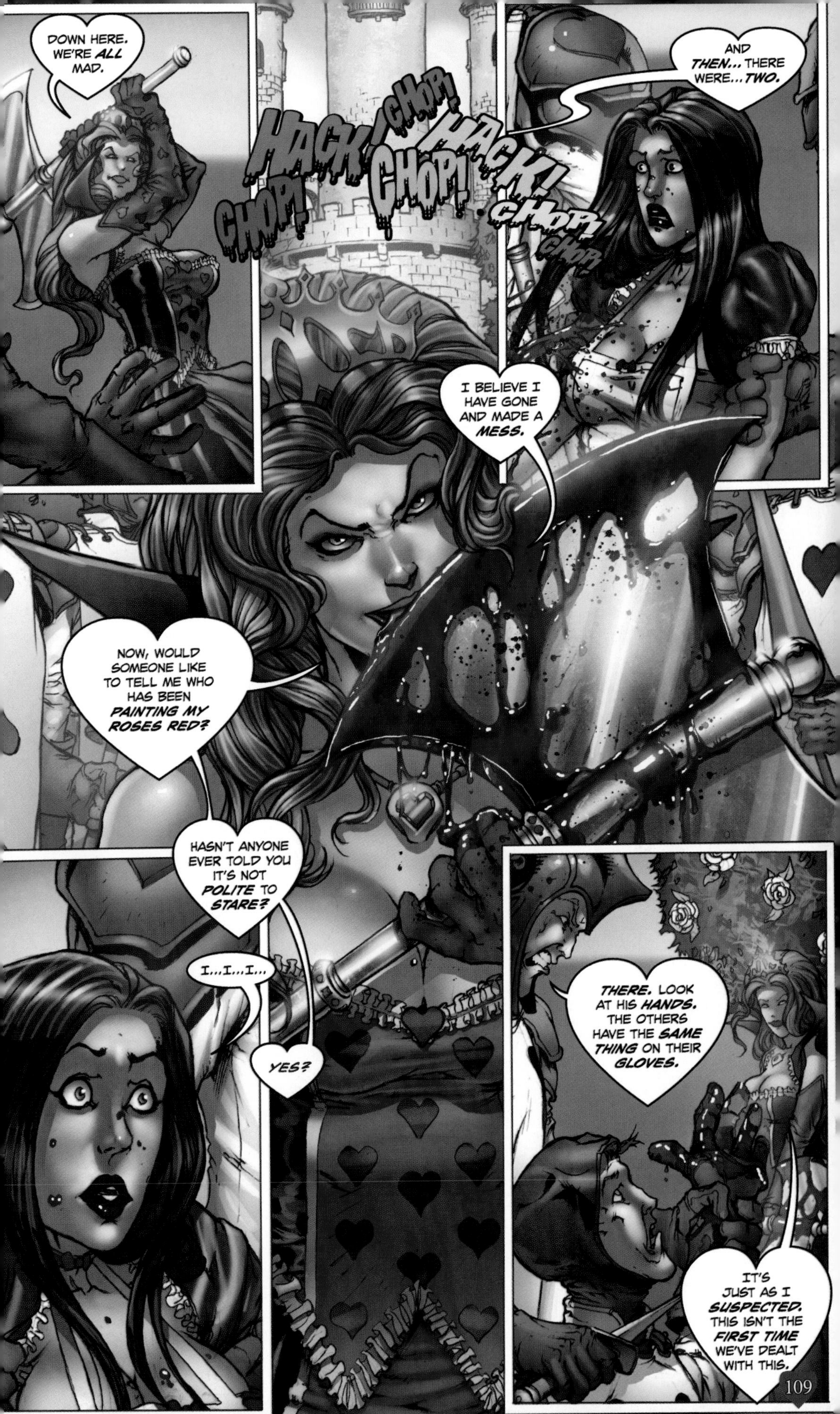

DOWN HERE. WE'RE ALL MAD.
HACK! CHOP! HACK! CHOP! CHOP! CHOP! CHOP
AND THEN... THERE WERE... TWO.
I BELIEVE I HAVE GONE AND MADE A MESS.
NOW, WOULD SOMEONE LIKE TO TELL ME WHO HAS BEEN PAINTING MY ROSES RED?
HASN'T ANYONE EVER TOLD YOU IT'S NOT POLITE TO STARE?
I...I...I...
YES?
THERE. LOOK AT HIS HANDS. THE OTHERS HAVE THE SAME THING ON THEIR GLOVES.
IT'S JUST AS I SUSPECTED. THIS ISN'T THE FIRST TIME WE'VE DEALT WITH THIS.

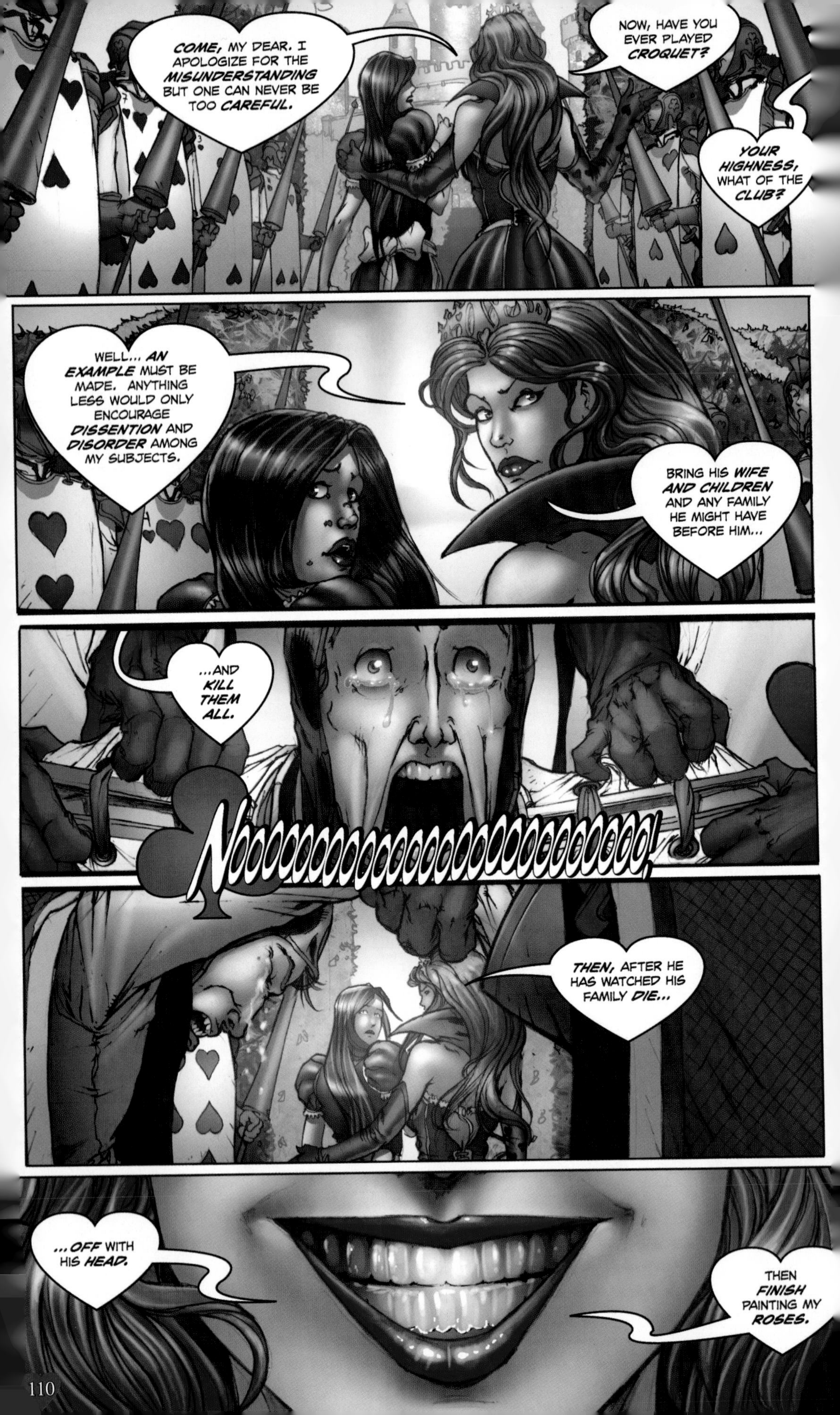
COME, MY DEAR. I APOLOGIZE FOR THE MISUNDERSTANDING BUT ONE CAN NEVER BE TOO CAREFUL.
NOW, HAVE YOU EVER PLAYED CROQUET?
YOUR HIGHNESS, WHAT OF THE CLUB?
WELL... AN EXAMPLE MUST BE MADE. ANYTHING LESS WOULD ONLY ENCOURAGE DISSENTION AND DISORDER AMONG MY SUBJECTS.
BRING HIS WIFE AND CHILDREN AND ANY FAMILY HE MIGHT HAVE BEFORE HIM...
...AND KILL THEM ALL.
NOOOOOOOOOOOOOOOOOOOOOOOOOO!
THEN, AFTER HE HAS WATCHED HIS FAMILY DIE...
...OFF WITH HIS HEAD.
THEN FINISH PAINTING MY ROSES.

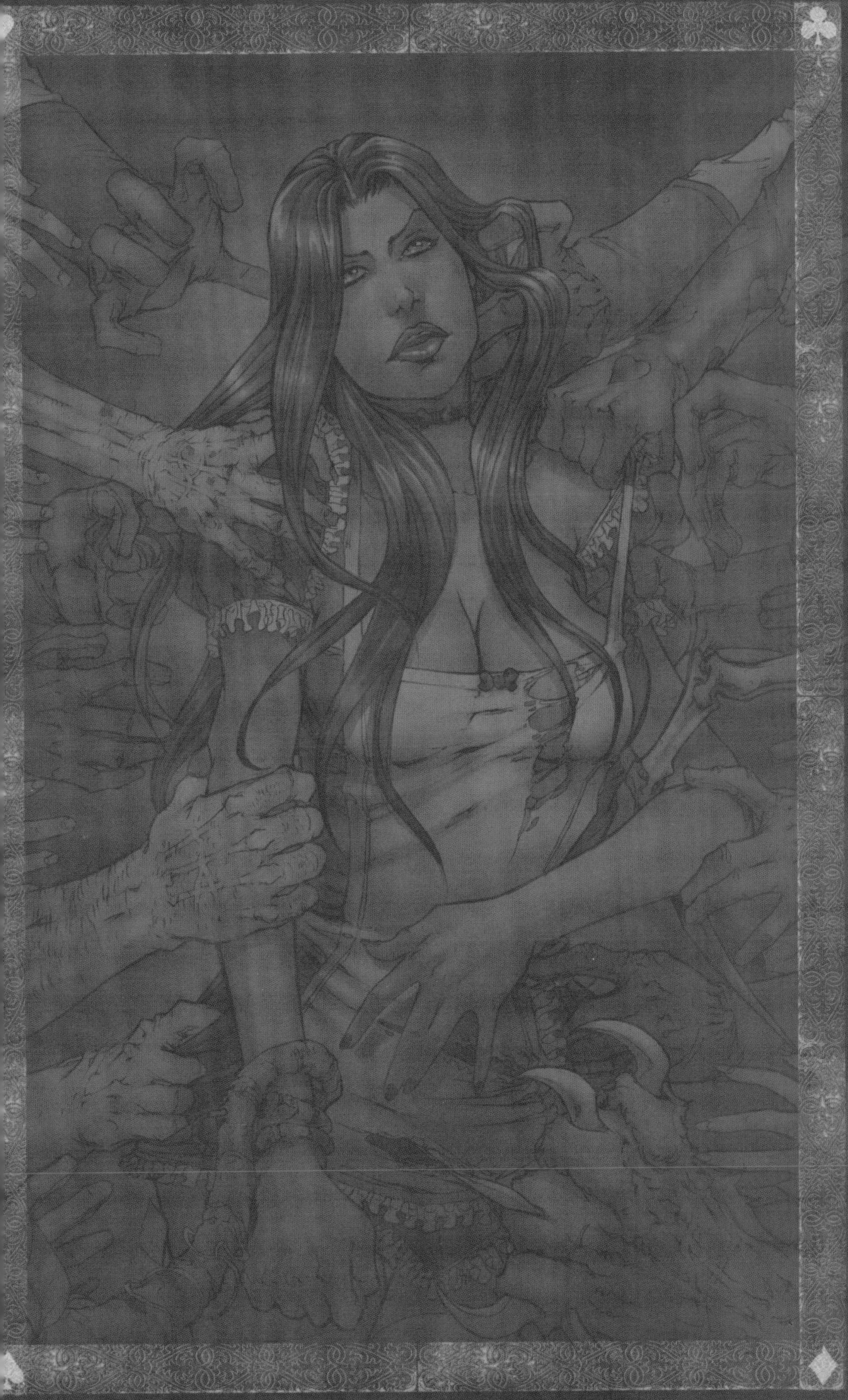

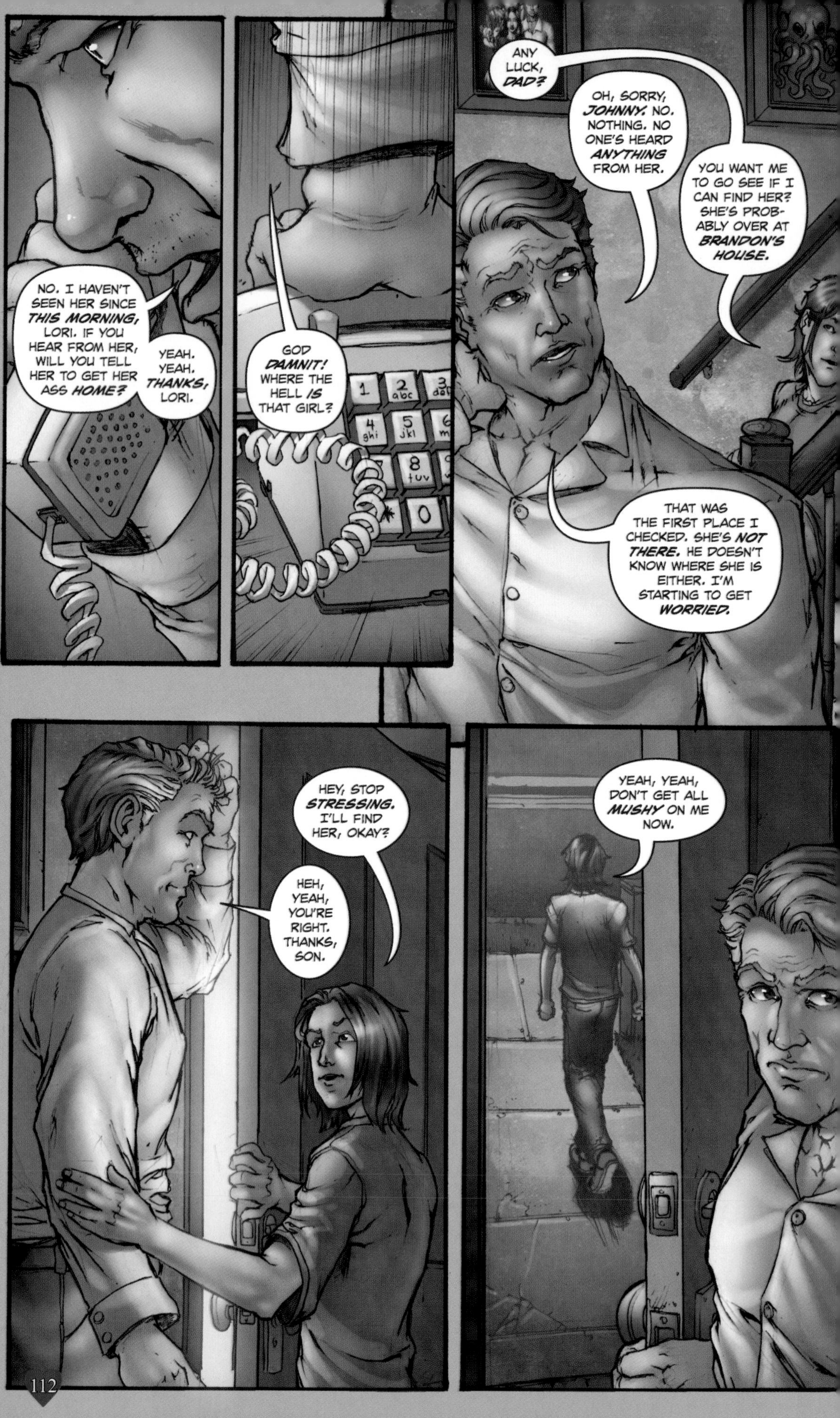
NO. I HAVEN'T SEEN HER SINCE THIS MORNING, LORI. IF YOU HEAR FROM HER, WILL YOU TELL HER TO GET HER ASS HOME?
YEAH. YEAH. THANKS, LORI.
GOD DAMNIT! WHERE THE HELL IS THAT GIRL?
ANY LUCK, DAD?
OH, SORRY, JOHNNY. NO. NOTHING. NO ONE'S HEARD ANYTHING FROM HER.
YOU WANT ME TO GO SEE IF I CAN FIND HER? SHE'S PROBABLY OVER AT BRANDON'S HOUSE.
THAT WAS THE FIRST PLACE I CHECKED. SHE'S NOT THERE. HE DOESN'T KNOW WHERE SHE IS EITHER. I'M STARTING TO GET WORRIED.
HEY, STOP STRESSING. I'LL FIND HER, OKAY?
HEH, YEAH, YOU'RE RIGHT. THANKS, SON.
YEAH, YEAH, DON'T GET ALL MUSHY ON ME NOW.

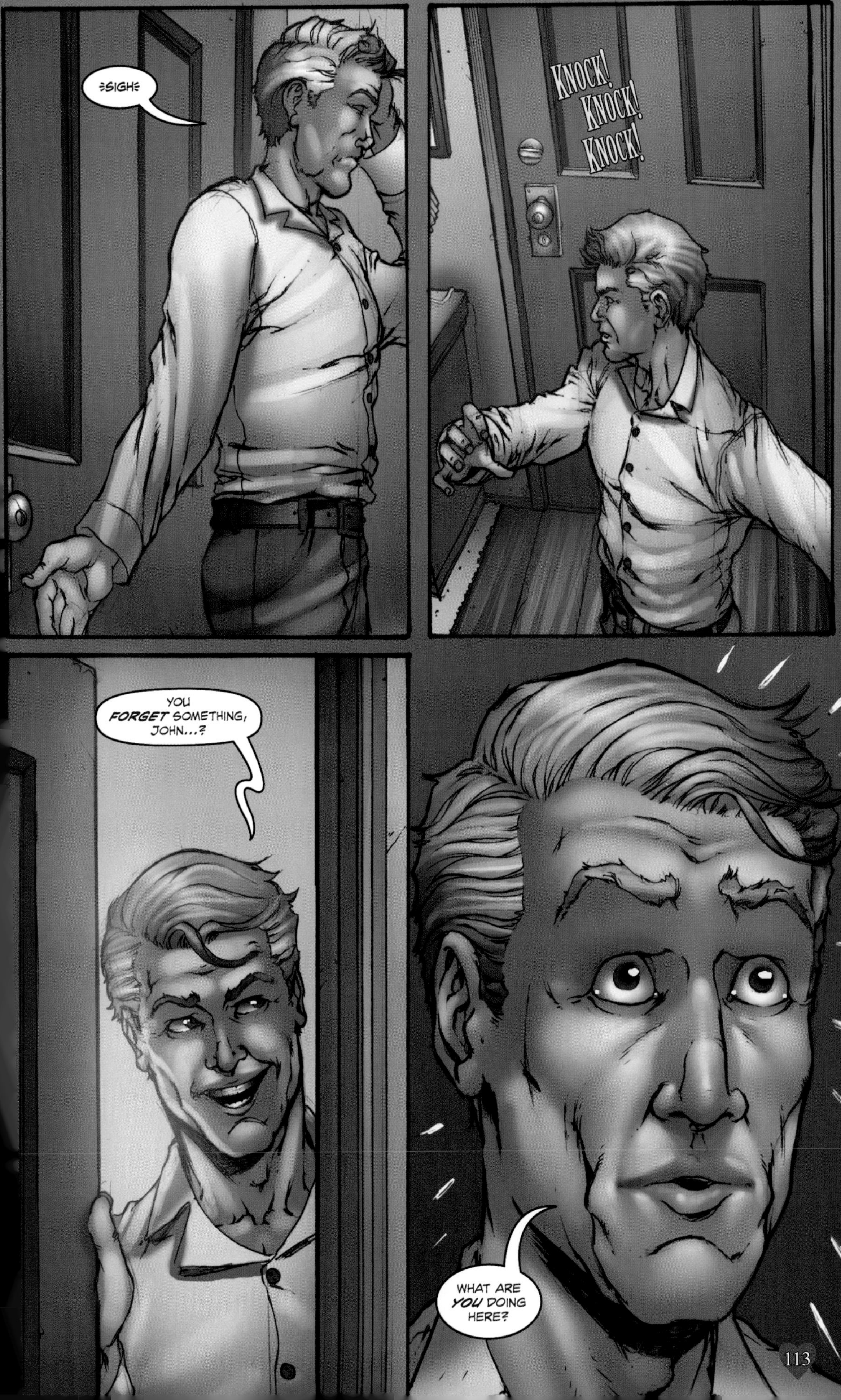

SIGH
KNOCK! KNOCK! KNOCK!
YOU FORGET SOMETHING, JOHN...?
WHAT ARE YOU DOING HERE?

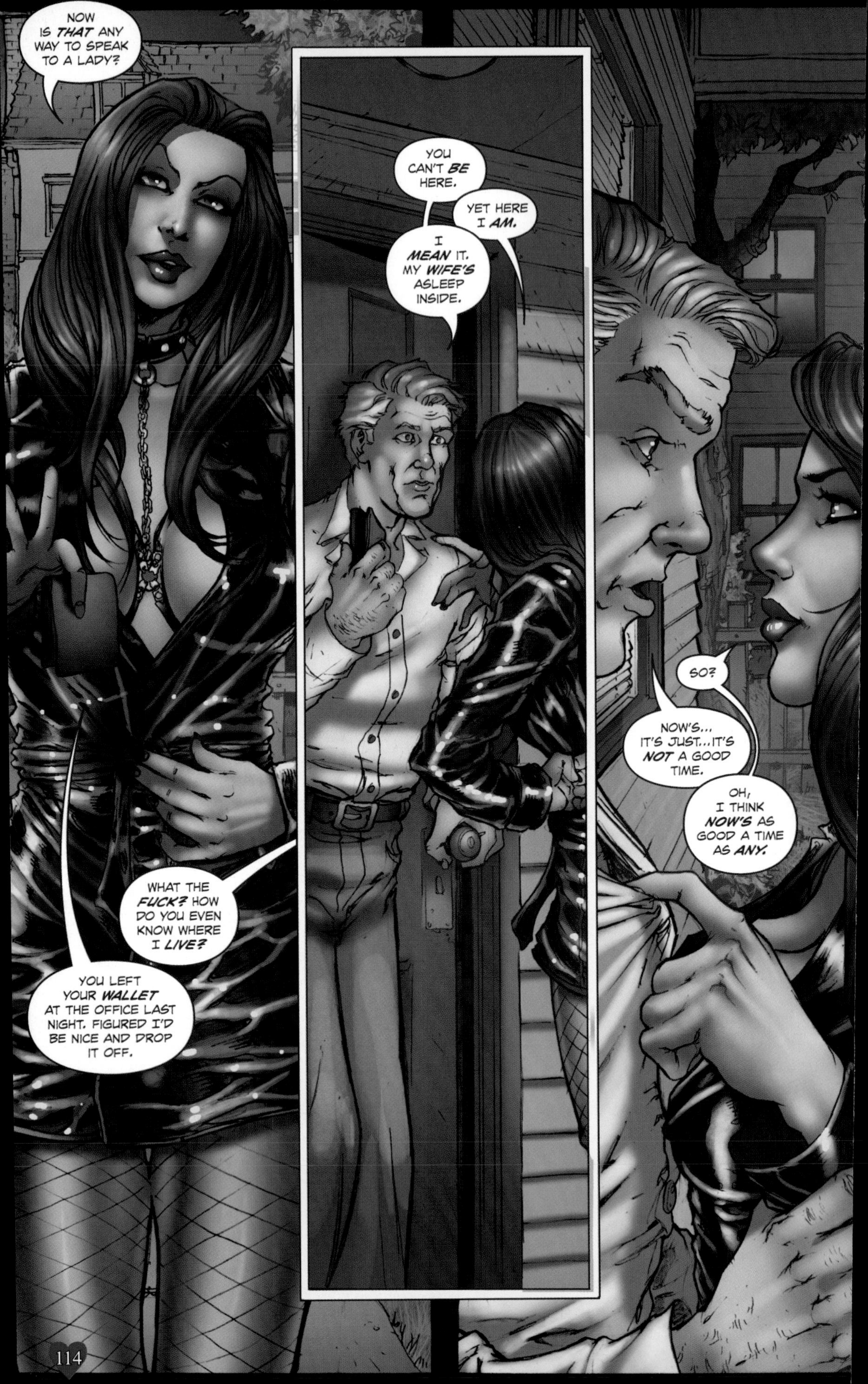
NOW IS THAT ANY WAY TO SPEAK TO A LADY?
YOU CAN'T BE HERE.
YET HERE I AM.
I MEAN IT. MY WIFE'S ASLEEP INSIDE.
SO?
NOW'S... IT'S JUST...IT'S NOT A GOOD TIME.
OH, I THINK NOW'S AS GOOD A TIME AS ANY.
WHAT THE FUCK? HOW DO YOU EVEN KNOW WHERE I LIVE?
YOU LEFT YOUR WALLET AT THE OFFICE LAST NIGHT. FIGURED I'D BE NICE AND DROP IT OFF.

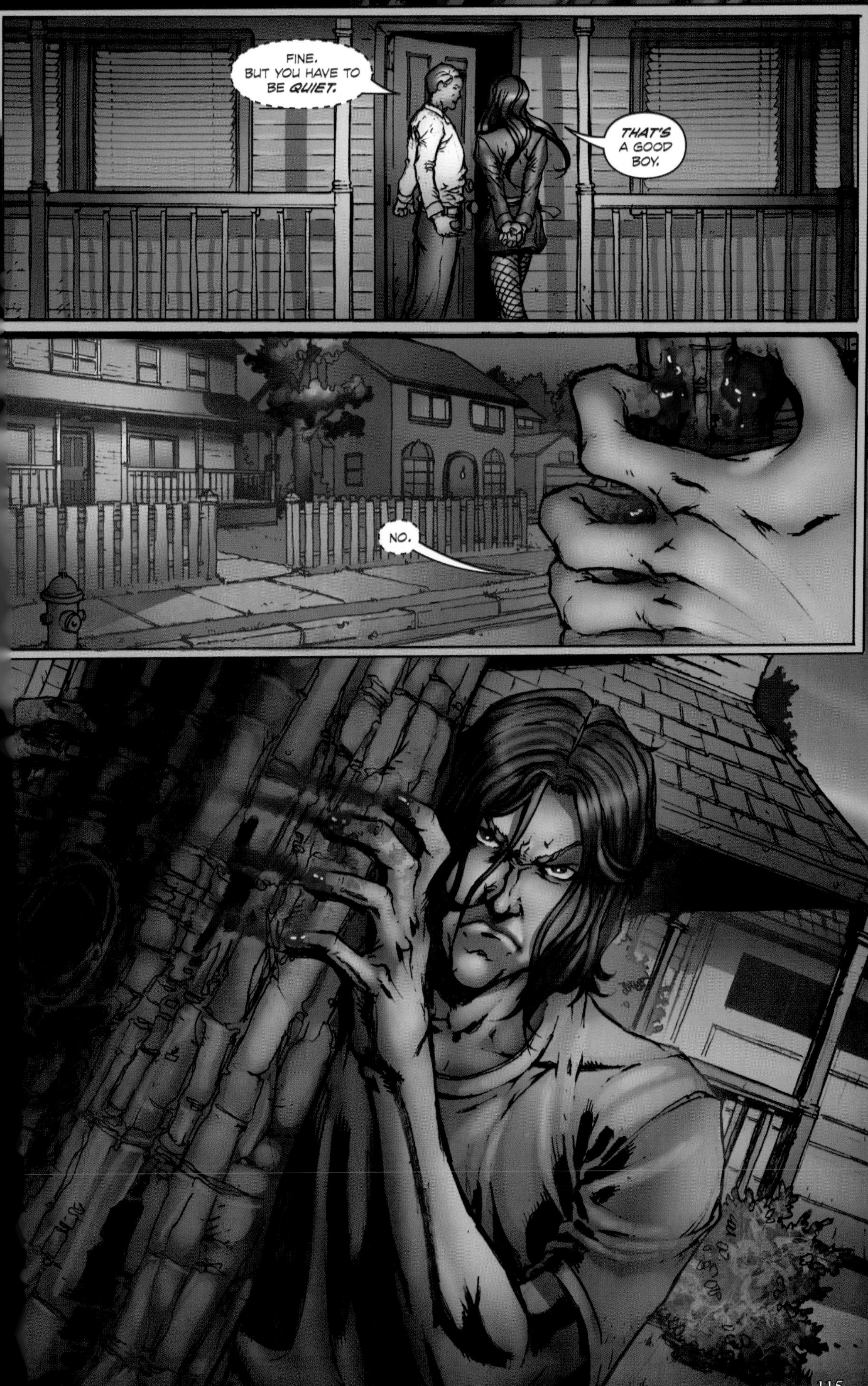
FINE. BUT YOU HAVE TO BE *QUIET.*
THAT'S A GOOD BOY.
NO.

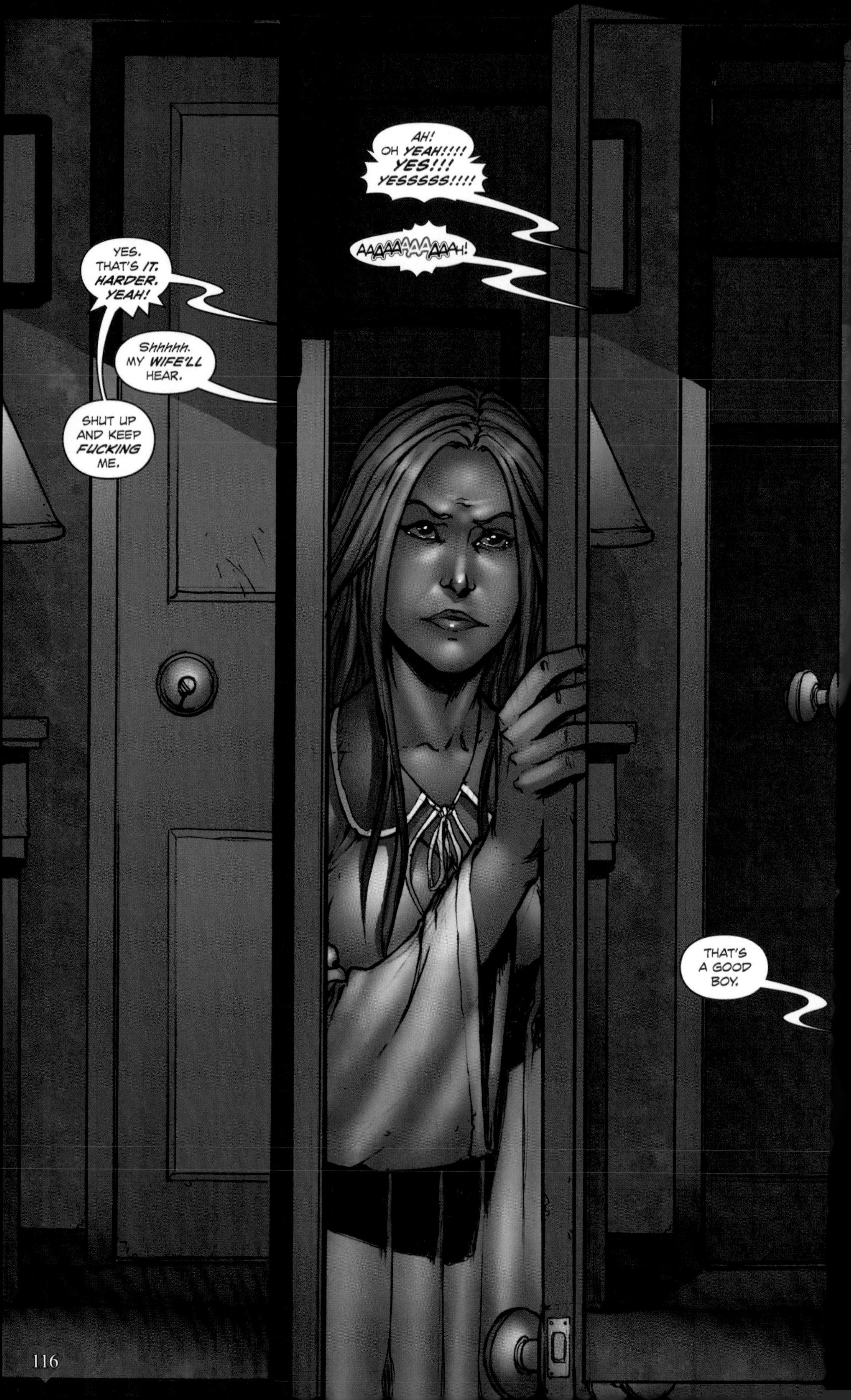
AH! OH YEAH!!!! YES!!! YESSSSS!!!!
AAAAAAAAAAAH!
YES. THAT'S IT. HARDER. YEAH!
Shhhhh. MY WIFE'LL HEAR.
SHUT UP AND KEEP FUCKING ME.
THAT'S A GOOD BOY.

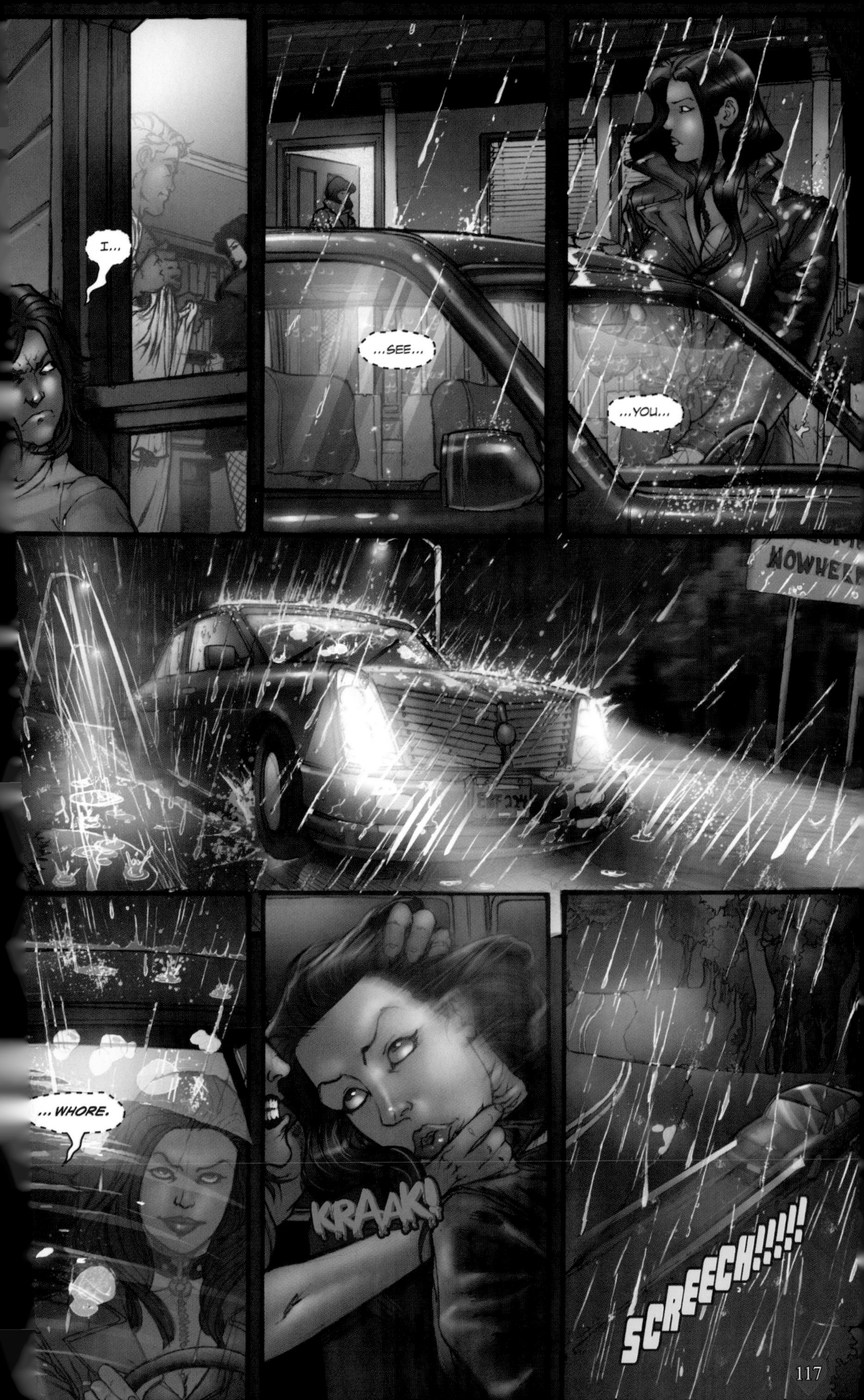
I...
...SEE...
...YOU...
NOWHERE
...WHORE.
KRAAK!
SCREECH!!!!!!

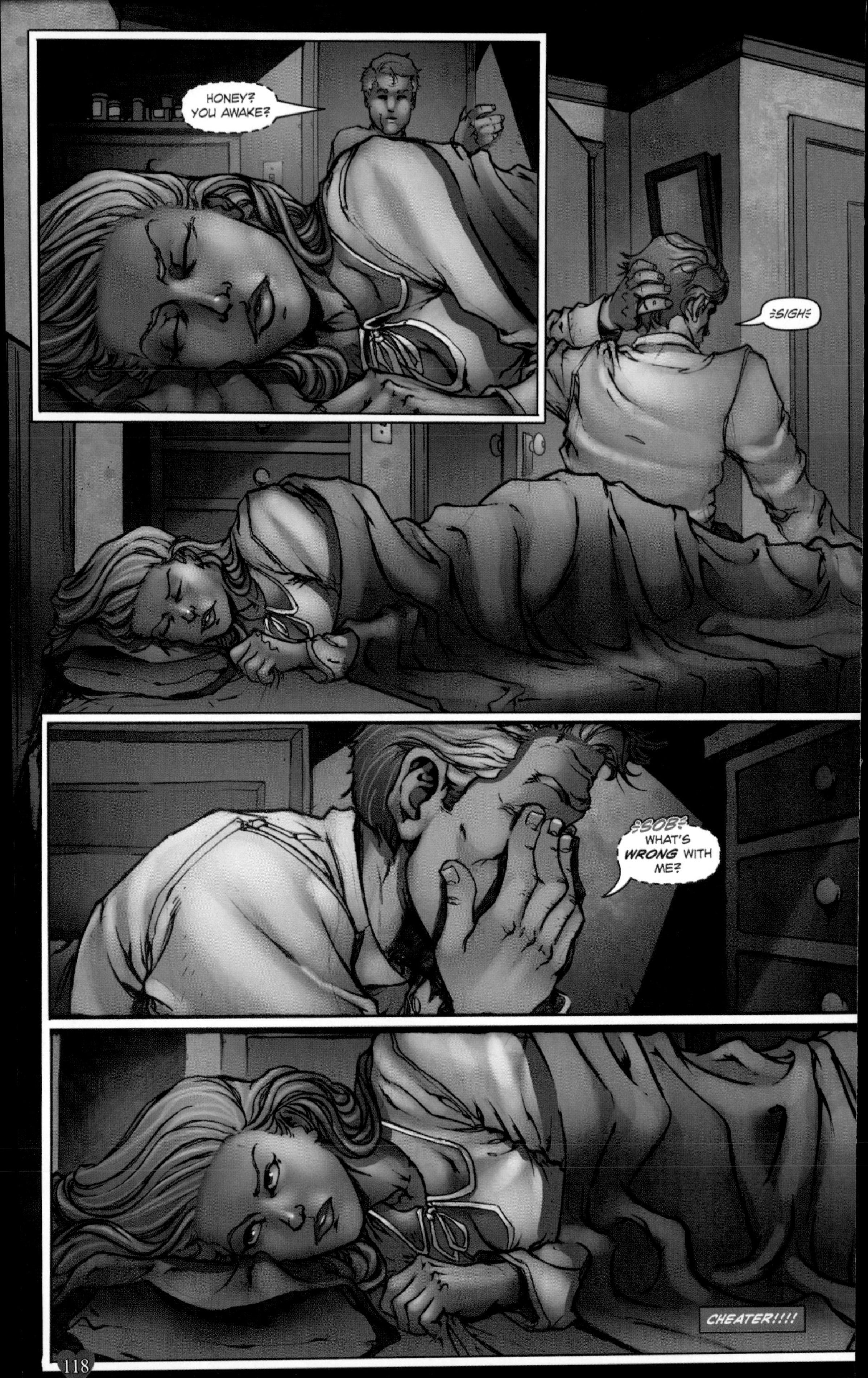
HONEY? YOU AWAKE?
SIGH
SOB WHAT'S WRONG WITH ME?
CHEATER!!!!

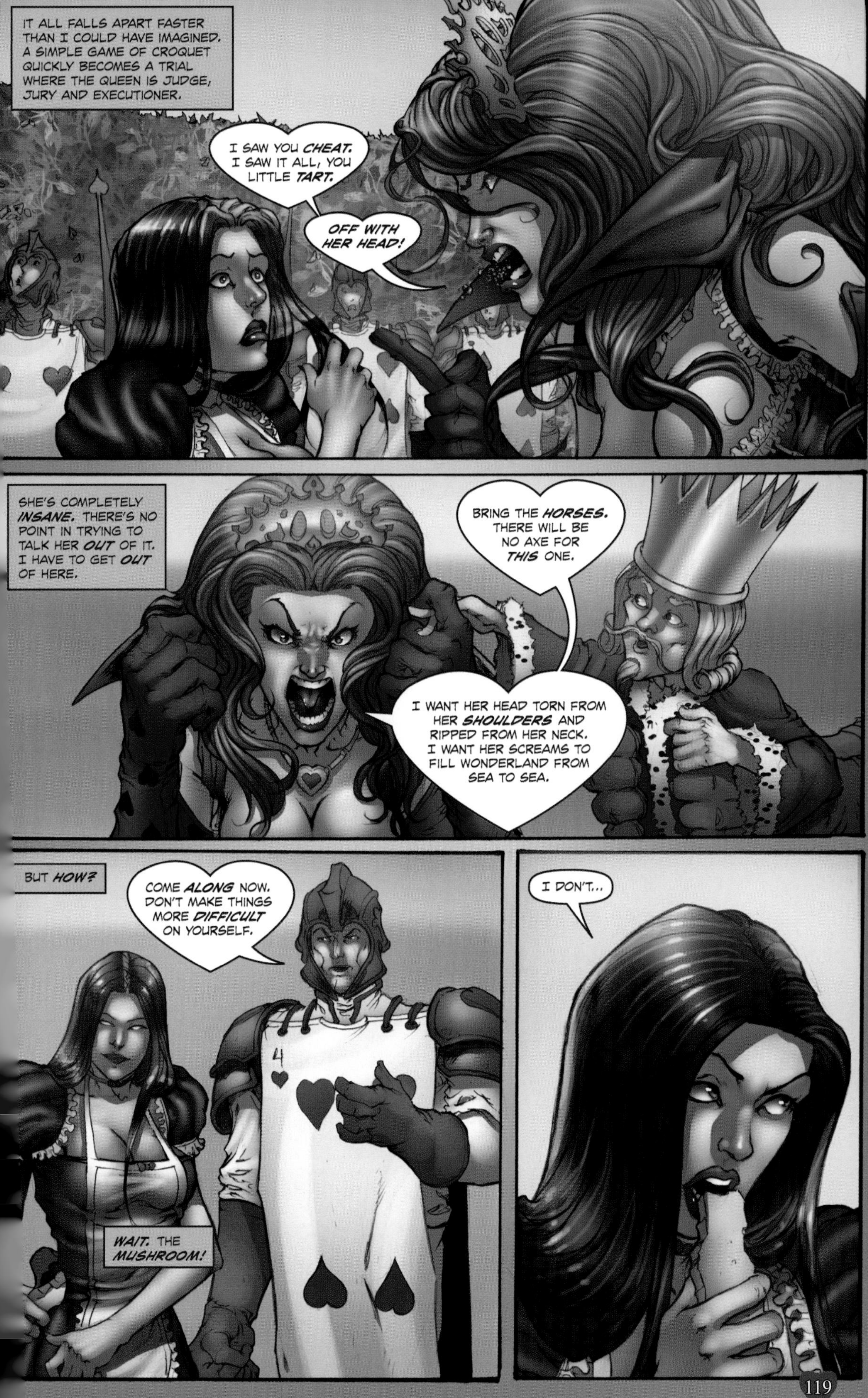
IT ALL FALLS APART FASTER THAN I COULD HAVE IMAGINED. A SIMPLE GAME OF CROQUET QUICKLY BECOMES A TRIAL WHERE THE QUEEN IS JUDGE, JURY AND EXECUTIONER.
I SAW YOU CHEAT. I SAW IT ALL, YOU LITTLE TART.
OFF WITH HER HEAD!
SHE'S COMPLETELY INSANE. THERE'S NO POINT IN TRYING TO TALK HER OUT OF IT. I HAVE TO GET OUT OF HERE.
BRING THE HORSES. THERE WILL BE NO AXE FOR THIS ONE.
I WANT HER HEAD TORN FROM HER SHOULDERS AND RIPPED FROM HER NECK. I WANT HER SCREAMS TO FILL WONDERLAND FROM SEA TO SEA.
BUT HOW?
COME ALONG NOW. DON'T MAKE THINGS MORE DIFFICULT ON YOURSELF.
WAIT. THE MUSHROOM!
I DON'T...

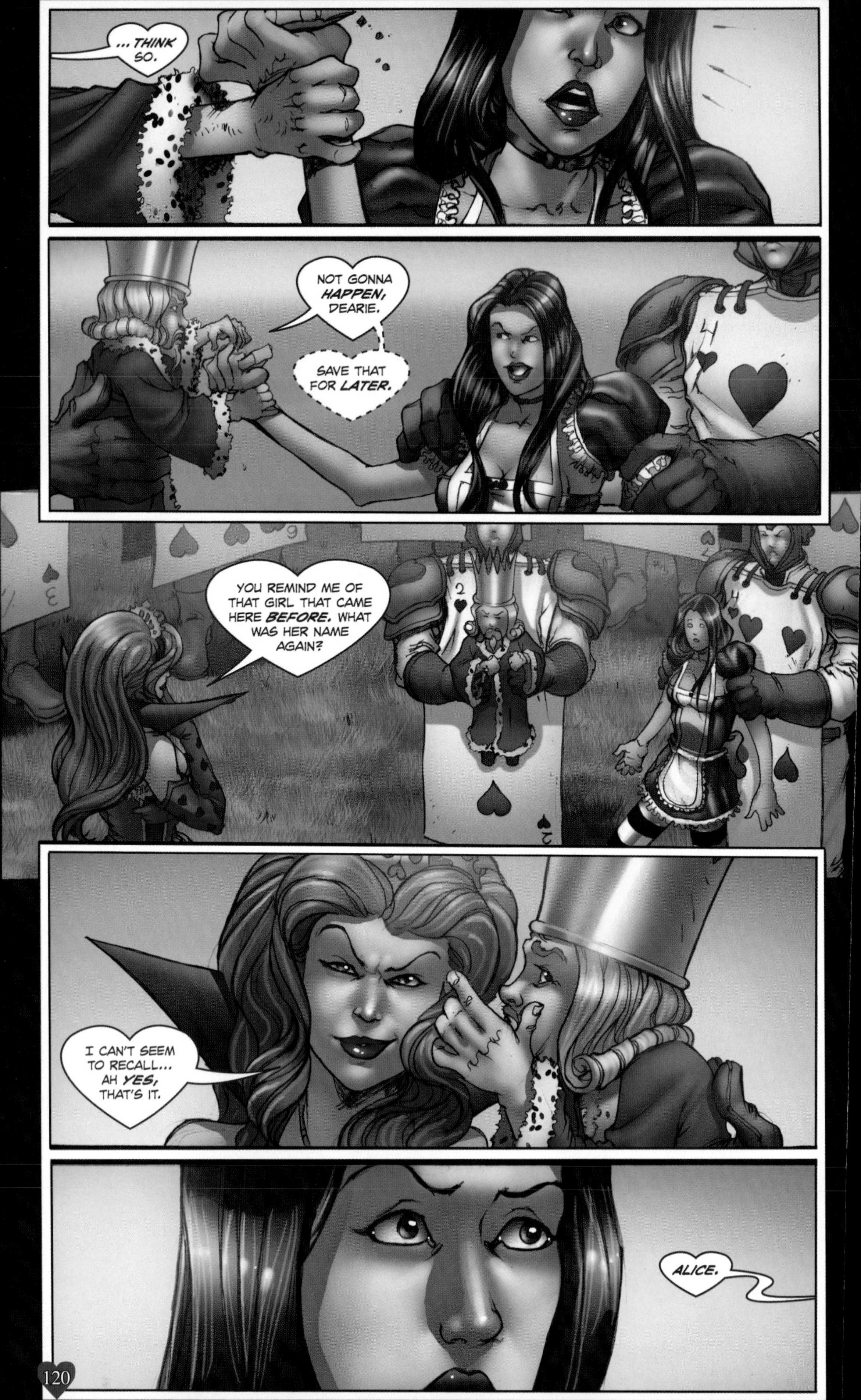

...THINK SO.
NOT GONNA *HAPPEN,* DEARIE.
SAVE THAT FOR *LATER.*
YOU REMIND ME OF THAT GIRL THAT CAME HERE *BEFORE.* WHAT WAS HER NAME AGAIN?
I CAN'T SEEM TO RECALL... AH *YES,* THAT'S IT.
ALICE.

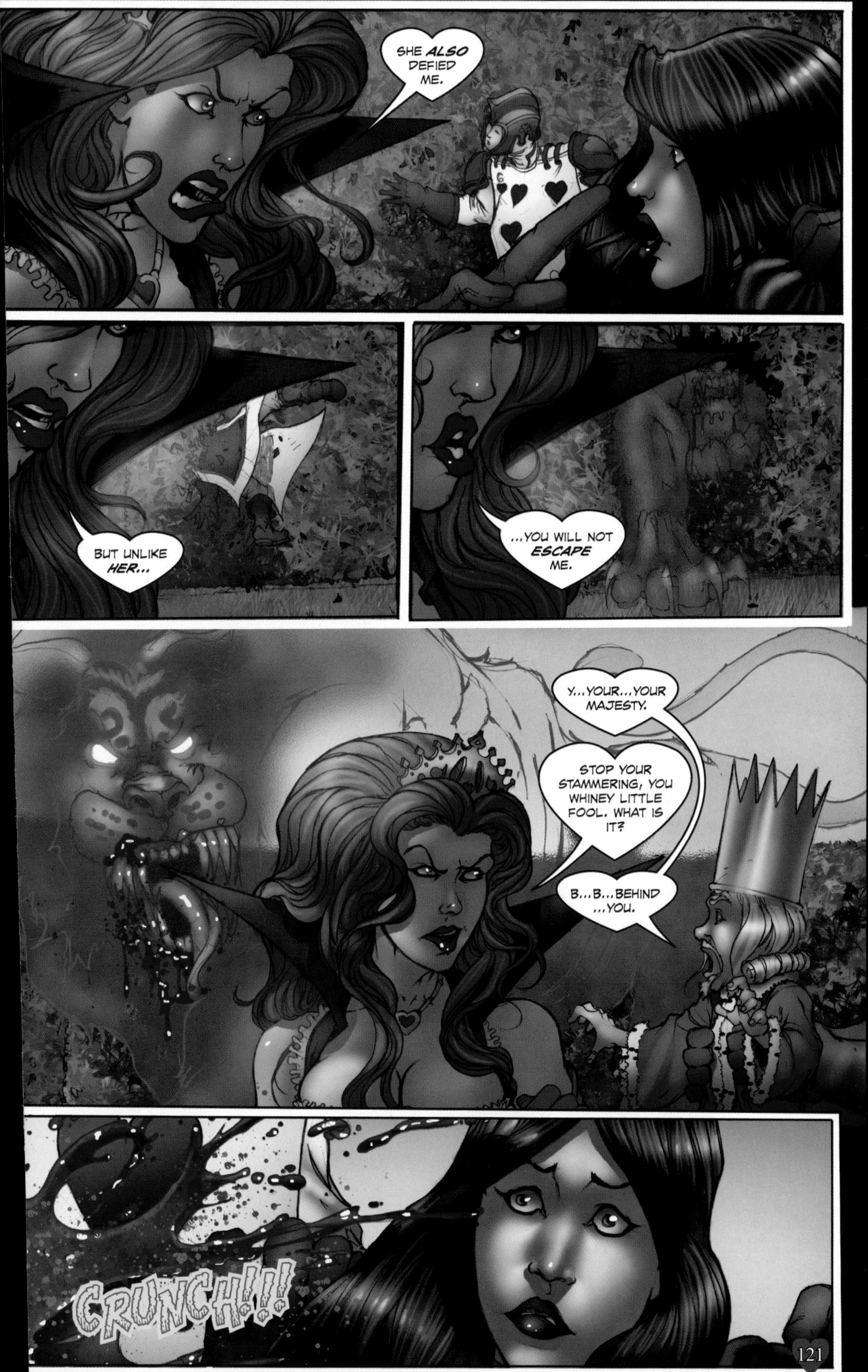
SHE ALSO DEFIED ME.
BUT UNLIKE HER...
...YOU WILL NOT ESCAPE ME.
Y...YOUR...YOUR MAJESTY.
STOP YOUR STAMMERING, YOU WHINEY LITTLE FOOL. WHAT IS IT?
B...B...BEHIND ...YOU.
CRUNCH!!!

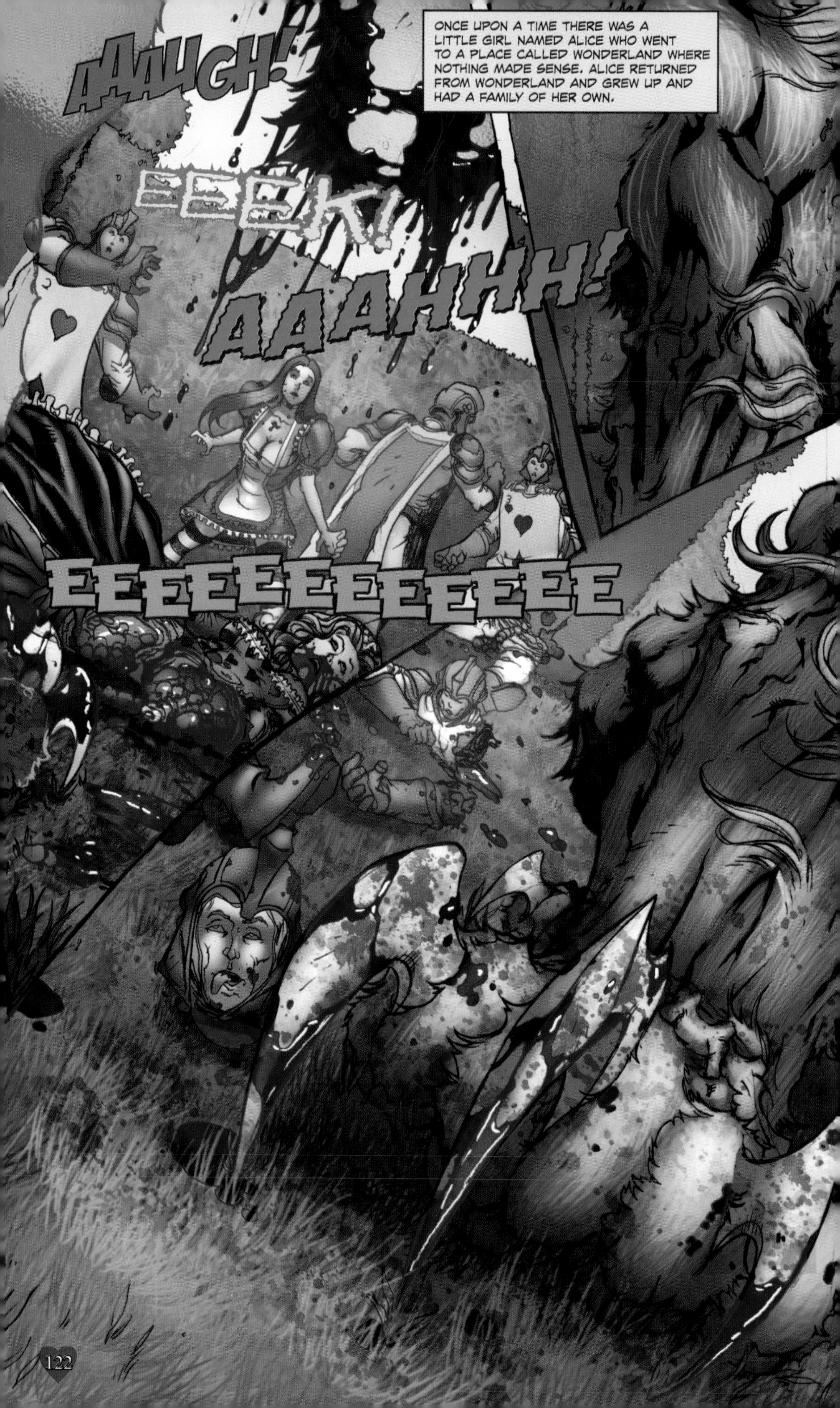
ONCE UPON A TIME THERE WAS A LITTLE GIRL NAMED ALICE WHO WENT TO A PLACE CALLED WONDERLAND WHERE NOTHING MADE SENSE. ALICE RETURNED FROM WONDERLAND AND GREW UP AND HAD A FAMILY OF HER OWN.
AAAUGH!
EEEEK!
AAAHHH!
EEEEEEEEEEEEE

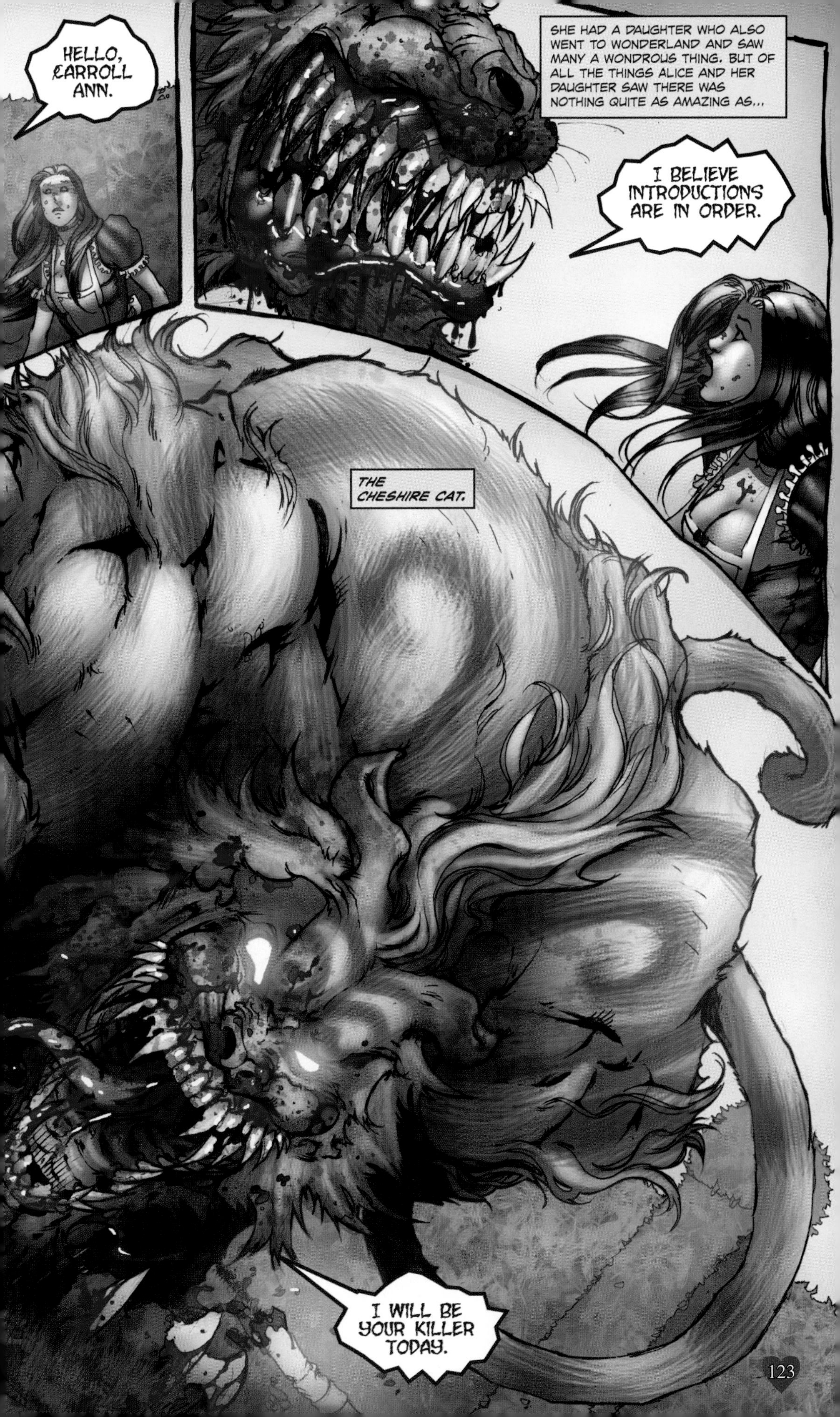
HELLO, CARROLL ANN.
SHE HAD A DAUGHTER WHO ALSO WENT TO WONDERLAND AND SAW MANY A WONDROUS THING. BUT OF ALL THE THINGS ALICE AND HER DAUGHTER SAW THERE WAS NOTHING QUITE AS AMAZING AS...
I BELIEVE INTRODUCTIONS ARE IN ORDER.
THE CHESHIRE CAT.
I WILL BE YOUR KILLER TODAY.

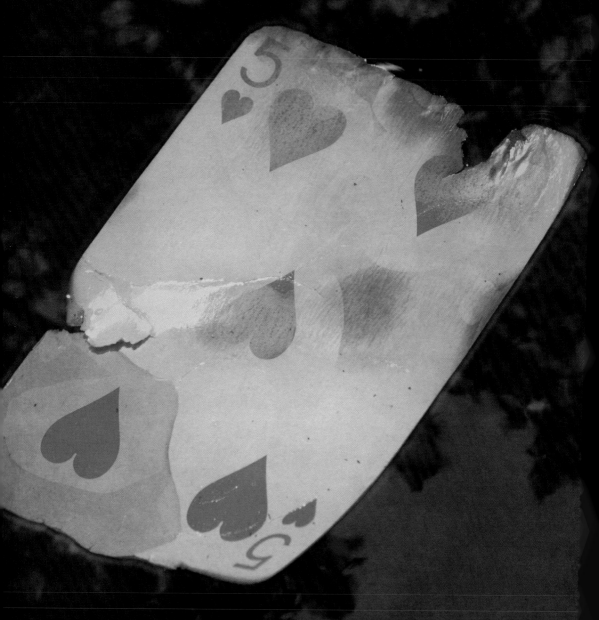

five

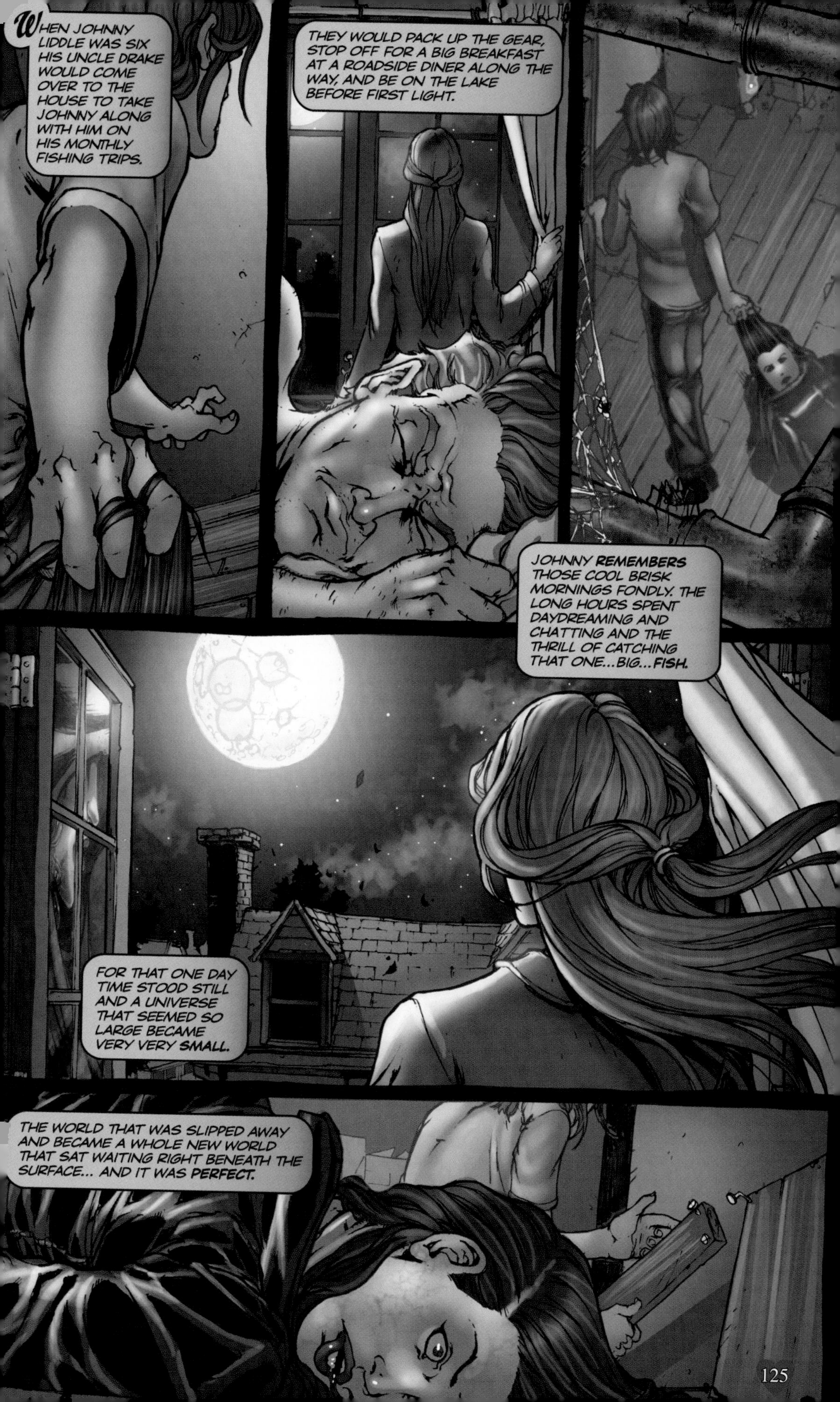
WHEN JOHNNY LIDDLE WAS SIX HIS UNCLE DRAKE WOULD COME OVER TO THE HOUSE TO TAKE JOHNNY ALONG WITH HIM ON HIS MONTHLY FISHING TRIPS.
THEY WOULD PACK UP THE GEAR, STOP OFF FOR A BIG BREAKFAST AT A ROADSIDE DINER ALONG THE WAY, AND BE ON THE LAKE BEFORE FIRST LIGHT.
JOHNNY REMEMBERS THOSE COOL BRISK MORNINGS FONDLY. THE LONG HOURS SPENT DAYDREAMING AND CHATTING AND THE THRILL OF CATCHING THAT ONE...BIG...FISH.
FOR THAT ONE DAY TIME STOOD STILL AND A UNIVERSE THAT SEEMED SO LARGE BECAME VERY VERY SMALL.
THE WORLD THAT WAS SLIPPED AWAY AND BECAME A WHOLE NEW WORLD THAT SAT WAITING RIGHT BENEATH THE SURFACE... AND IT WAS PERFECT.

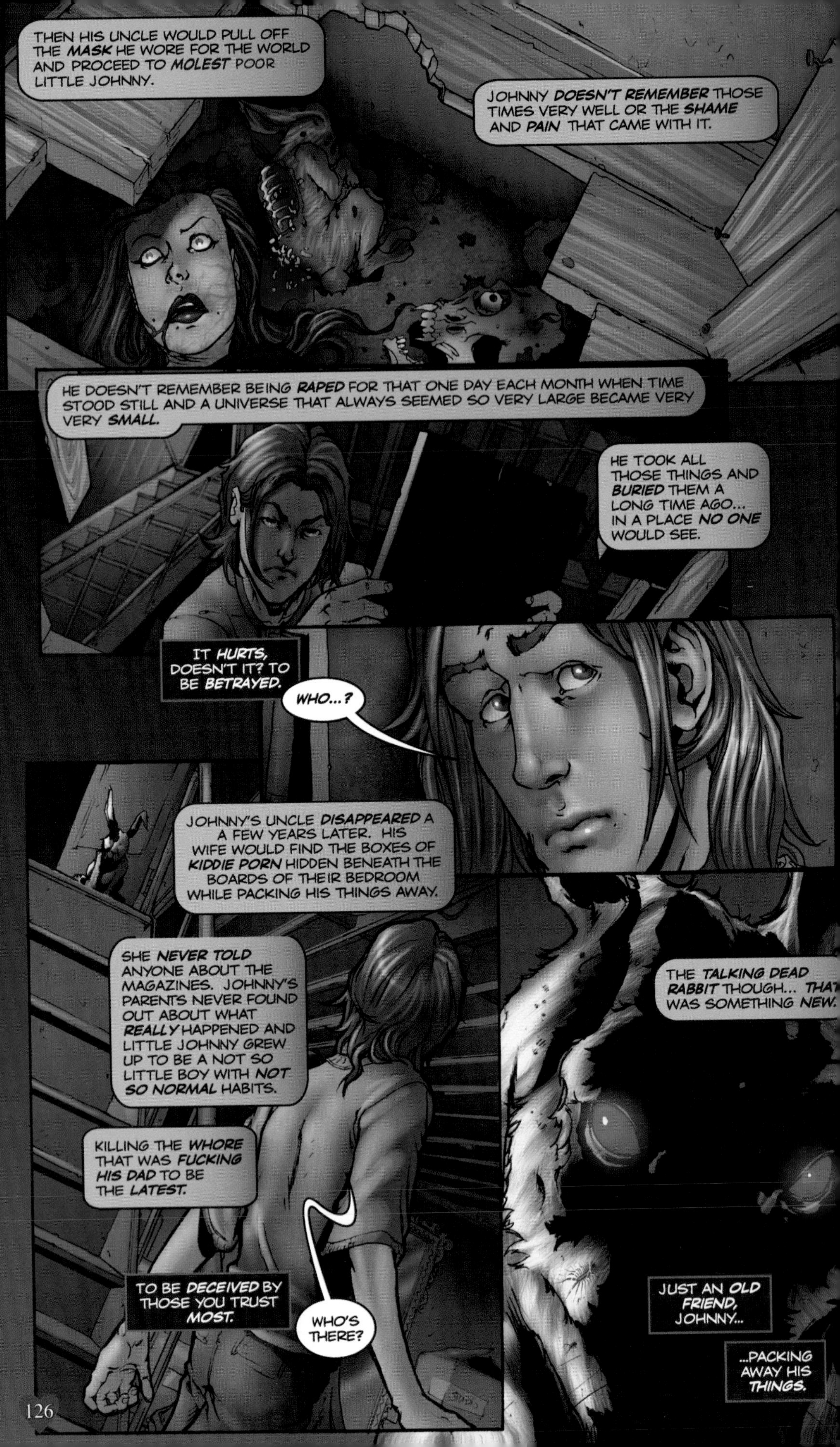

THEN HIS UNCLE WOULD PULL OFF THE MASK HE WORE FOR THE WORLD AND PROCEED TO MOLEST POOR LITTLE JOHNNY.
JOHNNY DOESN'T REMEMBER THOSE TIMES VERY WELL OR THE SHAME AND PAIN THAT CAME WITH IT.
HE DOESN'T REMEMBER BEING RAPED FOR THAT ONE DAY EACH MONTH WHEN TIME STOOD STILL AND A UNIVERSE THAT ALWAYS SEEMED SO VERY LARGE BECAME VERY VERY SMALL.
HE TOOK ALL THOSE THINGS AND BURIED THEM A LONG TIME AGO... IN A PLACE NO ONE WOULD SEE.
IT HURTS, DOESN'T IT? TO BE BETRAYED.
WHO...?
JOHNNY'S UNCLE DISAPPEARED A A FEW YEARS LATER. HIS WIFE WOULD FIND THE BOXES OF KIDDIE PORN HIDDEN BENEATH THE BOARDS OF THEIR BEDROOM WHILE PACKING HIS THINGS AWAY.
SHE NEVER TOLD ANYONE ABOUT THE MAGAZINES. JOHNNY'S PARENTS NEVER FOUND OUT ABOUT WHAT REALLY HAPPENED AND LITTLE JOHNNY GREW UP TO BE A NOT SO LITTLE BOY WITH NOT SO NORMAL HABITS.
KILLING THE WHORE THAT WAS FUCKING HIS DAD TO BE THE LATEST.
TO BE DECEIVED BY THOSE YOU TRUST MOST.
WHO'S THERE?
THE TALKING DEAD RABBIT THOUGH... THAT WAS SOMETHING NEW.
JUST AN OLD FRIEND, JOHNNY...
...PACKING AWAY HIS THINGS.

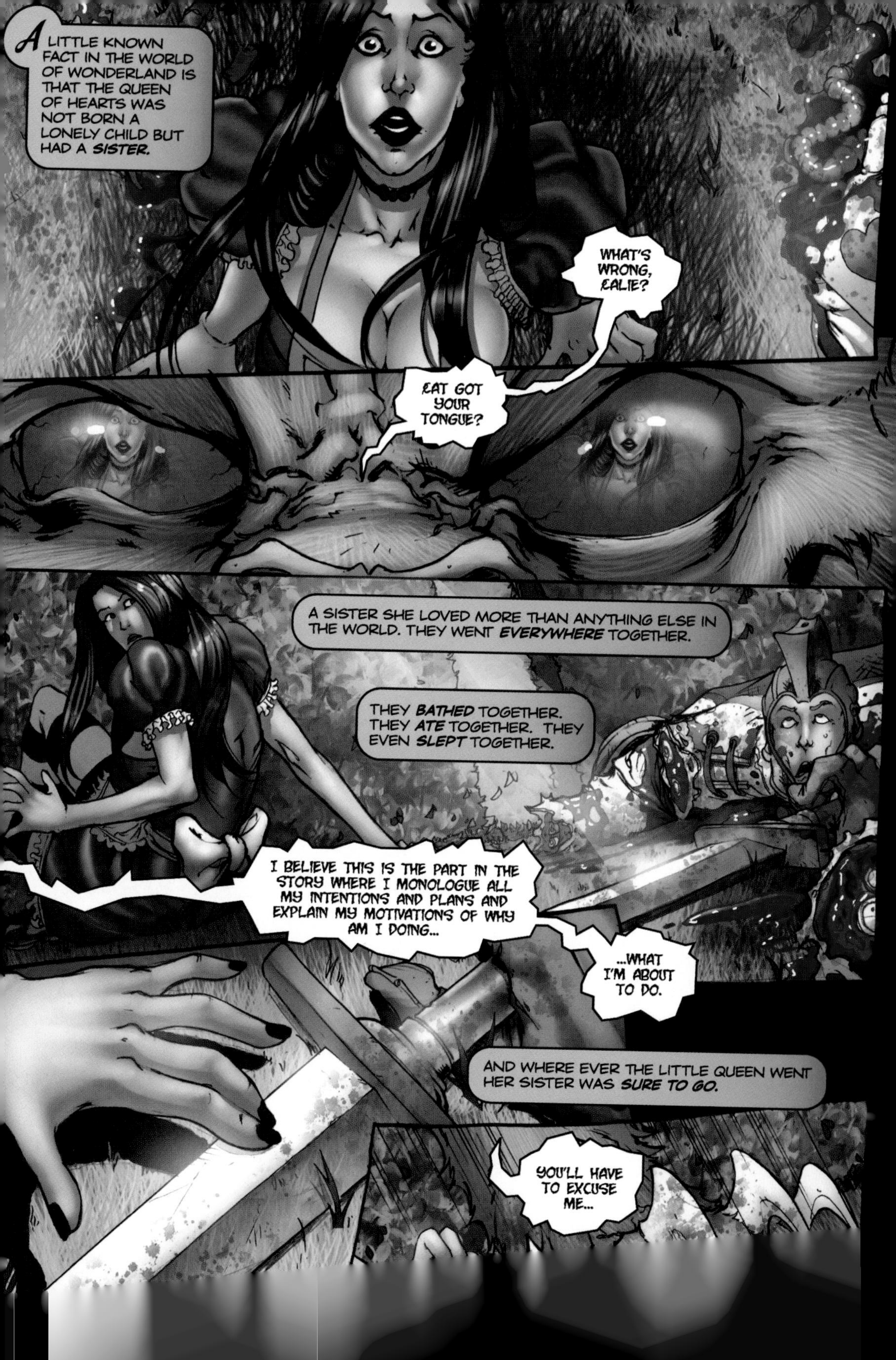
A LITTLE KNOWN FACT IN THE WORLD OF WONDERLAND IS THAT THE QUEEN OF HEARTS WAS NOT BORN A LONELY CHILD BUT HAD A *SISTER.*
WHAT'S WRONG, CALIE?
CAT GOT YOUR TONGUE?
A SISTER SHE LOVED MORE THAN ANYTHING ELSE IN THE WORLD. THEY WENT *EVERYWHERE* TOGETHER.
THEY *BATHED* TOGETHER. THEY *ATE* TOGETHER. THEY EVEN *SLEPT* TOGETHER.
I BELIEVE THIS IS THE PART IN THE STORY WHERE I MONOLOGUE ALL MY INTENTIONS AND PLANS AND EXPLAIN MY MOTIVATIONS OF WHY AM I DOING...
...WHAT I'M ABOUT TO DO.
AND WHERE EVER THE LITTLE QUEEN WENT HER SISTER WAS *SURE TO GO.*
YOU'LL HAVE TO EXCUSE ME...

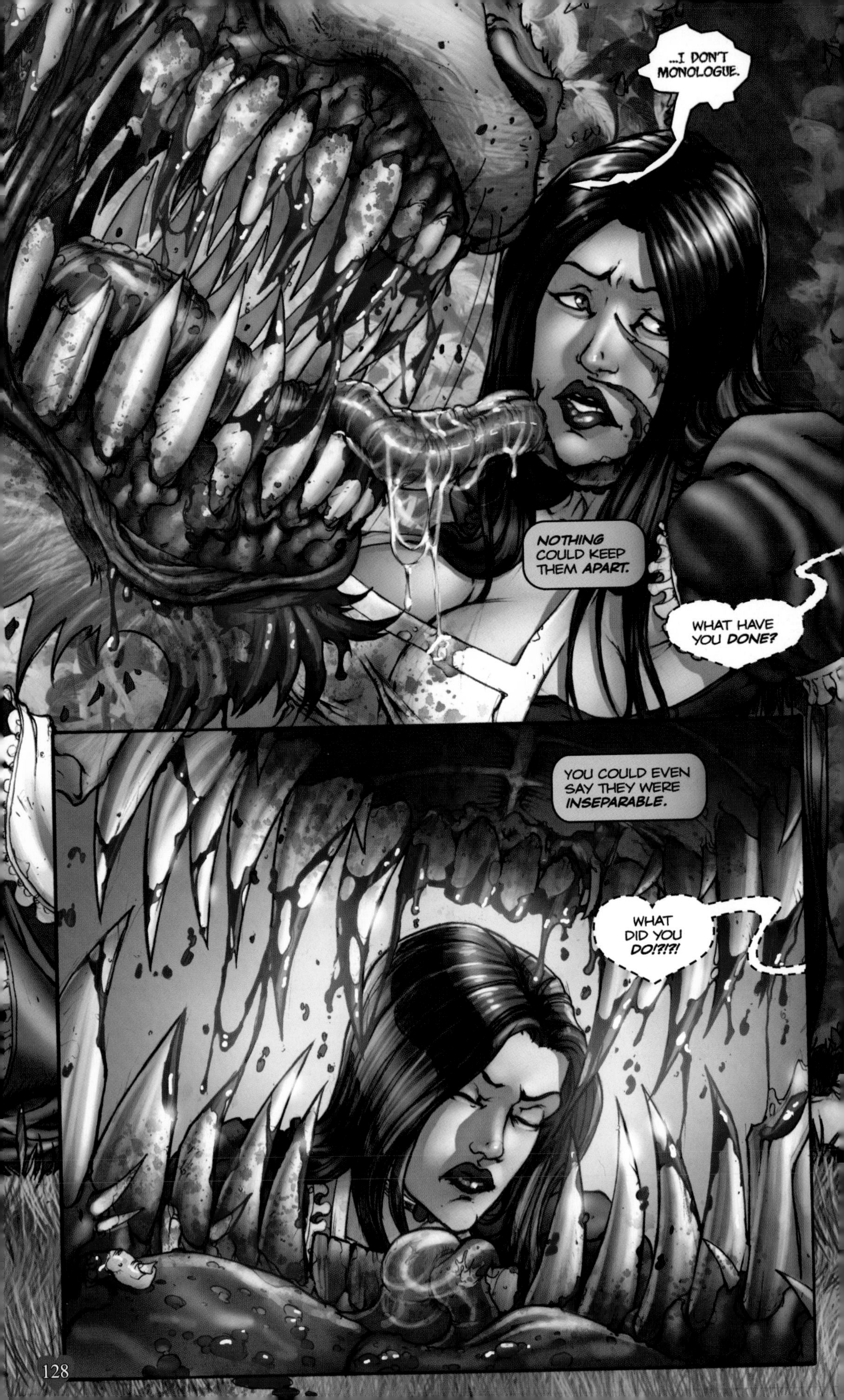
...I DON'T MONOLOGUE.
NOTHING COULD KEEP THEM APART.
WHAT HAVE YOU DONE?
YOU COULD EVEN SAY THEY WERE INSEPARABLE.
WHAT DID YOU DO!?!?!

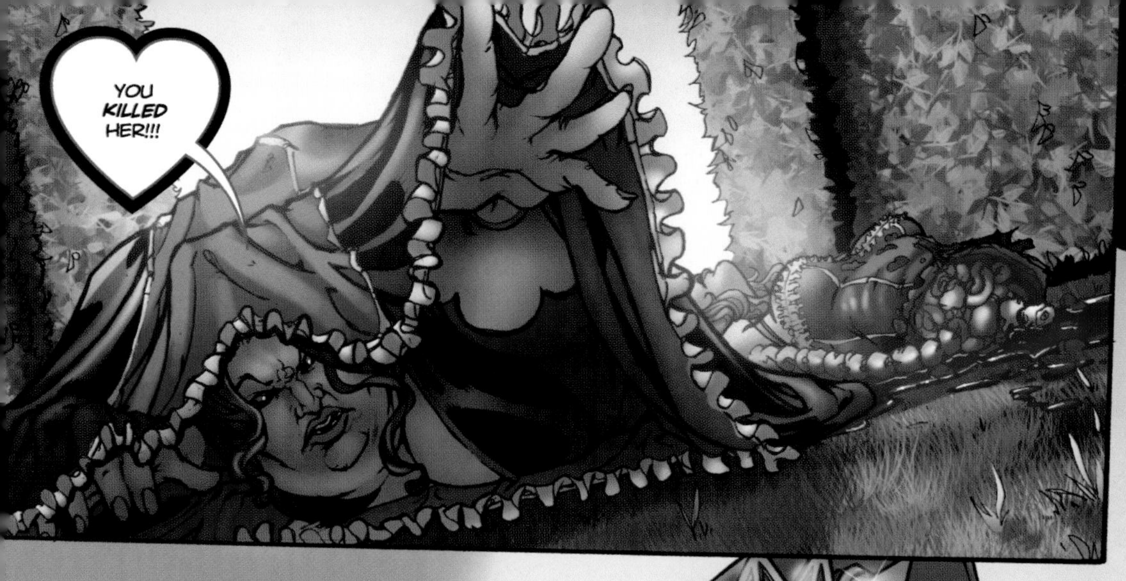
YOU KILLED HER!!!

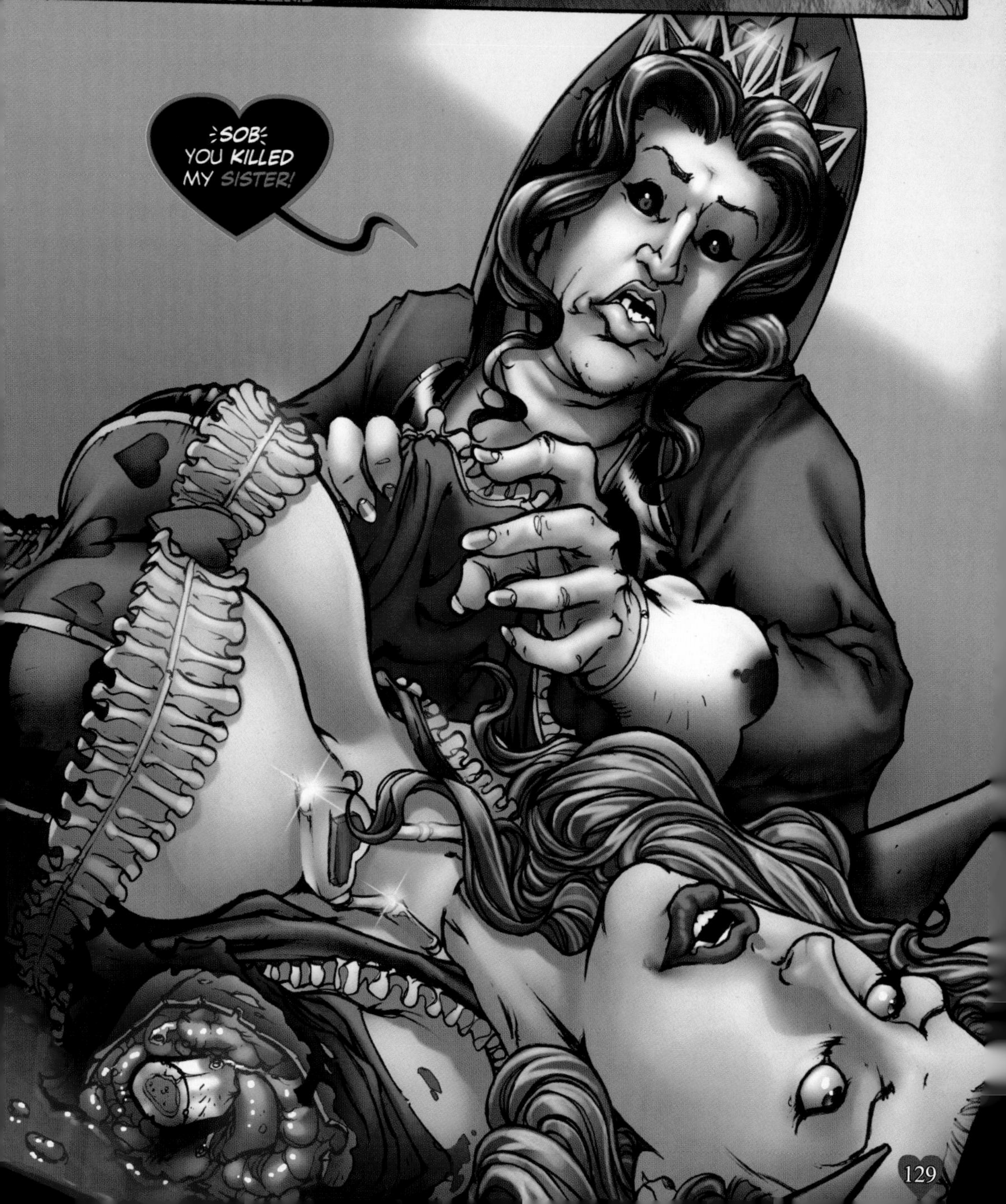
SOB
YOU KILLED MY SISTER!

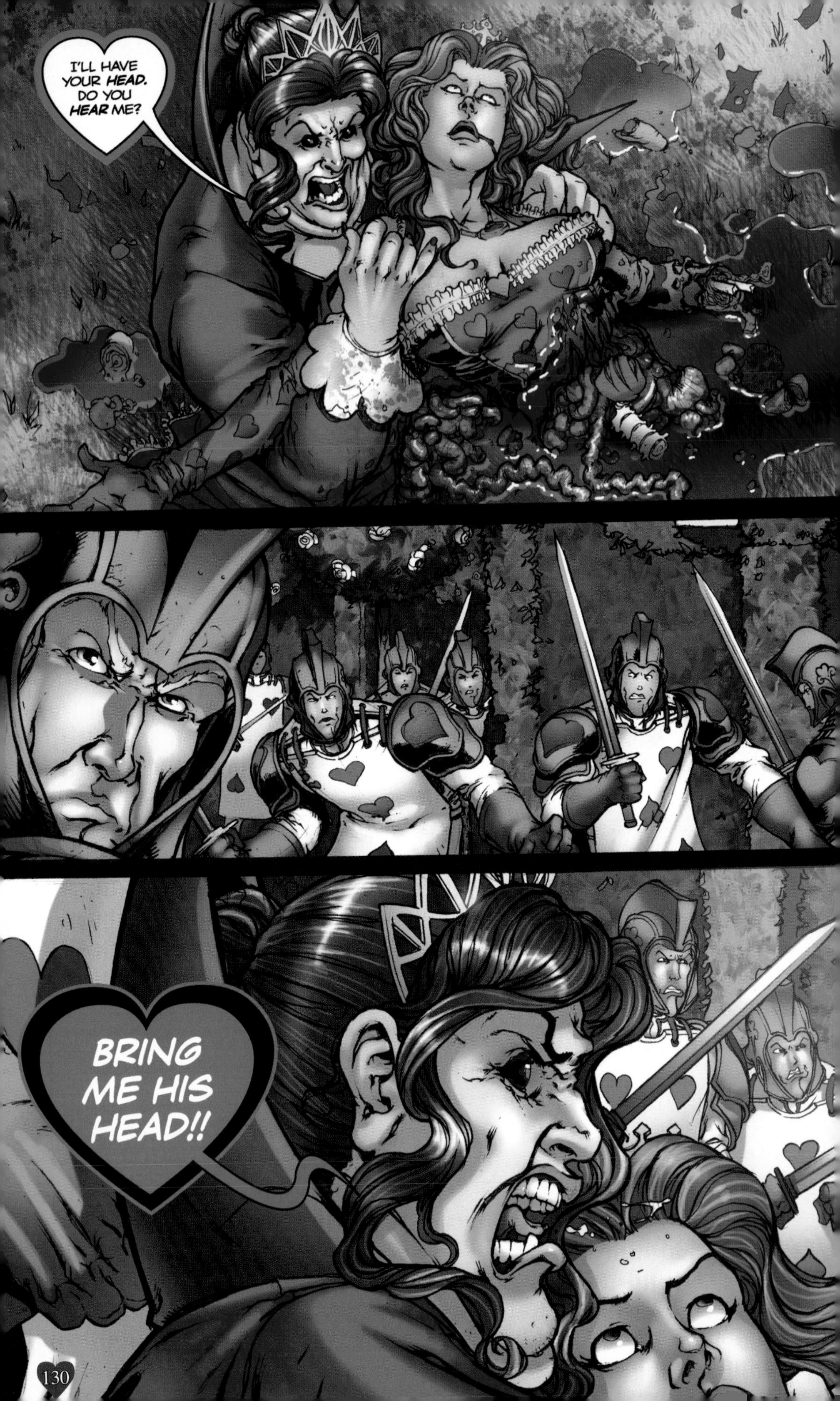
I'LL HAVE YOUR HEAD. DO YOU HEAR ME?
BRING ME HIS HEAD!!

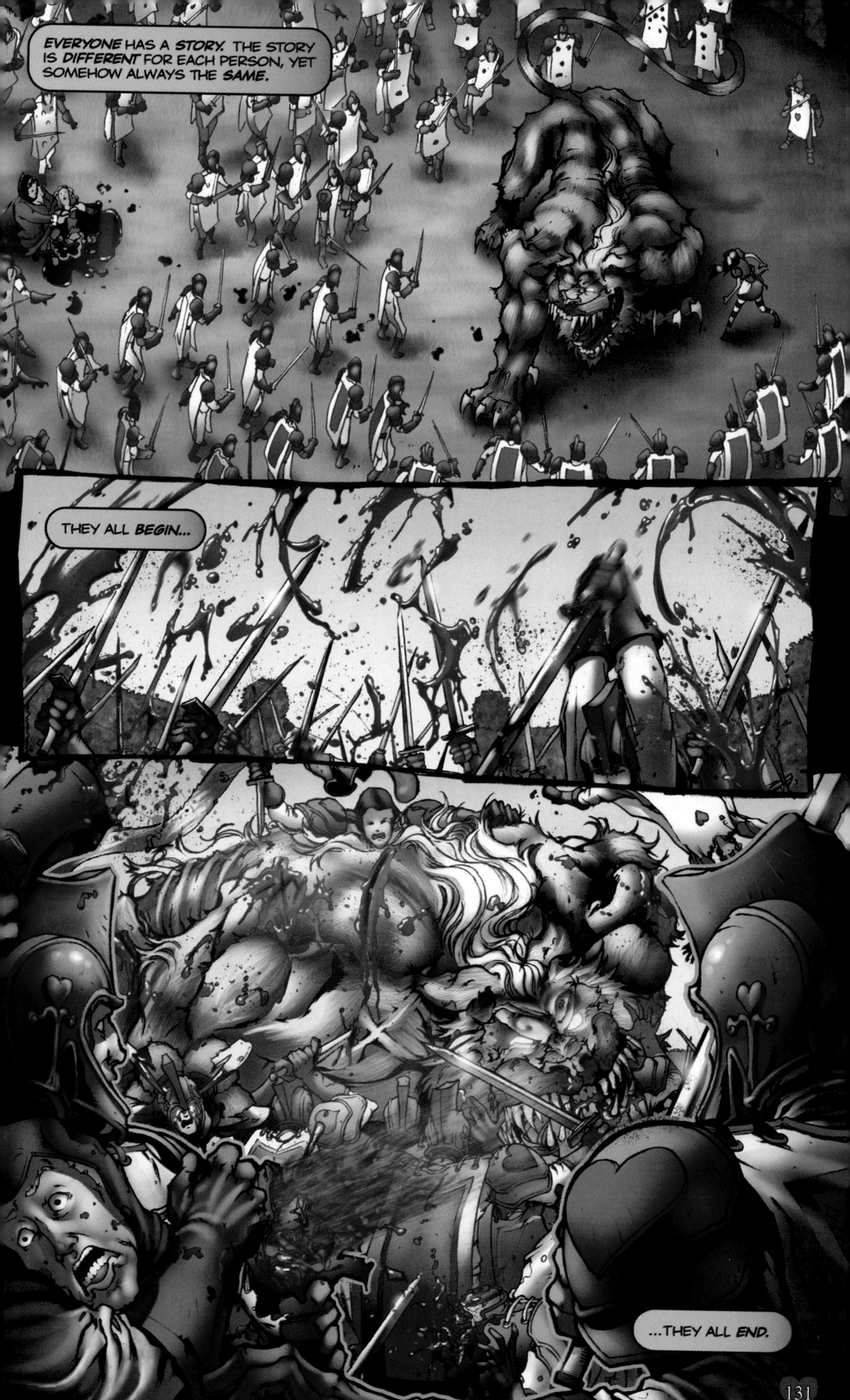
EVERYONE HAS A STORY. THE STORY IS DIFFERENT FOR EACH PERSON, YET SOMEHOW ALWAYS THE SAME.
THEY ALL BEGIN...
...THEY ALL END.

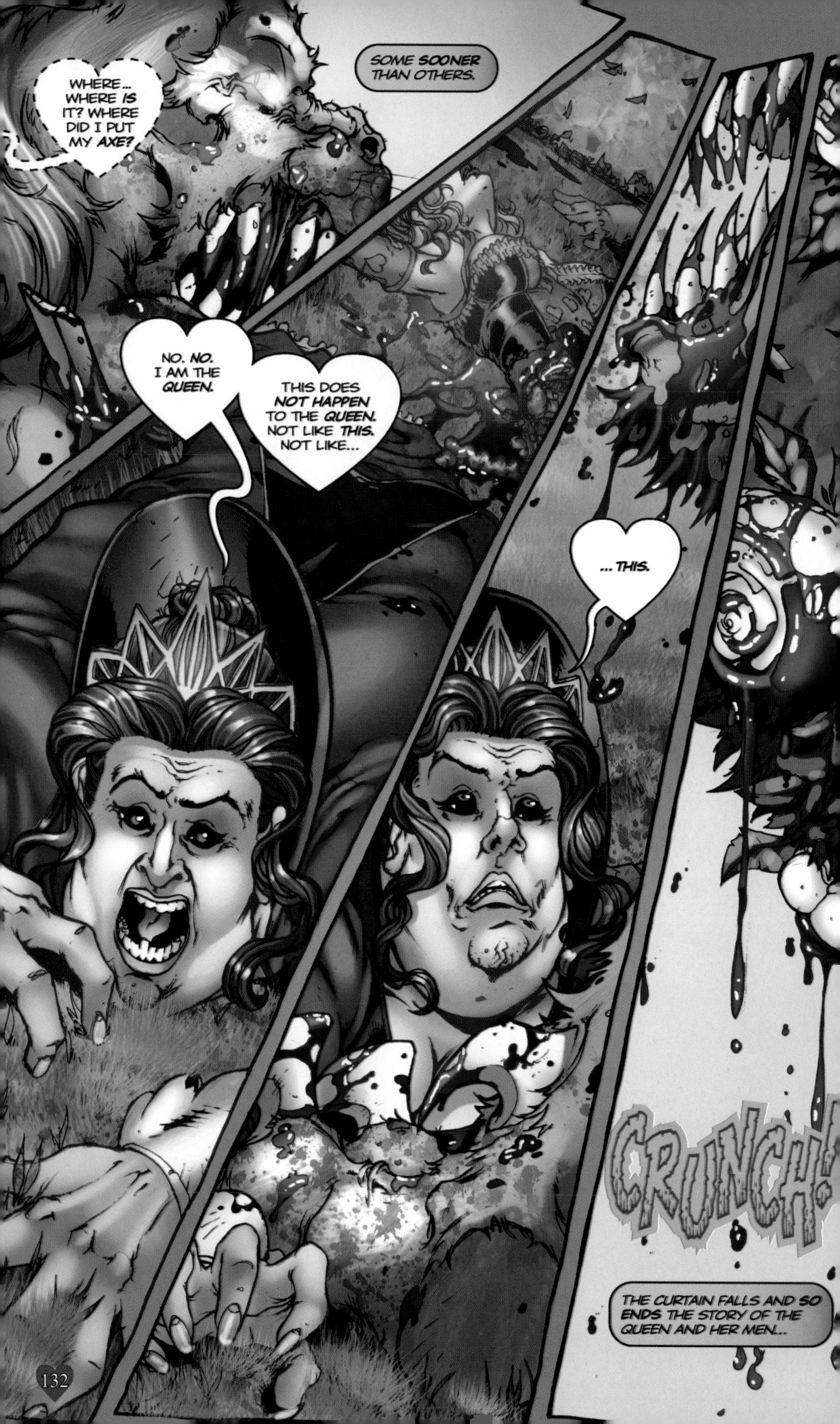
WHERE... WHERE IS IT? WHERE DID I PUT MY AXE?
SOME SOONER THAN OTHERS.
NO. NO. I AM THE QUEEN.
THIS DOES NOT HAPPEN TO THE QUEEN. NOT LIKE THIS. NOT LIKE...
...THIS.
CRUNCH!
THE CURTAIN FALLS AND SO ENDS THE STORY OF THE QUEEN AND HER MEN...

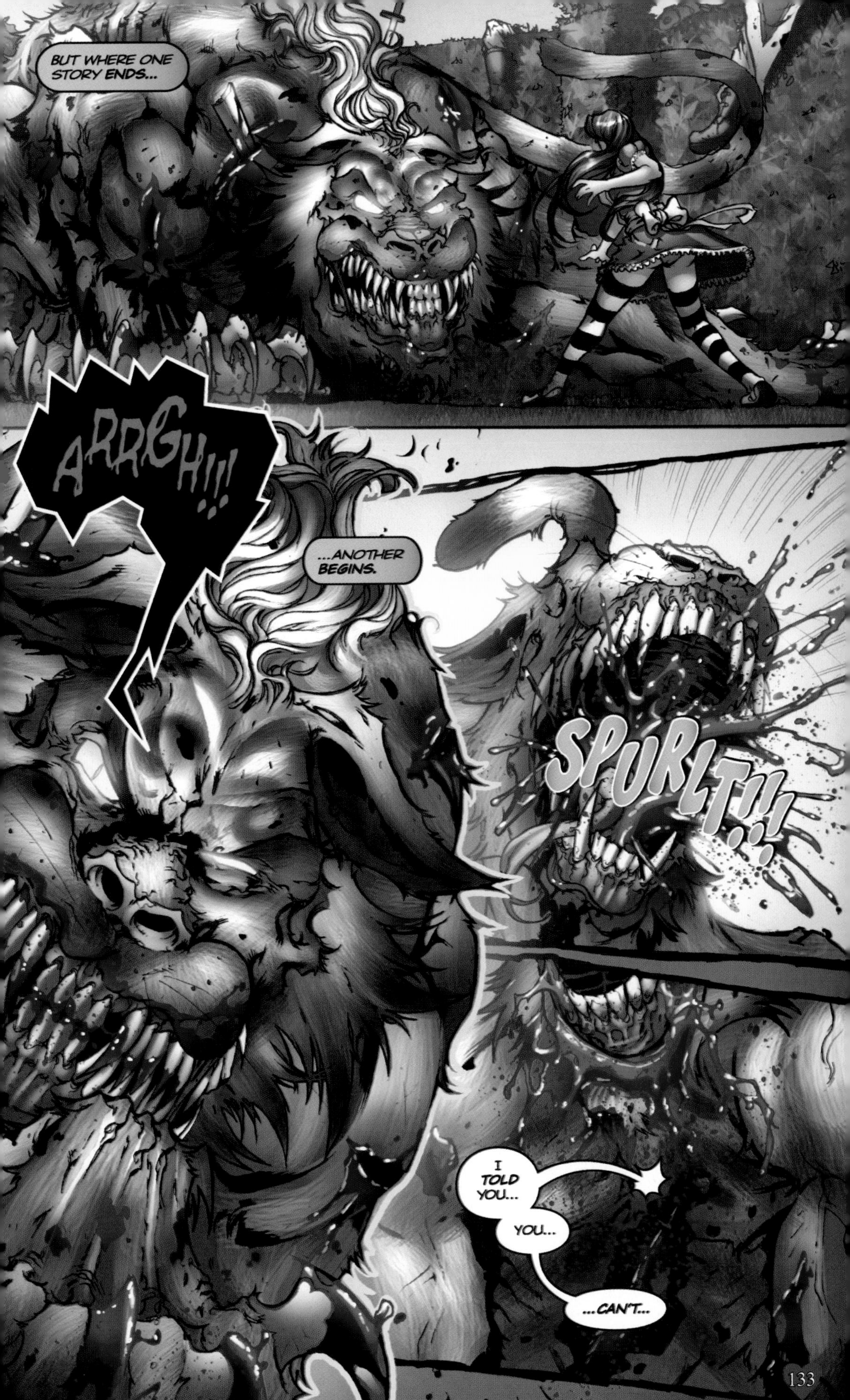

BUT WHERE ONE STORY ENDS...
ARRGH!!!
...ANOTHER BEGINS.
SPURLT!!!
I TOLD YOU...
YOU...
...CAN'T...

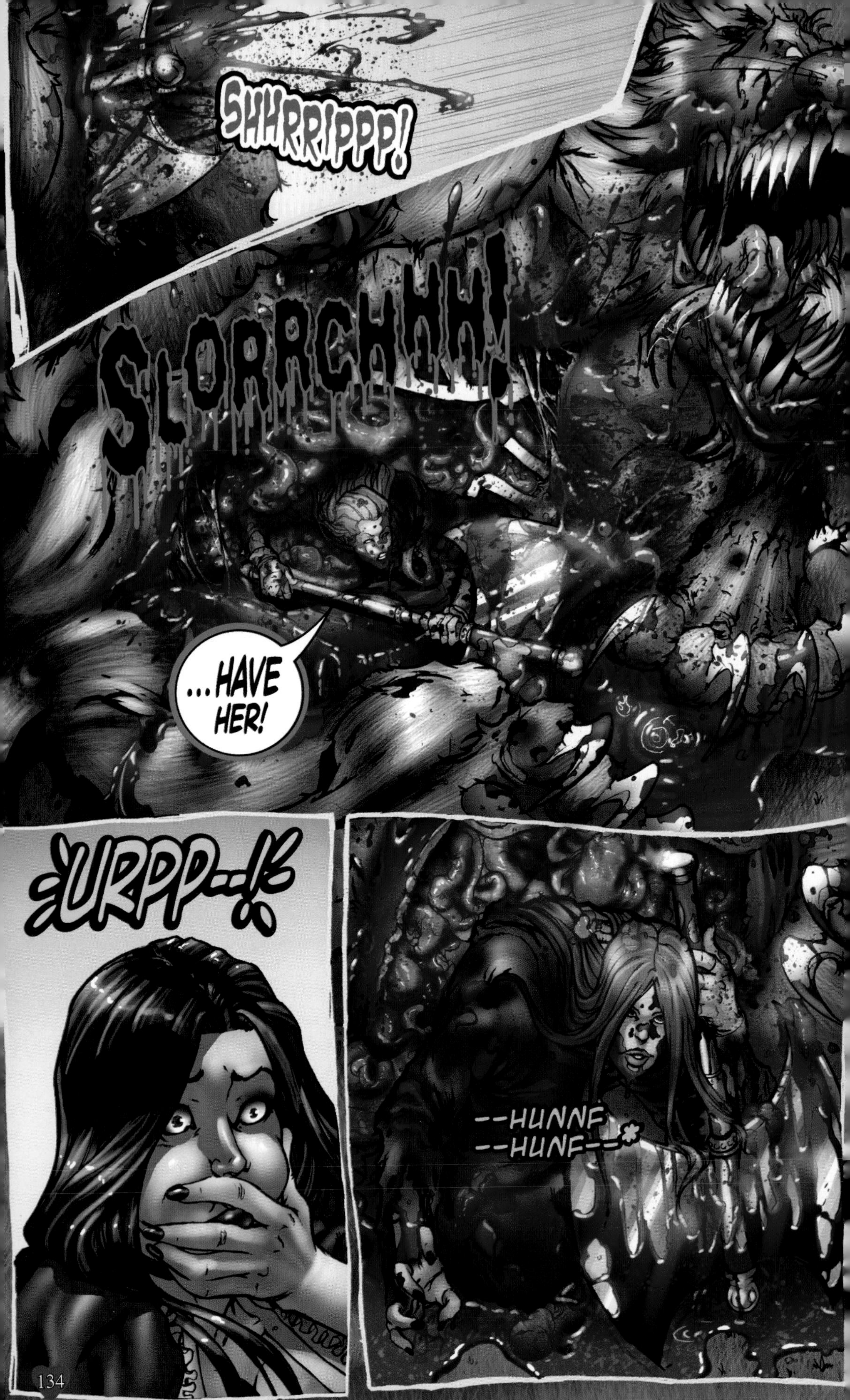
SHHRRIPPP!
SLORRCHHH!
...HAVE HER!
-URPP--!-
--HUNNF
--HUNF--

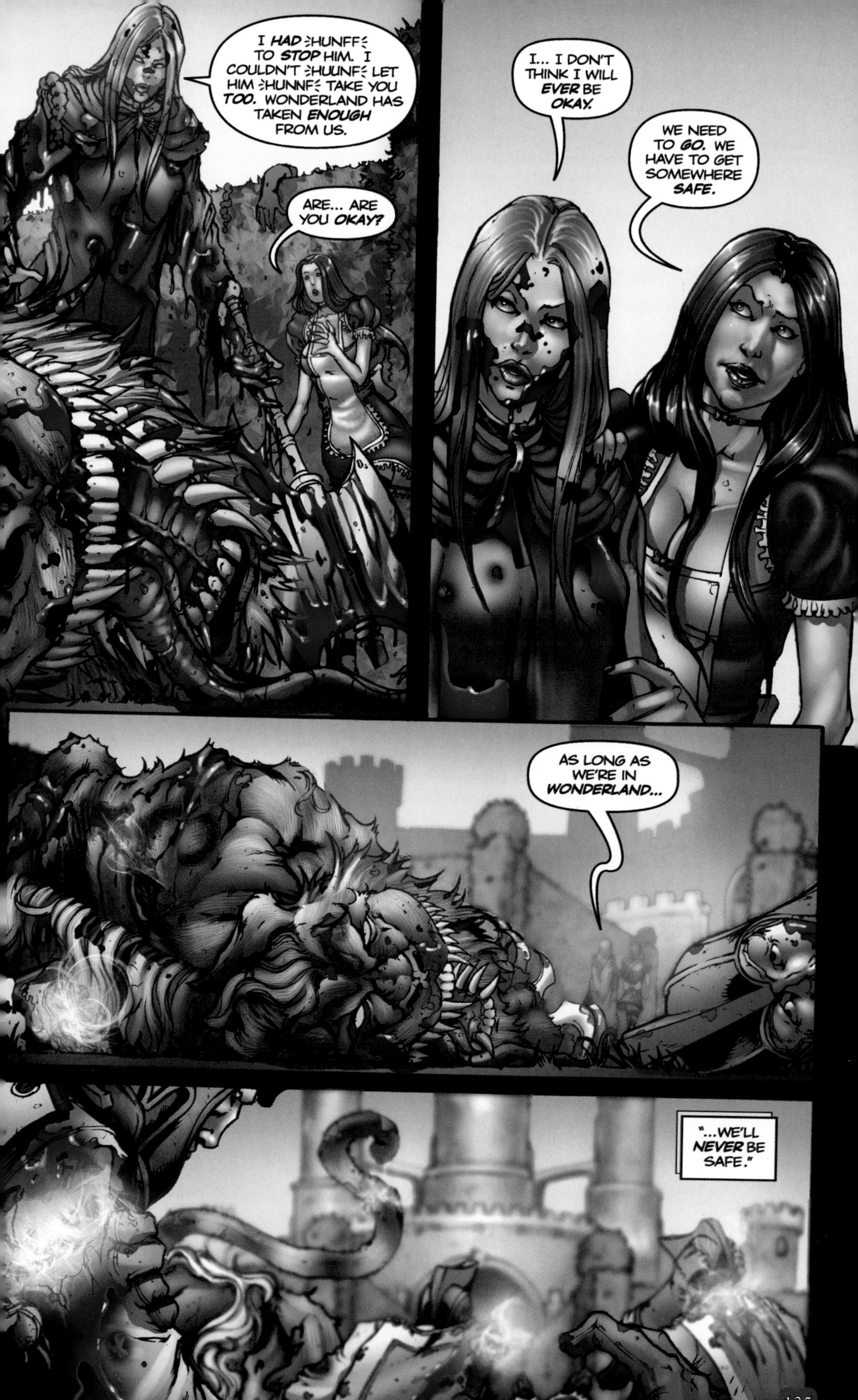
I HAD ⁂HUNFF⁂ TO STOP HIM. I COULDN'T ⁂HUUNF⁂ LET HIM ⁂HUNNF⁂ TAKE YOU TOO. WONDERLAND HAS TAKEN ENOUGH FROM US.
ARE... ARE YOU OKAY?
I... I DON'T THINK I WILL EVER BE OKAY.
WE NEED TO GO. WE HAVE TO GET SOMEWHERE SAFE.
AS LONG AS WE'RE IN WONDERLAND...
"...WE'LL NEVER BE SAFE."

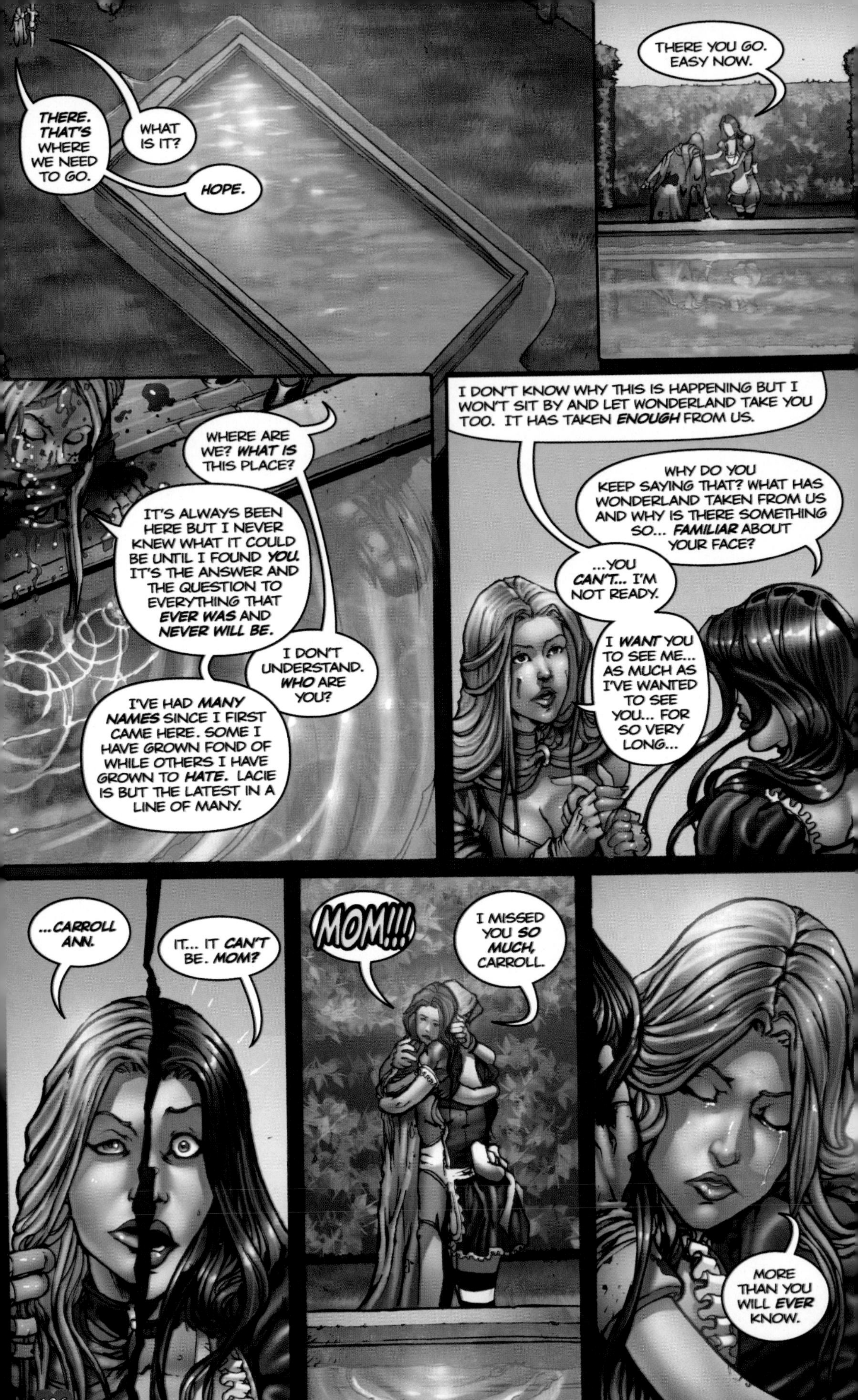
THERE. THAT'S WHERE WE NEED TO GO.
WHAT IS IT?
HOPE.
THERE YOU GO. EASY NOW.
WHERE ARE WE? WHAT IS THIS PLACE?
IT'S ALWAYS BEEN HERE BUT I NEVER KNEW WHAT IT COULD BE UNTIL I FOUND YOU. IT'S THE ANSWER AND THE QUESTION TO EVERYTHING THAT EVER WAS AND NEVER WILL BE.
I DON'T UNDERSTAND. WHO ARE YOU?
I'VE HAD MANY NAMES SINCE I FIRST CAME HERE. SOME I HAVE GROWN FOND OF WHILE OTHERS I HAVE GROWN TO HATE. LACIE IS BUT THE LATEST IN A LINE OF MANY.
I DON'T KNOW WHY THIS IS HAPPENING BUT I WON'T SIT BY AND LET WONDERLAND TAKE YOU TOO. IT HAS TAKEN ENOUGH FROM US.
WHY DO YOU KEEP SAYING THAT? WHAT HAS WONDERLAND TAKEN FROM US AND WHY IS THERE SOMETHING SO... FAMILIAR ABOUT YOUR FACE?
...YOU CAN'T... I'M NOT READY.
I WANT YOU TO SEE ME... AS MUCH AS I'VE WANTED TO SEE YOU... FOR SO VERY LONG...
...CARROLL ANN.
IT... IT CAN'T BE. MOM?
MOM!!!
I MISSED YOU SO MUCH, CARROLL.
MORE THAN YOU WILL EVER KNOW.

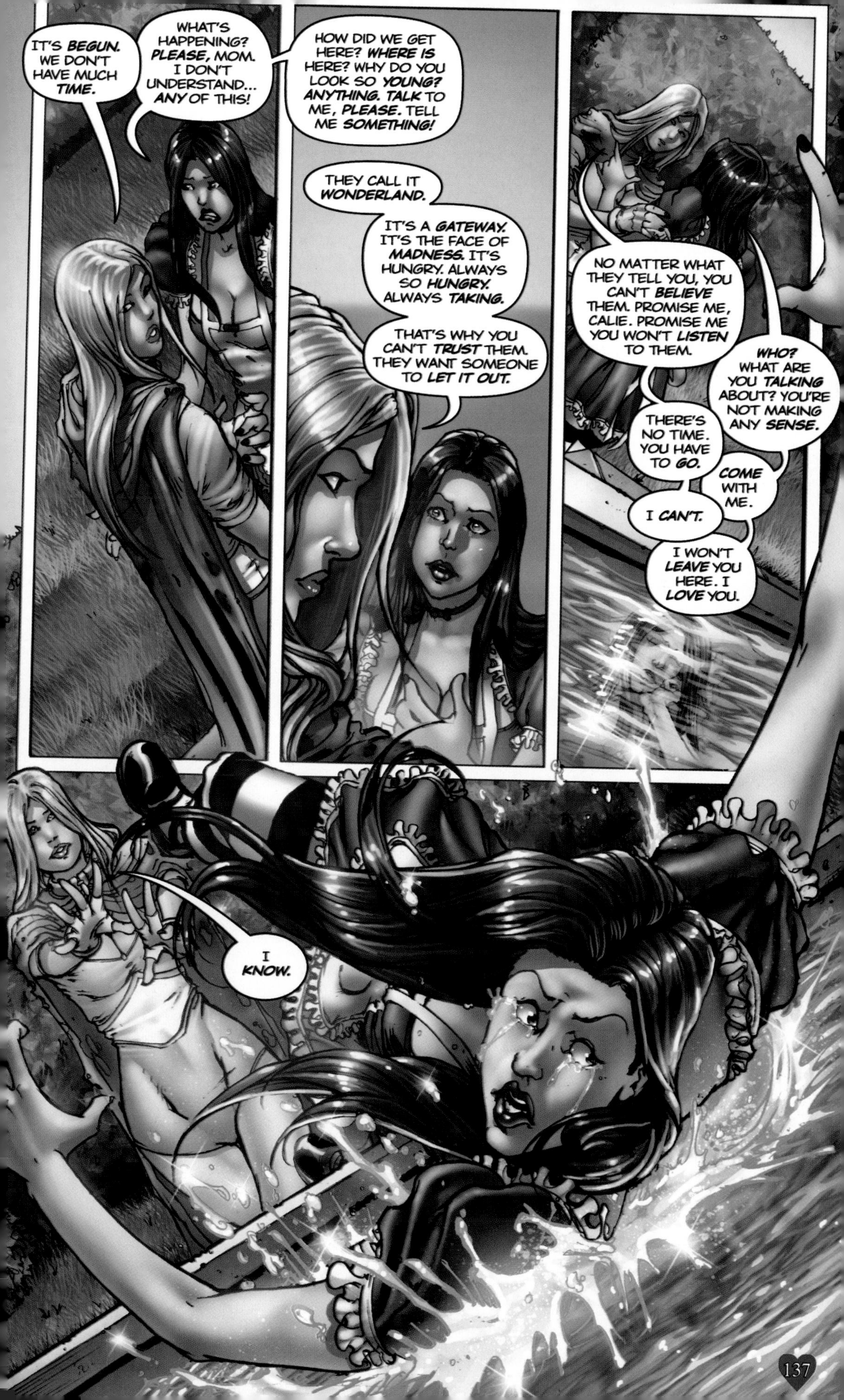
IT'S BEGUN. WE DON'T HAVE MUCH TIME.
WHAT'S HAPPENING? PLEASE, MOM. I DON'T UNDERSTAND... ANY OF THIS!
HOW DID WE GET HERE? WHERE IS HERE? WHY DO YOU LOOK SO YOUNG? ANYTHING. TALK TO ME, PLEASE. TELL ME SOMETHING!
THEY CALL IT WONDERLAND.
IT'S A GATEWAY. IT'S THE FACE OF MADNESS. IT'S HUNGRY. ALWAYS SO HUNGRY. ALWAYS TAKING.
THAT'S WHY YOU CAN'T TRUST THEM. THEY WANT SOMEONE TO LET IT OUT.
NO MATTER WHAT THEY TELL YOU, YOU CAN'T BELIEVE THEM. PROMISE ME, CALIE. PROMISE ME YOU WON'T LISTEN TO THEM.
WHO? WHAT ARE YOU TALKING ABOUT? YOU'RE NOT MAKING ANY SENSE.
THERE'S NO TIME. YOU HAVE TO GO.
COME WITH ME.
I CAN'T.
I WON'T LEAVE YOU HERE. I LOVE YOU.
I KNOW.

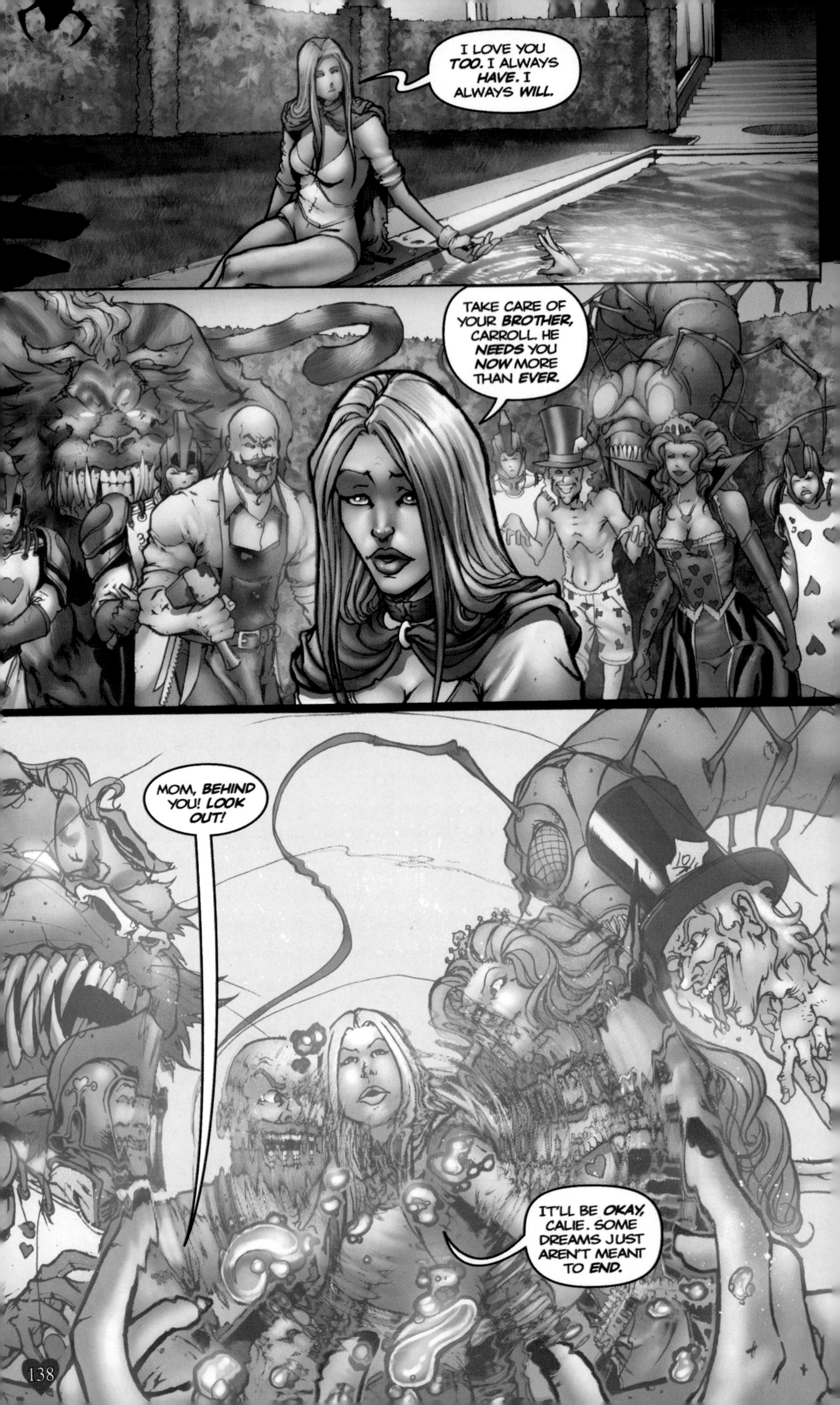
I LOVE YOU TOO. I ALWAYS HAVE. I ALWAYS WILL.
TAKE CARE OF YOUR BROTHER, CARROLL. HE NEEDS YOU NOW MORE THAN EVER.
MOM, BEHIND YOU! LOOK OUT!
IT'LL BE OKAY, CALIE. SOME DREAMS JUST AREN'T MEANT TO END.

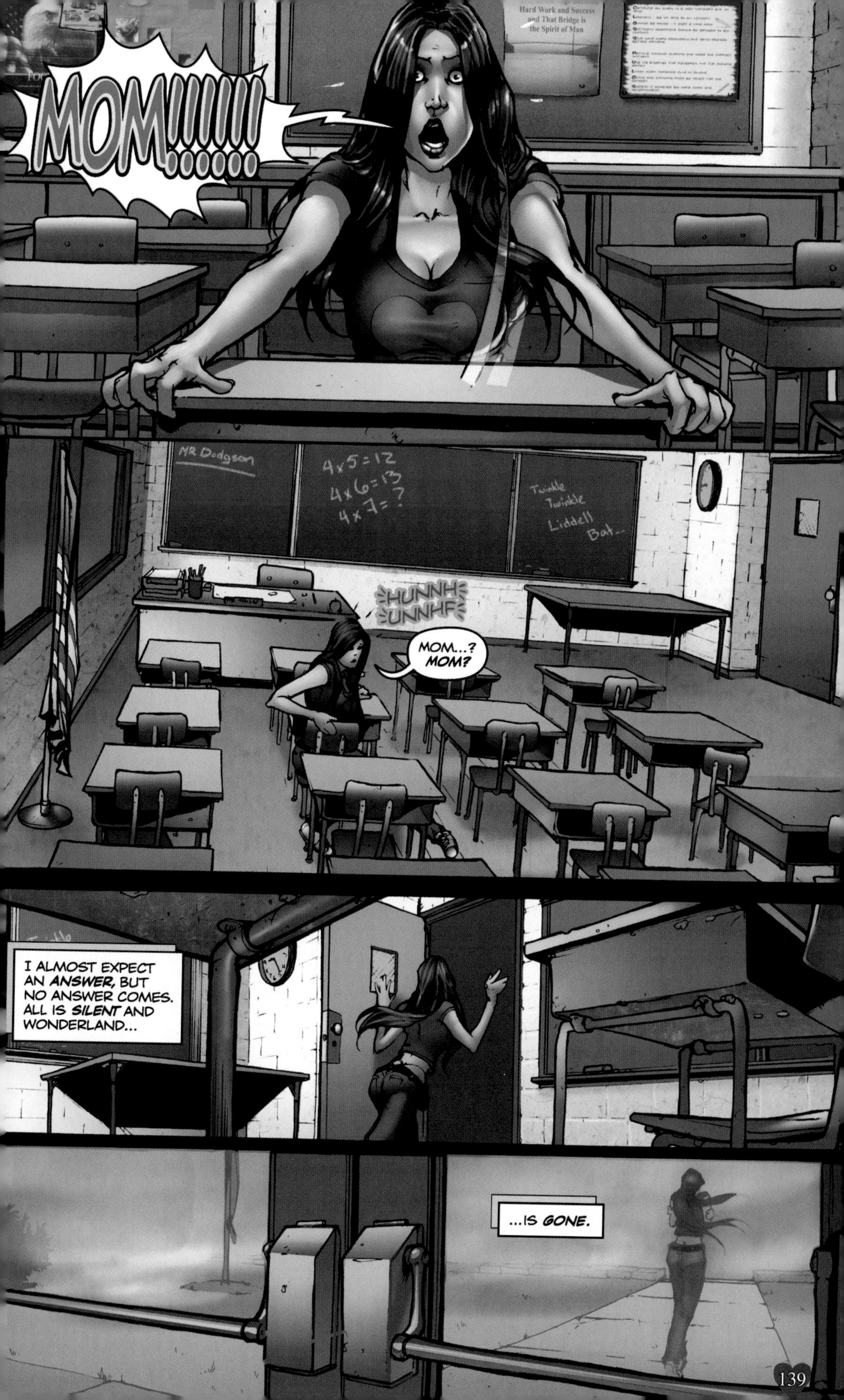
Hard Work and Success
and That Bridge is
the Spirit of Man
MOM!!!!!!!.......
MR Dodgson
4x5=12
4x6=13
4x7=?
Twinkle
Twinkle
Liddell
Bat...
HUNNH
UNNHF
MOM...?
MOM?
I ALMOST EXPECT AN ANSWER, BUT NO ANSWER COMES. ALL IS SILENT AND WONDERLAND...
...IS GONE.

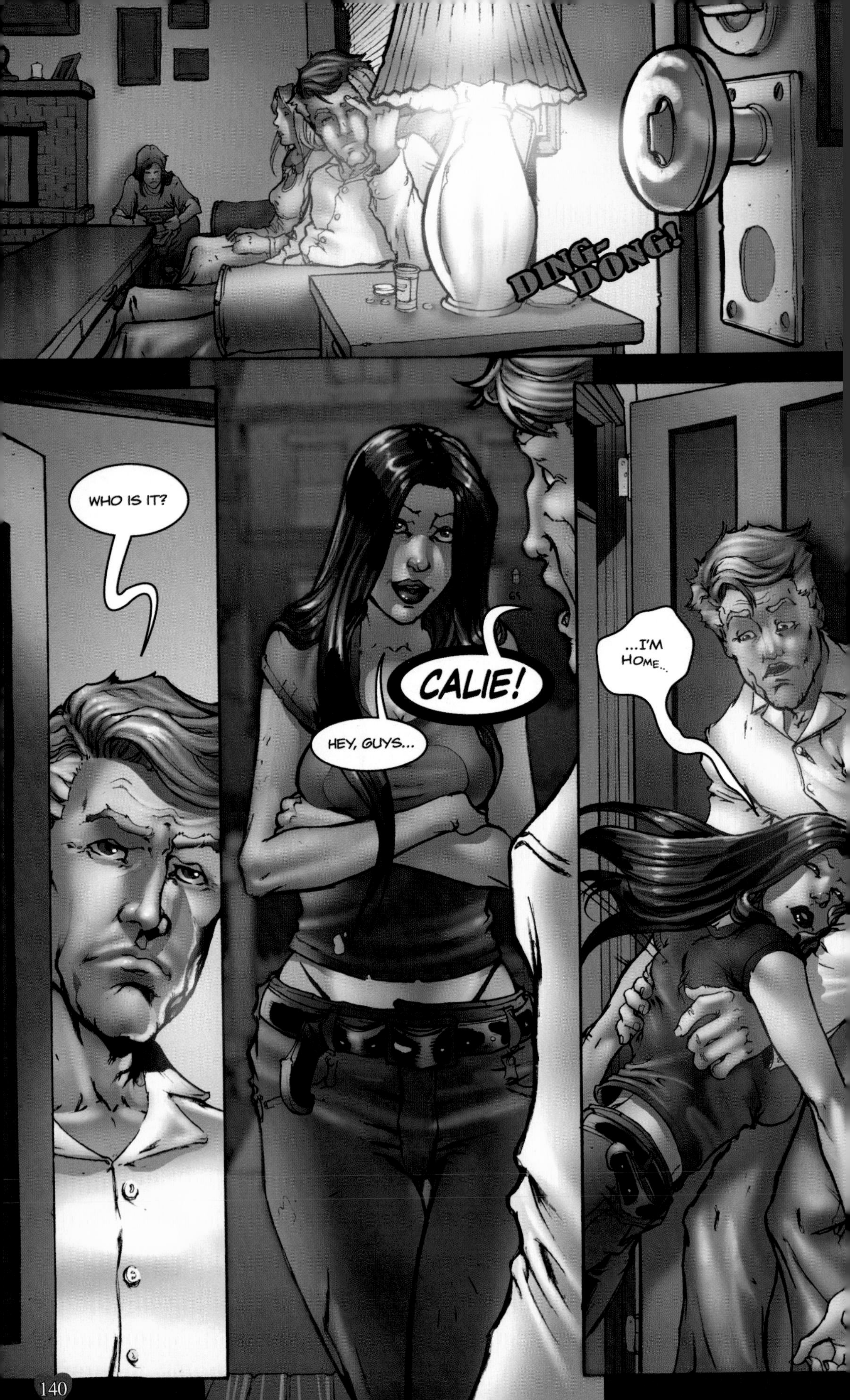
DING-DONG!
WHO IS IT?
CALIE!
HEY, GUYS...
...I'M HOME...

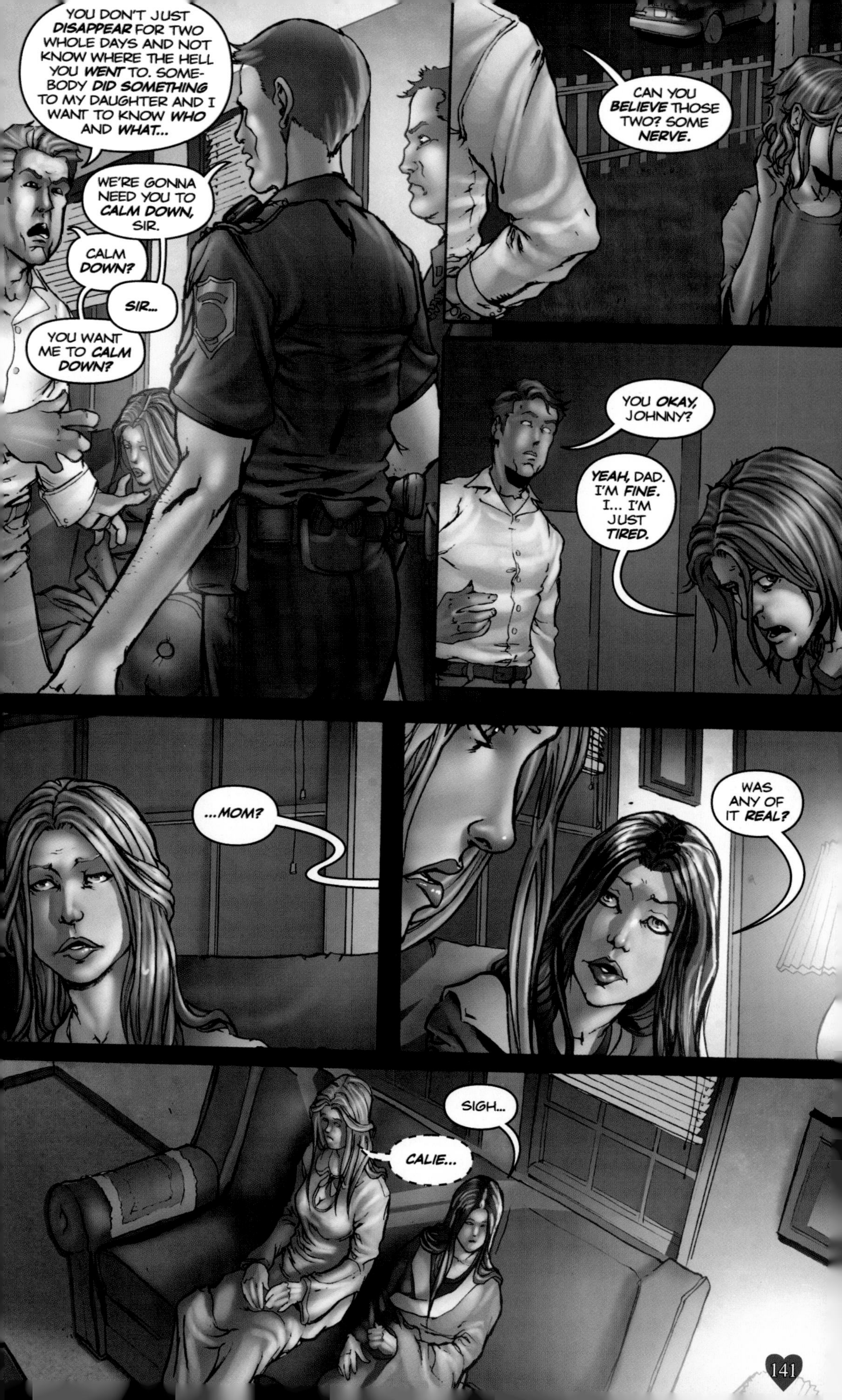

YOU DON'T JUST DISAPPEAR FOR TWO WHOLE DAYS AND NOT KNOW WHERE THE HELL YOU WENT TO. SOMEBODY DID SOMETHING TO MY DAUGHTER AND I WANT TO KNOW WHO AND WHAT...
WE'RE GONNA NEED YOU TO CALM DOWN, SIR.
CALM DOWN?
SIR...
YOU WANT ME TO CALM DOWN?
CAN YOU BELIEVE THOSE TWO? SOME NERVE.
YOU OKAY, JOHNNY?
YEAH, DAD. I'M FINE. I... I'M JUST TIRED.
...MOM?
WAS ANY OF IT REAL?
SIGH...
CALIE...

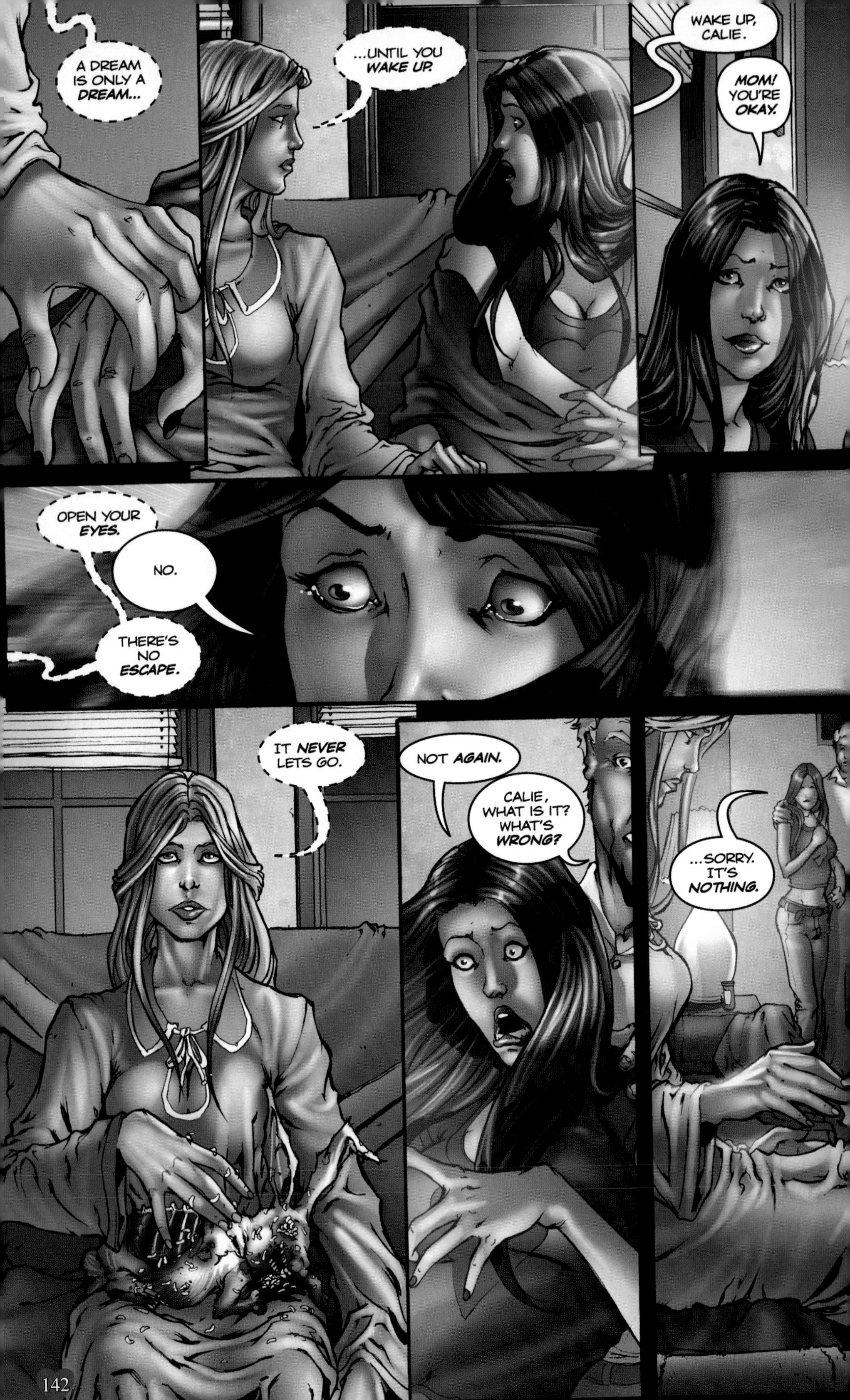
A DREAM IS ONLY A DREAM...
...UNTIL YOU WAKE UP.
WAKE UP, CALIE.
MOM! YOU'RE OKAY.
OPEN YOUR EYES.
NO.
THERE'S NO ESCAPE.
IT NEVER LETS GO.
NOT AGAIN.
CALIE, WHAT IS IT? WHAT'S WRONG?
...SORRY. IT'S NOTHING.

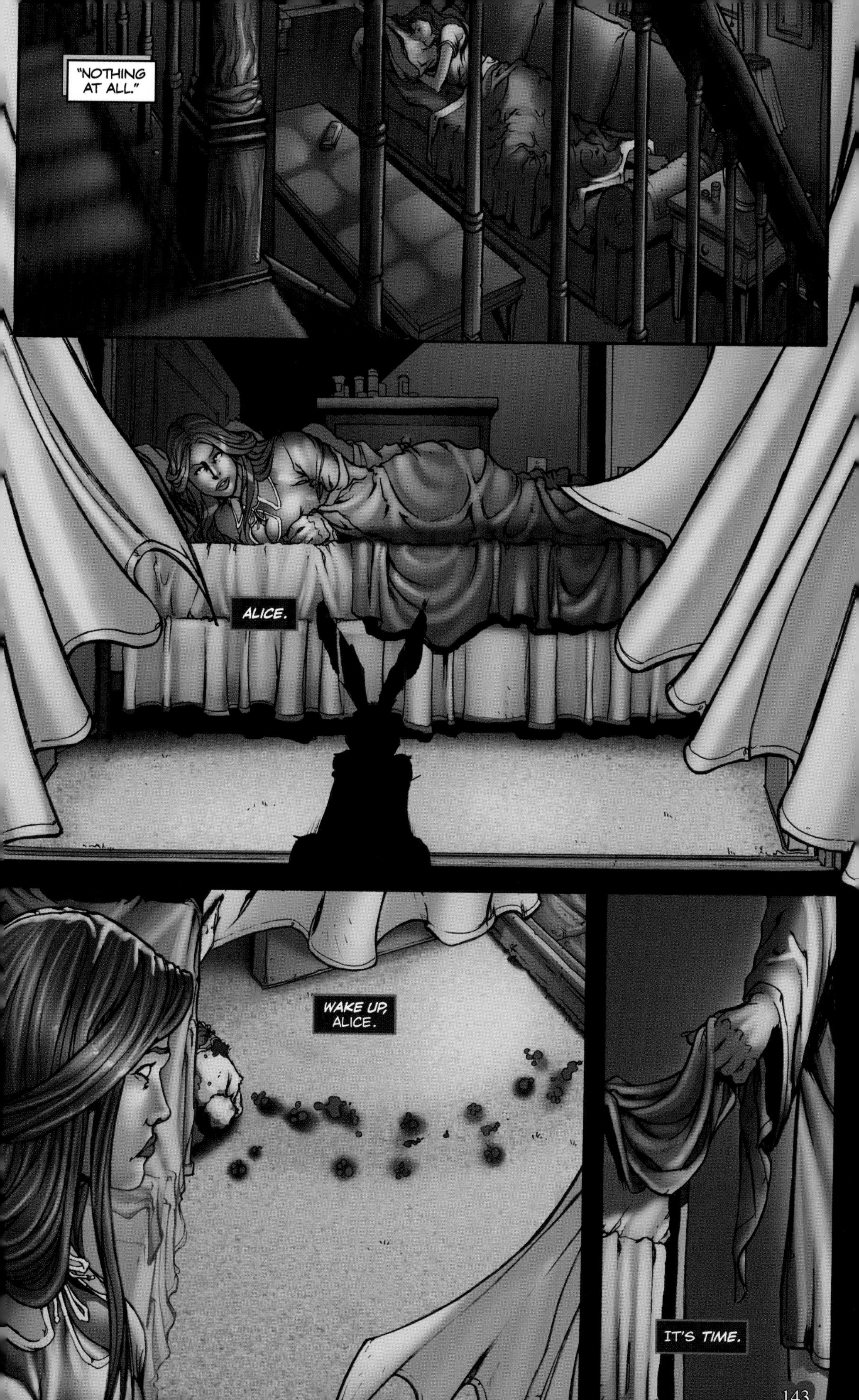
"NOTHING AT ALL."
ALICE.
WAKE UP, ALICE.
IT'S TIME.

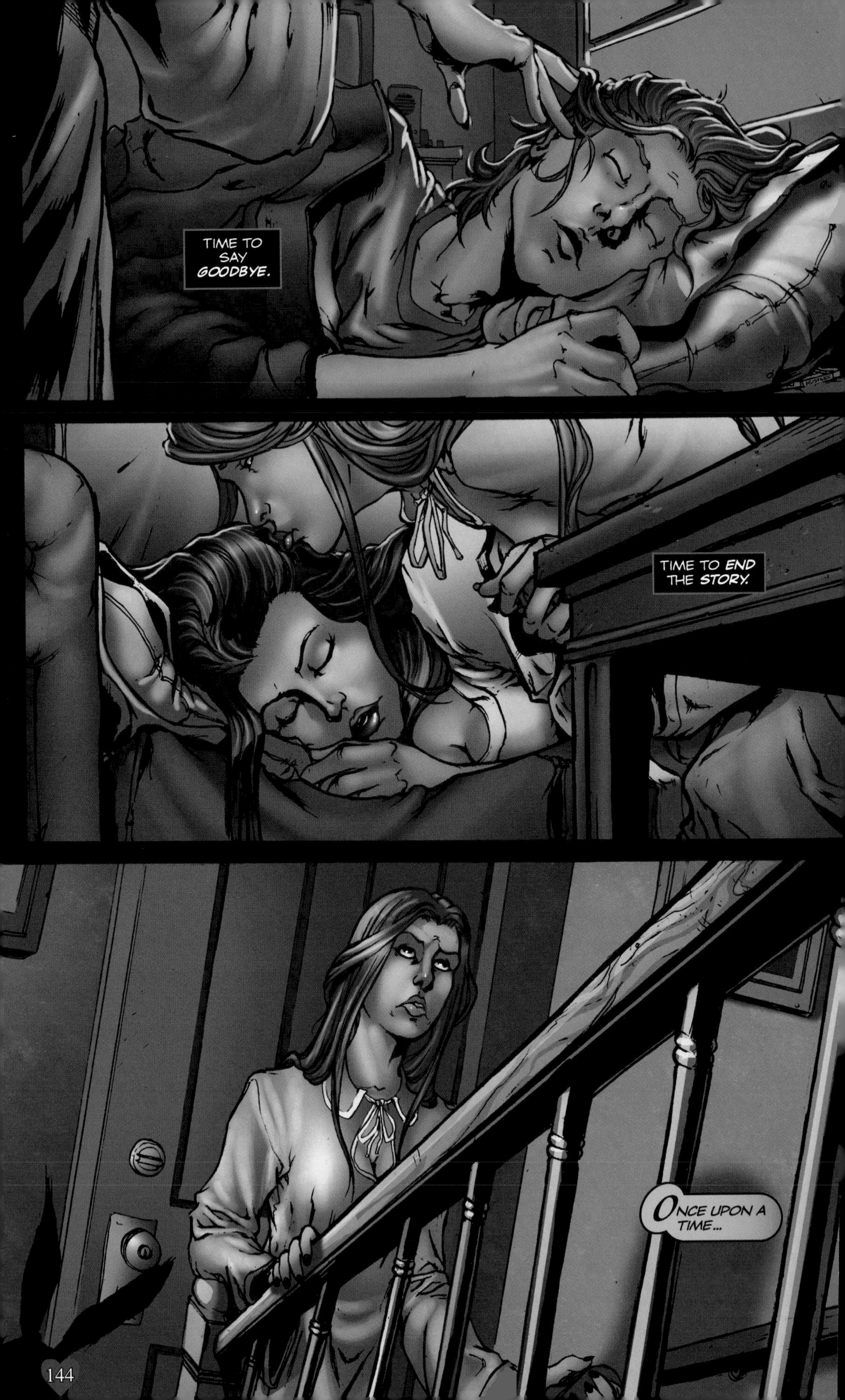
TIME TO SAY GOODBYE.
TIME TO END THE STORY.
ONCE UPON A TIME...

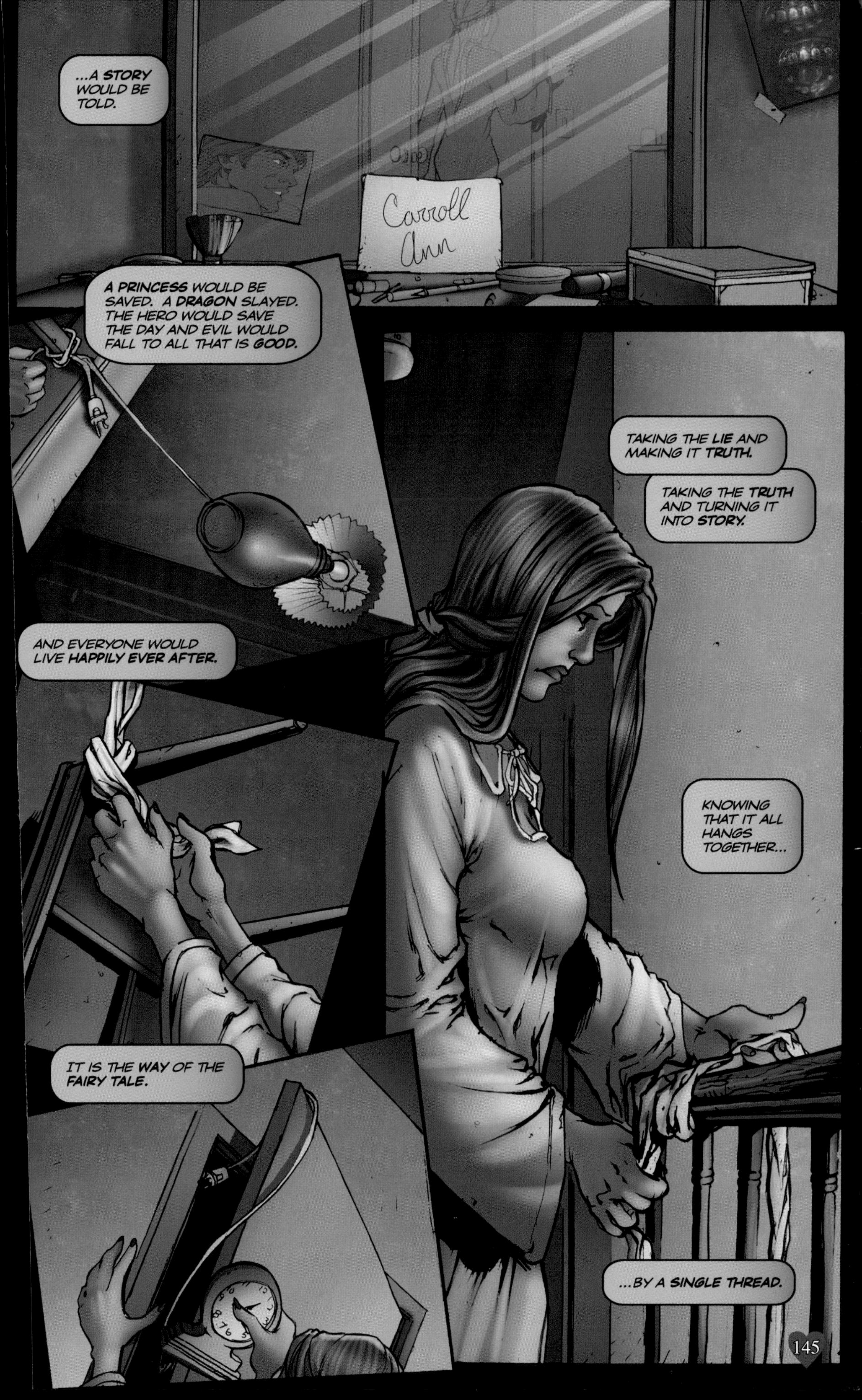

...A STORY WOULD BE TOLD.
Carroll Ann
A PRINCESS WOULD BE SAVED. A DRAGON SLAYED. THE HERO WOULD SAVE THE DAY AND EVIL WOULD FALL TO ALL THAT IS GOOD.
TAKING THE LIE AND MAKING IT TRUTH.
TAKING THE TRUTH AND TURNING IT INTO STORY.
AND EVERYONE WOULD LIVE HAPPILY EVER AFTER.
KNOWING THAT IT ALL HANGS TOGETHER...
IT IS THE WAY OF THE FAIRY TALE.
...BY A SINGLE THREAD.

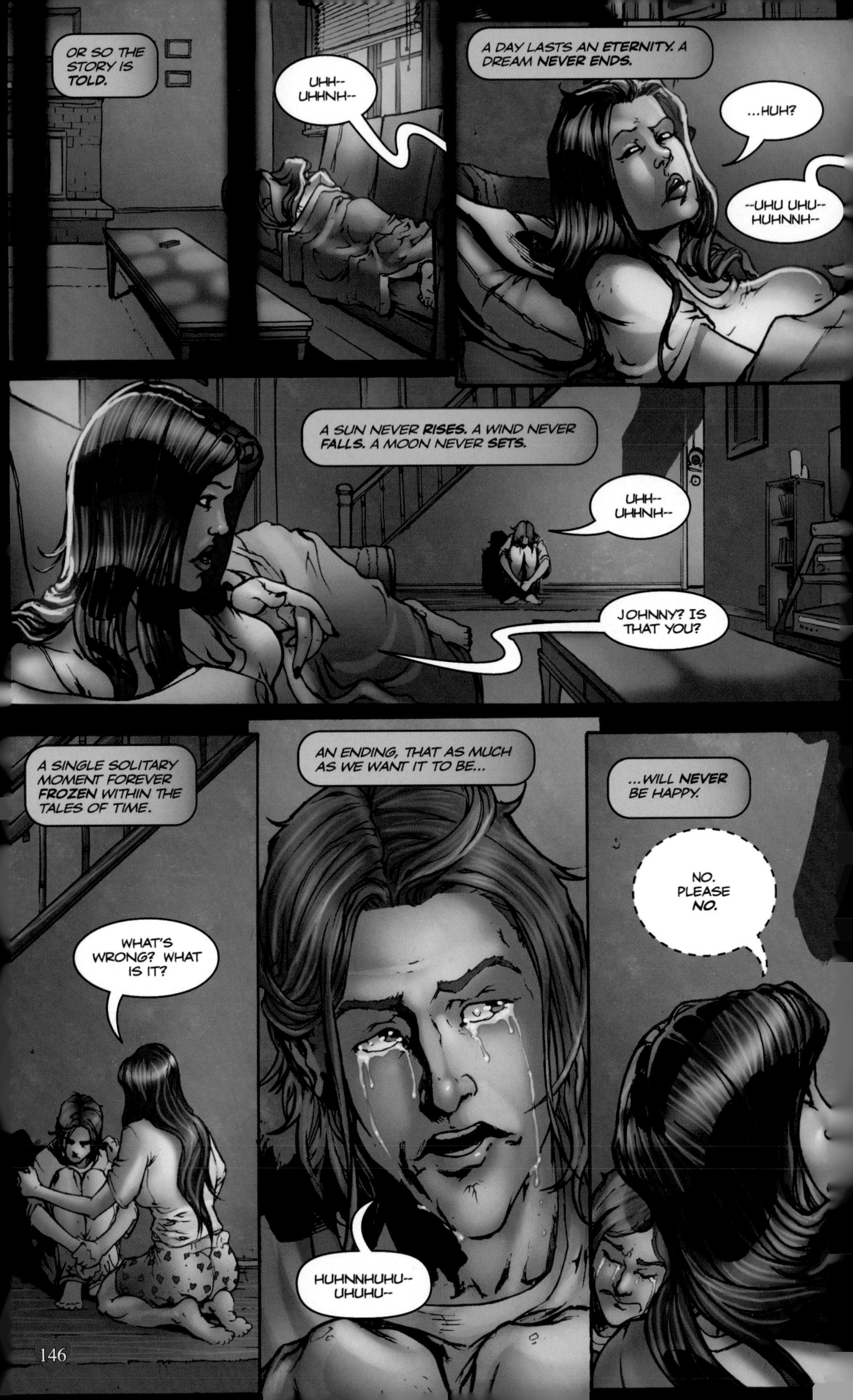

OR SO THE STORY IS TOLD.
UHH-- UHHNH--
A DAY LASTS AN ETERNITY. A DREAM NEVER ENDS.
...HUH?
--UHU UHU-- HUHNNH--
A SUN NEVER RISES. A WIND NEVER FALLS. A MOON NEVER SETS.
UHH-- UHHNH--
JOHNNY? IS THAT YOU?
A SINGLE SOLITARY MOMENT FOREVER FROZEN WITHIN THE TALES OF TIME.
WHAT'S WRONG? WHAT IS IT?
AN ENDING, THAT AS MUCH AS WE WANT IT TO BE...
HUHNNHUHU-- UHUHU--
...WILL NEVER BE HAPPY.
NO. PLEASE NO.

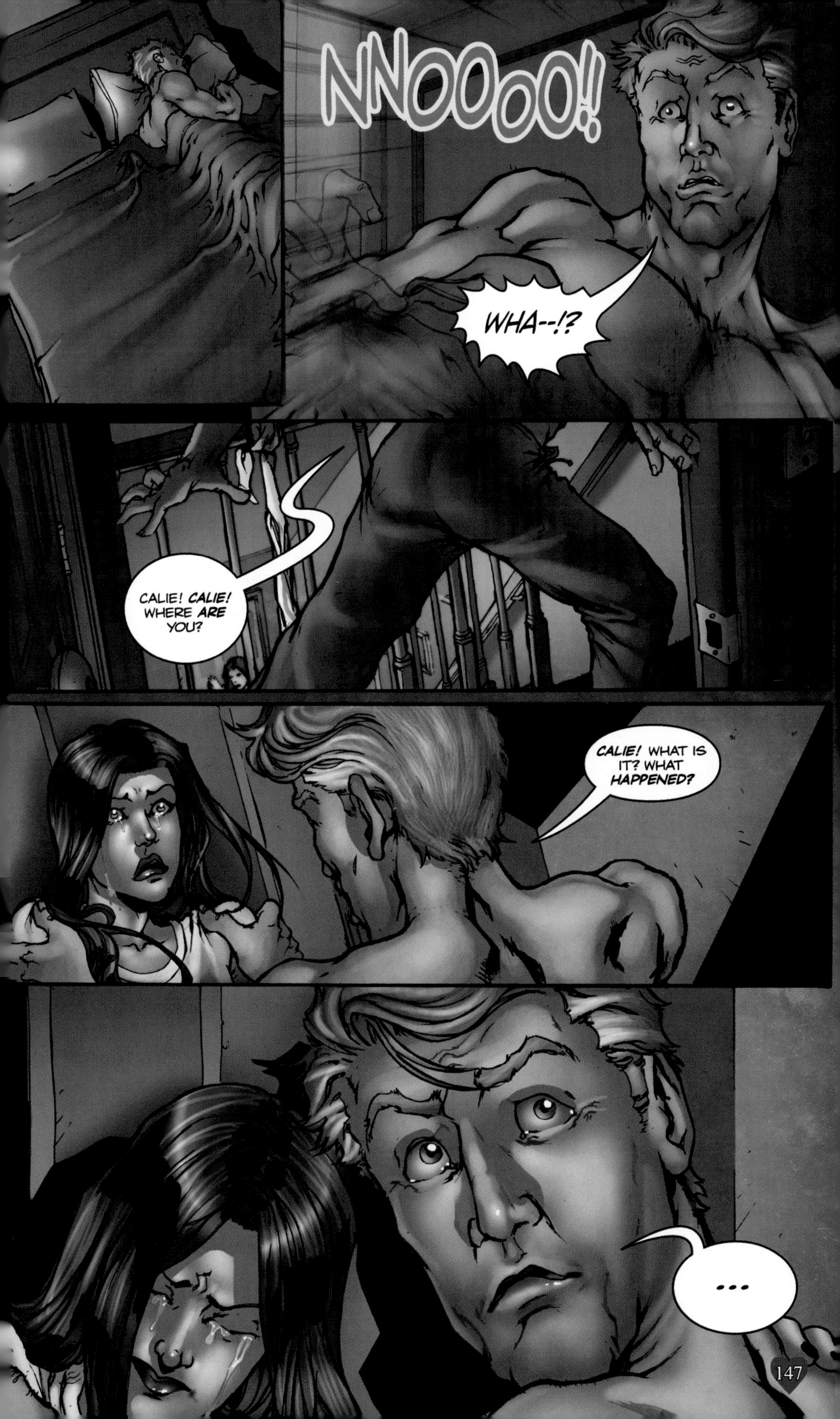
NNOOOOO!!
WHA--!?
CALIE! CALIE! WHERE ARE YOU?
CALIE! WHAT IS IT? WHAT HAPPENED?
...

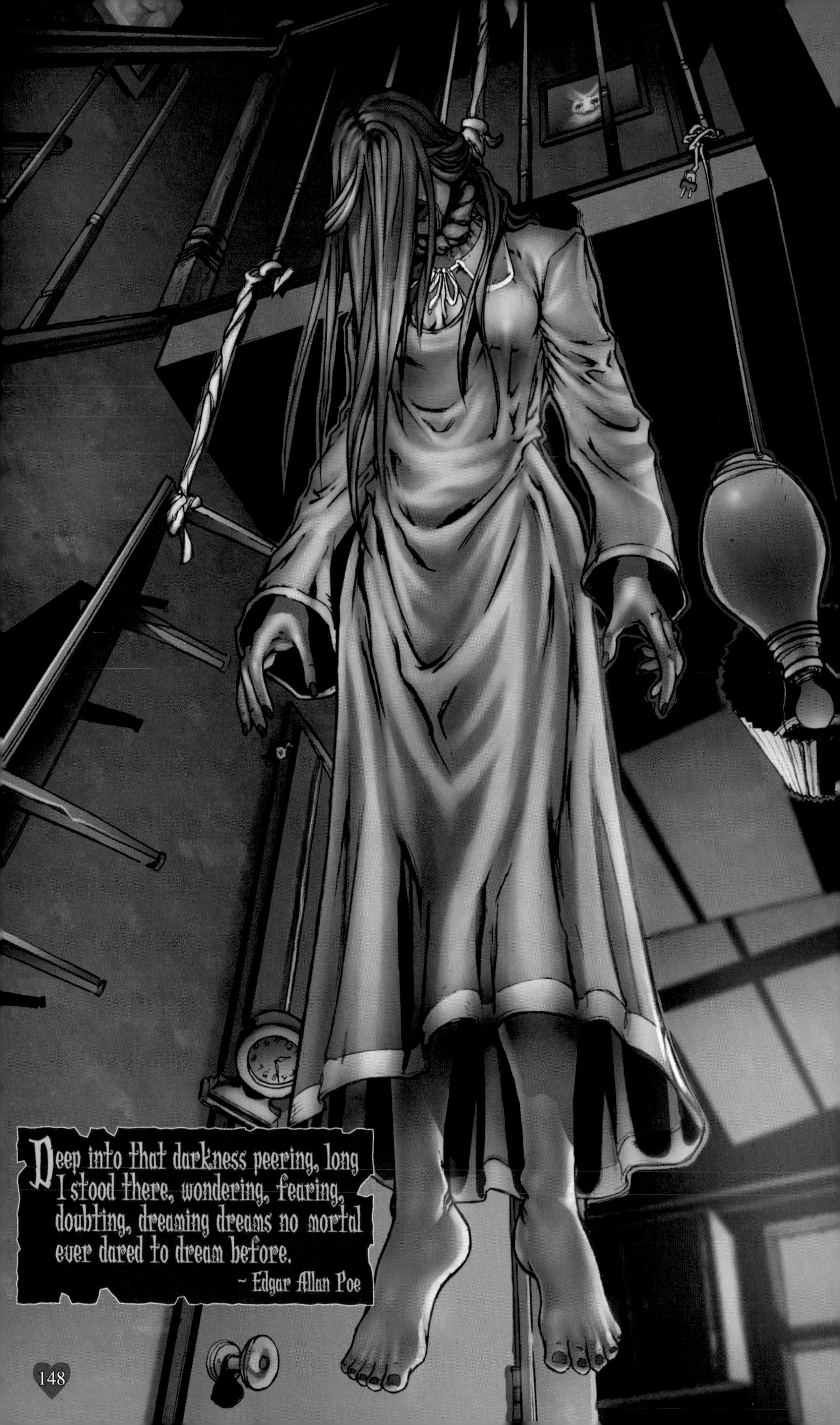
Deep into that darkness peering, long I stood there, wondering, fearing, doubting, dreaming dreams no mortal ever dared to dream before.
~ Edgar Allan Poe

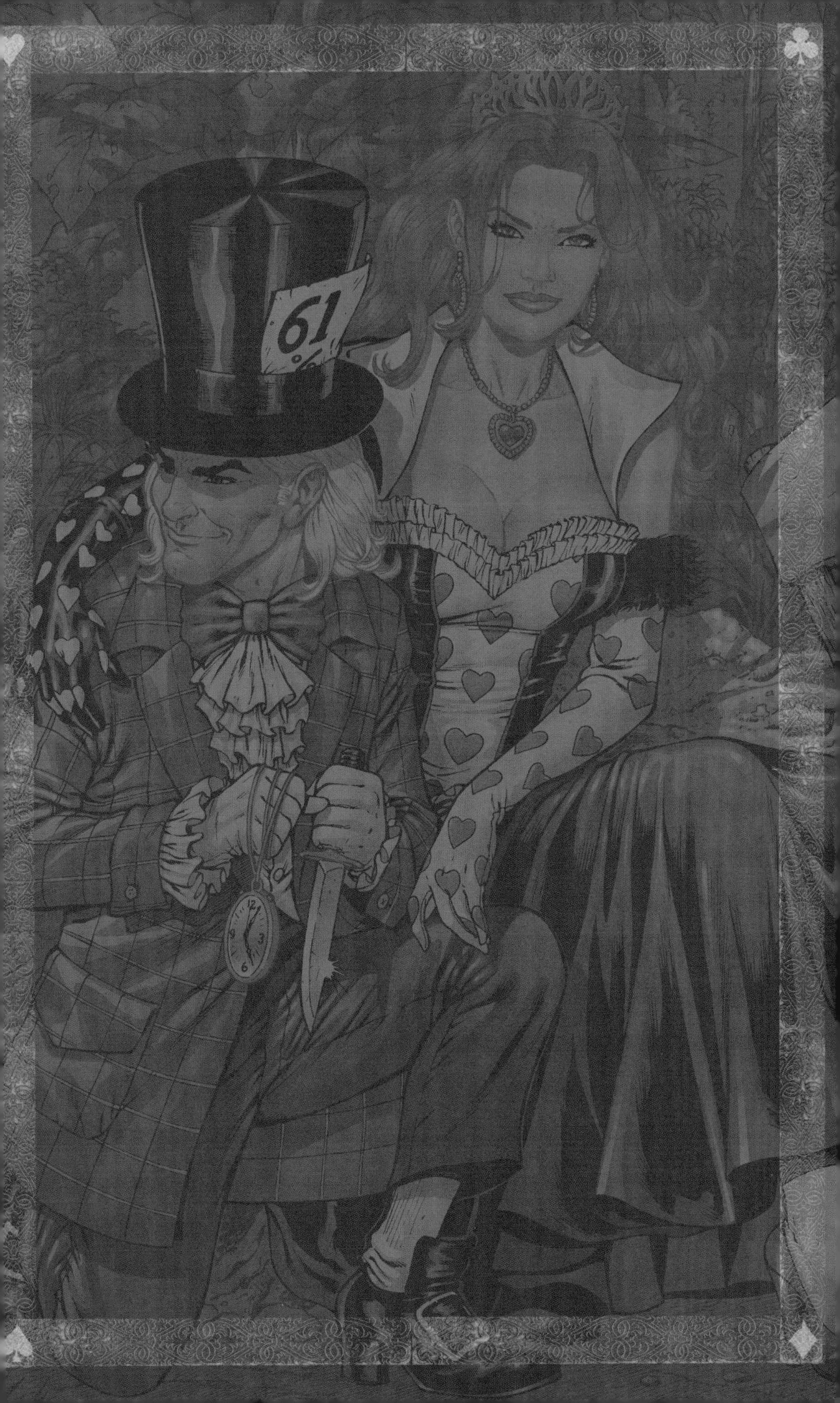
61

Johnny's Blog

26 March 2007
Backgrounds! Ha Ha very funny!

So after weeks of my sister Calie, and my girlfriend Megan persistent protests to join up on myspace here I am. Now if someone can please show me how to change my background I'd really appreciate it. Ha ha, Calie. Very fucking funny. Smart ass. I'm surprised you didn't throw in a few cute cuddly puppies. I should have known better than to let you set this shit up for me. By the way, I emailed Brandon pictures of you before you dyed your hair black. You know the ones where you have on the glasses and look like something straight out of the Brady (does that show even come on anymore) Bunch. You know, your pre wanna be alternative goth phase. I do hope you realize that this means war:)

28 March 2007
Endings

Megan broke up with me today. She told me she just wants to be friends. Bitch. I can't even bring myself to hate her. I wish I could just disappear. I'm going to the baseball game with my dad tomorrow. A fun filled day of pretending to give a shit about people trying to hit a ball with a piece of wood. Anything more mundane and I'd be in a boredom induced coma. sigh. Maybe it'll take my mind off things.

29 March 2007
Erase me

I erased the pictures of you off my computer today. Sent them to recycle. A click of a button and the images disappear into the emptiness of that section of cyberspace where unwanted things go. The pictures we took at the mall. The ones where you kissed my lips and held me close are burning in an ashtray as we speak. The smoke drifts out on a silent breeze as your face turns black and smog like gray. The ashes are carried away to the place where all memories eventually fade to dust in the wind. If only it was so easy to erase the memory of you from my mind. Erase all that is me so that none of you remains. Cut out all the pain and misery you have left me with so that what was is all that remains instead of what never will be. I want to forget you. Forget everything you ever were to me. I want to move on and not be held down by the memory that is you.

29 March 2007
Missing in action

My sister ran off who knows where. Like I really need this shit right now. Mom's been acting weirder than she normal does. We found her in the basement today after the game. Calie wasn't here.

30 March 2007
Still missing

Calie's still gone. Dad's getting worried about her. I'm getting worried too. I know I give her a lot of shit but whenever shit hit the fan she's always been there for me. After mom lost it...well...anyway... She doesn't usually pull this kinda shit. Even her boy toy Brandon doesn't know where she's at. Dad's been calling all her friends all day trying to find her. I'm gonna head out in a little bit and see if I can find her myself.

About me

Email me

People I
don't mind

Calie
Beth
Eric
Chiodos
Linda Ly
~I Am Who I Am~
Jenna
The one and only
Raven Gregory
Nei
RTeddy
Dingo
BENDIS!
Warren Ellis
Wonderland
Kat Von D
Enter Shikari
Seidman
Dane

Johnny's Blog

30 March 2007
HURT HURT HURT HURT HURT HURT HURT

I couldn't find Calie. I...I couldn't. But I found...
I found out that this world is an ugly and dirty place. It's filled with horrible ugly people. People who wear masks to trick you into thinking they're safe when in reality they are all waiting to betray you. It's hurts. I want to hurt it back. My head won't stop hurting. It only stops when...

01 April 2007
Homecoming

Calie came home today. She said she doesn't remember what happened or where she went. She said it's all a blur. My head still hurts. It gets hard to think at times. Sometimes I think I might be losing my mind. I keep seeing strange shadows. Hearing things...things that can't be there. It's happening again. Just like before when mom tried to kill herself. The...the shadow...it's back. It's back again. Or maybe it's just the stress. I've been really stressed out lately. Yeah...that's probably it.

01 April 2007
I wonder

It's getting late and it's been a long day. What with Calie coming home and dealing with the cops and all that stuff. And no I'm not losing my mind. Just think the stress has been getting to me lately. But that's not what I wanted to talk about. What I wanted to talk about was this...
How do you know I am who I say I am? Just because I say my name is Johnny Liddle does that really prove anything? Just because you can click on pictures of me does that make me really there on the other end of the screen? How do you know I'm even real? How do you even know I even exist? Just because I say I do. Is that really enough for you to believe in me? Maybe someone made me up? Maybe I'm some serial myspace killer looking for some innocent underage victim with whom I want to get on prime time television with. Maybe, just maybe, I'm nothing more than a dream. A character in someone else's story. Sometimes I wonder. What's real and what's really real?

02 April 2007
My mom is dead.

...

05 April 2007
Ever after

The shadow is back. Everything hurts. I miss my mom. It's all his fault. I know it is. I have nothing. No one. Nothing left but the hurt and the hurt and the hurt and shadows. Wait, no, that's not right. I still have my sister. She's the only one I have left. The only one I can trust. She's the only one who's still there for me. My Calie. At least I have her.

About me

Email me

People I
don't mind

Calie
Beth
Eric
Chiodos
Linda Ly
~I Am Who I Am~
Jenna
The one and only
Raven Gregory
Nei
RTeddy
Dingo
BENDIS!
Warren Ellis
Wonderland
Kat Von D
Enter Shikari
Seidman
Dane

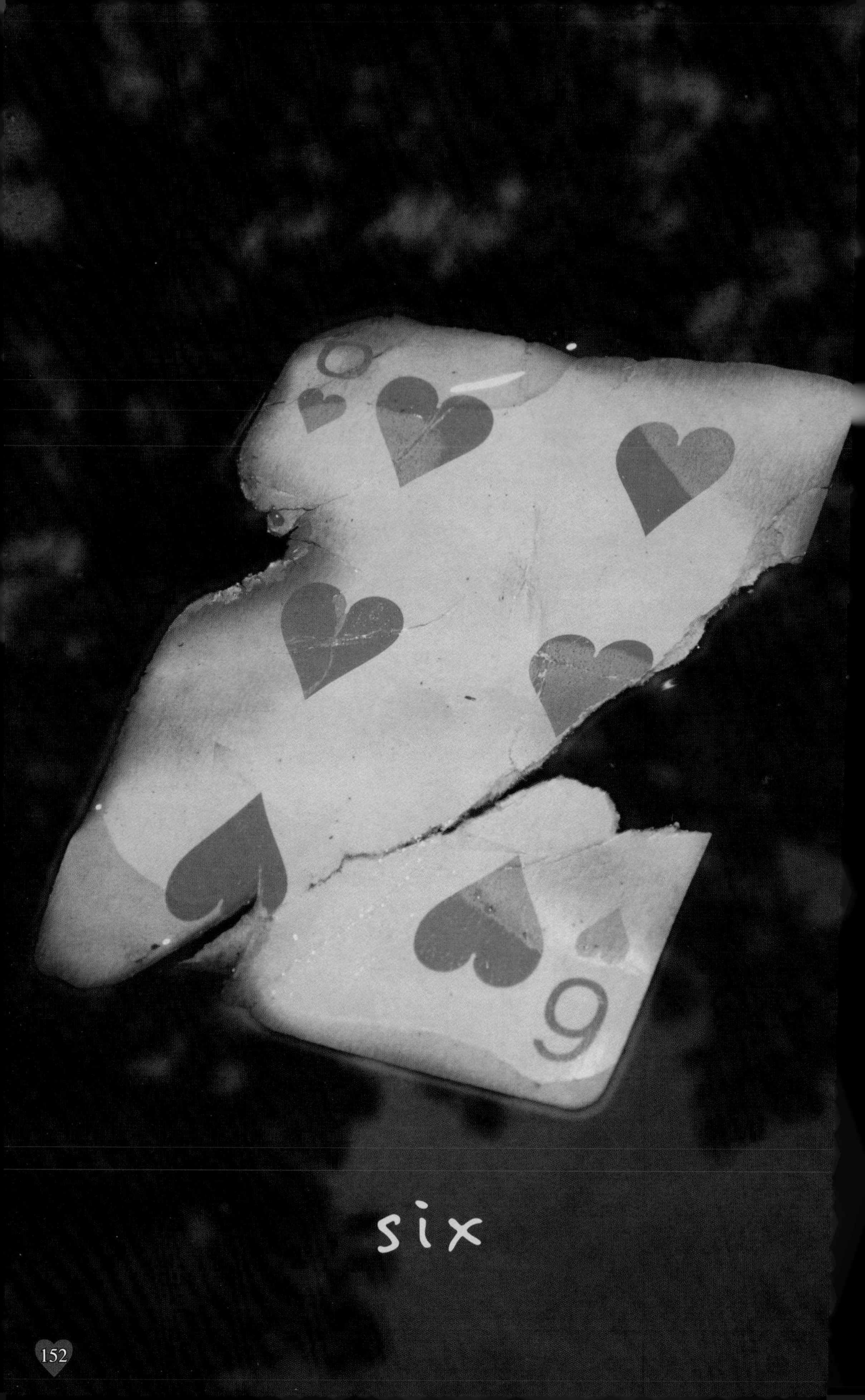

six

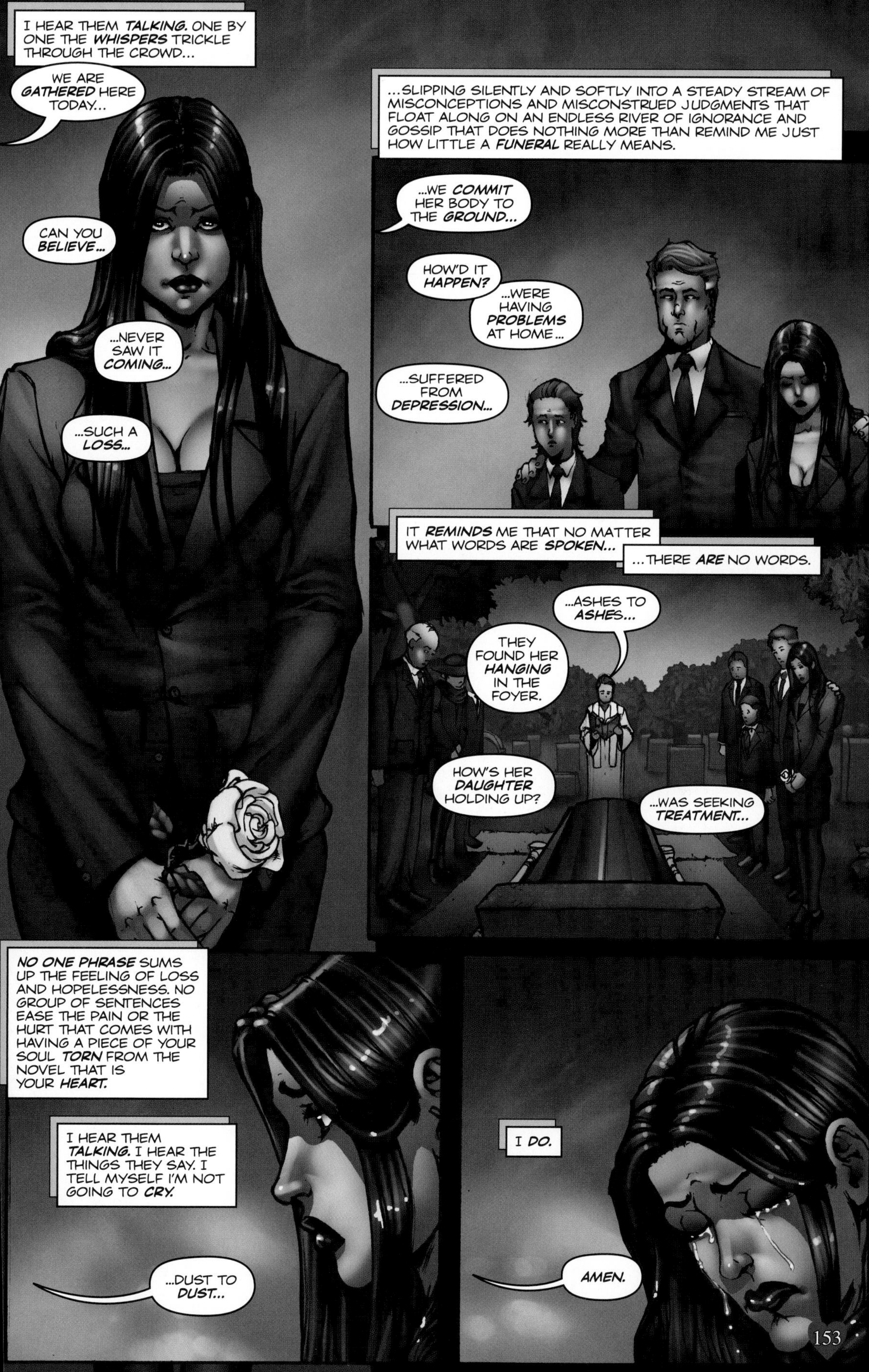

I HEAR THEM TALKING. ONE BY ONE THE WHISPERS TRICKLE THROUGH THE CROWD...
WE ARE GATHERED HERE TODAY...
CAN YOU BELIEVE...
...NEVER SAW IT COMING...
...SUCH A LOSS...
...SLIPPING SILENTLY AND SOFTLY INTO A STEADY STREAM OF MISCONCEPTIONS AND MISCONSTRUED JUDGMENTS THAT FLOAT ALONG ON AN ENDLESS RIVER OF IGNORANCE AND GOSSIP THAT DOES NOTHING MORE THAN REMIND ME JUST HOW LITTLE A FUNERAL REALLY MEANS.
...WE COMMIT HER BODY TO THE GROUND...
HOW'D IT HAPPEN?
...WERE HAVING PROBLEMS AT HOME...
...SUFFERED FROM DEPRESSION...
IT REMINDS ME THAT NO MATTER WHAT WORDS ARE SPOKEN...
...THERE ARE NO WORDS.
...ASHES TO ASHES...
THEY FOUND HER HANGING IN THE FOYER.
HOW'S HER DAUGHTER HOLDING UP?
...WAS SEEKING TREATMENT...
NO ONE PHRASE SUMS UP THE FEELING OF LOSS AND HOPELESSNESS. NO GROUP OF SENTENCES EASE THE PAIN OR THE HURT THAT COMES WITH HAVING A PIECE OF YOUR SOUL TORN FROM THE NOVEL THAT IS YOUR HEART.
I HEAR THEM TALKING. I HEAR THE THINGS THEY SAY. I TELL MYSELF I'M NOT GOING TO CRY.
...DUST TO DUST...
I DO.
AMEN.

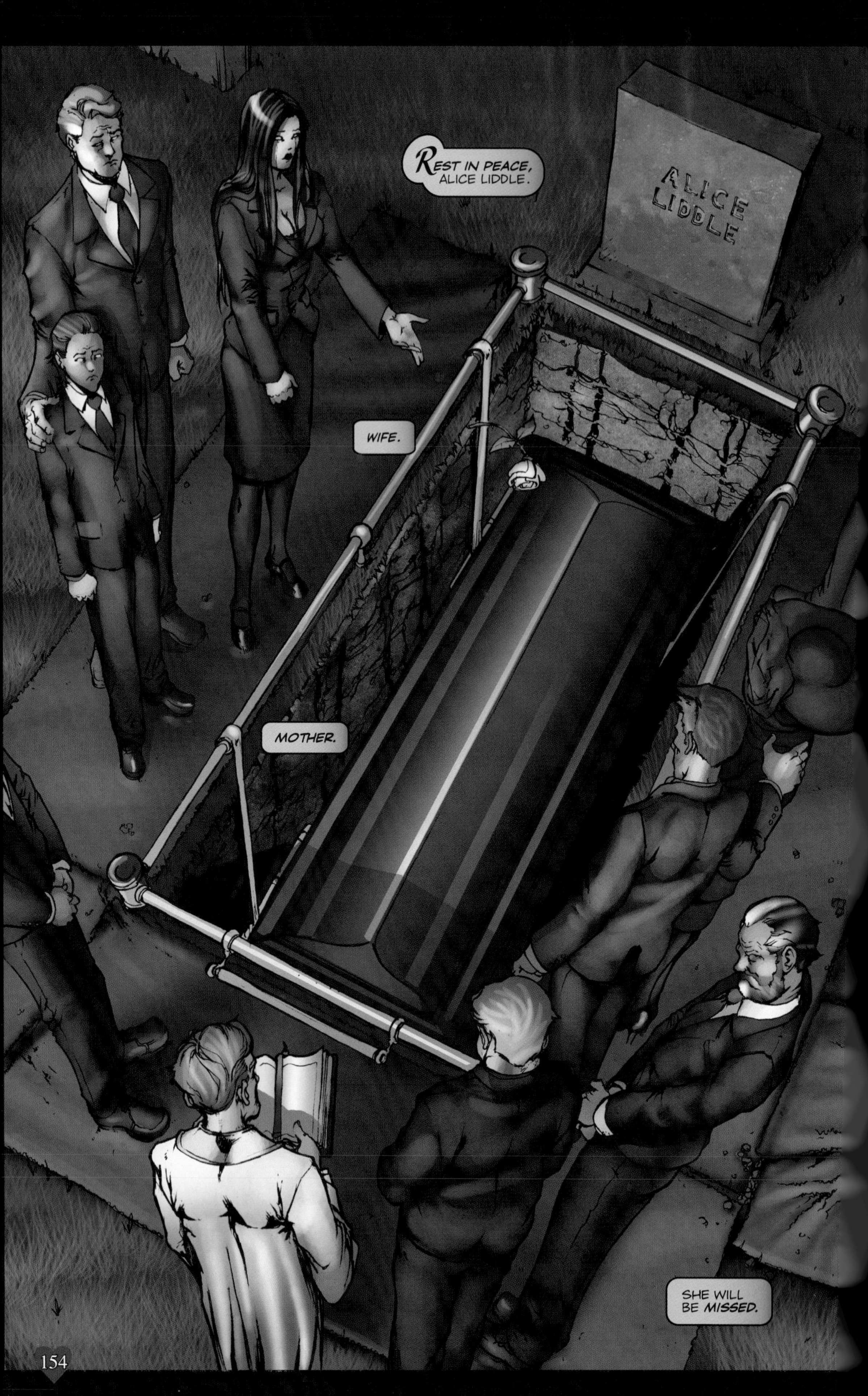
REST IN PEACE, ALICE LIDDLE.
ALICE LIDDLE
WIFE.
MOTHER.
SHE WILL BE MISSED.

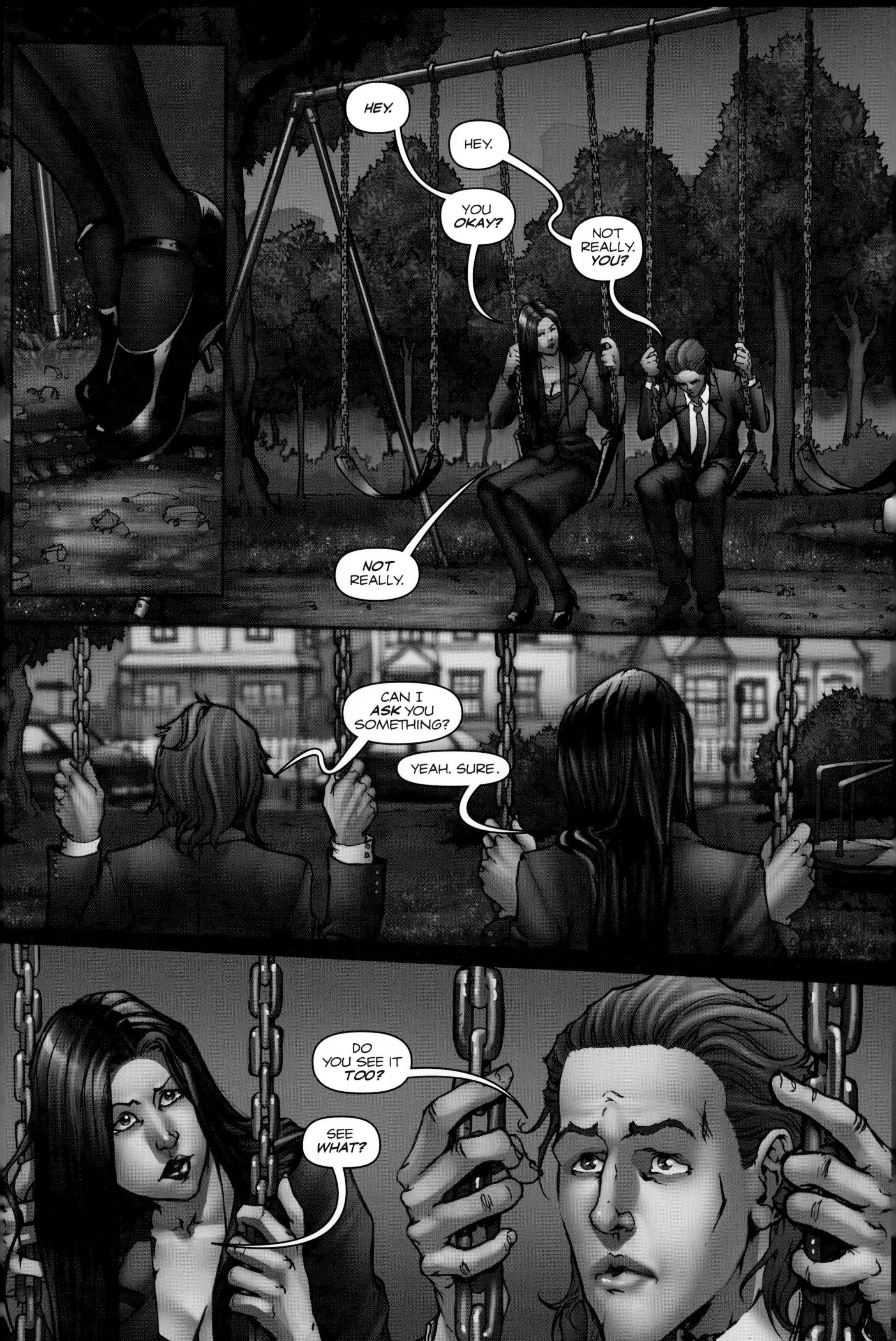
HEY.
HEY.
YOU OKAY?
NOT REALLY. YOU?
NOT REALLY.
CAN I ASK YOU SOMETHING?
YEAH. SURE.
DO YOU SEE IT TOO?
SEE WHAT?

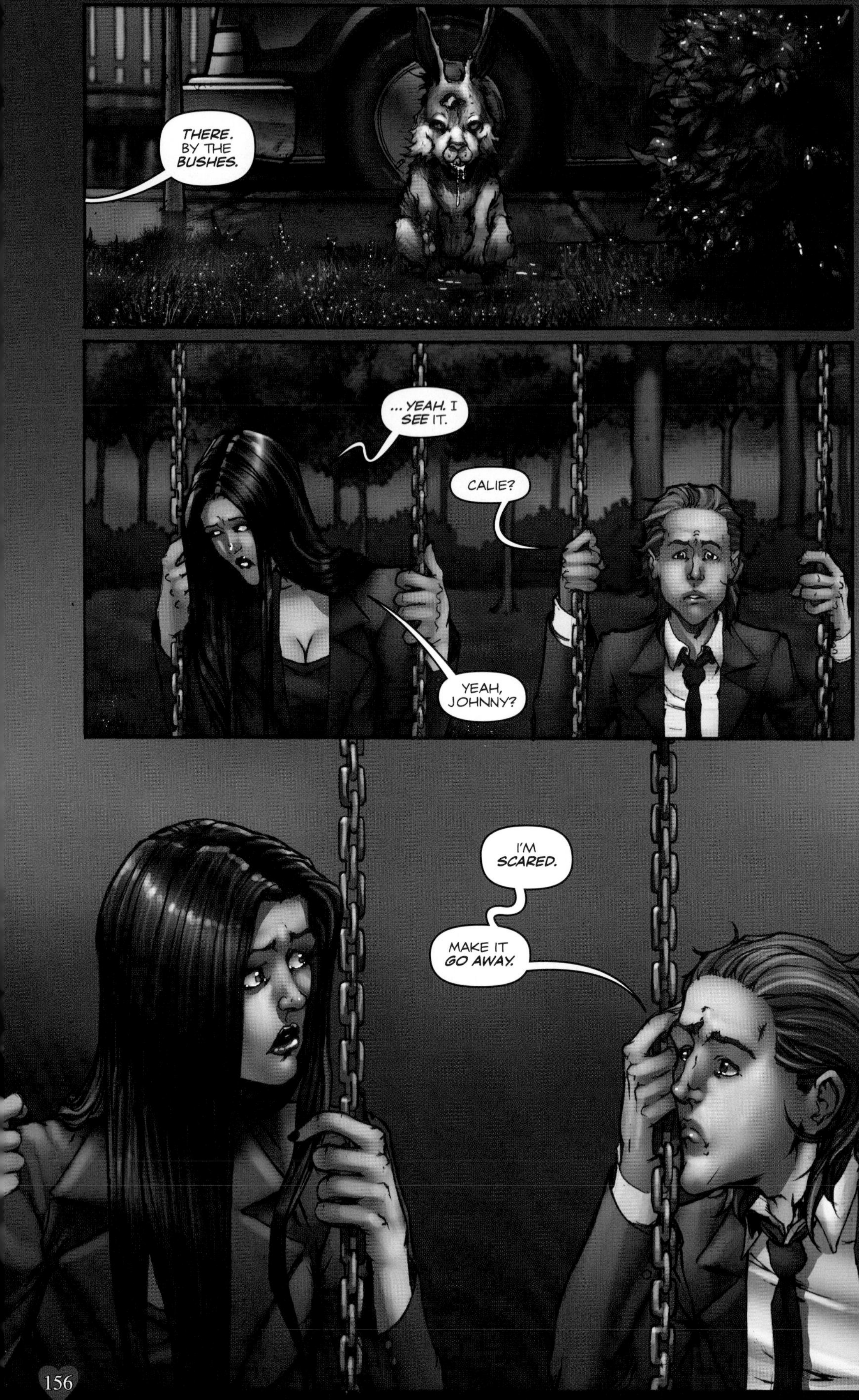
THERE. BY THE BUSHES.
...YEAH. I SEE IT.
CALIE?
YEAH, JOHNNY?
I'M SCARED.
MAKE IT GO AWAY.

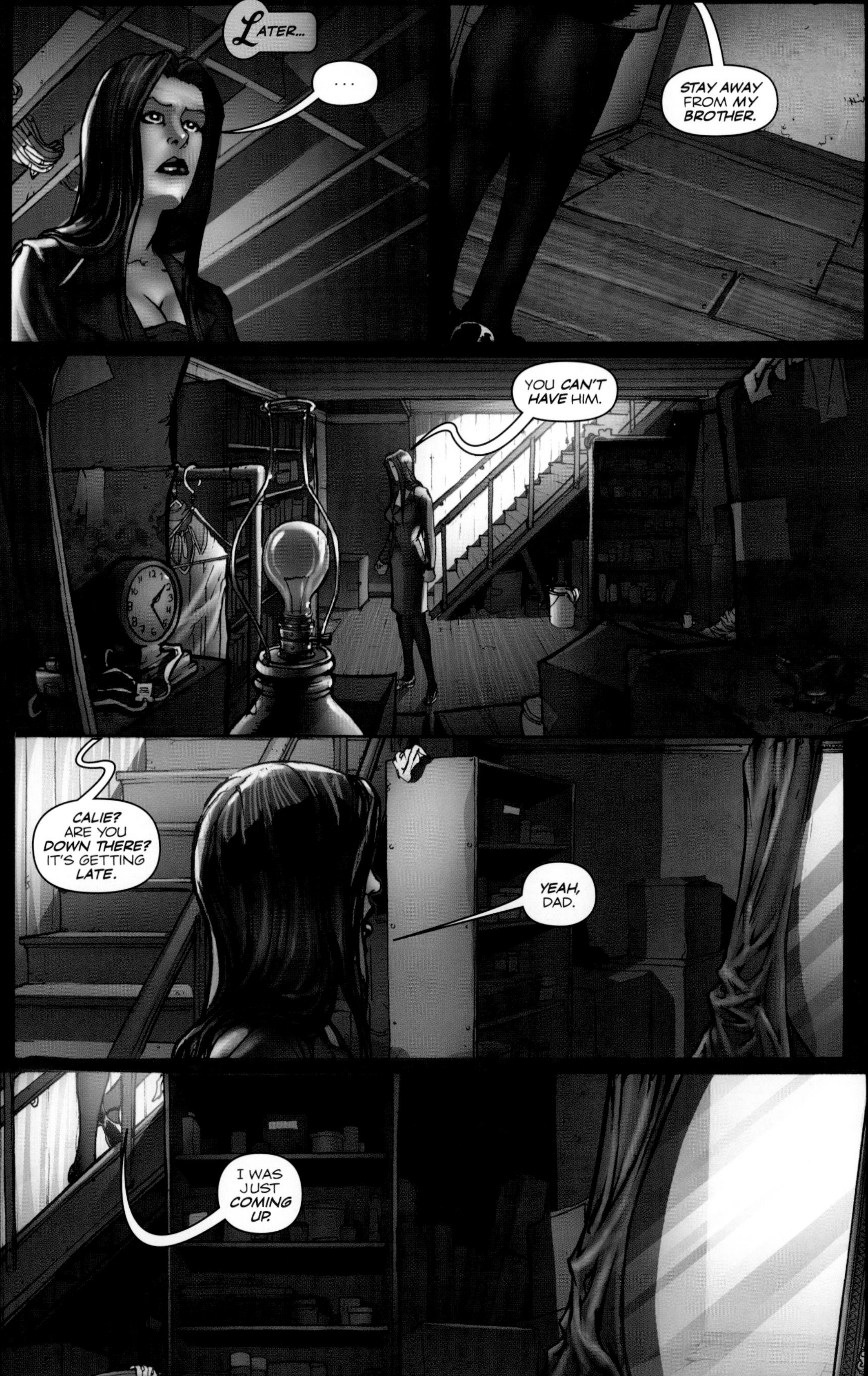
Later...
. . .
STAY AWAY FROM MY BROTHER.
YOU CAN'T HAVE HIM.
CALIE? ARE YOU DOWN THERE? IT'S GETTING LATE.
YEAH, DAD.
I WAS JUST COMING UP.

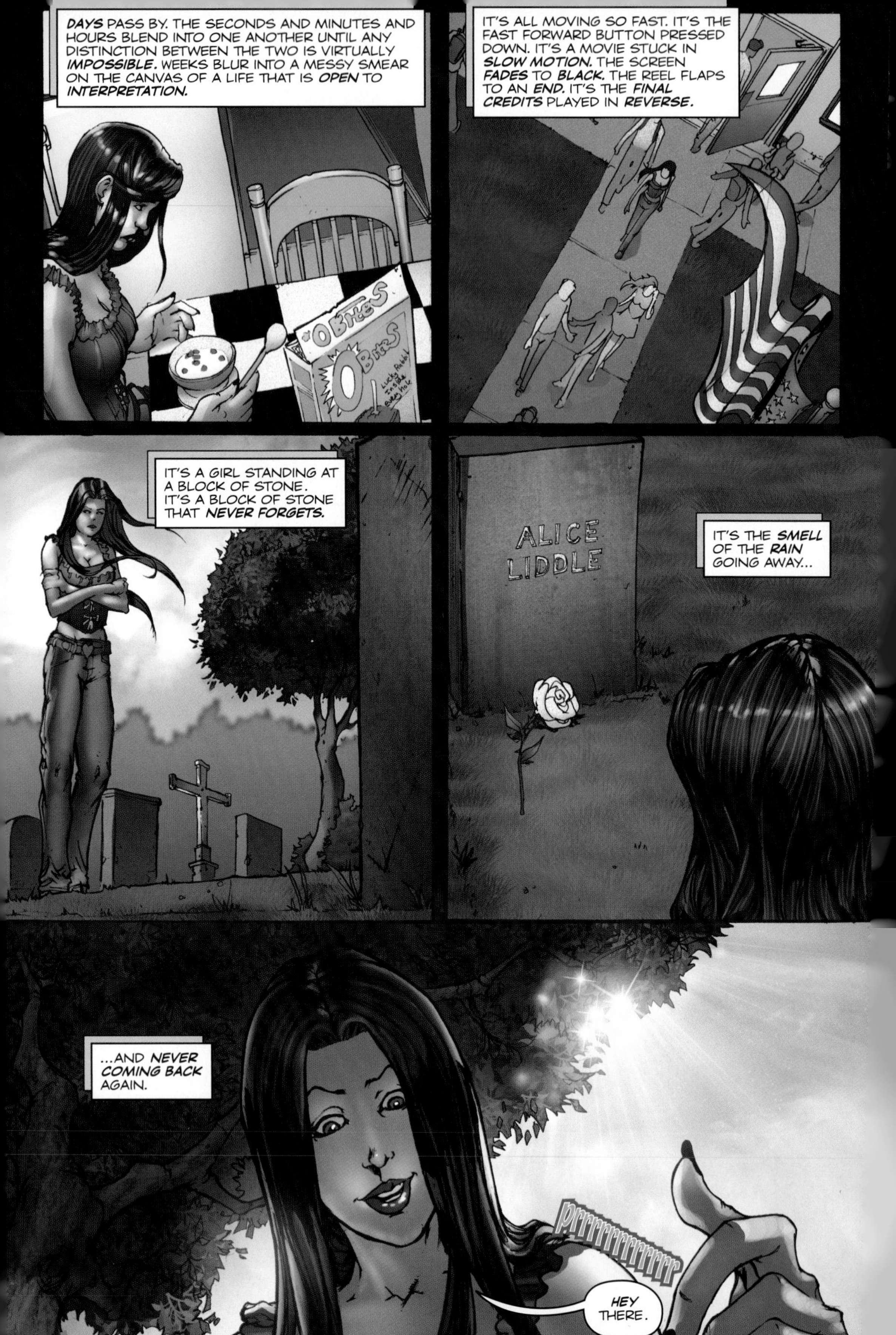

DAYS PASS BY. THE SECONDS AND MINUTES AND HOURS BLEND INTO ONE ANOTHER UNTIL ANY DISTINCTION BETWEEN THE TWO IS VIRTUALLY ***IMPOSSIBLE.*** WEEKS BLUR INTO A MESSY SMEAR ON THE CANVAS OF A LIFE THAT IS ***OPEN*** TO ***INTERPRETATION.***
IT'S ALL MOVING SO FAST. IT'S THE FAST FORWARD BUTTON PRESSED DOWN. IT'S A MOVIE STUCK IN ***SLOW MOTION.*** THE SCREEN ***FADES*** TO ***BLACK.*** THE REEL FLAPS TO AN ***END.*** IT'S THE ***FINAL CREDITS*** PLAYED IN ***REVERSE.***
IT'S A GIRL STANDING AT A BLOCK OF STONE. IT'S A BLOCK OF STONE THAT ***NEVER FORGETS.***
ALICE LIDDLE
IT'S THE ***SMELL*** OF THE ***RAIN*** GOING AWAY...
...AND ***NEVER COMING BACK*** AGAIN.
HEY THERE.

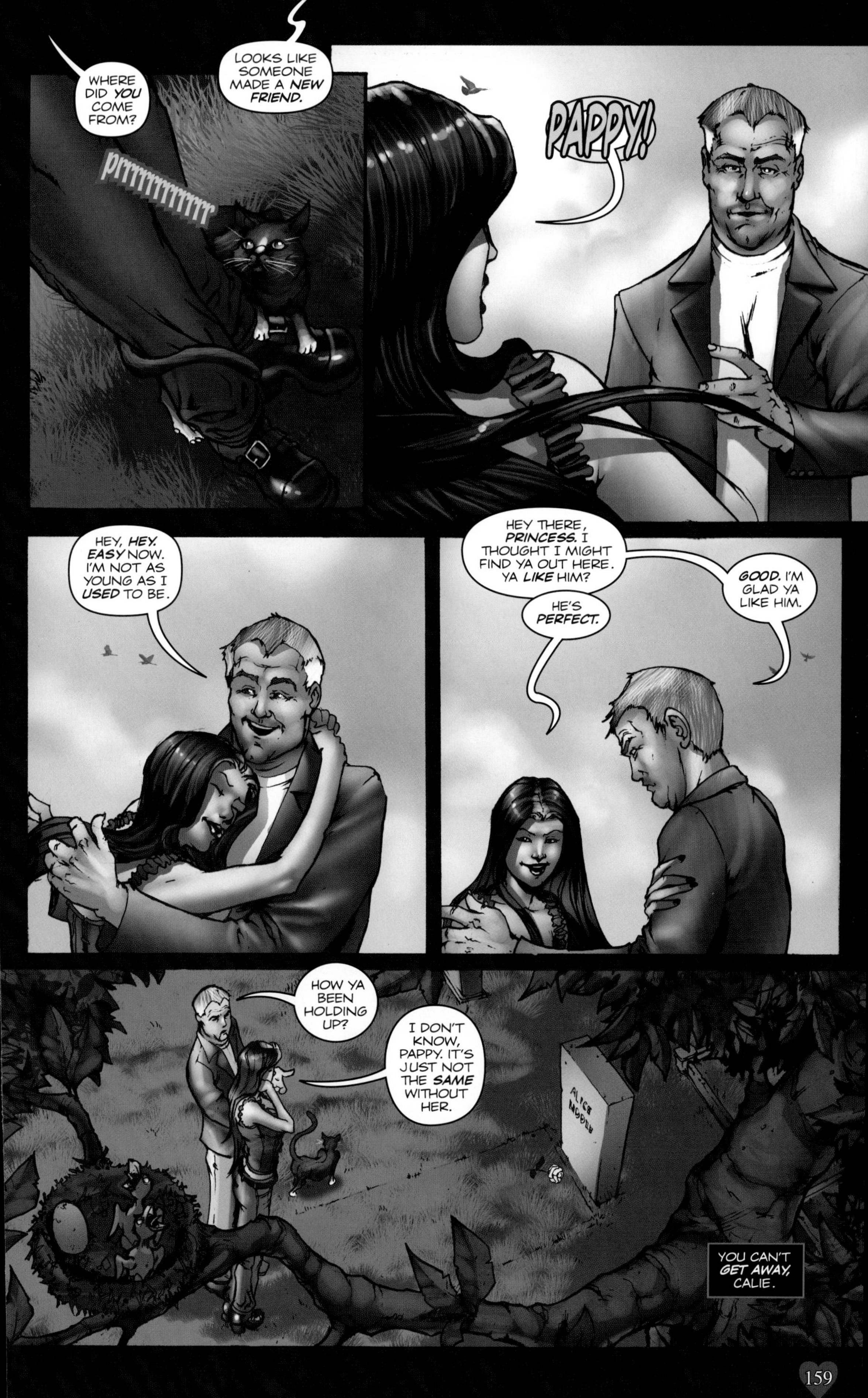
WHERE DID YOU COME FROM?
LOOKS LIKE SOMEONE MADE A NEW FRIEND.
prrrrrrrrrrrr
PAPPY!
HEY, HEY. EASY NOW. I'M NOT AS YOUNG AS I USED TO BE.
HEY THERE, PRINCESS. I THOUGHT I MIGHT FIND YA OUT HERE. YA LIKE HIM?
HE'S PERFECT.
GOOD. I'M GLAD YA LIKE HIM.
HOW YA BEEN HOLDING UP?
I DON'T KNOW, PAPPY. IT'S JUST NOT THE SAME WITHOUT HER.
YOU CAN'T GET AWAY, CALIE.

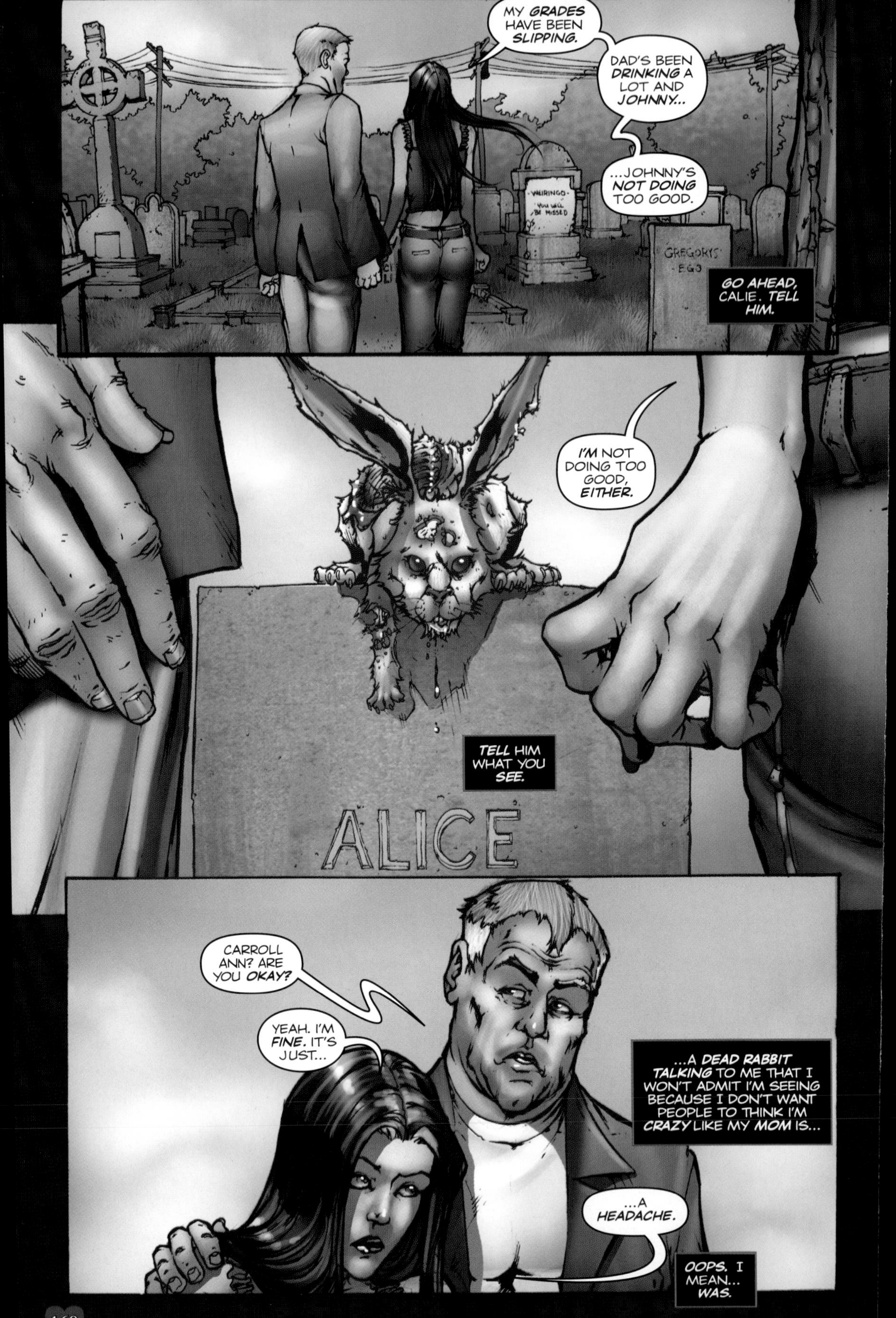
MY GRADES HAVE BEEN SLIPPING.
DAD'S BEEN DRINKING A LOT AND JOHNNY...
...JOHNNY'S NOT DOING TOO GOOD.
GREGORYS
GO AHEAD, CALIE. TELL HIM.
I'M NOT DOING TOO GOOD, EITHER.
TELL HIM WHAT YOU SEE.
ALICE
CARROLL ANN? ARE YOU OKAY?
YEAH. I'M FINE. IT'S JUST...
...A DEAD RABBIT TALKING TO ME THAT I WON'T ADMIT I'M SEEING BECAUSE I DON'T WANT PEOPLE TO THINK I'M CRAZY LIKE MY MOM IS...
...A HEADACHE.
OOPS. I MEAN... WAS.

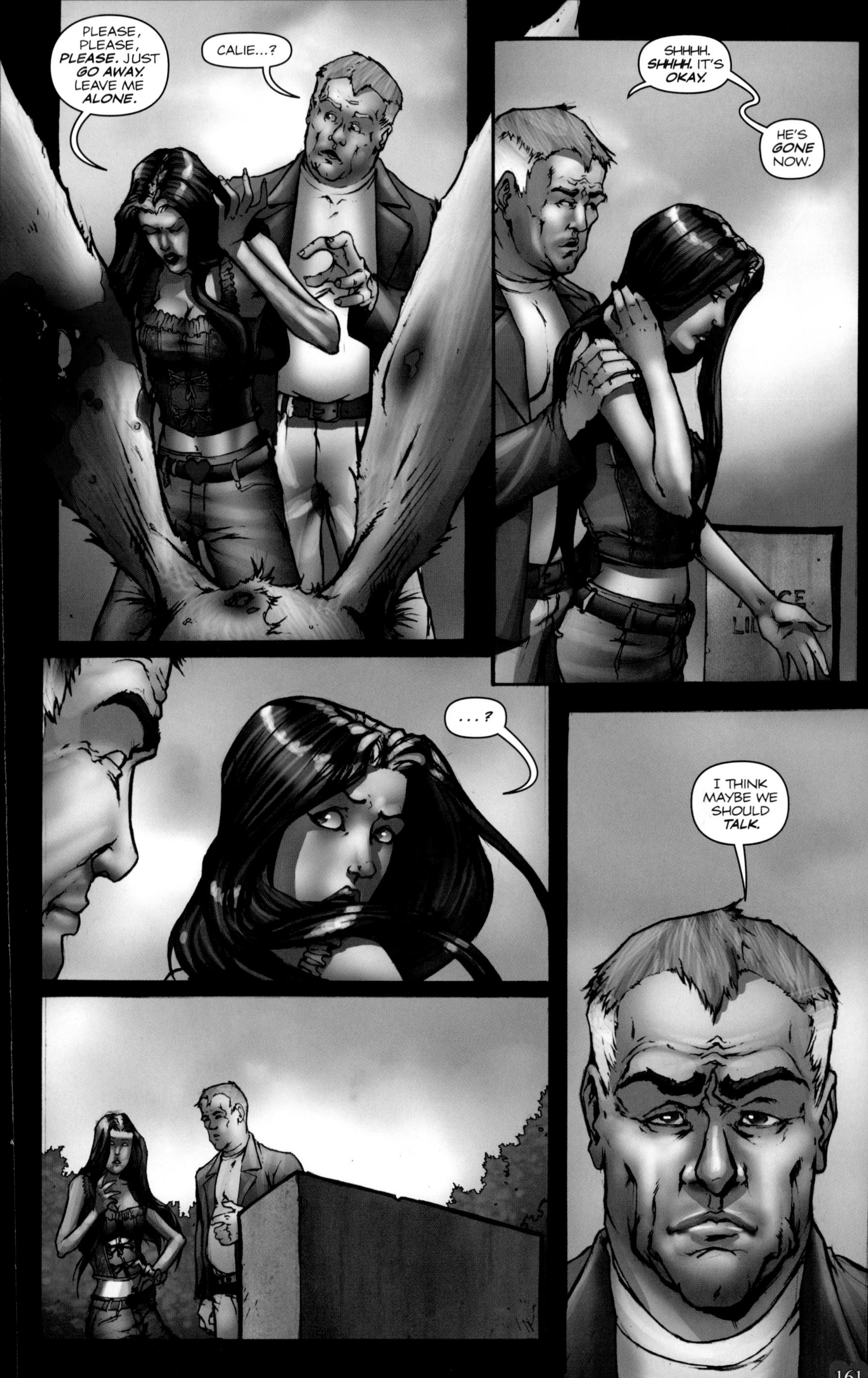

PLEASE, PLEASE, **PLEASE.** JUST ***GO AWAY.*** LEAVE ME ***ALONE.***
CALIE...?
SHHHH. ***SHHHH.*** IT'S ***OKAY.***
HE'S ***GONE*** NOW.
...?
I THINK MAYBE WE SHOULD ***TALK.***

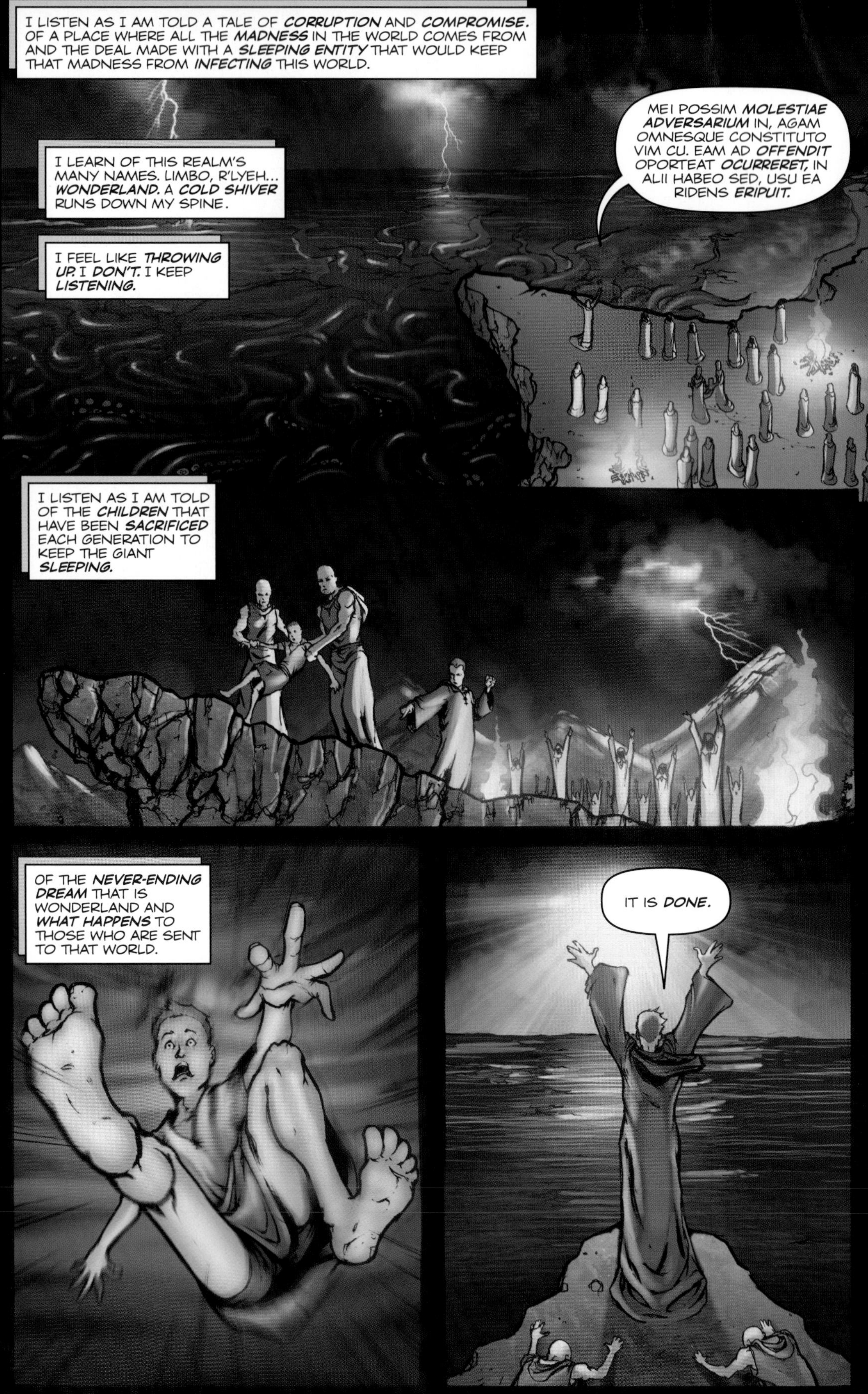
I LISTEN AS I AM TOLD A TALE OF CORRUPTION AND COMPROMISE. OF A PLACE WHERE ALL THE MADNESS IN THE WORLD COMES FROM AND THE DEAL MADE WITH A SLEEPING ENTITY THAT WOULD KEEP THAT MADNESS FROM INFECTING THIS WORLD.
I LEARN OF THIS REALM'S MANY NAMES. LIMBO, R'LYEH... WONDERLAND. A COLD SHIVER RUNS DOWN MY SPINE.
I FEEL LIKE THROWING UP. I DON'T. I KEEP LISTENING.
MEI POSSIM MOLESTIAE ADVERSARIUM IN, AGAM OMNESQUE CONSTITUTO VIM CU. EAM AD OFFENDIT OPORTEAT OCURRERET, IN ALII HABEO SED, USU EA RIDENS ERIPUIT.
I LISTEN AS I AM TOLD OF THE CHILDREN THAT HAVE BEEN SACRIFICED EACH GENERATION TO KEEP THE GIANT SLEEPING.
OF THE NEVER-ENDING DREAM THAT IS WONDERLAND AND WHAT HAPPENS TO THOSE WHO ARE SENT TO THAT WORLD.
IT IS DONE.

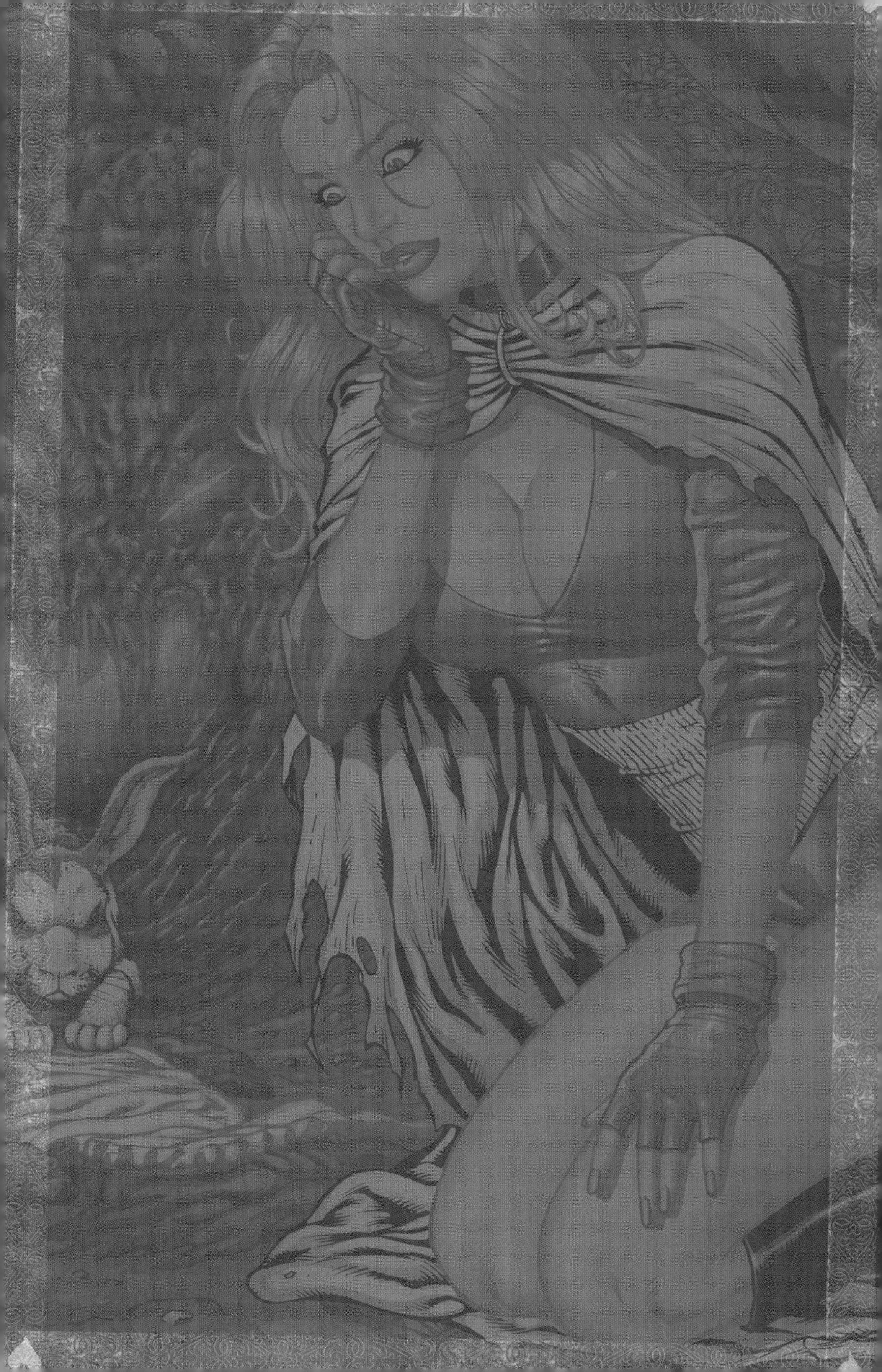

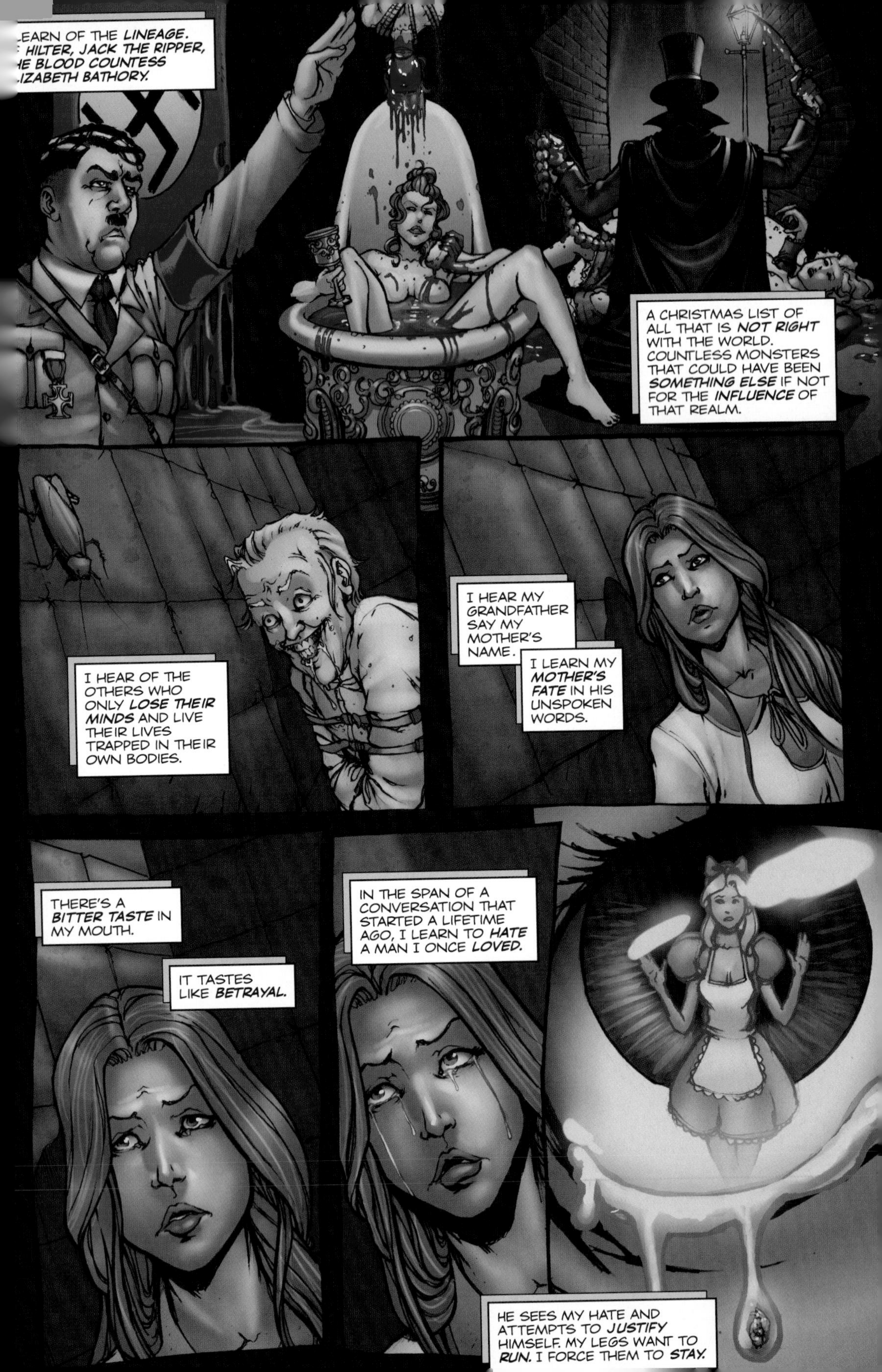

EARN OF THE LINEAGE. HILTER, JACK THE RIPPER, HE BLOOD COUNTESS IZABETH BATHORY.
A CHRISTMAS LIST OF ALL THAT IS NOT RIGHT WITH THE WORLD. COUNTLESS MONSTERS THAT COULD HAVE BEEN SOMETHING ELSE IF NOT FOR THE INFLUENCE OF THAT REALM.
I HEAR OF THE OTHERS WHO ONLY LOSE THEIR MINDS AND LIVE THEIR LIVES TRAPPED IN THEIR OWN BODIES.
I HEAR MY GRANDFATHER SAY MY MOTHER'S NAME.
I LEARN MY MOTHER'S FATE IN HIS UNSPOKEN WORDS.
THERE'S A BITTER TASTE IN MY MOUTH.
IT TASTES LIKE BETRAYAL.
IN THE SPAN OF A CONVERSATION THAT STARTED A LIFETIME AGO, I LEARN TO HATE A MAN I ONCE LOVED.
HE SEES MY HATE AND ATTEMPTS TO JUSTIFY HIMSELF. MY LEGS WANT TO RUN. I FORCE THEM TO STAY.

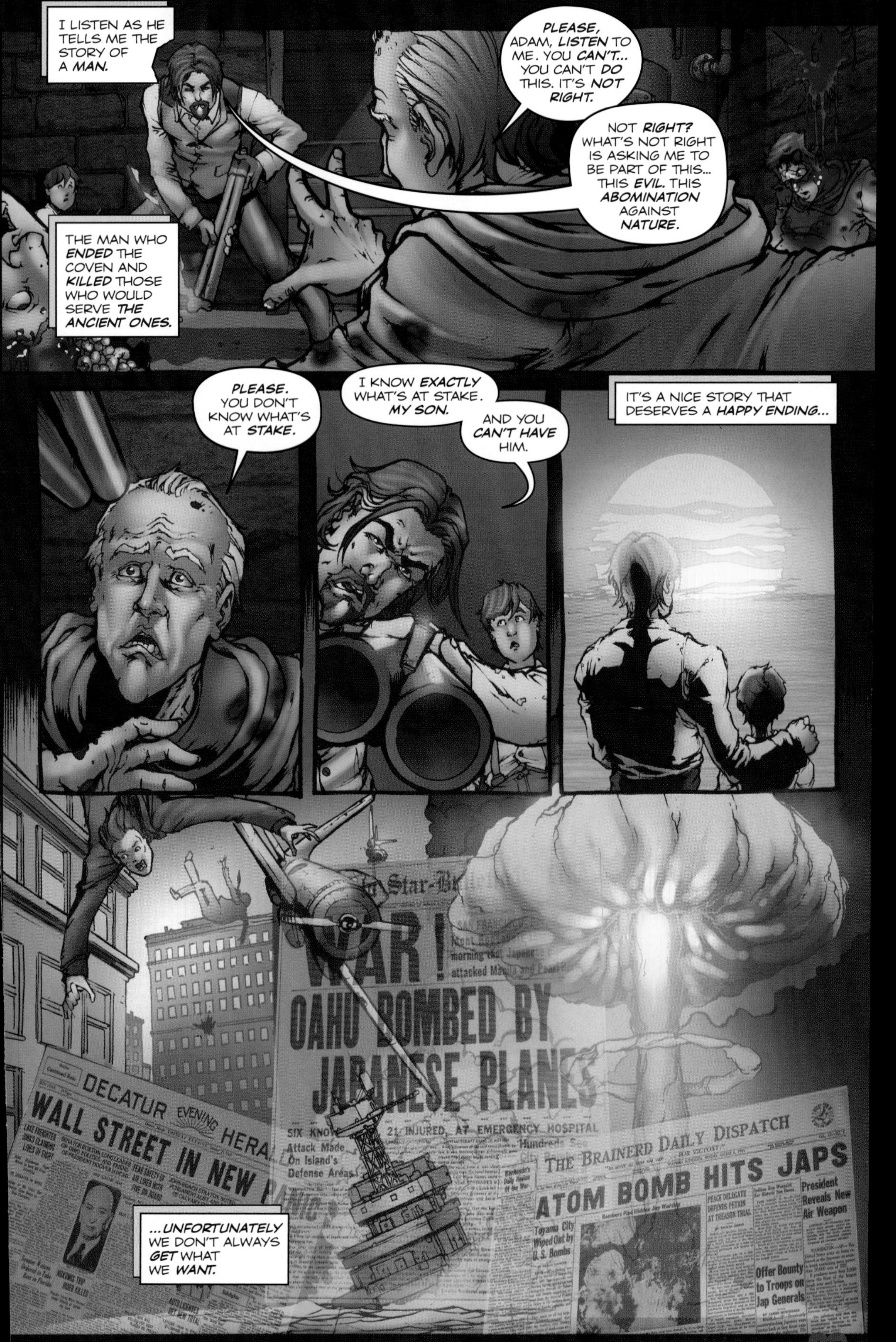

I LISTEN AS HE TELLS ME THE STORY OF A MAN.
PLEASE, ADAM, LISTEN TO ME. YOU CAN'T... YOU CAN'T DO THIS. IT'S NOT RIGHT.
NOT RIGHT? WHAT'S NOT RIGHT IS ASKING ME TO BE PART OF THIS... THIS EVIL. THIS ABOMINATION AGAINST NATURE.
THE MAN WHO ENDED THE COVEN AND KILLED THOSE WHO WOULD SERVE THE ANCIENT ONES.
PLEASE. YOU DON'T KNOW WHAT'S AT STAKE.
I KNOW EXACTLY WHAT'S AT STAKE. MY SON.
AND YOU CAN'T HAVE HIM.
IT'S A NICE STORY THAT DESERVES A HAPPY ENDING...
WAR!
OAHU BOMBED BY JAPANESE PLANES
DECATUR EVENING HERALD
WALL STREET IN NEW
THE BRAINERD DAILY DISPATCH
ATOM BOMB HITS JAPS
President Reveals New Air Weapon
Offer Bounty to Troops on Jap Generals
...UNFORTUNATELY WE DON'T ALWAYS GET WHAT WE WANT.

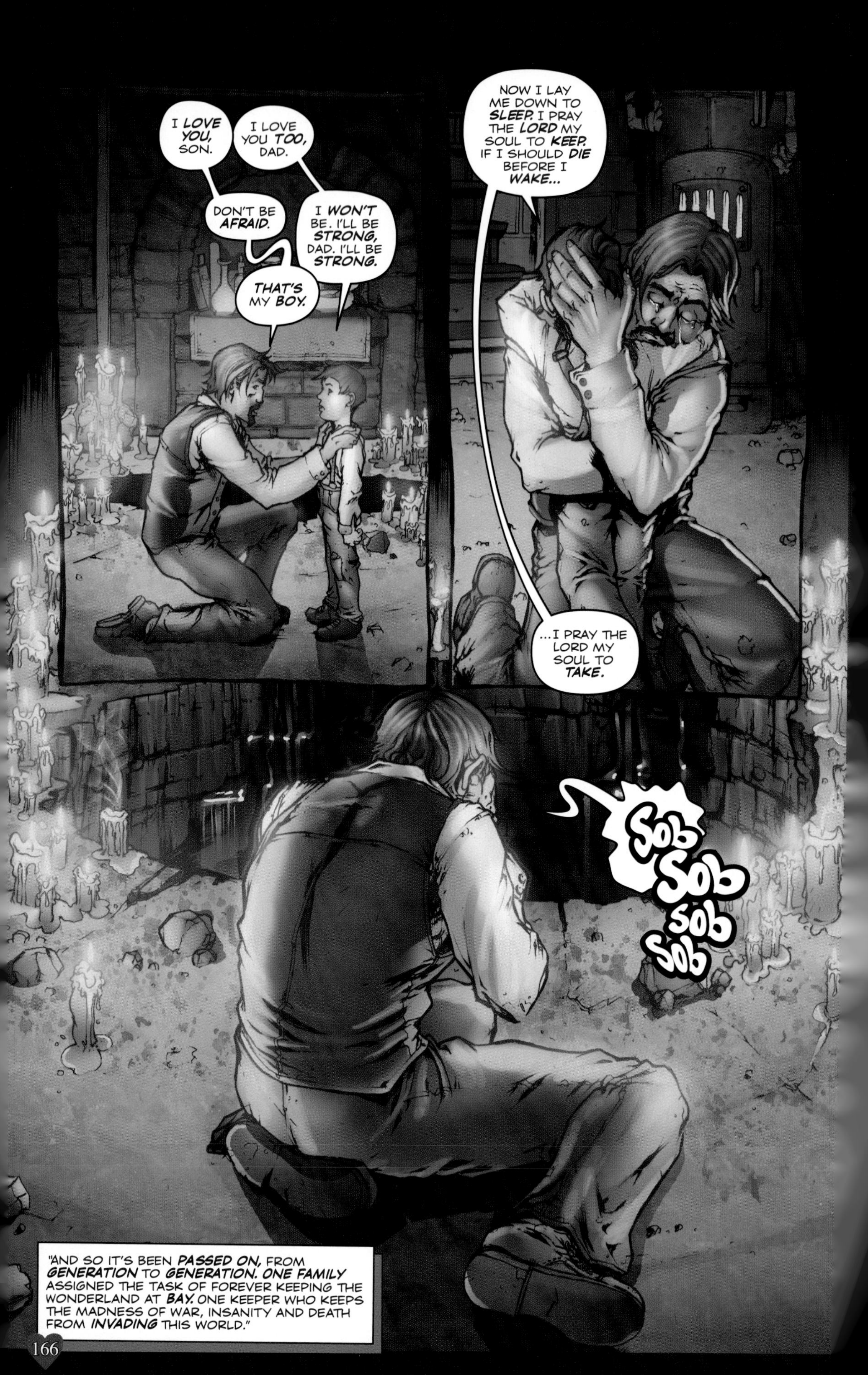
I LOVE YOU, SON.
I LOVE YOU TOO, DAD.
DON'T BE AFRAID.
I WON'T BE. I'LL BE STRONG, DAD. I'LL BE STRONG.
THAT'S MY BOY.
NOW I LAY ME DOWN TO SLEEP. I PRAY THE LORD MY SOUL TO KEEP. IF I SHOULD DIE BEFORE I WAKE...
...I PRAY THE LORD MY SOUL TO TAKE.
SOB SOB SOB SOB
"AND SO IT'S BEEN PASSED ON, FROM GENERATION TO GENERATION. ONE FAMILY ASSIGNED THE TASK OF FOREVER KEEPING THE WONDERLAND AT BAY. ONE KEEPER WHO KEEPS THE MADNESS OF WAR, INSANITY AND DEATH FROM INVADING THIS WORLD."

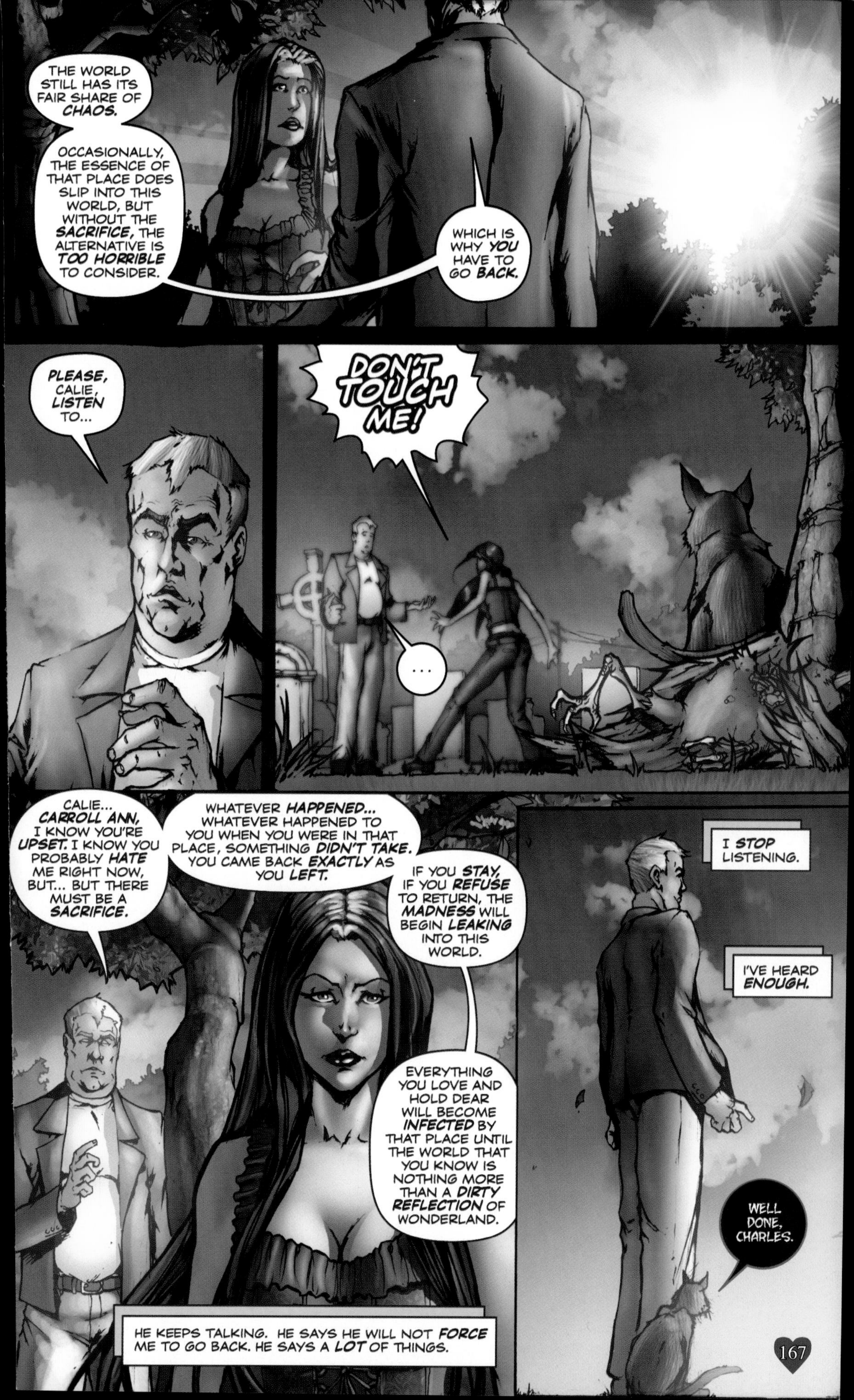
THE WORLD STILL HAS ITS FAIR SHARE OF CHAOS.
OCCASIONALLY, THE ESSENCE OF THAT PLACE DOES SLIP INTO THIS WORLD, BUT WITHOUT THE SACRIFICE, THE ALTERNATIVE IS TOO HORRIBLE TO CONSIDER.
WHICH IS WHY YOU HAVE TO GO BACK.
PLEASE, CALIE, LISTEN TO...
DON'T TOUCH ME!
...
CALIE... CARROLL ANN, I KNOW YOU'RE UPSET. I KNOW YOU PROBABLY HATE ME RIGHT NOW, BUT... BUT THERE MUST BE A SACRIFICE.
WHATEVER HAPPENED... WHATEVER HAPPENED TO YOU WHEN YOU WERE IN THAT PLACE, SOMETHING DIDN'T TAKE. YOU CAME BACK EXACTLY AS YOU LEFT.
IF YOU STAY, IF YOU REFUSE TO RETURN, THE MADNESS WILL BEGIN LEAKING INTO THIS WORLD.
EVERYTHING YOU LOVE AND HOLD DEAR WILL BECOME INFECTED BY THAT PLACE UNTIL THE WORLD THAT YOU KNOW IS NOTHING MORE THAN A DIRTY REFLECTION OF WONDERLAND.
HE KEEPS TALKING. HE SAYS HE WILL NOT FORCE ME TO GO BACK. HE SAYS A LOT OF THINGS.
I STOP LISTENING.
I'VE HEARD ENOUGH.
WELL DONE, CHARLES.

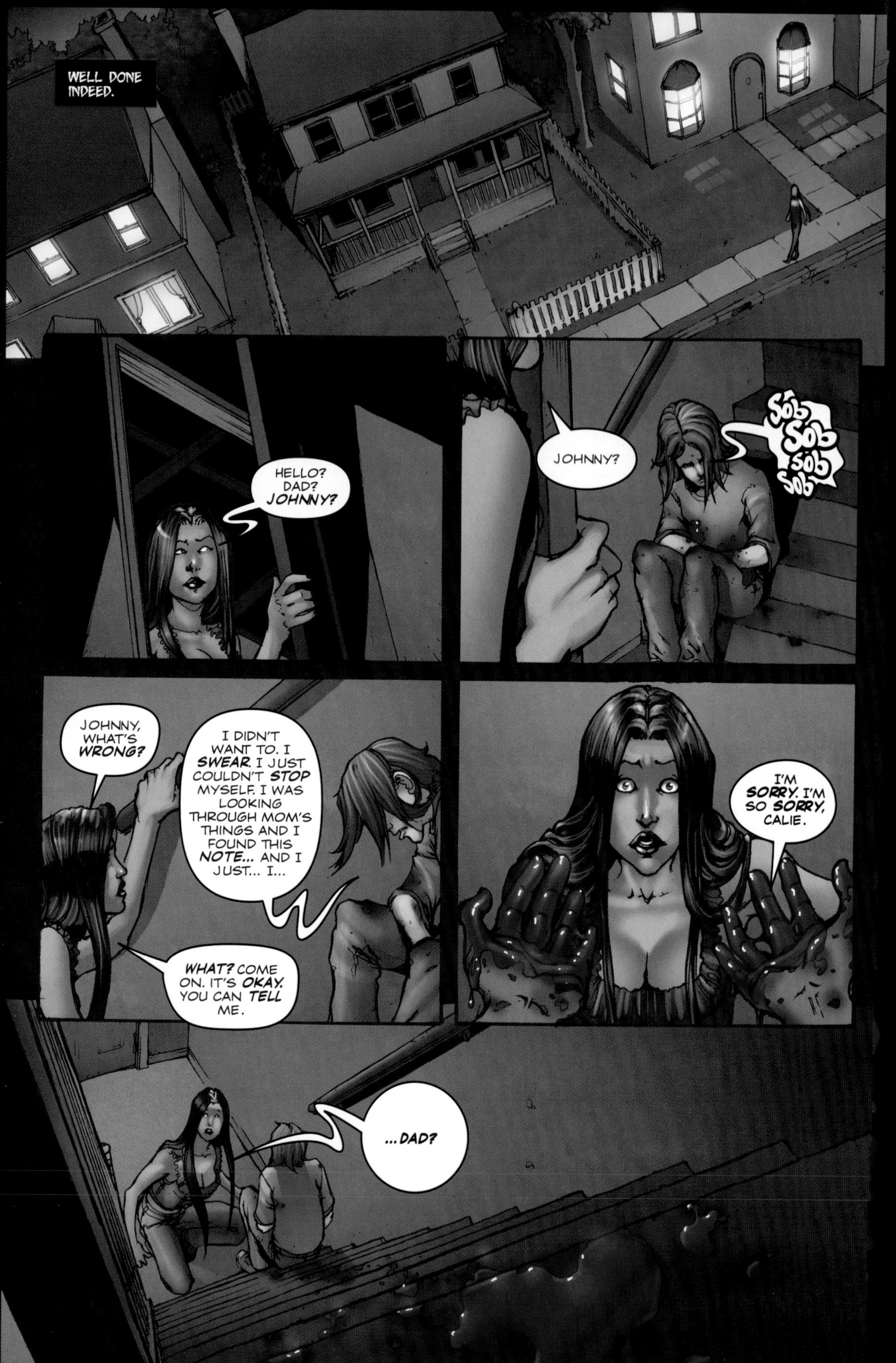
WELL DONE INDEED.
HELLO? DAD? JOHNNY?
JOHNNY?
SOB SOB SOB SOB
JOHNNY, WHAT'S WRONG?
I DIDN'T WANT TO. I SWEAR. I JUST COULDN'T STOP MYSELF. I WAS LOOKING THROUGH MOM'S THINGS AND I FOUND THIS NOTE... AND I JUST... I...
WHAT? COME ON. IT'S OKAY. YOU CAN TELL ME.
I'M SORRY. I'M SO SORRY, CALIE.
...DAD?

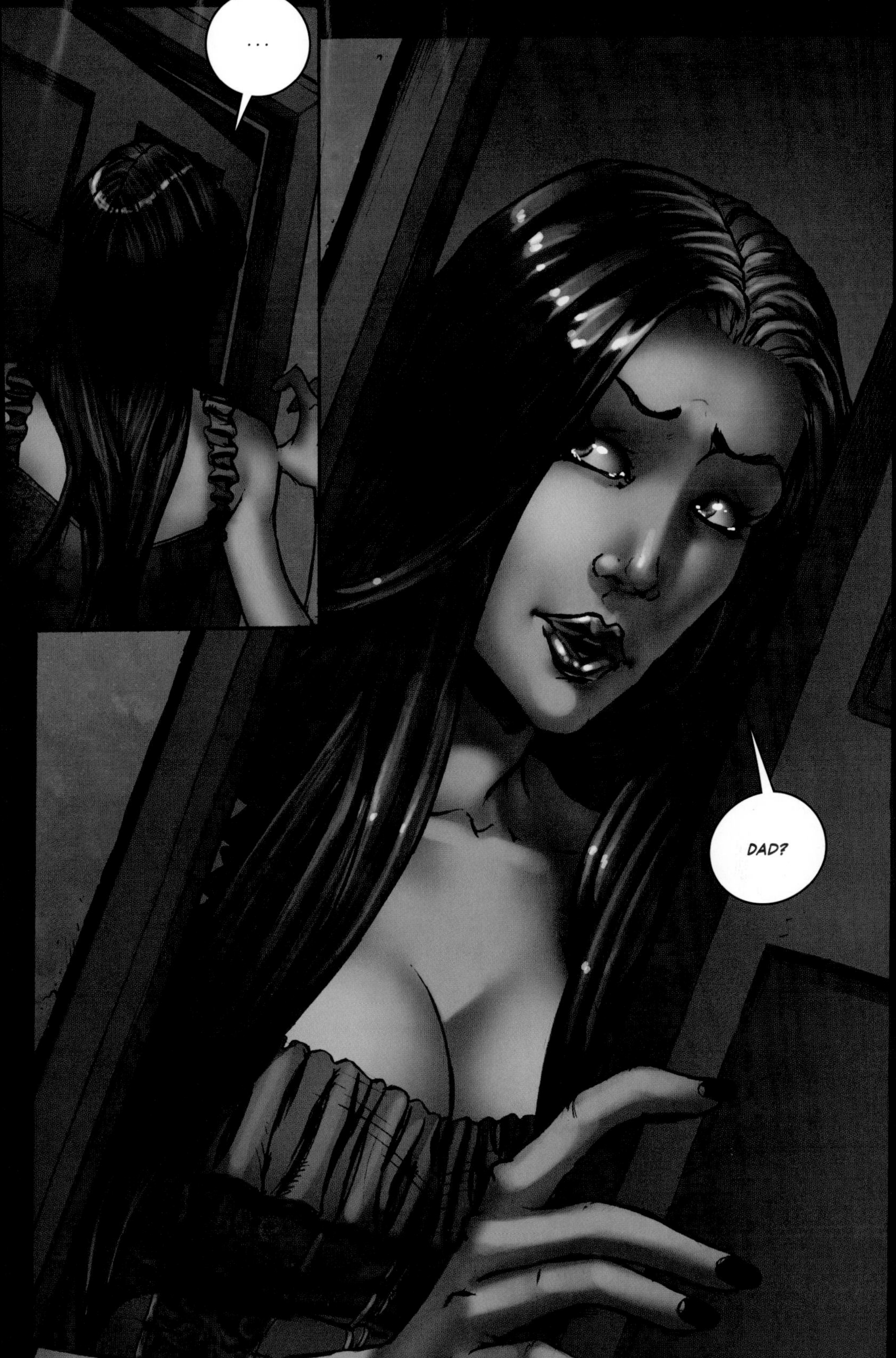
...
DAD?

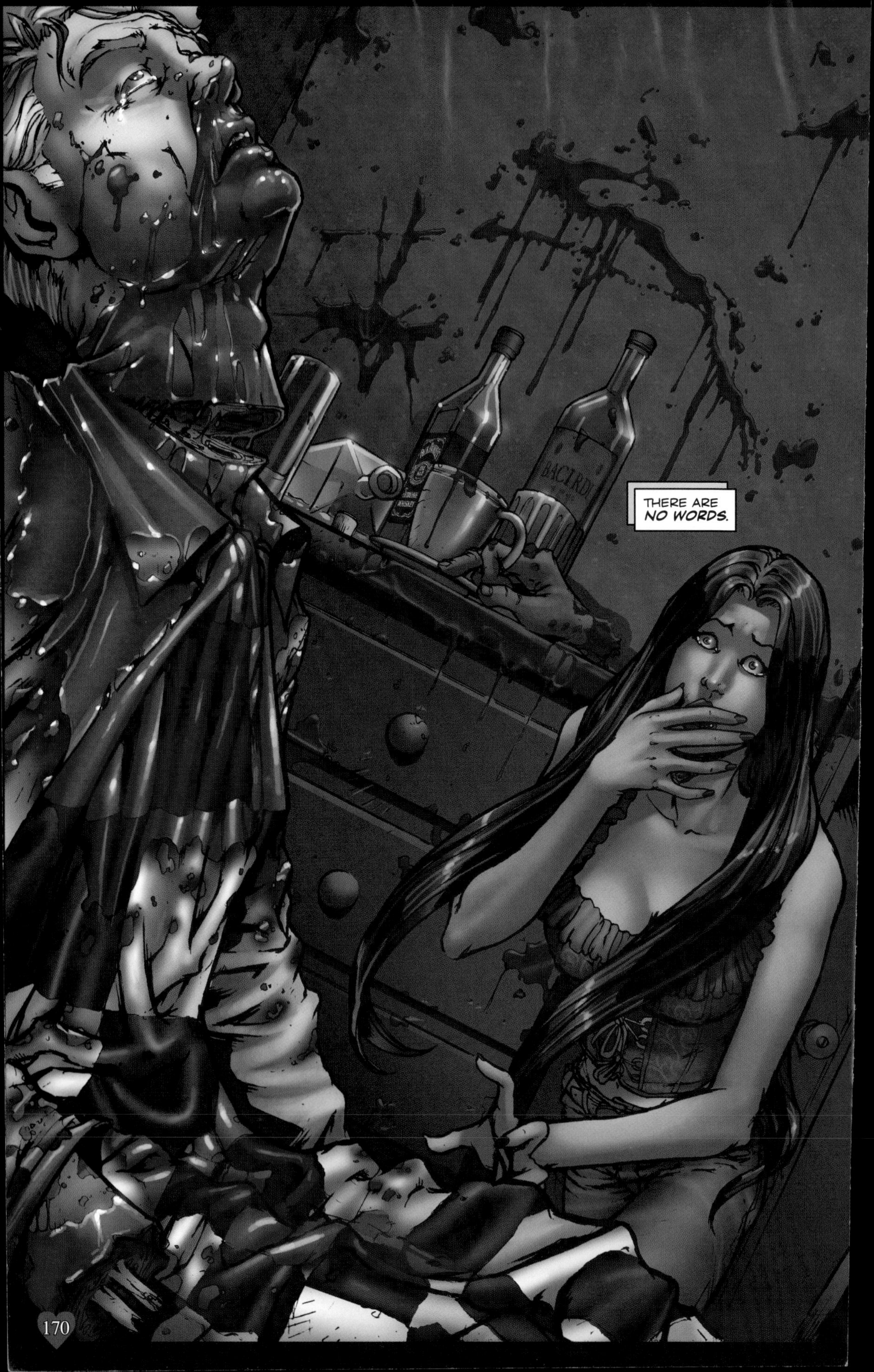
THERE ARE
NO WORDS.

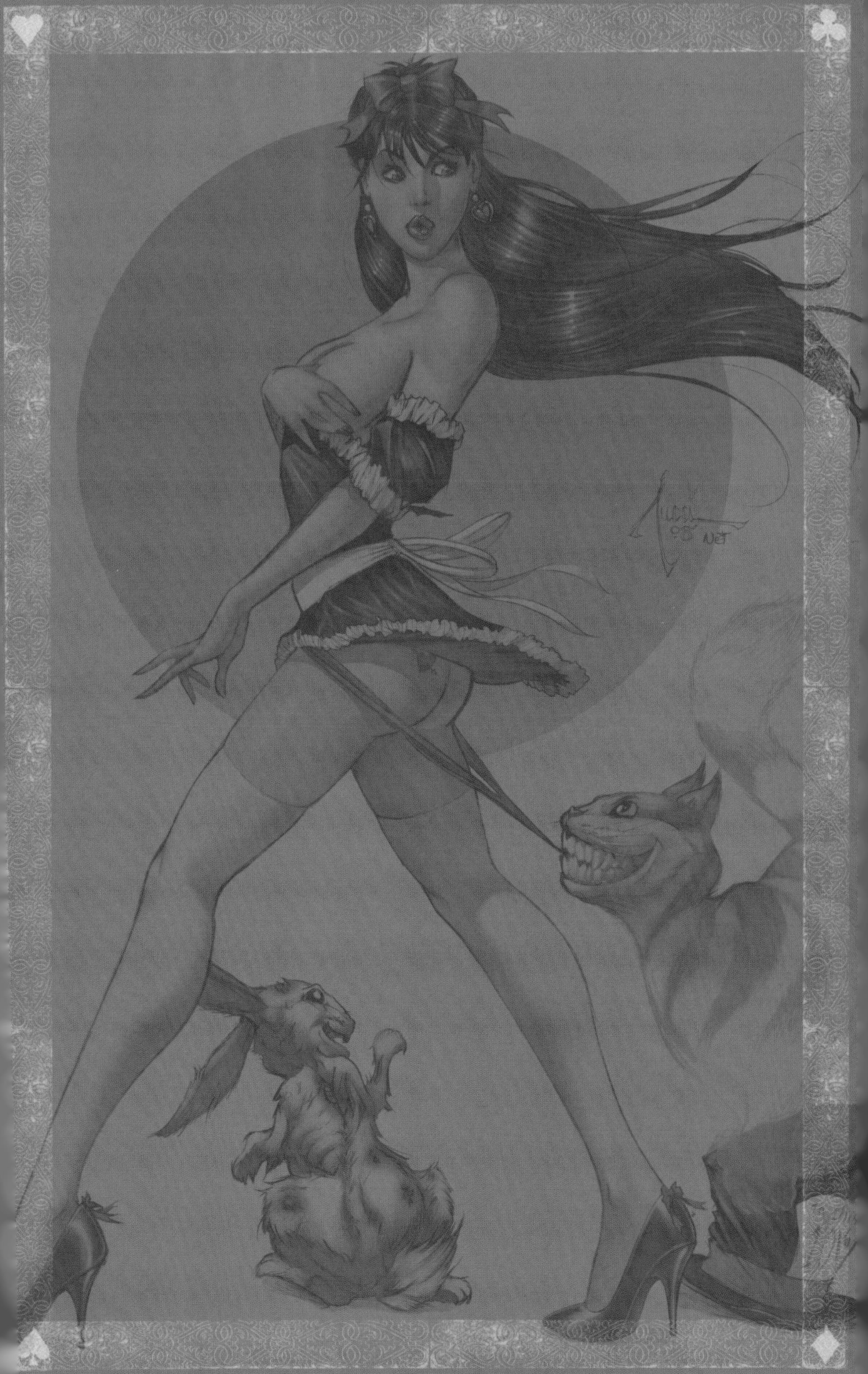

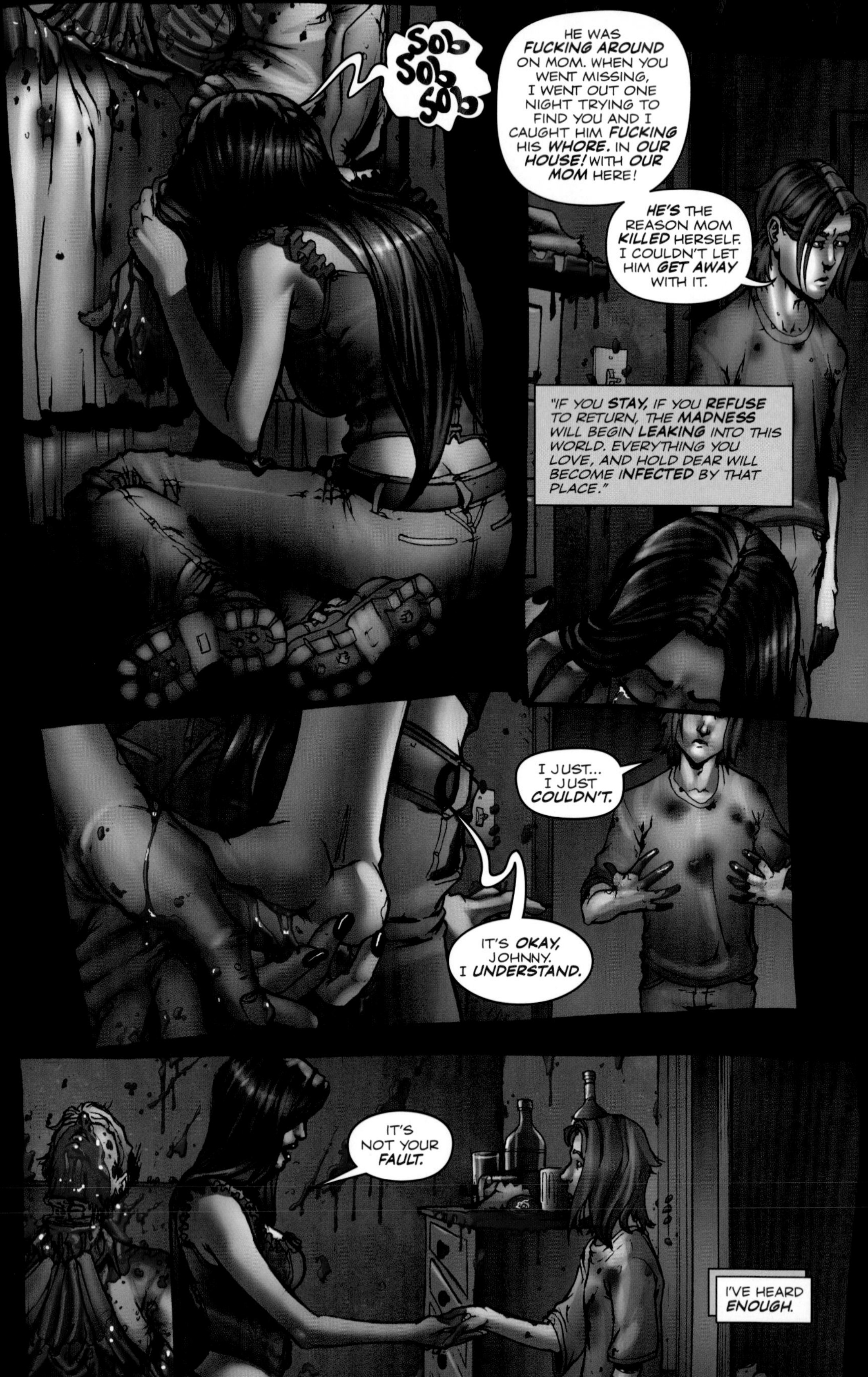
SOB SOB SOB
HE WAS FUCKING AROUND ON MOM. WHEN YOU WENT MISSING, I WENT OUT ONE NIGHT TRYING TO FIND YOU AND I CAUGHT HIM FUCKING HIS WHORE. IN OUR HOUSE! WITH OUR MOM HERE!
HE'S THE REASON MOM KILLED HERSELF. I COULDN'T LET HIM GET AWAY WITH IT.
"IF YOU STAY, IF YOU REFUSE TO RETURN, THE MADNESS WILL BEGIN LEAKING INTO THIS WORLD. EVERYTHING YOU LOVE, AND HOLD DEAR WILL BECOME INFECTED BY THAT PLACE."
I JUST... I JUST COULDN'T.
IT'S OKAY, JOHNNY. I UNDERSTAND.
IT'S NOT YOUR FAULT.
I'VE HEARD ENOUGH.

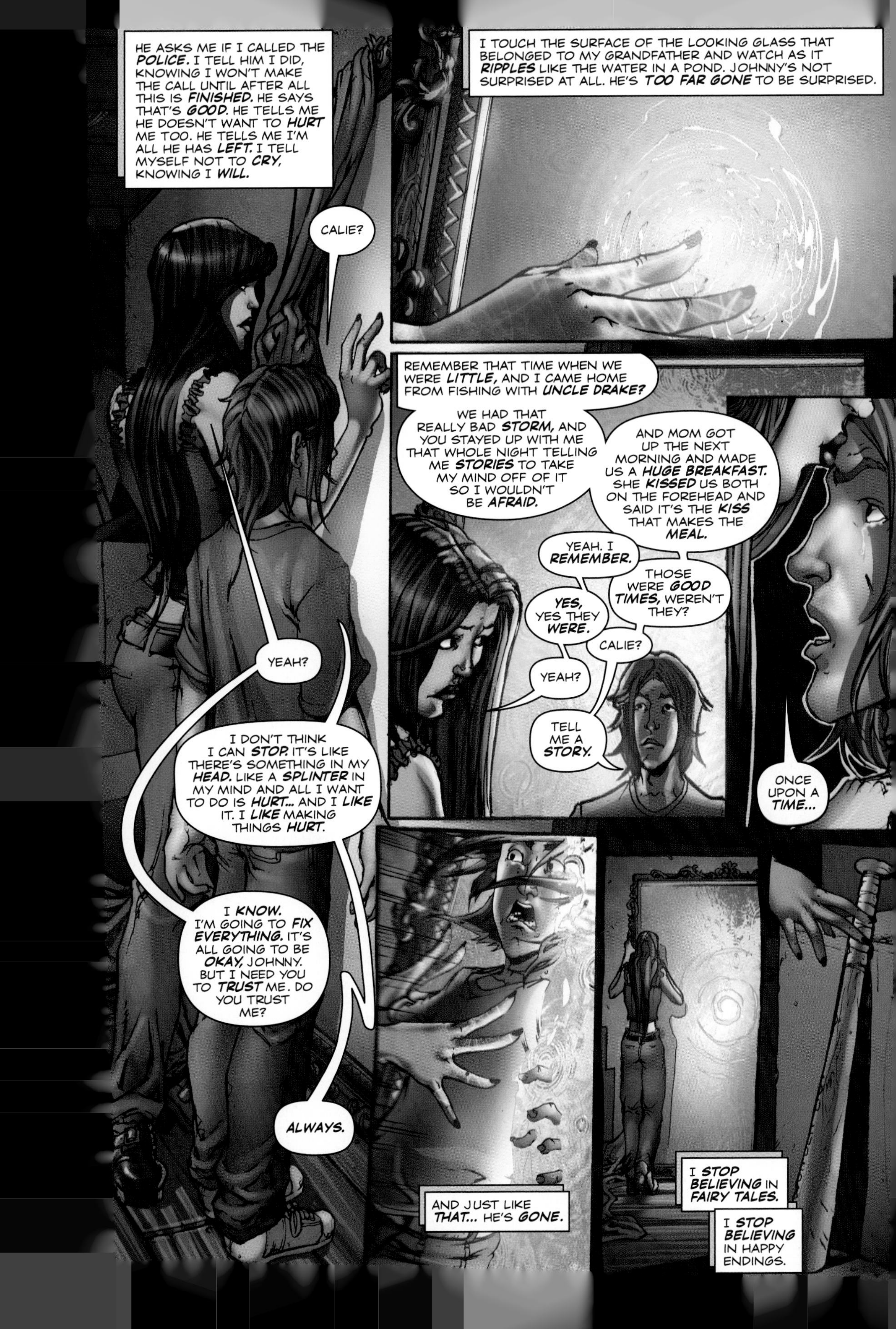
HE ASKS ME IF I CALLED THE POLICE. I TELL HIM I DID, KNOWING I WON'T MAKE THE CALL UNTIL AFTER ALL THIS IS FINISHED. HE SAYS THAT'S GOOD. HE TELLS ME HE DOESN'T WANT TO HURT ME TOO. HE TELLS ME I'M ALL HE HAS LEFT. I TELL MYSELF NOT TO CRY, KNOWING I WILL.
CALIE?
YEAH?
I DON'T THINK I CAN STOP. IT'S LIKE THERE'S SOMETHING IN MY HEAD. LIKE A SPLINTER IN MY MIND AND ALL I WANT TO DO IS HURT... AND I LIKE IT. I LIKE MAKING THINGS HURT.
I KNOW. I'M GOING TO FIX EVERYTHING. IT'S ALL GOING TO BE OKAY, JOHNNY. BUT I NEED YOU TO TRUST ME. DO YOU TRUST ME?
ALWAYS.
I TOUCH THE SURFACE OF THE LOOKING GLASS THAT BELONGED TO MY GRANDFATHER AND WATCH AS IT RIPPLES LIKE THE WATER IN A POND. JOHNNY'S NOT SURPRISED AT ALL. HE'S TOO FAR GONE TO BE SURPRISED.
REMEMBER THAT TIME WHEN WE WERE LITTLE, AND I CAME HOME FROM FISHING WITH UNCLE DRAKE?
WE HAD THAT REALLY BAD STORM, AND YOU STAYED UP WITH ME THAT WHOLE NIGHT TELLING ME STORIES TO TAKE MY MIND OFF OF IT SO I WOULDN'T BE AFRAID.
AND MOM GOT UP THE NEXT MORNING AND MADE US A HUGE BREAKFAST. SHE KISSED US BOTH ON THE FOREHEAD AND SAID IT'S THE KISS THAT MAKES THE MEAL.
YEAH. I REMEMBER.
THOSE WERE GOOD TIMES, WEREN'T THEY?
YES, YES THEY WERE.
CALIE?
YEAH?
TELL ME A STORY.
ONCE UPON A TIME...
AND JUST LIKE THAT... HE'S GONE.
I STOP BELIEVING IN FAIRY TALES.
I STOP BELIEVING IN HAPPY ENDINGS.

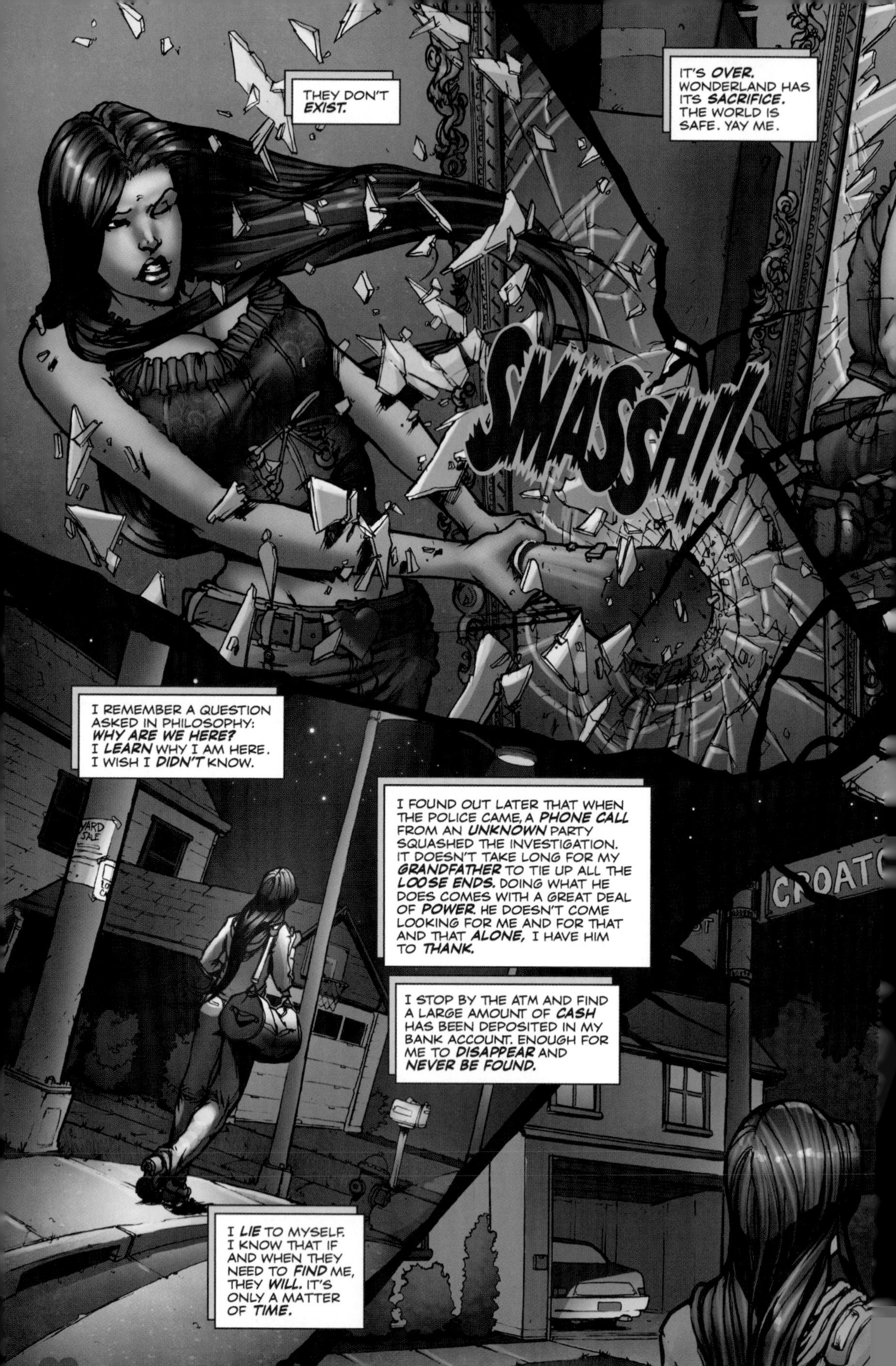
THEY DON'T EXIST.
IT'S OVER. WONDERLAND HAS ITS SACRIFICE. THE WORLD IS SAFE. YAY ME.
SMASH!!
I REMEMBER A QUESTION ASKED IN PHILOSOPHY: WHY ARE WE HERE? I LEARN WHY I AM HERE. I WISH I DIDN'T KNOW.
I FOUND OUT LATER THAT WHEN THE POLICE CAME, A PHONE CALL FROM AN UNKNOWN PARTY SQUASHED THE INVESTIGATION. IT DOESN'T TAKE LONG FOR MY GRANDFATHER TO TIE UP ALL THE LOOSE ENDS. DOING WHAT HE DOES COMES WITH A GREAT DEAL OF POWER. HE DOESN'T COME LOOKING FOR ME AND FOR THAT AND THAT ALONE, I HAVE HIM TO THANK.
YARD SALE
CROATO
I STOP BY THE ATM AND FIND A LARGE AMOUNT OF CASH HAS BEEN DEPOSITED IN MY BANK ACCOUNT. ENOUGH FOR ME TO DISAPPEAR AND NEVER BE FOUND.
I LIE TO MYSELF. I KNOW THAT IF AND WHEN THEY NEED TO FIND ME, THEY WILL. IT'S ONLY A MATTER OF TIME.

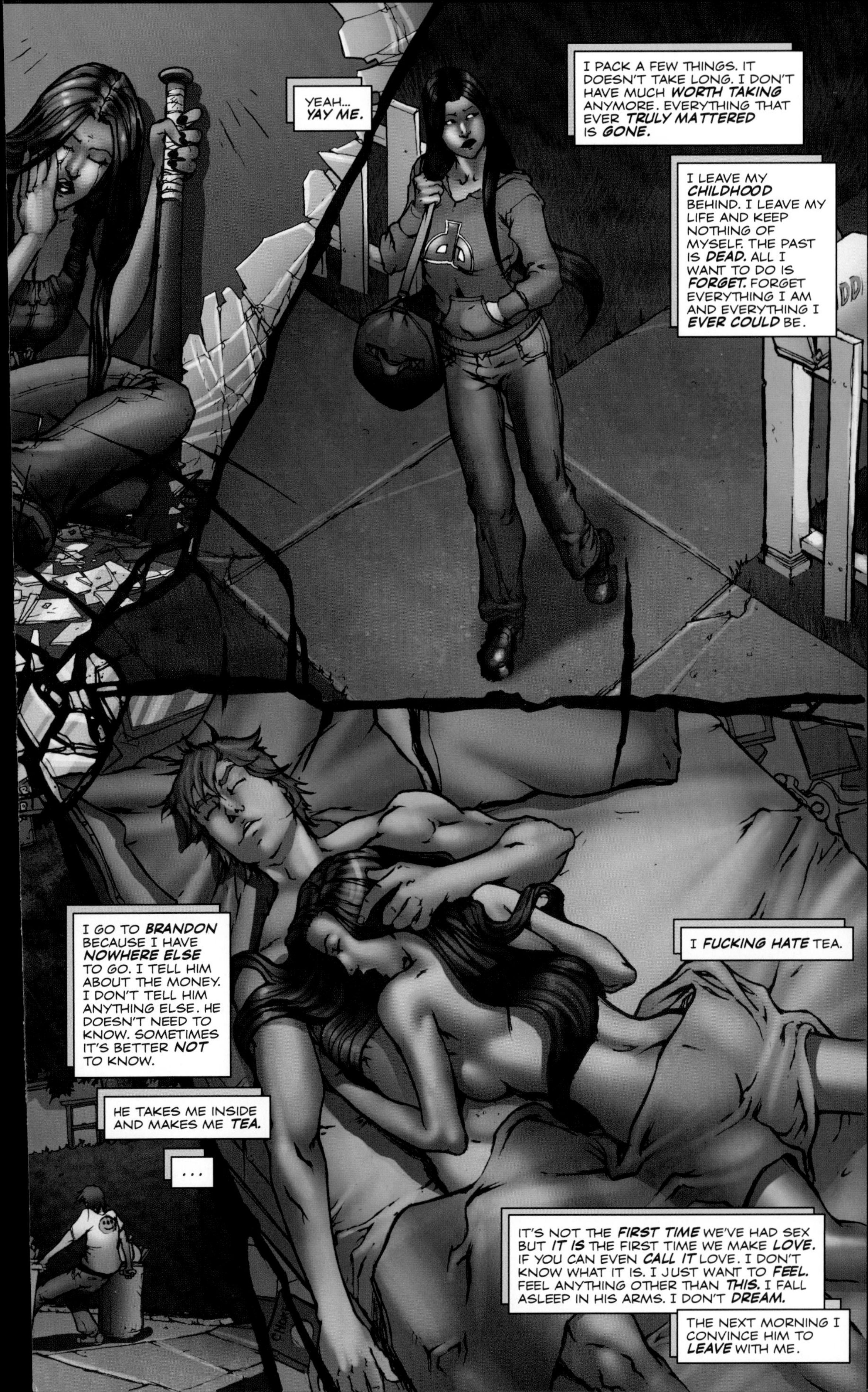
YEAH... YAY ME.
I PACK A FEW THINGS. IT DOESN'T TAKE LONG. I DON'T HAVE MUCH WORTH TAKING ANYMORE. EVERYTHING THAT EVER TRULY MATTERED IS GONE.
I LEAVE MY CHILDHOOD BEHIND. I LEAVE MY LIFE AND KEEP NOTHING OF MYSELF. THE PAST IS DEAD. ALL I WANT TO DO IS FORGET. FORGET EVERYTHING I AM AND EVERYTHING I EVER COULD BE.
I GO TO BRANDON BECAUSE I HAVE NOWHERE ELSE TO GO. I TELL HIM ABOUT THE MONEY. I DON'T TELL HIM ANYTHING ELSE. HE DOESN'T NEED TO KNOW. SOMETIMES IT'S BETTER NOT TO KNOW.
HE TAKES ME INSIDE AND MAKES ME TEA.
...
I FUCKING HATE TEA.
IT'S NOT THE FIRST TIME WE'VE HAD SEX BUT IT IS THE FIRST TIME WE MAKE LOVE. IF YOU CAN EVEN CALL IT LOVE. I DON'T KNOW WHAT IT IS. I JUST WANT TO FEEL. FEEL ANYTHING OTHER THAN THIS. I FALL ASLEEP IN HIS ARMS. I DON'T DREAM.
THE NEXT MORNING I CONVINCE HIM TO LEAVE WITH ME.

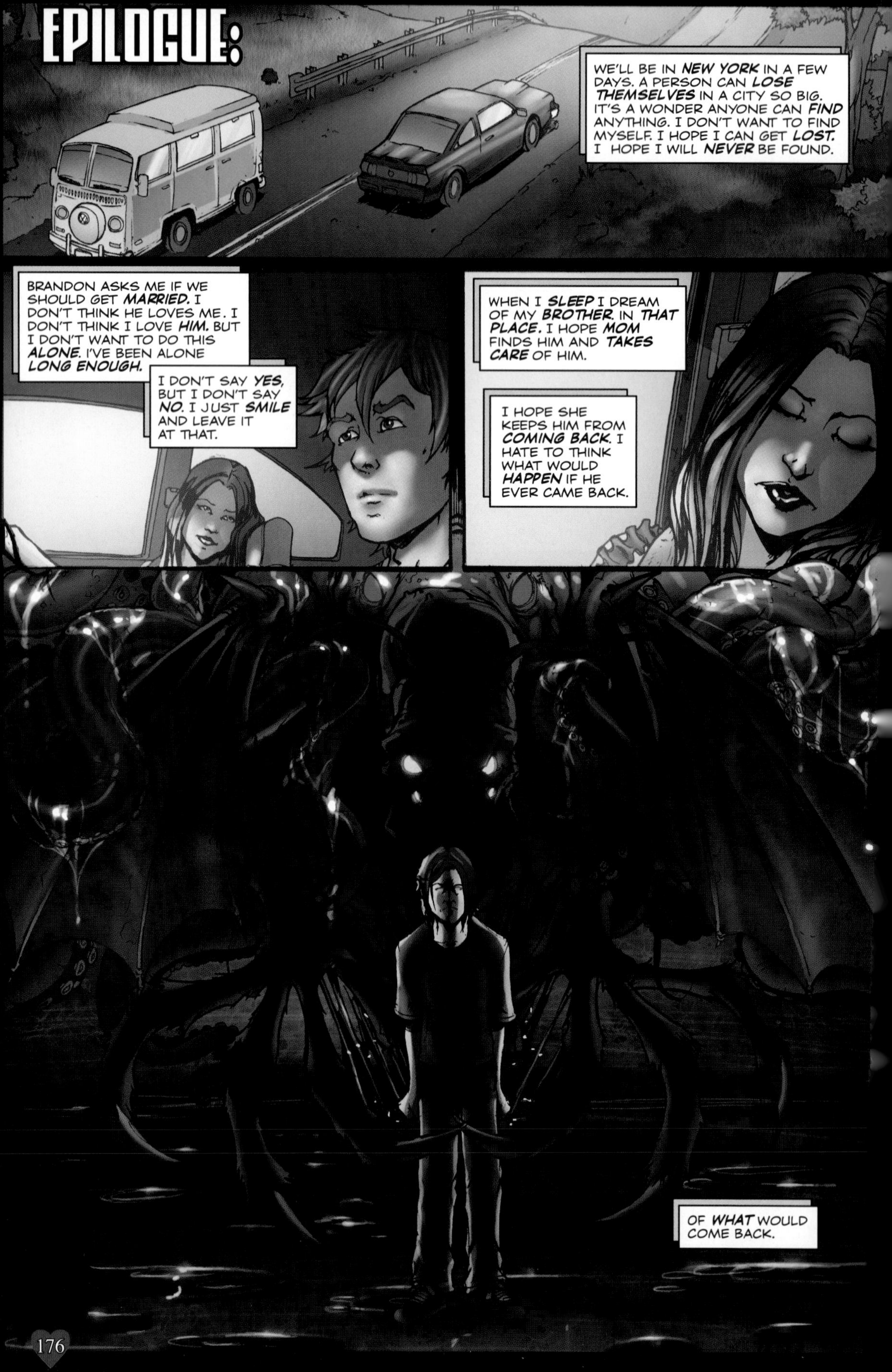
EPILOGUE:
WE'LL BE IN NEW YORK IN A FEW DAYS. A PERSON CAN LOSE THEMSELVES IN A CITY SO BIG. IT'S A WONDER ANYONE CAN FIND ANYTHING. I DON'T WANT TO FIND MYSELF. I HOPE I CAN GET LOST. I HOPE I WILL NEVER BE FOUND.
BRANDON ASKS ME IF WE SHOULD GET MARRIED. I DON'T THINK HE LOVES ME. I DON'T THINK I LOVE HIM. BUT I DON'T WANT TO DO THIS ALONE. I'VE BEEN ALONE LONG ENOUGH.
I DON'T SAY YES, BUT I DON'T SAY NO. I JUST SMILE AND LEAVE IT AT THAT.
WHEN I SLEEP I DREAM OF MY BROTHER. IN THAT PLACE. I HOPE MOM FINDS HIM AND TAKES CARE OF HIM.
I HOPE SHE KEEPS HIM FROM COMING BACK. I HATE TO THINK WHAT WOULD HAPPEN IF HE EVER CAME BACK.
OF WHAT WOULD COME BACK.

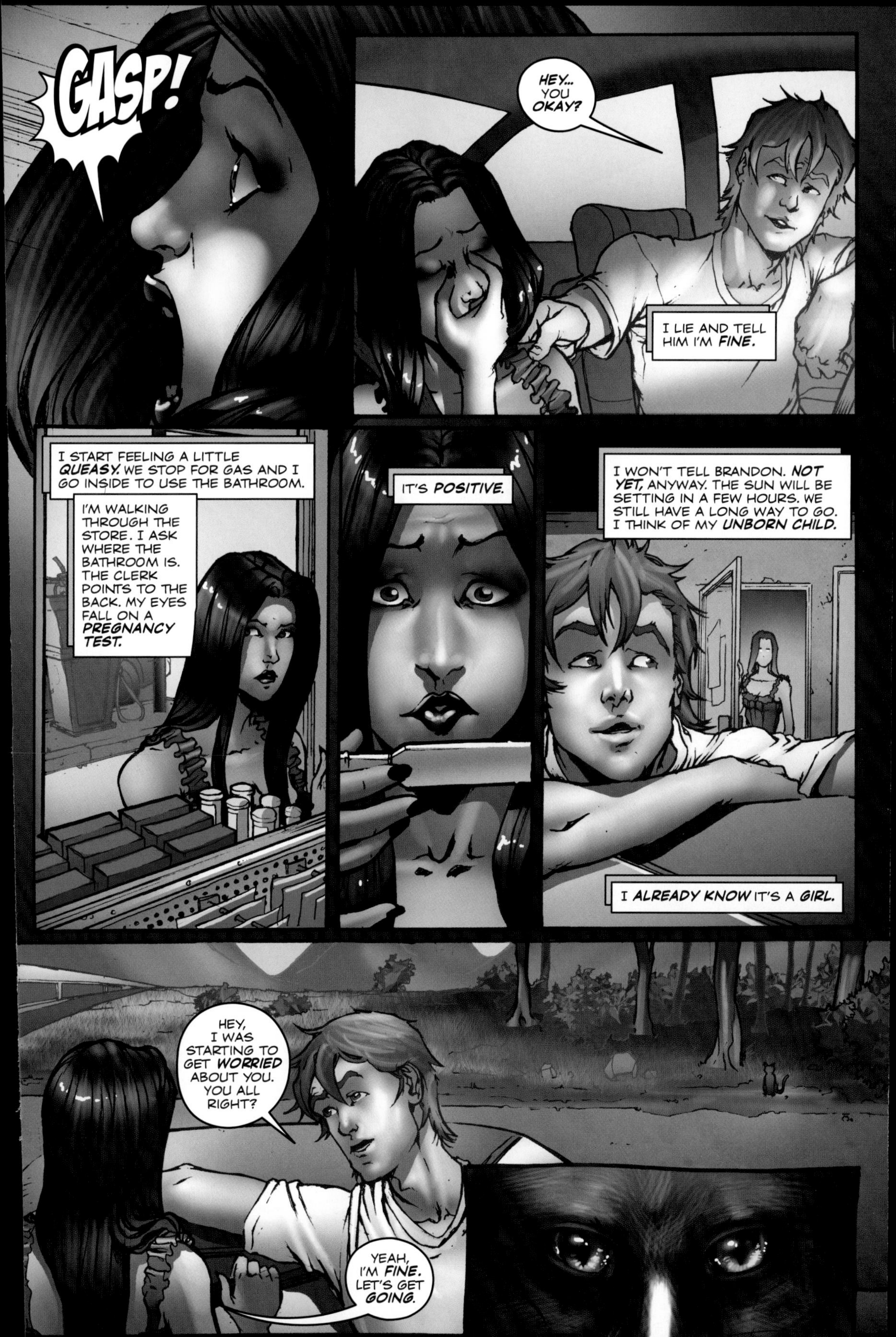
GASP!
HEY... YOU OKAY?
I LIE AND TELL HIM I'M FINE.
I START FEELING A LITTLE QUEASY. WE STOP FOR GAS AND I GO INSIDE TO USE THE BATHROOM.
I'M WALKING THROUGH THE STORE. I ASK WHERE THE BATHROOM IS. THE CLERK POINTS TO THE BACK. MY EYES FALL ON A PREGNANCY TEST.
IT'S POSITIVE.
I WON'T TELL BRANDON. NOT YET, ANYWAY. THE SUN WILL BE SETTING IN A FEW HOURS. WE STILL HAVE A LONG WAY TO GO. I THINK OF MY UNBORN CHILD.
I ALREADY KNOW IT'S A GIRL.
HEY, I WAS STARTING TO GET WORRIED ABOUT YOU. YOU ALL RIGHT?
YEAH, I'M FINE. LET'S GET GOING.

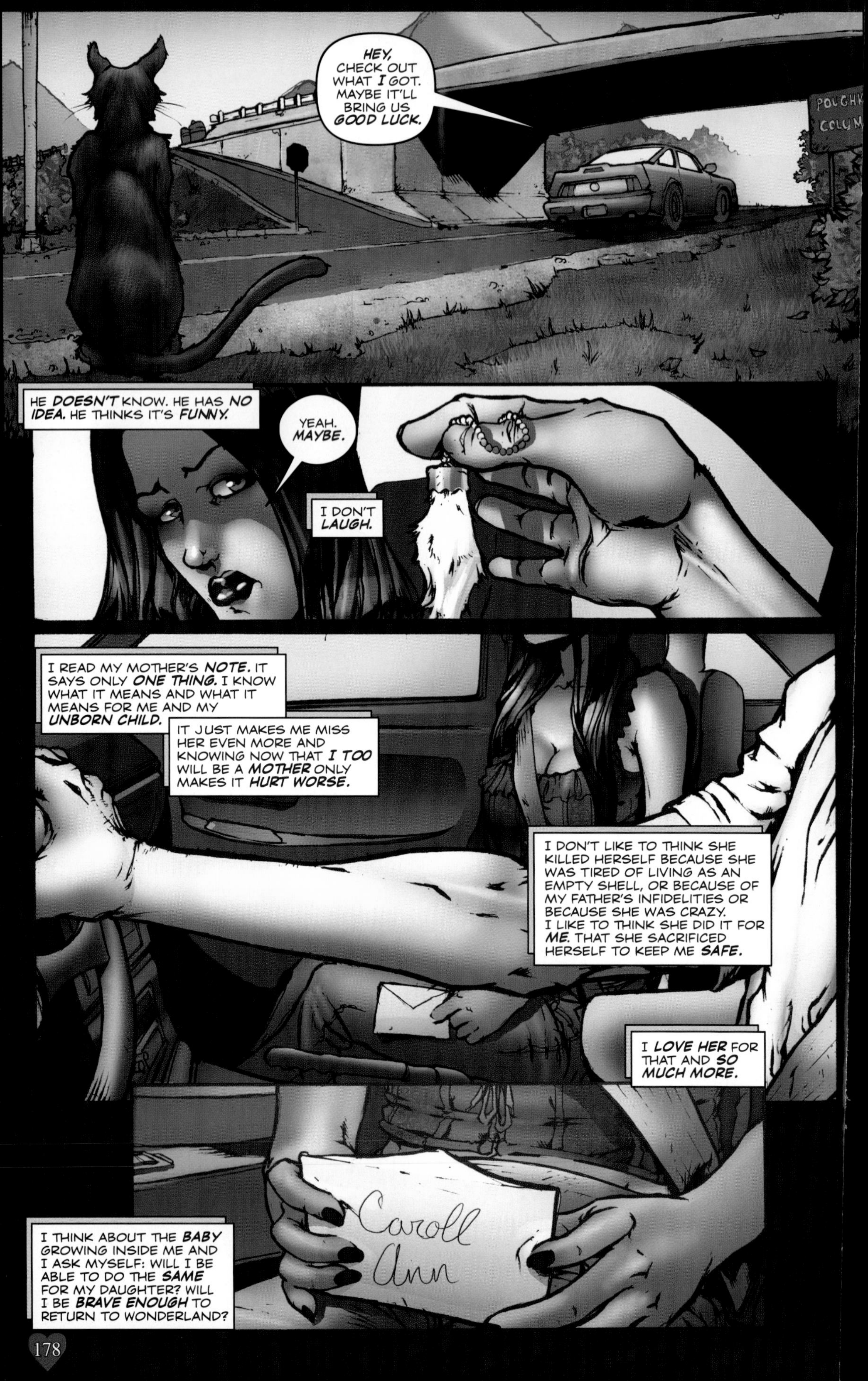
HEY, CHECK OUT WHAT I GOT. MAYBE IT'LL BRING US GOOD LUCK.
POUGHK
COLUM
HE DOESN'T KNOW. HE HAS NO IDEA. HE THINKS IT'S FUNNY.
YEAH. MAYBE.
I DON'T LAUGH.
I READ MY MOTHER'S NOTE. IT SAYS ONLY ONE THING. I KNOW WHAT IT MEANS AND WHAT IT MEANS FOR ME AND MY UNBORN CHILD.
IT JUST MAKES ME MISS HER EVEN MORE AND KNOWING NOW THAT I TOO WILL BE A MOTHER ONLY MAKES IT HURT WORSE.
I DON'T LIKE TO THINK SHE KILLED HERSELF BECAUSE SHE WAS TIRED OF LIVING AS AN EMPTY SHELL, OR BECAUSE OF MY FATHER'S INFIDELITIES OR BECAUSE SHE WAS CRAZY. I LIKE TO THINK SHE DID IT FOR ME. THAT SHE SACRIFICED HERSELF TO KEEP ME SAFE.
I LOVE HER FOR THAT AND SO MUCH MORE.
Caroll Ann
I THINK ABOUT THE BABY GROWING INSIDE ME AND I ASK MYSELF: WILL I BE ABLE TO DO THE SAME FOR MY DAUGHTER? WILL I BE BRAVE ENOUGH TO RETURN TO WONDERLAND?

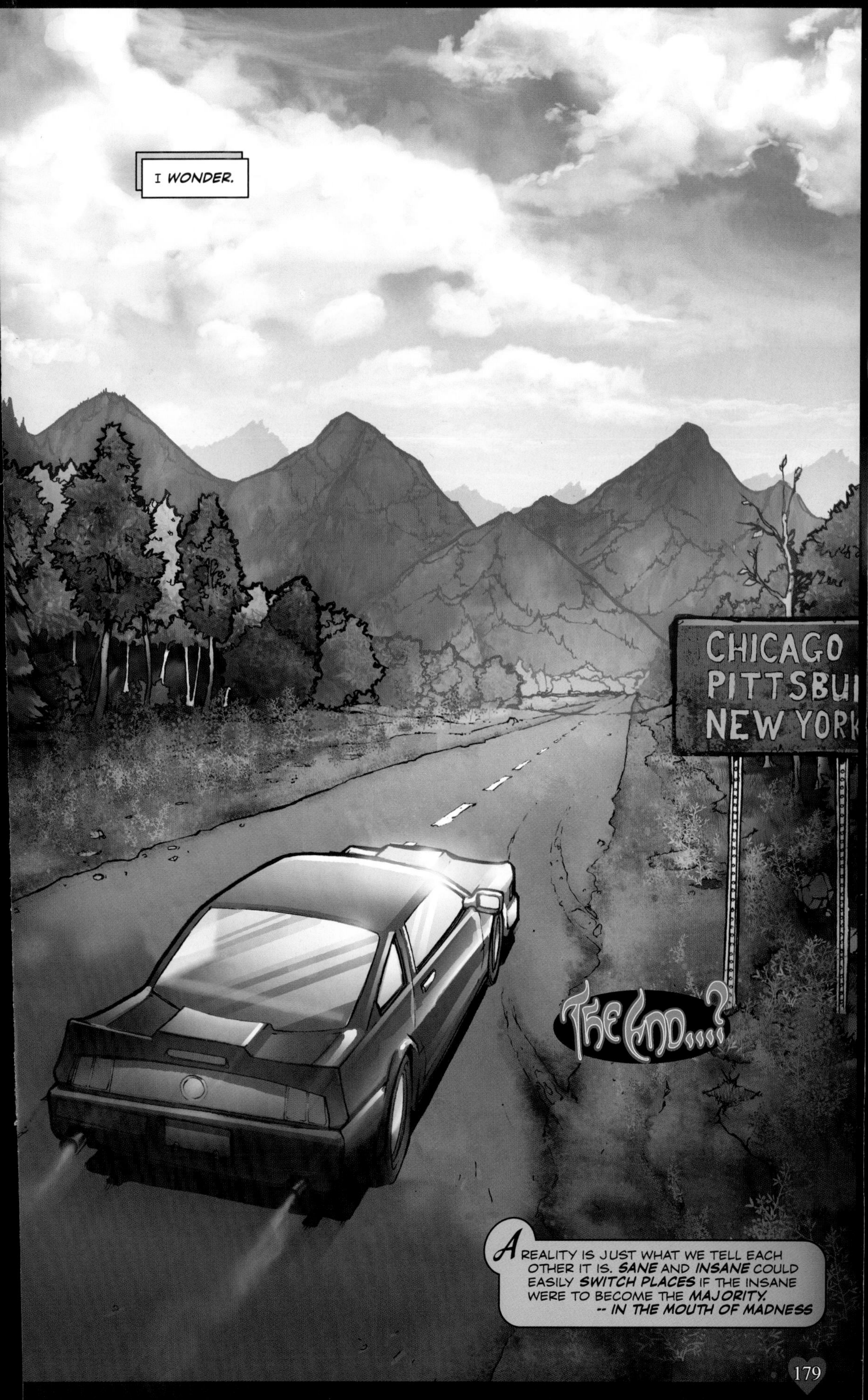
I WONDER.
CHICAGO
PITTSBU
NEW YORK
THE END...?
A REALITY IS JUST WHAT WE TELL EACH OTHER IT IS. SANE AND INSANE COULD EASILY SWITCH PLACES IF THE INSANE WERE TO BECOME THE MAJORITY.
-- IN THE MOUTH OF MADNESS